Advertising, Promotion, and New Media

Advertising,

Promotion,

and

New Media

EDITED BY
MARLA R. STAFFORD
RONALD J. FABER

M.E.Sharpe
Armonk, New York
London, England

The following chapters were originally published in
the *Journal of Advertising* in the following issues:
Vol. 31, No. 3 (Fall 2002): Chapters 2, 6, 7, 8, 9, 10, 11; and
Vol. 31, No. 4 (Winter 2002): Chapter 5.

Library of Congress Cataloging-in-Publication Data

Advertising, promotion, and new media / edited by Marla R. Stafford and Ronald J. Faber
   p. cm.
Includes bibliographical references and index.
ISBN 0-7656-1315-8 (cloth: alk. paper)
   1. Internet advertising 2. Advertising. 3. Interactive multimedia. 4. Interactive
marketing.
   I. Stafford, Marla R., 1960– II. Faber, Ronald J., 1948–

HF6146.I58A39 2004
659.14'4—dc22   2004004069

Printed in the United States of America

The paper used in this publication meets the minimum requirements of
American National Standard for Information Sciences
Permanence of Paper for Printed Library Materials,
ANSI Z 39.48-1984.

BM (c)   10   9   8   7   6   5   4   3   2   1

Contents

Preface

Advertising, Promotion, and the New Media

Although the term "new media" may immediately elicit the idea of digital technology, in fact, the new media were first born in the 1800s. Until the first telegraph line opened in 1844, introducing the world to modern media, communication and transportation were inseparable (Czitrom 1982); information could be delivered only as fast as transportation allowed. From their earliest introduction, the new media have continued to evolve. In 1920, radio was introduced. In the 1940s, television appeared on the scene; each of these new media was clearly an improvement over the previous version, with enhanced technologies accompanying each new entrant into the field. But even with the doors of modern communications opening, no doubt the people of the mid-1800s would be surprised by the communications improvements we have witnessed in recent years.

Enhanced technologies and innovative product development provide an ongoing barrage of new communications that join the ever-growing list of existing media transforming rapidly into old media. New media can be defined as media that are interactive and integrate computers with multimedia; they seem to greet us wherever we turn.

Today's new media continue to emerge as a function of digital technology, ranging from the now ubiquitous Internet, to mobile phones and online games. Along with the growth of new media channels comes the need to understand new advertising opportunities and how they can be used to communicate effectively with customers. This book, based partly on the special issue of the *Journal of Advertising* on "Advertising and New Media," addresses these emerging technologies and their use by advertisers.

The book is organized into five parts. Part I, "Defining, Understanding, and Measuring New Media Advertising," includes four distinct chapters. In his opening chapter, Leckenby provides an overview of the new media, how they have emerged from the old media, and how the new and old media interact together. In doing so, Leckenby merges his discussion with implications for current media planning. This opening chapter sets the stage for subsequent chapters in the book that investigate a myriad of new media types and their role in advertising and promotion.

In Chapter 2, "The Netvertising Image: Netvertising Image Communication Model (NICM) and Construct Definition," Stern, Zinkhan, and Holbrook present a model and definition of advertising images on the Internet. This model, called the "netvertising image," facilitates the construction of a formal language system for theory development and hypothesis testing specific to images in the multimedia context. The authors offer a range of topics for building a stream of research in this area.

Chapter 3, written by Rodgers, examines some of the biases that are associated with Internet research. Rodgers presents the results of two studies that suggest the need to carefully develop representative and appropriate experimental stimuli in Internet research. Bhat, Bevans, and Sengupta wrote the final chapter in this section, which provides a detailed list of measurement tools for evaluating and measuring advertising on the World Wide Web. This comprehensive list of measures is a helpful primer for anyone using or researching Internet advertising.

Part II of the book focuses on "Important Elements of Internet Advertising," including issues such as interactivity and telepresence. Liu and Shrum's opening chapter defines and clarifies the concept of interactivity and the implications of interactivity on the effectiveness of advertising. McMillan and Hwang offer a validated measure of perceived interactivity and the specific influences that affect it. These two chapters help the reader to better understand the role and importance of interactivity as a key component of the new media.

In Chapter 7, Li, Daugherty, and Biocca examine the relationship between 3-D advertising and telepresence. Their findings suggest that increased sensory information such as 3-D advertising can enhance telepresence and ultimately influence product knowledge, attitudes, and intentions. This section closes with a chapter by Menon and Soman, who investigate the role of curiosity in Web advertising. Their results suggest that, as compared to ads containing detailed product information, a curiosity-generating advertising approach increases interest and learning. Curiosity is also related to the quality—but not the quantity—of search.

Traditional Web media such as banners, pop-ups, and online sponsorship are the focus of Part III. Shen reports on how a sample of interactive advertising media directors price, evaluate, and pretest banner ads. His results indicate that click-throughs and outcomes are more preferred than exposures in evaluating banner advertising effectiveness. Shen also identifies the critical issues associated with the use of Internet banner advertising.

Pop-up ads remain a popular form of Web advertising, and in Chapter 10, Edwards, Li, and Lee examine how consumers react to forced exposure of pop-ups. The authors use perceived intrusiveness to understand consumers' irritation of pop-up ads and their potential avoidance. Results offer both insight and implications for increasing the effectiveness of pop-up advertising.

Another common type of online advertising is placing a link for one business on another's host site. Selecting a proper affiliate to execute this advertising is critical to its ultimate effectiveness. In Chapter 11, Papatla and Bhatnagar offer an empirical model for selecting the most appropriate affiliate based on product category.

More recent additions to new media forms include mobile advertising and advergames, the focus of Part IV of this book. Mobile devices are the new and compelling outlet for promotional communication in a society that is ever more on the move. In Chapter 12, Perlado and Barwise summarize key issues in mobile advertising research and provide a framework for future research on this growing phenomenon. In Chapter 13, Stafford examines the issues with promotion targeted to mobile devices, specifically considering the likely emerging portal model for mediating access to consumer mobile devices.

Two chapters on advergames round out this section with Hernandez and her colleagues examining the effectiveness of brand placement in two online games across players from four different countries. Results suggest that the script format affects recall; expertise level and perceived goal difficulty, however, did not have any effect on recall. In Chapter 15, Youn and Lee examine motivations for advergame play. Their results suggest that escapism, competition, boredom relief, and fun were all positively related to attitude toward the advergame; curiosity had a negative relationship with attitude toward the advergame. Moreover, attitude toward the advergame was related to both attitude toward the site and relationship-building with the site.

The book concludes with the chapter, "The Future of Consumer Decision Making in the Age of New Media Promotions and Advertising." This chapter summarizes the current trends in new media, offers insight into how new media affect information search, and presents challenges that advertisers are currently facing with regard to the new media. This chapter also discusses how sales promotions can be integrated with the new media.

The new media continue to permeate our environment. *Advertising, Promotion, and the New Media* represents a compilation of state-of-the-art, thought-provoking research on some of the most recent trends in the digital media and how they are used to communicate effectively with their customer. Our goal for this book is not only to contribute to current thought on advertising, promotion, and new media, but also to stimulate additional research in the new and ever-evolving media.

Marla Royne Stafford
Ronald J. Faber

Reference

Czitrom, Daniel J. (1982), *Media and the American Mind, from Morse to McLuhan*, Chapel Hill: University of North Carolina Press.

Part I

Defining, Understanding, and Measuring New Media Advertising

1

The Interaction of Traditional and New Media

John D. Leckenby

The development of new types of media such as the Internet and the World Wide Web is a process often surrounded and enveloped by exciting events that go far beyond the new medium itself. Radio is an outstanding example of this phenomenon; while the building of this new medium would have provided enough excitement in and of itself, the accompanying social and economic times ensured it would be a time to remember throughout history. At the pinnacle of the evolution of radio as a new medium, the Great Depression occurred in the United States. This history shows that the development of radio was not disconnected from the social, political, and economic events; radio became part of the system that soon allowed millions to become involved in stock market trading with up-to-the-minute reports on stock movements. It is often thought the crash of the stock market led to the succeeding depression in the economy.

Radio is but one example of the great spike that new media types inject into the world, both causing and caused by great events in history. It is this composite of historical events, not just the advent of the new medium and its technical wonderments, that makes "new media" such an important and noteworthy point of immense interest. While today this interest is almost exclusively centered on the Internet, comparable levels of interest could be uncovered in previous historical epochs, for example, with the introduction of television, radio, telephony, magazines, and newspapers.

It is desirable, therefore, to put any new media development into proper historical perspective by comparing and contrasting the "new" one with the "old" ones. Further, there are indications that the development of a new medium does not occur in a vacuum unrelated to the old media developments that have already taken place. It is tempting to accept the proposition that because they are "old," the old media have been developed by some point in time and do not change thereafter. Of course, this is untrue. Each of these old media is constantly evolving over time. For example, party lines in telephony give way to private lines as technology continually evolves. And the fact that old media change over time leads to the proposition that the old media "interact" with the new media during the process of the new media's development to make the new medium something other than it might have been in the absence of the old media types. For example, Standage (1998) mentioned that the telegraph was a precursor to the Internet in terms of its two-way wired communication. Parallels between the development of the radio and the Internet have also been identified, based on cultural history (Douglas 1987; Lappin 1995).

It is the purpose of this discussion to explore primarily the idea of the interaction between media types as they develop over time. How has the fact that the Internet has been developed after television and radio, for example, affected its development? How has the development of the Internet affected the evolutionary change of television and radio? Are there identifiable phases in the development of media types along these lines?

Each of the above questions, as well as further comparisons and contrasts, will be addressed in this discussion. In addition, implications and connections with the field of media planning will be considered. This exposition is motivated, of course, by the introduction of a new medium in the 1990s, the Internet and its associated components.

What Is "Old" and What Is "New" in Media?

It is worthwhile at the onset to note the definitions used by media planners in the field of advertising with respect to media issues. Kelly and Juggenheimer (2003, 104) offer the following:

Media Unit: A specific physical size or time unit for the placement of an advertisement such as "full-page, four-color, bleed in *Better Homes & Gardens* magazine for the December 2003 issue."

Media Vehicle: A particular "named carrier" for the placement of an advertisement, such as *Better Homes & Gardens* magazine.

Media Type: A category of named carriers such as magazines.

When advertising media planners refer to "media types," they are concerned with the broadest categories of media, such as magazines, television, radio, and the Internet. This is the broadest level of discussion. When the term "media" is used in this discussion, it will refer to "media type" by default and not to vehicles or to units, unless noted. So, an "old" medium might be radio and a "new" medium might be the Internet.

The first thing to note about "new" media is that they are not completely new. They have, in many instances, been growing out of the old media over time, so that there is a need for historical perspective in the discussion of new media. Marvin (1988, 3) wrote: "New technology is a historically relative term. We are not the first generation to wonder at the rapid and extraordinary shifts in the dimensions of the world and the human relationships it contains as a result of new forms of communication."

Historical linkages between new and old media have been consciously attempted by some researchers. As an example, Leonhirth, Mindich, and Straumanis (1997) compared the mailing list with the telegraph, the round table, and the bonfire. Moreover, Murray (1997, 67) indicated that the newly emerging medium of the Internet is still relying on formats derived not from exploiting its own extensive power but from earlier technologies. Thus, the Internet is still in its early stages.

McMillan (2001, 164) provides an excellent overview of the new and old media question. She notes that "many observers tend to write about 'new media' such as networked commuting and telecommunications as if they had been recently discovered in their fully developed state." Williams, Strover, and Grant (1994) defined new media as those that offered new services or enhancement to old services and included such applications as microelectronics, computers, and telecommunications. Negroponte (1995) suggested that new and old media differ, based upon the transmission of digital rather than physical atoms. Choice and control have been pointed out as features of new media (Pavlik 1998). As noted earlier, "interactivity" has often been construed to be the primary differentiating factor between the Internet and other media.

Stern (1995, 127) indicated that "television is a linear, passive, time-constrained medium. The television is time-constrained, unless your viewer has carefully videotaped your commercials for playback at a more convenient time. Accessing the World Wide Web can be done at any time."

Interaction also indicates that users can get information instead of its being given to them (Stern 1995). Williams and colleagues noted, in addition to interactivity, demassification and asynchronicity as factors critical to new media. Demassification means that "a certain degree of the control of mass communication systems moves from the message producer to the media consumer" (Williams, Rice and Rogers 1988, 13).

"Asynchronicity allows for the sending and receiving of messages at a time convenient for the individual user rather than requiring all participants to use the system at the same time" (Williams, Rice, and Rogers 1988, 13). For instance, people can receive electronic messages in their offices or homes whenever they log onto a host computer.

According to Rice and Williams (1984), new media tend to form a link between mass media and interpersonal media to a greater extent than did their forerunners. Cathcart and Gumpert (1983) indicated that "mediated interpersonal communication" has been facilitated by new technologies.

The term "old" holds some pejorative meaning for many cultures. And, clearly, "old" and "new" are not mutually exclusive categories but rather represent a continuum. The "old" does not disappear but melds into the "new." For example, data from Nielsen NetRatings indicate that use of the Internet does not eliminate television exposure but rather complements it (Nielsen NetRatings 2003). The American Internet User Survey (FIND/SVP 1997) found that some Internet users report a decrease in television viewing, but a large number of Internet users report no change in their television habits. According to Coffey and Stipp (1997), the study conducted by Statistical Research, Inc. in 1996 indicated that over 40 percent of computer owners have both a television and a computer in the same room, allowing them to use both media at the same time, or to go back and forth between a television and a computer easily. Coffey and Stipp (1997, 61) noted: "Radio did not replace newspapers; TV did not replace the movies or radio; satellites and cable did not replace broadcast TV."

"The new medium did not wipe out the old. People who listened to news broadcasts on the radio would still buy a newspaper" (Winston 1998, 86). The "old" media have kept on prospering because of unique attributes that satisfy different audience needs (Coffey and Stipp 1997).

It might be more appropriate to refer to "traditional" media rather than old media. This term, "traditional," implies that the media in reference have been in existence for some time. In the Merriam Webster Online Dictionary (www.merriam-webster.com), "tradition" is defined as "an inherited, established, or customary pattern of thought, action, or behavior (as a religious practice or a social custom)." In the context of this discussion, "established" is the critical part of the above definition of the meaning of "traditional." An "old" medium is an established medium and is, therefore, an entity that has become traditional. Television, for example, is an established medium. But just as with religious and social practices and customs, television and other "traditional" media change and evolve over time.

It is worthwhile to note in passing that "old" media typically do not disappear over time. They may become less important or changed but usually do not disappear from the scene.

"New" media, on the other hand, are those that, according to the above definition of "traditional," are not yet fully established as customary institutions in a society. They are not yet considered to be mature in their development. New and traditional are points on the time continuum with respect to development and the evolutionary change of that development. However, new media are required to suggest some significant improvements over existing media if they are to reform relationships between audience and content-maker and thus prove the value of their own individual existence as media to be used in addition to the traditional media (Fredin 1989).

It is worthwhile to examine the development of some traditional media first to understand how they developed in the context of "old" media at the time of their inception. This will provide a backdrop against which the introduction of the new medium of the Internet can be considered.

The Development of Traditional Media: Radio and Television

Winston (1998, 67) notes that "the radio is the clearest example in these histories of a machine already in existence—'invented'—but not recognized as such." Sir William Crookes made the first published record of the concept of radio. His vision was of "telegraphy without wires, posts, cables, or any of our present costly appliances." He considered radio a person-to-person system, with "all the requirements . . . well within the possibility of discovery" (Marvin 1988, 156; Beck 1967, 95). In 1922, journalists wrote jubilant articles about the radio, the newest development in wireless technology. Politicians saw radio as the latest invention of American entrepreneurial genius. In 1921, only five stations had acquired the new "broadcast class" licenses issued by the Department of Commerce for transmissions of music, concerts, markets, weather reports, lectures, and so forth. That number had increased to 576 by 1923 (Lappin 1995). In 1922, radio sets were a high-priced novelty: The average radio set cost US$50; less than 0.2 percent of American households had a radio at that time. But that situation quickly changed, too.

Radio rapidly became the main patron of music and musicians because the radio was a very economical way to access music. Radio also influenced the film industry; film scholars agree that Warner's sound film initiative was strongly influenced by the radio business.

However, the sudden popularity of radio increased operating costs to account for—even after the station was built and running—equipment maintenance, staff salaries, and compensation for performers and musicians. All expenses were paid by broadcast station owners, while broadcast listeners did not pay for the programming they enjoyed—a similar problem that many poor Web site administrators should have recognized. But few broadcasting station owners were prepared to support these costs indefinitely. The radio broadcast landscape of the 1920s might seem strangely familiar to many if a suffix of .edu, .gov, .org, or .com was tacked onto the call letters of each radio station. In 1923, 39 percent of radio broadcast stations were owned by firms that sold radio hardware and equipment or manufactured it, so that their broadcasts were funded by the sale of the equipment necessary to access them.

But things were changing rapidly. By 1930, almost 46 percent of American homes owned a radio. The commercial networks controlled the broadcast airwaves and few of the wireless community or the amateurs had any power (Lappin 1995).

Television broadcasting is also a great invention and is not merely the product of a science related to light, electronics, and sound. Vladimir Zworykin's is the most convincing claim to the invention of television, which was first built under the aegis of four major electrical manufacturers. Every basic view of modern television systems agrees with Zworykin's original patent description of 1923. He worked to refine the devices and develop those ideas in the 1930s (Winston 1998, 106). Television is the creature of an economy able to produce and distribute goods on a huge scale, and of a society so complicated that its business is unable to operate with person-to-person communication (Bogart 1958). Television rode in on the pinnacle of an increasing wave of interest in the existing media, and television broadcasting developed rapidly under the aegis of the leading radio networks for its first few years. When television service in the United States was launched, television had to be created to fit into a media system adapting live events from print, films, and radio. In particular, the television was specially designed for the home delivery of movies after the first public television demonstration in the United States. In 1936, the Academy of Motion Picture Arts and Sciences stated: "There appears to be no danger that television will burst upon an unprepared motion picture industry" (Waldrop and Borkin 1938, 126).

Television was contributing to 70 percent of broadcasting advertising revenues by 1952, by which time the broadcasting industry had developed and changed from radio to television. Winston (1998, 122) stated: "Nearly every audio-caterpillar had successfully become a video-butterfly in 1952." It could be said that television had eventually arrived in the early 1950s.

Nonetheless, the arrival of television did not lure away whatever interested parties had been radio fans. Radio-producing entities changed to television, but there were no victims in the radio industry (Winston 1998).

The phases of the invention of new media can happen either synchronously with or subsequently to the important supervening necessity that ensures diffusion. The invention of television is synchronous with some fundamental supervening necessities. These would include the general drive to adapt the development of entertainment, which had underpinned the development of radio and cinema.

During the 1950s, leisure gave indications of replacing work as the major focus of living. The big growth in leisure meant an increasing opportunity and a rising demand for the mass media (Schramm 1960). The home delivery of movies was the main television research objective.

Nonetheless, the growth of the mass media cannot be understood merely as an effect of the increase in leisure time. The mass media have themselves extended prevailing awareness of what makes a good life (Schramm 1960). At the end of World War II, there were other components to underpin television and the drive toward greater consumerism (Winston 1998).

The introduction of new media is an important and significant historical occasion when patterns anchored in older media are challenged, reexamined, and defended. New media are supposed to form new social groups, that is, "audiences" and to encourage new uses based on novel technological properties. The history of a new medium starts when audiences come together around these uses. Viewed in this light, the history of the Internet as a new medium began with the creation of "online communities."

The Introduction of a New Medium: The Internet

The widespread adoption of the Internet and other components in the mid-1990s provoked a good deal of excitement, some of which carries over to the present time. As has so often been noted, the Internet has been the fastest-growing new medium ever. The Internet is experiencing exponential growth in the number of networks, number of hosts, and volume of traffic (Stern 1995)—having a total of 134 million estimated users as of August 1998 and of 605.60 million estimated users worldwide as of September 2002 (Nua Internet Surveys 2003). Among the many segments of the Internet, advertising became one of the fastest growing, with $906 million spent for online advertising in 1997 (Interactive Advertising Bureau 1998) and $5 billion in online expenditures projected by the year 2000 (Jupiter Communication 1997).

It is worthwhile to put the Internet into context with respect to advertising expenditures for "old" media types. Advertising is one indicator of the growth of a medium, along with the penetration of the medium into the population of a society. Robert Coen of McCann-Erickson Worldwide is considered the "guru" of advertising expenditure projections and recordkeeping for the advertising industry worldwide, and his data appear regularly in the trade publication, *Advertising Age*. His data on U.S. advertising expenditures for 2000 to 2002 are shown in Table 1.1.

Table 1.1

U.S. Advertising Expenditures for 2000–2002

	2000 (final)		2001 (final)		2002 (final)	
	millions of $s	% of total	millions of $s	% of total	millions of $s	% of total
Newspaper						
National	7,229	2.9	6,615	2.9	6,806	2.9
Local	41,821	16.9	37,640	16.3	37,225	15.7
Total	49,050	19.8	44,255	19.1	44,031	18.6
Magazines	12,370	5.0	11,095	4.8	10,995	4.6
Broadcast TV						
Four TV networks	15,888	6.4	14,300	6.2	15,000	6.3
(3 TV networks)	−14,256	−5.8	−12,795	−5.5	(13,256)	(5.6)
Syndication*	3,108	1.3	3,102	1.3	3034	1.3
Spot (national)	12,264	5.0	9,223	4.0	10,920	4.6
Spot (Local)	13,542	5.5	12,256	5.3	13114	5.6
Total	44,802	18.1	38,881	16.8	42,068	17.8
Cable TV						
Cable networks	11,765	4.8	11,777	5.1	12,071	5.1
Spot (local)	3,690	1.5	3,959	1.7	4,226	1.8
Total	15,455	6.2	15,736	6.8	16,297	6.9
Radio						
Network	780	0.3	711	0.3	775	0.3
Spot (national)	3,668	1.5	2,956	1.3	3,340	1.4
Spot (local)	14,847	6.0	14,194	6.1	14,762	6.2
Total	19,295	7.8	17,861	7.7	18,877	7.9
Yellow pages						
National	2,093	0.8	2,087	0.9	2,087	0.9
Local	11,135	4.5	11,505	5.0	11,689	4.9
Total	13,228	5.3	13,592	5.9	13,776	5.8
Direct mail	44,591	18.0	44,725	19.3	46,067	19.4
Business papers	4,915	2.0	4,468	1.9	3,976	1.7
Out of home						
National	2,068	0.8	2,051	0.9	2,061	0.9
Local	3,108	1.3	3,083	1.3	3,114	1.3
Total	5,176	2.1	5,134	2.2	5,175	2.2
Internet	6,507	2.6	5,645	2.4	4,883	2.1
Miscellaneous						
National	24,418	9.9	23,042	9.9	23,414	9.9
Local	7,665	3.1	6,853	3.0	7,316	3.1
Total	32,083	13.0	29,895	12.9	30,730	13.0
National total	151,664	61.3	141,797	61.3	145,429	61.4
Local total	95,808	38.7	89,490	38.7	91,446	38.6
Grand total	247,472	100.0	231,287	100.0	236,875	100.0

Source: Prepared for Universal/McCann by Robert J. Coen; available at: www.mccann.com/insight/bobcoen.html
  *Includes UPN,WB, and Pax.

Table 1.2

The Outlook for 2003 National Advertising

	% Change over 2002	2003 Projections ($000,000)
Four TV networks	+ 4.0	$15,600
Spot TV	− 1.0	10,811
Cable TV	+ 10.0	13,275
Syndication TV	+ 8.0	3,276
Radio	+ 4.2	4,288
Magazines	+ 7.0	11,765
Newspapers	+ 5.5	7,180
Consumer media subtotal	**+ 5.2**	**66,195**
Direct mail	+ 6.5	49,061
Yellow pages	+ 1.5	2,118
Internet	+ 5.0	5,127
Other national media	+ 3.8	30,563
Total national	**+ 5.2**	**$153,064**

Source: Prepared for Universal McCann by Robert J. Coen; available at www.universal mccann.com/InsidersReport0603.pdf

The data in Table 1.1 show that the Internet hovers in recent years at about 2 percent of the total advertising expenditures in the media in the United States. This is about the same order as business papers and out-of-home media, including outdoor advertising. It is much more than network radio, for example. But this is small in comparison to the 20 percent for newspapers and 18 percent for television. Table 1.2 shows Coen's projections for advertising expenditures for the United States for 2003 for these media types.

Clearly, the Internet has grown dramatically in a short period of time. Yet, with respect to advertising support and expenditures, as shown in Tables 1.1 and 1.2, the excitement about this medium has been out of proportion to its importance as an advertising medium. Newspapers have historically constituted the largest advertising medium in the United States (18.6 percent of the total advertising expenditures in 2002). The Internet is far behind, at 2.1 percent of the total. Direct marketing, including so-called junk mail, is huge by comparison at 19.4 percent. Yet, the Internet is comparable in size as an advertising medium to out-of-home media, including outdoor advertising, at 2.2 percent. The Internet is larger by far than network radio as an advertising medium with its 0.3 percent of total advertising expenditures.

As a "rule of thumb" among media planners in the advertising field, a new medium is thought to be a viable and standard advertising media type, in league with newspapers and others noted above, when its penetration among the population of any interest group reaches 70 percent. The Internet had not reached this point in the United States and Canada as of 2002 (see Table 1.3).

Table 1.3

Estimated Number of Internet Users, September 2002 (in millions)

World total	605.60
Africa	6.31
Asia/Pacific	187.24
Europe	190.91
Middle East	5.12
Canada and United States	182.67
Latin America	33.35

Source: Adapted from www.nua.ie/surveys/how_many_online?

Nua Internet Surveys (2003) notes that in September 2002, 182.67 million people in the United States and Canada were online; this represents 65.13 percent of the population of those two countries. But this is close enough to the 70 percent mark suggesting that, from the media planning perspective in the field of advertising, the Internet has become a major media type. According to Forrester Research (1998), goods and services of over $22 billion would be exchanged on the Internet during 1999; the number was projected to be $3.2 trillion in the year 2003. Clearly, there has been substantial growth in electronic commerce since the commercialization of the Internet in the early 1990s. Huge reach and different interactive abilities have made the Internet a crucial marketing and trading medium for many businesses. There has arisen an astounding adoption of the practice of using the Web for marketing, promoting, and transacting services and products with consumers. Organizations traded US$20 billion worth of services and products online and this number was projected to reach US$184 billion in the year 2004.

Why are people excited about the Internet? One of the critical reasons might be the unique characteristic of the Internet as an "interactive" medium, compared with the other mass media. These interactive features may provide people with vast opportunities to communicate with each other beyond time and spatial restrictions (Miller 1996).

It has already been widely documented that the Internet as a new medium has fundamentally transformed the traditional source-oriented advertising paradigm and that "interactivity" is at the core of this change (Bezjian-Avery, Calder, and Iacobucci 1998; Hoffman and Novak 1996). "Interactivity suggests that the reasons consumers seek, self-select, process, use, and respond to information are critical for understanding responses to comumunications. Search and self-selection of the sources from which information may be obtained, as well as the way this information is processed, has long been recognized as an important determinant of consumer behavior" (Stewart and Pavlou, 2002, 380).

According to Bezjian-Avery, Calder, and Iacobucci (1998, 24), "interactivity is fundamentally the ability to control information. Whereas in traditional advertising, the presentation is linear and the consumer is passively exposed to product information, for interactive advertising, the consumer instead actively traverses the information."

Like the Internet, such traditional media as television and radio are also devices for wireless communication; however, these are only one-way communication. Interactivity is one of the most important features of the wireless communication now possible via the Internet.

When it comes to the media these days, such interactivity is the most frequently discussed issue, and this is a multidimensional concept. The first conceptualization of interactivity comes from an interpersonal communication perspective (Ha and James 1998). Here, interactivity is defined as the facility for individuals and organizations to communicate directly with one another, regardless of distance or time (Blattberg and Deighton 1991; Ha and James 1998). The second conceptualization of interactivity comes from a mechanical perspective (Ha and James 1998). This is the approach viewing interactivity as a given technological characteristic of a medium. Steuer (1992) defines interactivity as the extent to which users can participate in modifying the form and content of a mediated environment in real time, and he classifies a variety of media, based on three interactivity levels (high/medium/low). Additionally, Steuer focuses on the functioning of three elements in interactivity: the speed with which content can be manipulated, the range of ways in which content can be manipulated, and mapping (Steuer 1992).

Sohn and Leckenby (2002) explain interactivity in terms of social communication. They propose that interactivity is a process-dependent concept, not a static attribute-based concept: Individuals' active participation in social communication processes is a crucial factor for increasing the perceived interactivity of the Internet. However, other researchers view interactivity as the control of the information flow, or the possibility of the user to travel over information (Bezjian-Avery, Calder, and Iacobucci 1998). With respect to interactivity, the chief goal of a system-centered perspective is finding the best guidelines for the design of technology, while a user-centered perspective studies the interaction between humans and the technology (Unz and Hesse 1999). Studies have found that the interactive capability of the medium offers uses and gratifications including convenience, diversion, relationship development, and intellectual appeal.

In the online environment, consumers have control over their entire communication experiences: consumers initiate, sustain, and terminate communication with commercial Web sites. "Interactive advertising places the consumer at the center of the study of marketing communication because its effectiveness hinges not only on how the marketer's message influences the consumer, but also on how the consumer shapes the interaction" (Stewart and Pavlou 2002: 10). Also, Duncan and Moriarty (1998, 1) said that "communication is (rather than persuasion) the foundation of consumer-marketer relationships in an increasingly interactive context." This change from one-way persuasion to two-way interaction suggests that the meaning of traditional measures of consumer reactions to marketing communications may be transformed in interactive conditions (Stewart and Pavlou 2002).

Hence, what is of particular importance is not only the consumer's response to the advertising message, but also the "mutual interaction and correspondence" between the consumer and the advertiser—two interrelating entities with different goals (Leckenby and Li 2000).

As the possibilities of two-way interaction between consumer and advertiser have become a major theme of advertising research, many researchers have attempted to examine the concept of interactivity in relation to interactive advertising effectiveness (Coyle and Thorson 2001; Lombard and Snyder-Duch 2001; Macias 2003; Wu 1999; Cho 1999; Cho and Leckenby 1997). Their pioneering studies have illuminated how the interactivity construct, along with other constructs such as those of involvement and attitude, can be incorporated into an existing framework of consumer information processing.

There is general agreement that the Internet is now a "new" medium and that it is important in advertising and other spheres of world concern, and some of these reasons have been noted above. But what is it that makes a "new" medium? And what constitutes an "old" medium?

Radio as a Traditional Medium and the Internet as a New Medium

It is instructive to briefly examine and compare the radio and Internet media to show some similarities in traditional and new media development with respect to these two media types.

The following statements were made early on regarding the development of the radio medium:

> It has helped to create a vast new audience of a magnitude which was never dreamed of. . . . This audience, invisible but attentive, differs not only in size but in kind from any audience the world has ever known. It is in reality a linking-up of millions of homes.
> —Owen Young

*The miracle of [it]. I cannot tell you how it transformed our
lives. . . . Television never has its me-to-you intimacy.*
                                                    —Alan Jenkins

Sicart (2000) notes that the above quotes are not about the Internet but
about radio. The first he excerpted from a 1929 report prepared for the Radio
Corporation of America by Owen Young, then chairman of General Electric.
The second is from a memoir of the 1920s by Alan Jenkins (1974). Taken
together, the comments indicate the manner in which it was perceived that
radio was revolutionizing people's perception of space and time in a manner
similar to the way the Internet is perceived to be doing today.

The enthusiasm demonstrated for radio in its first developments can be
seen today in the comments made by advertising people about the Internet.
The following quotes about the Internet are instructive:

*In a relationship-driven world, the key ingredient to successful
media will be interactivity.*
                              —Peter Georgescu, CEO, Young & Rubicam
                                           [*Advertising Age*, April 14, 1997]

*After the 20th century Industrial Age, we are shifting our global
focus for the 21st century to our relationships and how we
interact.*
                           —Jack Myers, Chairman, The Myers Group, New York
[*Technology and the World of International Marketing Communications*,
                                                            April 2000]

While there can be little doubt about the importance of interactivity as a
critical part of understanding the development of the Internet, it is also the
case that the enthusiasm expressed above for this new medium does not
exceed that shown for radio in its infancy. For example, Geoffrey Perrett
(1982) believed the reaction of Americans to the radio in the 1920s to be a
phenomenon unlike any before, because of the remarkable breadth and
speed of radio's success.

The Internet's development as a medium will undoubtedly promote interaction through the digital exchange of information. Humankind may grow
closer as a community and become freer by exchanging information. Nonetheless, "this is not the first time a new medium has come along, promising
to radically transform the way we relate to one another. It isn't even the first
time a fellowship of amateur trailblazers has led the charge across the new
media hinterland" (Lappin 1995).

The commercialization of a medium is often taken to be one of the characteristics that indicates that the trajectory toward maturity has been reached. While Gugliclmo Marconi certainly invented the initial "wireless" technology upon which radio was based, it was his employee, David Sarnoff, who had the vision that led to radio as it is understood today. It is worthwhile to note a few points about Sarnoff and his work. First, he was a young man when he came across the idea of setting up a one-to-many version of the wireless or radio. He was nineteen years of age when he began his work with Marconi. It should be noted that the digital pioneers of the Internet as a commercial enterprise in Silicon Valley, for example, tended to be very young people not unlike Sarnoff was at the time he developed his major ideas about the direction radio should take. So, while it is true that the Internet was invented by "older" and "more grounded" physical scientists to share information about their work, it was the young commercial entrepreneurs who commercialized the Internet (Winston 1998).

Sicart (2000) has produced an interesting comparison between the behavior of the stock of RCA, the largest U.S company in the radio business in the 1920s, and that of AOL Time Warner in the late 1990s and early 2000s. Figure 1.1 shows this comparison.

The figure shows the similarity of the trajectories of the stocks of the largest company in the radio business and the largest company in the Internet business. At minimum, this chart suggests a similarity in the commercial aspects of these two media as they developed during their early stages.

The interaction of the new medium of radio with the traditional medium of newspapers was evident during the episode of the sinking of the *Titanic*. Sarnoff received the transmissions from rescue ships like the *Californian* and relayed this information to newspapers so that listeners in New York, where he established his radio station, quickly became aware of what was happening (Winston 1998). For example, lists of survivors were transmitted to the public in this manner—essentially from radio to newspapers to the public. There has clearly been an interaction of the Internet with traditional media in its early development. Web TV clearly connected the Internet with television early on. The content of newspapers has been "published" on the Internet for some time now. E-mail is a prominent application that merges the idea of older "letter-writing" and "memo-writing" through the post or other means of transmission from sender to receiver with the technology of the Internet. In fact, it is clear now that almost all forms of traditional media messages can be transformed and conveyed through the Internet.

It is interesting to note that broadcast audience measurement was invented by the sociologist and chair of the sociology department at Columbia Uni-

Figure 1.1   **AOL Time Warner vs. RCA**

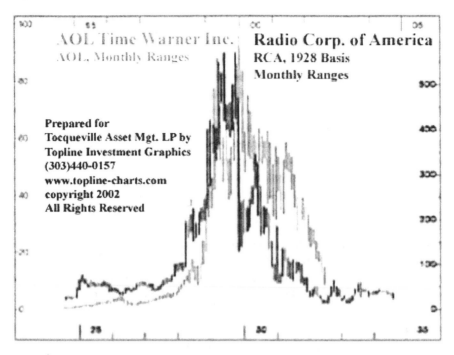

versity, Raymond Lazarsfeld, at the behest of Sarnoff. Estimation of the size of a medium's audience was recognized by him as critical to commercialization because there is a direct relationship between estimated audience size and the amount of money advertisers are willing to pay the medium for running their ads. Sarnoff's concept of audience measurement is the basis for television and Internet audience measurement today. Nielsen NetRatings and ComScore MediaMetrix use essentially the same concepts as those invented by Lazarsfeld and Sarnoff.

Finally, interactivity is often cited as the primary distinguishing characteristic of the Internet, for example, by the editors of the *Journal of Interactive Advertising* (Leckenby and Li 2000), yet historical records show that this concept was identified with the development of radio as well. William Crookes created the first published record of the concept of radio. He envisioned a medium that would allow person-to-person communication without the wires, posts, and other expensive paraphernalia that telegraphy required. Moreover, he believed the requisites for such a system lay well within the realm of possible discoveries (Marvin 1988, 156; Beck 1967, 95).

Also, Lappin (1995) mentioned:

Radio started out the same way as with the Internet. It was a truly interactive medium. It was user-dominated and user-controlled.

Thus, the Internet is not the first medium to be viewed as "revolutionary" because it involved the concept of interactivity.

The relationships noted above between the development of the radio medium and the Internet medium lead to the proposition that a new medium does not develop in a vacuum but rather builds in interesting ways upon traditional media. Further, there are suggestions that this process of building media types is not a linear one but rather one involving complex interactions among the media types as they develop over time. The "Media Interaction Cycle" based upon these ideas is discussed below.

The Media Interaction Cycle

As noted by McMillan (2001), there tends to be a "flow" among media types as they develop, rather than a discrete invention of one type and subsequently an invention of another type, and so forth. Flow consists of a process by which an experience is achieved, after the establishment beforehand of the requisite conditions. Additionally, the process of this experience must be followed by resultant consequences (Csikszentmihalyi and LeFevre 1989, 816). That is to say, there appears to be an "interaction" among media types during and after their initial development. One such characterization suggested by Leckenby (in Goldfarb 1999) is illustrated in Figure 1.2.

Today's ubiquitous online banner ads are simply a product of taking known methods and ideas and transferring them to the new media from the traditional media, a common occurrence with the advent of a new medium. This is Phase I of the media cycle, "Transference." Motion pictures, in their early phase of development, often looked like films of a Broadway stage play. Techniques and ideas had not yet been invented to take specific advantage of the technology that movies brought with them. There is some historical evidence of a similar evolutionary path for the Internet:

> Among the prerequisite activities for the successful creation of the Internet was the long-distance operation of a single computer via telephone wire, initially accomplished by George Stibitz in 1940 with the IBM Model 1. Thus, the concept of remotely operating a computer, using a keyboard and telephone line, preceded the first true computers by a number of years. Only some twenty years later, GE and Tymeshare, a specialized firm, were selling systems that used telephone links to permit remote access to computers. (Winston 1998)

Figure 1.2 **Phases of the Media Interaction Circle**

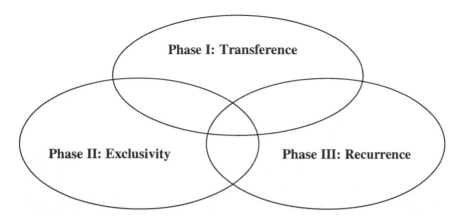

Similarly, each "new" medium has developed through interaction between it and traditional media in terms of technology.

As another example, the radio was a far more economical method to access music than the previous methods had been. This is similar to the Internet, where users can download free music from applications like KaZaA and Morpheus. This shows both new media and traditional media sharing a similar concept—economical pleasure and entertainment. But this does not necessarily mean that the traditional media will be abandoned in favor of the new; Internet users still utilize several media because of the different benefits of each medium.

Before NBC and Microsoft launched their new cable Internet news and information services, they heavily promoted these new offerings in all the media, especially on NBC television. The MSNBC Web site became a very frequently accessed information site after its launching (Coffey and Stipp 1997). This example is a clear indication that Internet users are also users of other media such as television and radio, which may additionally serve as powerful methods to promote Web sites. In short, there are important connection points between the media.

In Phase II, "Exclusivity," however, there are invariably new tools and ideas developed exclusively to answer unique problems that surround the new medium. Such ideas and tools are being developed and understood now for the Internet, for example, user-centric audience measurement methods.

Compared with other media, the Internet medium model has not yet been conceptually developed. For example, log data that can track the routes of Internet users are analyzed in extremely detailed ways today, but it is often very difficult to determine the duration and times of connection, reach/frequency, and click-through. The specific natures of these problems had not been clearly established until now, so companies that measure Internet audience have been free to give any interpretation they like to the data. New methods and ideas are now being developed to solve the problems that are perceived to be exclusive to this new medium.

Phase III, "Recurrence," will be apparent when techniques and ideas for the new medium "turn back" to the older formats. For example, television ads that look like Web interactive ads are an indication of this phase, but there are numerous other instances of the Internet's effects on the traditional media.

The television industry is certainly immense, but it receives very little feedback from its audiences and must rely upon program ratings and the like as measures of audience size (Schramm, Lyle, and Parker 1961). However, with digital television, a method that substitutes a television for a personal computer monitor to access the Internet is being developed. As this method is commercialized, many people who are not adept at using a PC can nonetheless still use the Internet. Then Internet advertisement effectiveness and subsequent consumer behavior will become the center of interest. The standardization of measuring Internet advertising effectiveness may also be a meaningful step on the path toward more successful traditional advertising.

"By being able to track consumer behavior, the Internet may provide a better picture of how consumers behave in response to advertising; this knowledge can be used to understand more traditional media where it was not possible to accurately monitor consumer behavior" (Stewart and Pavlou 2002, 383).

Some television stations have experimented with computers hooked up to audiences' television sets. Audiences are asked questions, and they answer using the PC. The answers are directly received by the television station linked to the television by cable so that, for example, users can play along with a game show just as though it were an online game. Audiences can also record a football game and watch it whenever they want.

Consumer goals and the structural context in which communications have their effects have been critical determinants of advertising effectiveness, but such matters have been regarded as "noise" because of the inability to accurately capture them with traditional media (Stewart and Pavlou 2002). However, determining the answers to such questions becomes possible through the special capabilities of the Internet.

By taking fuller advantage of the unique features of the Internet, filmmakers will be able to reach equally large but more specialized audiences scattered around the world. They will be able to appeal to the special interests and curiosities of individuals anywhere, anytime, through the Internet, rather than making lowest-common-denominator appeals to the masses (Gilder 1994).

The Internet has already transformed the cinema audience, just as radio and television had transformed their audiences. Before they go to the theater, Internet users may see the preview of a movie or reviews written by other Internet users who have already watched it. This is another illustration of the impact of the Internet on other media. Along a similar line, television and radio programs can also be rebroadcast through the Internet so that Internet users can enjoy them whenever they want.

This Media Interaction Cycle is envisioned as a process that may have no easily discernible and discrete starting and ending time for any one medium. It is probably the case that all three of the phases noted above are, to some extent, apparent at any point in media development. In Figure 1.2, the three phases of the Media Interaction Cycle are pictured in an overlapping manner in Venn diagram form and not as distinct entities. This pictorial representation is intended to convey the fact that the three phases of the Media Interaction Cycle are not mutually exclusive events but, rather, dependent upon one another. With respect to the time dimension, this also indicates that at some points in time all three phases may be occurring simultaneously in some mix of each other. At other times, perhaps only one phase of the Media Interaction Cycle can be observed.

With respect to advertising and related fields, what are the possible implications of the Media Interaction Cycle? Initially, with the advent of a new medium, most interest probably centers on the "Transference Phase." Managers of advertising campaigns confront a confusing situation when a new medium comes upon the scene. How can this new "thing" be dealt with? The easy path is to rely upon existing knowledge about how to do things as they have been done in the medium judged to be most "similar" to the new one. If users of the Internet do not want to see a whole page of ads, then only a small part of the page can have ads. And this means small ad space. Outdoor advertising is the model for "short talk" in advertising with a rule of thumb spanning many decades of media and creative practice in advertising; only eight words or less are ordinarily used in outdoor advertisements. So, from a creative perspective and a media planning perspective, at first Internet ads are treated as outdoor ads.

As the medium develops, there is a sense that the outdoor format is limiting both from a creative perspective ("It's like designing matchbook covers") and from a media planning perspective ("Always put the banner ad at the top of the page"). There is the sense that something "unique" is happening in the new medium unlike anything before in other media types. For example, as broadband and wireless capabilities in the user community develop, there is the sense that the Internet really has characteristics in one medium of all the other media that preceded it. And, in this "Exclusivity Phase," this leads to the idea that totally new forms of creative and media planning need to be developed in this situation. An ad becomes a mini-video game and requires media planners to make connections to new issues in their field such as online order fulfillment operations.

As the new medium develops, there may come a time when the formats of creative work and the aspects of media planning developed for the new medium become "hip." That is, there is a desire to mimic the advertising work in the new medium in traditional media. This may be "envy" on the part of managers of the traditional medium. So, creative people develop messages that look like Internet ads but are run on television. Media planners may wish to transfer some of the knowledge about audience measurement (e.g., "click-throughs") to television audience measurement. In this "Recurrence Phase," advertising people get the idea that what has been going on in the new medium, such as the Internet, may have utility in the traditional medium as well. It is a feedback effect.

Advertising ideas and practices are contingent upon the development of new media types. Yet, advertising people participate in the development of the new media. There is an intimate connection between how a medium develops and how advertising people deal with this development. In this sense, the Media Interaction Cycle is important for advertising people to understand both from a managerial perspective, as noted in the above examples, and from the broader perspective of self-understanding of their role in media-type development processes.

In this context, it is important to attempt to understand how the phases of the Media Interaction Cycle can be observed at any given point in time for a given media type in its development phases. Some of these characteristics are explored in the following discussion.

Dimensions of Media Development

While it is not possible to generalize about all the possible characteristics of media development, the following three may be worth noting: technical, material, and commercial. Upon the bases of the above three dimensions, the maturity of a medium may be judged on the traditional-to-new continuum. It is also upon these dimensions that it may be possible to identify which phases of the Media Interaction Cycle characterize a media type at any given time.

With respect to the technical aspects, it can be said that radio was not invented with the advent of Marconi's wireless technology, but that the medium of radio became recognizable only upon Sarnoff's establishment of one-to-many radio sets broadcasts. Yet, the development of the technology is itself a continuum. Sarnoff could not have developed the idea of a radio station and a radio network, had it not been for the first technology invented by Marconi. Similarly, the Internet as it is known today in consumer and business use could not exist without the initial ARPANET of the late 1960s, as developed by the military in the United States and opened to the public in 1992. Content or material change over time as a dominant mode in media (Winston 1998).

Initially, up until about 1919, radio content was about communicating with ships at sea, and later offered classical music and sports and stocks results. Only in 1922 did advertising content emerge in radio. On the Internet, the first content prior to 1992 tended to be scientific discussions among academicians using the network set up by the military establishment. Only later did entertainment through visual and audio content come to the fore on the Internet. Moreover, it should be noted that "personalities" also become part of a medium. Previously, most of us read books, listened to the radio, watched television, and entertained ourselves with hobbies. Now the Internet has become the way that many people entertain themselves (Sanders 1991). As Lappin mentioned:

> As more and more listeners began hearing an ever-growing variety of radio broadcasts, programming tastes became increasingly sophisticated. Newcomers didn't want to hear radio geeks chatting among themselves in Morse code. Like newbies on America Online, they wanted their information to arrive in neatly wrapped packages. They wanted to be entertained and informed. That meant live music. And speeches. Sporting events. (Lappin 1995)

Sarnoff essentially had the vision of how to commercialize the radio in order to make it a financially viable medium. Prior to his vision, most people looked upon radio as a harmless eccentricity and as something practical only in the narrowest sense. To prevent Great Britain's Marconi from monopolizing the expansion of the new technology, the United States Navy pressured Westinghouse, the United Fruit Company, General Electric, and the American Telegraph & Telephone Company to pool their patents into a powerful cartel known as the Radio Corporation of America (Winston 1998). The same type of centralization of commercial power can be observed in the development of the Internet. During the dot-com explosion of the late 1990s, Microsoft and AOL, among others, grew to prodigious size, in part through the acquisition of small players in the field. The selling of products online, as well as advertising for them online, became a major component of the Internet in the late 1990s.

Meeker (1997) noted the following common characteristics in the development of new media, giving some indication that more than the above three dimensions are at work in the media development process:

1. New technologies create new opportunities (e.g., the printing press);
2. Young people drive new media (e.g., David Sarnoff in radio);
3. Content tends over time to focus on some theme;
4. As new media develop, major brands are created (e.g., NBC);
5. Advertising pays the bill—low consumer costs are key to consumer acceptance of new media;
6. New talents and celebrities underlie the success of the new media (e.g., Edgar Allen Poe and Nathaniel Hawthorne in magazines); and
7. New media properties consolidate over time.

Benjamin Franklin wrote, "In this world nothing can be said to be certain, except death and taxes." Sanders (1991) added the change of communication technology to that list of certainties. Media development is dynamic, and the changing nature of technology provides new opportunities as well as new challenges. The recent proliferation of the Internet has made it possible for a wide variety of people to have direct access to a broad array of information. Although the number of people who use the Internet is increasing, Internet usage among people older than age fifty-five is low, compared with other age groups: Relatively young people direct new media. The Internet is a major topic of popular new culture, and, as such, it has also become an arena for popular culture. Media stars, for example, use the Internet to communicate with their fans (Charness, Parks, and Sabel 2001).

However, while Internet use has proliferated, there is still little clarity as to who is going to pay for usage and service of the Internet, just as radio broadcasters had to figure out a way to make money from radio broadcasting. This is just the beginning of the creation of another enormous media system whose worth will rely on the uses people make of it: Online media allow audience members to be both suppliers of electronic media content and consumers; thus, Internet users have the opportunities both to create the worth of this medium and to determine how it will be funded.

The history of new media is based not only on usage, but also on social practices. However, the invention of the Internet as a new medium is still experimental and its exact shape in terms of social satisfaction for the public is still to be decided. The new medium's need to be built to support a scheme of social satisfaction has already incurred and sometimes already met numerous contemporary challenges.

Summary and Conclusion

The primary point of this discussion is that there is an interaction, here called "The Media Interaction Cycle," between media types as they develop over time. New media are not invented in a vacuum. They come about based upon a "platform" of traditional media that have preceded them. As such, their development is influenced by those traditional media, which, nonetheless, do not disappear upon the introduction of the new medium. This is referred to as the "Transference Phase" of media development. At some point, new methods and ideas are developed to solve problems that are perceived to be exclusive to the new medium; this is called the "Exclusivity Phase." Finally, in the "Recurrence Phase," the new ideas and methods invented for the new medium come to be applied to traditional media; the ideas and methods of the new media turn back to the old media.

To fully understand the development of a new medium, it is clear that understanding of the traditional media must first be obtained. It should be possible to more fully understand the new media by making a careful study of traditional media from a compare-and-contrast standpoint and from a broader historical perspective. Advertising scholars and practitioners, in particular, could benefit from a more precise study of this nature. Such study should make it easier to deal with the inevitable upsets and confusion that occur surrounding the introduction and development of a new medium for the carrying of advertising messages.

It may also be the case that the three characteristics noted in the discussion of media dimensions—technical, material, and commercial—may play a large part in the determination of the dominance of each of the phases of the Media Interaction Cycle. Future empirical and historical research would help in exploring this hypothesis.

With respect to empirical research on media issues, it is fairly clear in the field of advertising that while there has been some study concerning the characteristics of a media type and how this should impact media planning practices, there has been relatively little research concerning the interaction of media types and how this may impact media planning implementation. Most media plans for national brands involve the usage of more than one media type. It would be helpful, therefore, to understand the "flow" of the characteristics between these media types in planning the campaign. The same approach may or may not be appropriate between any two media in a media plan, depending upon the dominant phase of interaction between those two types extant at any given point in time. For example, in the "Transference Phase" of Internet development, it may be the case that outdoor advertising served as the basis for banner ads on the Internet. Clearly, an advertising campaign involving outdoor and the Internet would have similarities both in media planning and in creative execution. What would these be and how would they be identified? In the "Recurrence Phase," for example, it may be that television adopts some of the practices of the Internet advertising process both from a media and a creative perspective. At that point, television advertising would benefit from a full understanding of Internet advertising practices. Research could help lead to this understanding.

There is the temptation to believe invariably that a new medium is totally new at the time of its introduction. An understanding of the Media Interaction Cycle could help overcome this tendency among those interested in advertising and other related fields dependent upon media development. More research is needed, especially of a historical nature, to document precisely over time the extent to which the three phases of the Media Interaction Cycle can be observed. Of particular importance would be to develop some evidence of the "overlaps" of each phase, for example, between pairs of media types and how these overlaps impinge upon media planning and other advertising-related issues. What is the implication for advertising media planning if all three phases are observed simultaneously for television and the Internet versus the case when only one or two phases are observed? How will it be known when these phases are operating? That is, what characteristics determine exactly the distinct and overlapping operation of the phases? It may well be that careful and detailed examination of the dimensions of media (technical, material, and commercial) could provide a start on answering these questions.

This discussion provides us with only a hint at the answers to the above questions. More study of the Media Interaction Cycle in historical and empirical contexts will possibly help those interested in understanding the usage of media to better "blend" the media types together in their thinking rather than viewing them in isolated, developmental fashion.

References

Beck, A.H.W. (1967), *Words and Waves*, London: Weidenfeld and Nicolson.

Bezjian-Avery, Alexa, Bobby Calder, and Dawn Iacobucci (1998), "New Media Interactive Advertising vs. Traditional Advertising," *Journal of Advertising Research*, 38 (4), 23–32.

Blattberg, R.C. and J. Deighton (1991), "Interactive Marketing: Exploring the Age of Addressability," *Sloan Management Review*, 33 (1), 5–14.

Bogart, Leo (1958), *The Age of Television*, New York: Frederick Ungar.

Cathcart, Robert and Gary Gumpert (1983), "Mediated Interpersonal Communication: Toward a New Typology," *Quarterly Journal of Speech*, 69 (3), 267–277.

Charness, Neil, Denise C. Parks, and Bernhard A. Sabel (2001), *Communication, Technology and Aging Opportunities and Challenges for the Future*, New York: Springer.

Cho, Chang-Hoan (1999), "How Advertising Works on the WWW: Modified Elaboration Likelihood Model," *Journal of Current Issues and Research in Advertising*, 21 (1), 33–50.

———— and John D. Leckenby (1997), "Internet-Related Programming Technology and Advertising," Paper presented to the annual meeting of the American Academy of Advertising, St. Louis, March, 25pp.

Coen, Robert (2003), *Advertising Expenditure Reports*, McCann-Erickson Advertising, New York [www.universalmccann.com/InsidersReport0603.pdf].

Coffey, Steve and Horst Stipp (1997), "The Interactions Between Computer and Television Usage," *Journal of Advertising Research*, 37 (2), 61–66.

Coyle, James R. and Esther Thorson (2001), "The Effects of Progressive Levels of Interactivity and Vividness in Web Marketing Sites," *Journal of Advertising*, 30 (3), 65–78.

Csikszentmihalyi, M. and J. LeFevre (1989), "Optimal Experience in Work and Leisure," *Journal of Personality and Social Psychology*, 56 (5), 815–822.

Douglas, Susan J. (1987), *Inventing American Broadcasting: 1899–1922*. Baltimore: Johns Hopkins University Press.

Duncan, Tom and S.E. Moriarty (1998), "A Communication-Based Marketing Model for Managing Relationships," *Journal of Marketing*, 62, 1–13.

FIND/SVP (1997), "The American Internet User Survey," [www.findsvp.com].

Forrester Research (1998), "Worldwide Internet Commerce Will Reach As High As $3.2 Trillion in 2003," [www.forrester.com].

Fredin, Eric S. (1989), "Interactive Communication Systems, Values, and the Requirement of Self-Reflection," in *Communication Yearbook* (Vol. 12), M. Burgoon, ed., Beverly Hills, CA: Sage.

Georgescu, Peter A. (1997), "Looking at the Future of Marketing: Marketers, Shops Won't Be 'Feeling Fine' Unless They Change, Says Y&R's Leader," Young and Rubicam, *Advertising Age* (April 14), 30.

Gilder, George (1994), "Life After Television, Updated," *Forbes ASAP*, 153 (5), S94–105.

Goldfarb, Jeff (1999), "Forecasting the Future: What Do the Next 50 Years Have in Store for the Industry?" *American Advertiser*, 16–20.

Ha, L., and E.L. James (1998), "Interactivity Reexamined: A Baseline Analysis of Early Business Web Sites," *Journal of Broadcasting and Electronic Media*, 42 (4), 457–469.

Hoffman, Donna L. and Thomas P. Novak (1996), "Marketing in Hypermedia Computer-Mediated Environments: Conceptual Foundations," *Journal of Marketing*, 60, 39–68.

Interactive Advertising Bureau (1998), [www.iab.net/resources/adrevenue/pr/1997-4ob.asp].

Jenkins, Alan (1974), *The Twenties*, London: Peerage Books.

Jupiter Communication (1997), [www.jupiterresearch.com/bin/item.pl/home].

Kelly, Larry and Donald Juggenheimer (2003), *Advertising Media Planning*, Armonk, NY: M.E. Sharpe.

Lappin, Todd (1995), "Déjà vu All Over Again," *Wired Magazine*, 3 (5), [www.wired.com/wired/archive/3.05/dejavu.html].

Leckenby, John D. and Hairong Li (2000), "From the Editors: Why We Need the *Journal of Interactive Advertising*," *Journal of Interactive Advertising* 1 (1), [www.jiad.org].

Leonhirth, William J., David T.Z. Mindich, and Andris Straumanis (1997), "Wanted . . . a Metaphor of History: Using Past Information Systems to Explain Internet Mailing

Lists," *Electronic Journal of Communication* 7 (4), [http://shadow.cios.org:7979/journals/EJC/007/4/007413.html].

Lombard, Matthew, and Jennifer Snyder-Duch (2001), "Interactive Advertising and Presence: A Framework," *Journal of Interactive Advertising,* [www.jiad.org].

Macias, Wendy (2003), "A Preliminary Structural Equation Model of Comprehension and Persuasion of Interactive Advertising Brand Web Sites," *Journal of Interactive Advertising,* 3 (2).

Marvin, C. (1988), *When Old Technologies Were New: Thinking about Communication in the Late Nineteenth Century*, New York: Oxford University Press.

Marvin, Carolyn and Quentin J. Schultze (1977), "CB in Perspective: The First Thirty Years," *Journal of Communication*, 27 (3), 104–117.

McMillan, Sally (2001), "Exploring Models of Interactivity from Multiple Research Traditions: Users, Documents, and Systems," in *Handbook of New Media*, L. Lievrouw and S. Livingston, eds., London: Sage, 163–182.

Meeker, Mary (1997), *The Internet Advertising Report*, New York: HarperBusiness.

Miller, Steven E. (1996), *Civilizing Cyberspace*, New York: ACM Press.

Murray, Janet H. (1997), *Hamlet on the Holodeck: The Future of Narrative in Cyberspace*, New York: Free Press.

Negroponte, Nicholas (1995), *Being Digital*, New York: Knopf.

Nielsen NetRatings (2003), [http://nielsen-netratings.com].

Nua Internet Surveys (2003), "How Many Online?" [www.nua.ie/surveys/how_many_online].

Pavlik, John V. (1998), *New Media Technology: Cultural and Commercial Perspectives*, 2d ed., Boston: Allyn and Bacon.

Perrett, Geoffrey (1982), *America in the Twenties: A History*, New York: Touchstone/Simon and Schuster.

Rice, Ronald E. and Frederick Williams (1984), "Theories Old and New: The Study of New Media," in *The New Media: Communication Research and Technology*, R.E. Rice, ed., Thousand Oaks, CA: Sage, 33–34.

Sanders, Mark (1991), *Communication Technology Today and Tomorrow*, Mission Hills, CA: Glencoe/Macmillan/McGraw-Hill.

Schramm Wilbur (1960), *Mass Communication*, Urbana: University of Illinois Press.

———, Jack Lyle, and Edwin B. Parker (1961), *Television in the Lives of Our Children*, Stanford, CA: Stanford University Press.

Sicart, Francois (2000), "AOL, RCA, and the Shape of History," [www.gold-eagle.com/research/sicartndx.html].

Sohn, D. and J.D. Leckenby (2002), "Social Dimensions of Interactive Advertising," *Proceedings of the Annual Conference of the American Academy of Advertising*, Jacksonville, FL, March.

Standage, Tom (1998), *The Victorian Internet*, New York: Walker.

Stern, Jim (1995), *World Wide Web Marketing*, New York: Wiley.

Stewart, David W. and Paul A. Pavlou (2002), "From Consumer Response to Active Consumer: Measuring the Effectiveness of Interactive Media," *Journal of the Academy of Marketing Science*, 30 (4), 376–396.

Steuer, J. (1992), "Defining Virtual Reality: Dimensions Determining Telepresence," *Journal of Communication*, 42 (2), 73–93.

Unz, D.C. and Hesse, F.W. (1999), "The Use of Hypertext for Learning," *Journal of Educational Computing Research*, 20, 279–295.

Waldrop, F.C. and J. Borkin (1938), *Television: A Struggle for Power*, New York: William Morrow.

Williams, Frederick, Ronald E. Rice, and Everett M. Rogers (1988), *Research Methods and the New Media*, New York: Free Press.

Williams, Frederick, Sharon Strover, and August E. Grant (1994), "Social Aspects of New Media Technologies," in *Media Effects: Advances in Theory and Research*, J. Bryant and D. Zillman, eds., Hillsdale, NJ: Lawrence Erlbaum Associates, 463–482.

Winston, Brian (1998), *Media Technology and Society*, London and New York: Routledge.

Wu, Guohua (1999), "Perceived Interactivity and Attitude toward Web site," Paper presented at the 1999 Annual Conference of the American Academy of Advertising, Albuquerque, March.

2

The Netvertising Image

Netvertising Image Communication Model (NICM) and Construct Definition

Barbara B. Stern, George M. Zinkhan, and Morris B. Holbrook

Research on Internet advertising, a phenomenon barely a decade old (Leigh 2000), lacks both a theoretically grounded definition of "image," here called the *netvertising image* (Stern 2001), and an image communication model. When the first model of computer-mediated communication (CMC) was presented in the mid-1990s, Hoffman and Novak (1996, 52) pointed out that "virtually no scholarly effort has been undertaken by marketing academics to understand hypermedia CMEs [computer-mediated environments] both as media for marketing communications and as markets in and of themselves." Since that time, even though research on the medium, marketing strategies (Zinkhan 2000), and online consumer behavior (Coupey 1999) has grown and a new journal—*Journal of Interactive Advertising*—has been established (2000), research on images is still at an embryonic stage.

This chapter aims at advancing image research by presenting a model and definition specifically derived for this newest and most rapidly growing advertising medium (Zeff and Aronson 1999). Since netvertising first appeared in 1994, its popularity has expanded geometrically, and until the end of 2000, the increase in revenues was robust. From a starting point of $.10 billion in 1995, revenue grew to $5.3 billion by 2000 (Reidman 2001); by 2001, it was expected to grow to $7.3 billion (Jupiter Media Matrix 2001). This relatively small increase indicates that revenue growth is slowing (Reidman 2001), attributable to both a sluggish economy and the impossibility of sustaining a

120 percent annual growth rate over the long term. Notwithstanding the economic downturn, some analysts still claim that revenue can be increased, but only if advertisers "get creative and innovative on how they attract their audience" (Reidman 2001, 74). In this regard, images are at the core of imaginative message design aimed at stimulating consumer responses such as attention and attitude toward the ad or toward the brand, as well as behavioral activity in the marketplace.

However, two obstacles hamper research on netvertising image design, processing, and effects. The first is the lack of an appropriate communication model, and the second is the lack of a generally agreed on definition of "image." To overcome these obstacles, this chapter first presents a model assembled from ordinary language meanings in the marketing literature and adapted to the netvertising context. It then revisits the definitions to transform them into a nominal definition that researchers can use to construct theory, derive hypotheses, and measure consumer responses.

Netvertising Image Communication Model

Whereas Hoffman and Novak's (1996) conceptual model of consumer behavior in hypermedia CMEs maps the network navigation process, the Netvertising Image Communication Model (NICM) shown in Figure 2.1 maps the stages in the communication process whereby marketer-generated images are converted into consumer responses. The model reflects the transitional process by which organized stimulus imagery leads to perceiver construction of mental images. It is based on prior conceptions of image in marketing, consumer behavior, and advertising research, where the term cuts across four domains (media, message, mind, and marketplace) and is variously used to refer to marketing phenomena such as advertisements, products, services, brands, retail stores, corporations, words and pictures, or consumption experiences (Bullmore 1984). Multiple marketing definitions have been incorporated into netvertising image meanings but have not yet been integrated into a communication model. We begin construction of an integrative model by identifying the prior disciplinary definitions that have influenced netvertising usage.

Marketing

In marketing research, the current focus is on brand image (Schmitt 1999; Schmitt and Simonson 1997), a term that is most often used as a singular or simple plural to denote a structure in the real world of the marketplace (Stern, Zinkhan, and Jaju 2002). That is, research focuses primarily on structural entities in the marketplace (stores, brands, corporations), and advertisements

Figure 2.1   **Stages in Image the Netvertising Communication Model (NICM)**

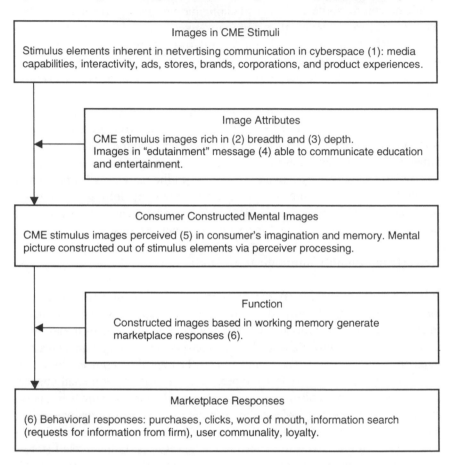

are considered the main vehicle for imparting or transferring images (Bullmore 1984) from these entities to pictures in the consumer's mind. The stimulus is the primary object of study, and images are assumed to be inherent in the entity or advertisement. Neither the message nor the consumer's construction of a mental image is of main interest.

Consumer Behavior

In contrast, consumer behavior research focuses primarily on the perceiver's construction of a mental image, with psychology the source of most theory about mental processes (Bettman 1979; Lynch and Srull 1982; Neisser 1976). The term most often used is the collective noun "imagery" (for review, see

MacInnis and Price 1987). Consumer researchers define this as "(1) a process (not a structure) by which (2) sensory information is represented in working memory" (MacInnis and Price 1987, 473; see also Bone and Ellen 1992). Mental imagery is considered "very like picturing and very unlike describing" (Fodor 1981, 76), for its inputs are sensory, including "sight, taste, sound, smell, and tactile sensations" (MacInnis and Price 1987, 474). However, most research has either addressed discursive processing, in which the inputs are language-like (words and numbers), or compared discursive versus pictorial processing. As a consequence, the study of "such basic issues as what factors stimulate imagery processing" has not developed fully (MacInnis and Price 1987, 486). To date, the process of mental image construction by the perceiver in response to sensory stimuli that include words, pictures, sounds, and movement has not been the focus of consumer behavior research.

Advertising

Advertising research differs in that it often aims at investigating relation-ships between advertisements and consumer responses, in which stimulus factors or elements are central to studies of media-message effects. Images are conceived of as media representations (Stern 1988, 1991) created out of multiple sensory inputs, which are examined by means of formalist literary criticism and semiotic theory, each of which treats different inputs. Whereas formalist criticism (Stern 1989) focuses primarily on the verbal message el-ement (the text) as a stimulus, semiotic criticism focuses on both verbal and visual elements (signs and symbols) as stimuli (Mick 1986, 1997). Semiotic research centers more on the communication process in which the sign is the basic unit, defined as "anything that can stand for something else to an ani-mate being (i.e., an interpreter) in some context" (Mick 1997, 250). How-ever, in both critical systems, image is a tangible or visible verbal and/or pictorial representation of something in the external world (Berger 1989, 38) that resembles the thing for which it stands but is not the actual thing. Thus, the terms "image" and "imagery" are used to refer to words and pictures, as well as music and other sensory inputs represented in a message (Stern 1988, 1991). In psycholinguistic research on advertising, "images" are inclusively defined as connotative references to "objects, persons, places or things that can be seen, heard, felt, smelled, or tasted" (Percy 1988, 271).

Netvertising

Netvertising usage draws from the prior conceptualizations but focuses spe-cifically on the unique characteristics of the Internet medium—notably media capabilities and interactivity (Hoffman and Novak 1996)—that influence advertisements designed for the CME. At first, CME image advertisements consisted of static pictorial banners on a Web page, which were quickly refined by the addition of dynamic pictorials such as moving pictures, animations, and computer-generated art (Kuegler 2000, 295). Banner images became sophisticated graphic devices designed to "act as a gateway to another page or Web site" (Vanden Bergh and Katz 1999, 451). Here, gateway is conceived of metaphorically as the image on the first screen of an advertisement that may or may not trigger immediate consumer action via click-throughs (Hoffman and Novak 1996; Kuegler 2000; Vanden Bergh and Katz 1999). The NICM shown in Figure 2.1 extends the image concept to describe the actions of all participants in the online environment by including the pre-gateway characteristics of created media-specific message stimuli and the post-gateway processes whereby consumers translate messages into mental pictures that in turn stimulate marketplace responses. In this way, the model aims at capturing the transactional process whereby stimulus images on the Web give rise to mental pictures that prompt market behaviors.

Dictionary, Historical, and Netvertising Definitions

"In [an image] one is trying to record the precise instant when a thing outward and objective transforms itself, or darts into a thing inward and subjective" (Pound 1916, 89).

What remains to be investigated is the other major obstacle to scientific research: the lack of a nominal definition. Prior research indicates that image is overdefined (Papineau 1979), for netvertising follows marketing usage based on everyday natural language meanings (Hempel 1970). The problem is that the abundance of meanings hampers a "refined understanding" of the concept (Dobni and Zinkhan 1990) necessary for a scientific language system. Abundance and variety stem from the fact that image, like many other ordinary language terms such as intelligence, emotion, or drama, cannot enter formal language systems with its "ordinary meaning unchanged" (Kyburg 1968, 90). Construction of a nominal definition depends on reduction of "the limitations, ambiguities, and inconsistencies of [a term's] ordinary usage by propounding a reinterpretation intended to enhance the clarity and precision of [its] meanings as well as [its] ability to function in hypotheses and theories with explanatory and predictive force" (Hempel 1970, 664). A nominal definition is needed to sustain communal research discourse and progress toward theory development and testing (Hempel 1970; Kyburg 1968), and ordinary definitions must be transformed into an attribute-based nominal definition applicable to the netvertising environment. The prerequisite for transformation is the abandonment of Humpty Dumpty's communication style, which expresses and exaggerates ordinary language definitions:

> "When *I* use a word," Humpty Dumpty said, in rather a scornful tone, "it means just what I choose it to mean—neither more nor less."

> "The question is," said Alice, "whether you *can* make words mean so many different things."

> "The question is," said Humpty Dumpty, "which is to be master—that's all" (Carroll 1896, 214).

The repository of ordinary language definitions is *The Oxford English Dictionary* (*OED*) (1933 [1989]), the dictionary of choice for etymological and historical information. According to the *OED,* the word "image" is derived from *ikon,* a technical term in Greek poetics that refers to the verbal creation of an almost visible representation of something in the "mind's eye," following the Greek Simonides's definition: "words are the images of things" (Bowra 1961, 363). Analytical image definitions in English dating back to the thirteenth century add up to a complex bundle of meanings—a "real semantic muddle" (Friedman 1953, 26)—that must be disentangled to identify the following image attributes relevant to netvertising.

Created Media Representations

The following definitions refer to images as created representations or media counterparts of items in the external world:

1. a thing in which the aspect, form, or character of another is reproduced; a counterpart, copy;
2. "a visible appearance" or a figure; and
3. a typical example or embodiment of something.

Sensory Elements and Vividness

The following definitions refer to words and pictures as elements of an image, which is considered a "vivid" representation of things in the external world:

4. verbal imagery, in rhetoric: simile, metaphor, or figure of speech; representation of something to the mind by speech or writing; a vivid or graphic description; and

5. pictorial/sensory image in art: an artificial imitation or representation of the external form of any object, especially of a person, such as a statue or portrait; an optical appearance or counterpart of an object, such as a reflection in a mirror or through a lens.

Mental Pictures

The following definition refers to the perceiver's creation in memory or imagination of a mental picture that is stimulated by the media representation:

6. a mental representation of something (especially a visible object), not by direct perception, but by memory or imagination; a mental picture or impression; an idea, conception.

To summarize, many dictionary definitions reveal diverse uses of "image" as a referent to created media representations that include verbal and/or pictorial elements aimed at influencing consumers' behavioral or attitudinal responses. However, the ordinary language definition is neither attribute-based nor specific to netvertising, and closer examination of "the meanings of [the term's] constituent expressions" (Hempel 1970, 660) is needed to identify the historical roots and netvertising applications of the term. The following attributes are derived from historical sources of analytical dictionary definitions modified to fit the netvertising context: (1) media representation; (2) number of message elements, multiple sensory inputs (words, pictures, movement, sound); (3) nature of message elements, vividness (concrete expressions); (4) format, "edutainment" (education and entertainment); (5) consumer response, mental picture; and (6) behavioral responses in the marketplace. In the following section, we examine the six key attributes.

Historical Sourcing of Attributes: Poetics and Philosophy

Everyday language definitions of image evolve from its original meanings in poetics and philosophy, relevant to netvertising as well as poetry in that both rely on evocative connotative language. The development of a nominal definition, considered a "hypothetical" concept, has also been called a "literary definition" (Underwood 1957, 54–55), apt in image research.

Media Representations

Netvertising images are media representations that are unlike other advertising representations in that they are located in cyberspace or virtual reality

(Hoffman and Novak 1996). Nevertheless, they are like other advertising images in that the representations are often viewed as more "real" than the objects that they represent. In this sense, advertising images are recent additions to the representation-as-reality category, traceable to Aristotle's aesthetics (Fergusson 1961) and updated by postmodernists (Firat and Venkatesh 1995). In the twentieth century, the modernist poetic and philosophical movement known as "Imagism" was the predecessor of postmodern usage.

Even though the Imagist Movement, a school of poetry that flourished from 1909 to 1917, was short-lived, its influence on advertising was profound (Gage 1981). T.E. Hulme's *Speculations* (1924) provided philosophical grounding for the concept of image as the fundamental reality, stating that "real communication between human beings is made only by means of images" (Pratt 1963, 27). He praised inventive imagery as the sole means of conveying the "spontaneous, intensive perception of reality," declaring the poetic mission to be the creation of innovative imagery capable of depicting a vivifying "*freshness* of impression" (Gage 1981, 163).

By the 1950s, long after the Imagists had been forgotten, advertising creatives took on the poetic task of "image creation" and "its legitimate offspring, 'image management'" (Leiss, Kine, and Jhally 1986, 239–240). The advertising industry is said to be responsible for the "poeticizing of consumption" (Hayakawa 1946, 262), and the "imagistic mode of communication" was used to construct advertising representations designed to be reconstructed as real pictures in the "mind's eye" (Puto and Wells 1984, p. 238). Netvertising continues the advertising mission of creating "art with commercial intent," in which "packaged commercial matter, born of creativity . . . courses through . . . the delivery process" (Leeabaert 1999, 3). In the virtual reality of cyberspace, created representations are conceived of metaphysically as "real."

Number of Message Elements: Multiple Sensory Inputs

The CME nourishes the production of images rich in breadth, which here refers to the number and kind of sensory dimensions that a netvertising message can include (Daft, Lengel, and Trevino 1987; Shih 1998; Steuer 1992). Sensory breadth and depth are made possible by the medium's capacity to provide "interactive access to both static (i.e., text, image, and graphics) and dynamic (audio, full-motion video, and animation) content" (Hoffman and Novak 1996, 53). Nonetheless, most early Internet researchers used "image" in a more limited way, referring primarily to visual elements but not other sensory inputs, perhaps because the research focus was on banner ads. More recently, researchers have extended "image" or "imagery" to refer to verbal material in brand-building banners, which "use imagery, animation, and succinct slogans" (Krishnamurthy 2000, p. 34). In current research, image is more broadly "defined as all digital subject matter on the site. This includes the form of the digital subject matter—text, video, audio, and graphics—as well as its domains, including product, service, and information offerings" (Rayport and Jaworski 2001, 115).

Nature of Message Elements: Vividness

The CME also facilitates production of vivid images with "representational richness" (Steuer 1992, 91) stemming from the elements or formal features of a message in a mediated environment (Shih 1998). The point of image vividness is to attract "a centering of attention on a limited stimulus field" (Hoffman and Novak 1996, 60) so that further processing can take place (Steuer 1992). Shih (1998) notes that higher levels of vividness stimulate higher levels of immersion in the media environment and more positive affect. The experiential power of vivid imagery lies in its presentation of "an intellectual and emotional complex in an instant of time" (Pound 1916, 86), for it has the capacity to render "particular moments and scenes out of color and objects" so vividly that they make perceivers instantly "see" things that are yet unseen (Benvenuto 1985, 120).

A comparison of the gateway screens for Hewlett-Packard and Canon (www.hp.com and www.canon.com) illustrates the nature of vivid versus pallid imagery. These are the opening screens on the corporate Web sites, intended to provide fun experiences and information (Vanden Bergh and Katz 1999). The vivid Hewlett-Packard screen (Figure 2.2) has a top slogan identifying the firm as the "leader in computing and imaging solutions and services" and a picture of a cute cartoon penguin in the upper left corner, on which the firm-relevant words, "hp linux evangelist opens doors to open source," are superimposed. Curiosity is aroused by the juxtaposition of picture and text, for there is no indication of what the penguin has to do with open sourcing. Furthermore, the phrase "opens doors" is a concrete expression, as are words such as "celebrating" in the picture below, "unveils" and "launch" in the "highlights" text, and "invent" in the slogan. Four paths are on the upper right, making it simple for viewers to click onto the next screen, and the combination of a brightly colored picture and concrete action verbs coalesces into a vivid image that represents Hewlett-Packard as an innovative, dynamic, and consumer-friendly firm.

In contrast, the pallid Canon opening screen (Figure 2.3) has a top slogan that tells the viewer "Welcome to Canon Worldwide Network," followed on the upper left by a list of corporate headquarters with language

Figure 2.2 **Hewlett-Packard Gateway Screen**

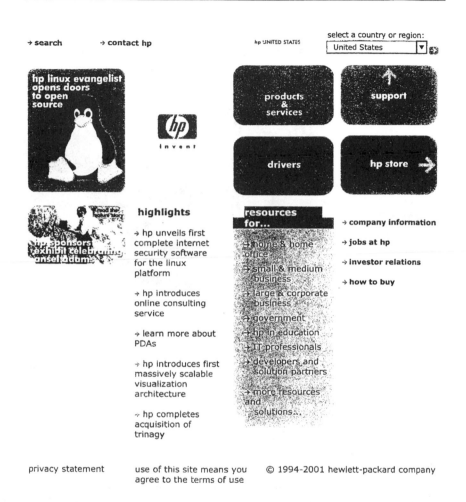

choices and geographic operations. The only other word in the copy is the abstract verb "welcome" used twice. The pictures on the upper right consist of hazy peripheral pastel photos of athletes playing golf and tennis; sea, sky, and clouds; and two people using a computer plus a shot of the keyboard. The central photo is a globe, with the slogan superimposed, and it ties together all of the verbal and visual images. However, the site is pallid in that it welcomes viewers only to the extent of telling them that the firm is worldwide, which does not differentiate Canon from competitors such as HP, Brother, Xerox, and others. Furthermore, the screen provides

Figure 2.3 **Canon Gateway Screen**

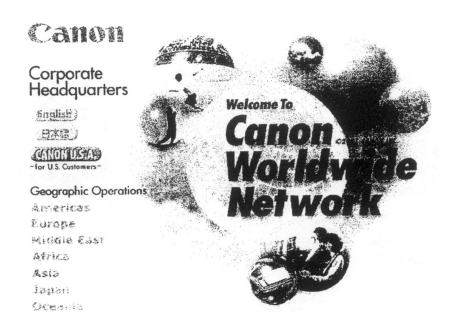

no obvious way to click onto the next screen, and the combination of vague
pictures, abstract text, and lack of pathways forms a pallid image that represents Canon as worldwide but firm-centered. The screen is, as they say,
"all about me."

To create vivid images, advertising copywriters follow the Imagists' lead
in using concrete language (Pratt 1963). Imagist poetry began the process of
discarding the "rigid, overblown, vague, sentimental, and unoriginal" (Gage
1981, 8) abstract language beloved by Victorian poets (Lentricchia 1990)
and using only concrete language to create vivid imagery. Concrete language
is defined in Amy Lowell's (1915, vii) how-to guide, *Some Imagist Poets,*
which sets forth rules for creating imagist works that are "hard and clear,
never blurred nor indefinite." Similarly, creatives responsible for netvertising
messages are urged "not just to build sites filled with product information
but to make the information so interesting, involving, and compelling as to
convince the consumer that these ads are the best source of product information" (Vanden Bergh and Katz 1999, 452). Vivid and attention-getting Web
sites are often called "sticky" and considered the best means for communicating a firm's core values and giving consumers a compelling purchase rationale (Rayport and Jaworski 2001).

Message Format: "Edutainment"

Communicating the core of companies and other sponsors occurs in netvertisements through the fusion of entertainment and education, which dates back to Aristotle's aesthetics. In the *Poetics*, representations are considered a source of learning as well as pleasure, for "why men enjoy seeing a likeness is that in contemplating it they find themselves learning or inferring" (Fergusson 1961, 5) something about the object being represented. A representation is considered artistic only insofar as it satisfies the human need to know and understand, which accompanies the need for pleasurable experiences (Else 1986; Golden and Hardison 1981). The Internet, then, is but the latest medium for education and entertainment—"edutainment" (Wind and Rangaswamy 2001, 24)—and netvertising images the latest expressions of creativity designed to fuse both (Hoffman and Novak 1996).

This time around, it is the CME that provides advertisers with "an unprecedented opportunity" to offer messages that include information in "a supporting knowledge environment" and entertainment in an enjoyable format (Wind and Rangaswany 2001, 24). In so doing, the medium overrides the boundary between telling and showing (Leiss, Kline, and Jhally 1986; Wells 1989), for as Rayport and Jaworski (2001, 114) point out, the netvertising context easily enables fusion of entertaining "virtual (and, to date, largely visual)" representations with educational and largely verbal "significant information." Thus, the format balances aesthetic content, in which visual elements provide a pleasant escape, and functional content, in which largely verbal elements provide information.

Consumer Response: Constructing Meaning and Mental Pictures

Prior marketing definitions converge in identifying the consumer creation of mental images of things not directly perceived but "seen" in memory or imagination (Brooks 1947; Gage 1981). Consumers are said to translate images of a brand, store, or corporation into a picture in the mind's eye. For example, corporate image is defined as "the mental construct developed by the consumer on the basis of a few selected impressions among the flood of total impressions; it comes into being through a creative process in which these selected impressions are elaborated, embellished and ordered" (Reynolds 1965, 70). Similarly, store image (Marks 1976, 37) is defined as "not merely the sum of objective individual dimensions associated with the store; rather, . . . a composite of dimensions that consumers perceive as the store." Brand image reaffirms this definition: "what people think and feel about it [the brand] . . . lies in the mind of the beholder, and is conditioned at least as much by the nature of the beholder as by the nature of the object itself" (Bullmore 1984, 236). Netvertising usage follows suit, with consumers viewed as active perceivers who respond to images in the interactive context (Hoffman and Novak 1996). Thus, there is uniformity in the conception of image as "a creation which fulfills its end in the mind" of the perceiver (Gage 1981, 1) and in the view of the "imagistic mode of communication" (Leiss, Kline, and Jhally 1986, 238) as a trigger for the transformation of consumption goods and experiences into vivid mental pictures (Puto and Wells 1984).

This transformation is based on consumer perception, for it is the consumer who "must construct meaning from the text through the act of interpretation" (Ritson and Elliott 1999, 266). That is, imagery recipients do not experience meaning as something closed or finite, but rather participate with the author in co-creating it. Nonetheless, the nature of image processing is more neglected than that of information processing and more controversial. At least three different views of the image construction process have been proposed. From the perspective of consumer construction, MacInnis and Price (1987) claim that "imagery" is a distinct type of processing mode used by persons to integrate bits of information about an object (or event) into a gestalt. Incoming information, rather than being stored as an image, is said to activate knowledge structures leading to the formation of a mental picture. Here, imagery is considered in the beholder's eye. Alternatively, from the perspective of imagery inherent in the stimulus, Unnava, Agarwal, and Haugtvedt (1996, 84) claim that "the modality of imagery and the modality of information presentation" may interact to facilitate or hamper learning. In this regard, stimulus factors such as the presentation of written or spoken information and visual imagery are posited as possible competitors for mental space. Another alternative from a blended perspective is Rayport and Jaworski's (2001) claim that the CME allows for a simultaneous combination of less cognitive processing (like viewing television images) and more (like reading print material). Here, the medium itself provides the opportunity for multisensory inputs that can be processed in many modalities at once.

In the scant research literature on consumer responses to interactive advertising, the information processing perspective dominates, with emphasis on the capacity of interactive technology to provide a greater "range and depth of information" that influences consumer processing strategies (Coupey 1999, 199). The research agenda reflects the need to examine possible "differences in the amount and depth of information processing" and the extent to which "information processing tends to be guided by the format in which information is presented" (Coupey 1999, 210). However, research "intended to elucidate the information processing behaviors of consumers in interactive media" (Coupey 1999, 205) has barely begun. Similarly, research on imagery processing in "advertising-oriented studies of reception" as part of meaning co-creation is in its infancy (Ritson and Elliott 1999, 274).

Behavioral Response: Marketplace Action

Perhaps the major reason for the lack of research on Internet imagery processing, aside from the newness of the field, is that the most compelling topic of interest has been external marketplace behavior, for as Rayport and Jaworski (2001, 124) point out, "mental space is marketspace." Images arc commonly used in "buy this" messages, in which the goal is an immediate behavioral response of order placement. But they also appear in softer-sell messages, also known as "image ads," for which the goal is the development of favorable attitudes to and relationships with firms and brands. These ads present "an image on a Web page that someone has paid to place there," in which banners serve the purpose of "trying to put forth some kind of image of the company represented" (Kuegler 2000, 295). Internet advertisements, especially on corporate Web sites, are seen as a way to "create an image and attempt to build an ongoing relationship with the consumer" (Hoffman and Novak 1996, 58). Thus, netvertising images can aim at short-term marketplace responses or longer-term attitude formation and relationship management.

To sum up, the following definition transforms the ordinary meanings in prior marketing research, dictionaries, and historical sources into an attribute-based nominal definition incorporating the stages in image communication shown in Figure 2.1:

> A netvertising image is a cyberspace (1) media representation in which (2) the message incorporates multiple sensory inputs as (3) vivid stimuli that fuse (4) entertainment and education to inspire (5) consumer creation of mental pictures that lead to (6) marketplace behavioral responses.

This definition, plus the related NICM, aim at contributing to a fuller understanding of the influence of unique cyberspace characteristics on image generation, transmission, and marketplace responses. Both the model and the nominal definition can contribute to managerial decisions about the success or failure of messages in a CME, as well as to future researchers' decisions about what to investigate. We now turn to identifying important underresearched areas of inquiry to provide suggestions for further research.

Future Research Directions

Among the blank or barely filled areas, those that stand out as particularly worthy of research are measurement issues, individual differences, memory, and attention versus intrusion.

Measurement

The methodological "dominance of experimental research in laboratory settings" (Ritson and Elliott 1999, 261) does not take into account the communal aspects of interactive communication or the influence of stimuli in the CME on meaning construction. Similarly, quantitative analysis of company Web sites (Ranchod, Hackney, and Gurau 1999) does not focus on the interpretation of image meaning. To address these issues, we propose the adaptation of interpretive methods (e.g., ethnographic interviews, *in-depth* interviews, onsite observation) to discover consumer responses, followed by qualitative data analysis to interpret response themes (Ritson and Elliott 1999). These methods, already used in research on print advertisements (Mick and Buhl 1992), are also well suited to elicit responses to netvertisements. Content analysis of responses (Kassarjian 1977) or iterative thematic analysis (Thompson, Locander, and Pollio 1989) may help to determine what consumers take away from the imaging process. Recently, Kozinets (1997, 470) introduced the term "netnography" to describe a form of qualitative research inquiry in which "the methods of cultural anthropology" are used to study cyberculture groups, called "tribes" (Cova and Cova 2002). Semiotic analysis has also been used to study print advertisements (Mick 1986), but at present, qualitative methods have not been used to study either the influence of netvertising advertisements on the Internet tribalization process or the role of images as identifying signs that link tribe members (Cova and Cova 2002).

So too is the brand-building potential of image ads virtually unexamined, with little known about their role in stimulating "partnership between the company and the tribe" (Cova and Cova 2002). Consequently, as a Jupiter Media Metrix (2001) report indicates, media planners seem to be "underestimating the branding power of online ads." The current measurement of the "power" of such ads by click-throughs is considered flawed in that it is merely "an intermediate behavioral measure that lacks meaning in and of itself" (Krishnamurthy 2000, 4). Even though the quantitative assessment of the number of clicks measures the capacity of a banner ad to attract the consumer's attention, it says nothing about responses such as derivation of ad meanings, attitude formation and change, or consumer-marketer relationships. The voluminous body of interpretive research in other marketing disciplines can be adapted to the netvertising context, in which multimethod techniques that combine qualitative and quantitative techniques are particularly applicable to the study of individual differences, as well as communal relationships.

Individual Differences

The study of individual differences is not yet well advanced, for most netvertising studies—similar to other image and information processing research (Luce, Bettman, and Payne 2001; MacInnis and Price 1987)—assume that mental and behavioral responses to images can be aggregated across subjects. However, as Leigh (2000) points out, individual factors, such as prior knowledge, predisposition/interest level, and cognitive capabilities, have been understudied, especially in media other than print. One exception is research on online auction behavior, in which questions about consumers' interest in and disposition to use auction sites—"what motivates them, and what will keep them coming back for more" (Herschlag and Zwick 2000, 14)—are addressed (Chui and Zwick 1999; Stafford and Stafford 2001; Wilcox 2000). Stafford and Stafford's (2001) findings indicate that participation in auctions is influenced by some of the individual factors mentioned by Leigh (2000): the level of technological proficiency, which relates to prior experience with the CME; attitude toward the CME, which relates to interest in online auctions; and involvement with the purchase situation. These findings can be adapted for netvertising research to measure individual differences such as interest in the search process itself, interest in learning about the informational content on a site, interest in new and unique site formats, desire for social aspects of interactive communication (chatting, friends, interaction, news groups, people) (Cova and Cova 2002; Kozinets 1997), and having fun by playing on the Internet.

Entertainment and Learning

Games, fun, and play in behavior on the Web have been compared to bricolage: the nonlinear, nonhierarchical, flexible mode of associative learning in which people assimilate ideas through play. The concept applies to advertisements on the Web, where individual users can play around with message order and organize the information in whatever way appeals to them (Shih 1998). This is viewed as active learning, a process whereby consumers are said to be able to internalize ideas and screen out unwanted information such that they can more efficiently store data in memory (Shih 1998). The process needs to be tested using netvertising images as stimuli, especially because the edutainment format fuses information and imagery.

Attention Versus Intrusion

Despite the gateway function of netvertising images, which is to capture the consumer's attention such that he or she clicks on the banner image to move to another page for additional information, there is surprisingly little research on the attention processes. Hoffman and Novak (1996, 60) call for additional research on "the role of the content characteristics of vividness and interactivity in attracting attention," usually defined as "the allocation of processing capacity or effort" to a stimulus (Bettman 1979, 77). Kozinets (1999, 257) calls for "new and innovative models of attention-seeking" and uses the phrase "attention marketing" to emphasize the importance of netvertising to attract attention in virtual communities of consumption. We suggest that a promising issue for additional research is the investigation of the attention-attracting role of image attributes such as vividness, entertainment, innovativeness, and ease of processing to determine not only what pulls consumers in, but also what drives them away.

In this regard, it is unlikely that consumers will want to block all Internet ads, for even though Junkbusters' ad-zapping software has been around since 1996, it is not widely used (Stamler 2001). However, it may grow in popularity, for when advertisers began questioning the effectiveness of banner ads, they began to create intentionally intrusive ads that consumers might very well want to avoid. The most aggressive ones at present are interstitial ads that automatically pop up between one Web page and another and force attention because a viewer must click on the window to get rid of it. Interstitials and other pop-ups irritate consumers (Meeker 1997; Rayport and Jaworski 2001), but neither managers nor researchers have more than impressionistic evidence about this irritation. Thus, the very newness of Internet research provides ample scope for examining the way that consumer processing is influenced by the creation of images and the way marketers can use this information to design and implement more effective campaigns.

References

Benvenuto, Richard (1985), *Amy Lowell*, Boston, MA: Twayne.
Berger, Arthur Asa (1989), *Seeing Is Believing: An Introduction to Visual Communication*, Mountain View, CA: Mayfield.
Bettman, James R. (1979), *An Information Processing Theory of Consumer Choice*, Reading, MA: Addison-Wesley.
Bone, Paula Fitzgerald and Pam Scholder Ellen (1992), "The Generation and Consequences of Communication-Evoked Imagery," *Journal of Consumer Research*, 19 (June), 93–104.

Bowra, C.M. ([1936] 1961), *Greek Lyric Poetry from Alcmon to Simonides*, Oxford, UK: Clarendon Press.

Brooks, Cleanth (1947), *The Well Wrought Urn: Studies in the Structure of Poetry*, New York: Harcourt, Brace.

Bullmore, J. (1984), "The Brand and Its Image Revisited," *International Journal of Advertising*, 1 (3), 235–238.

Carroll, Lewis ([1896] 1951), *Through the Looking-Glass*, in *The Complete Works of Lewis Carroll*, New York: Modern Library.

Chui, Kevin and Rami Zwick (1999), "Auction on the Internet—A Preliminary Study," [http://home.ust.hk/~mzwick/Internet_Auction.html].

Coupey, Eloise (1999), "Advertising in an Interactive Research Agenda," in *Advertising and the World Wide Web*, David W. Schumann and Esther Thorson, eds., Mahwah, NJ: Lawrence Erlbaum Associates, 197–215.

Cova, Bernard and Veronique Cova (2002), "The Tribalization of Society and Its Impact on the Conduct of Marketing," *European Journal of Marketing Special Issue: Societal Marketing in 2002 and Beyond*, [http://visionarymarketing.com/articles/cova/cova-tribe-2001.html].

Daft, Richard L., R.H. Lengel, and L.K. Trevino (1987), "Message Equivocality, Media Selection and Manager Performance: Implications for Information Systems," *MIS Quarterly*, 11 (1), 355–366.

Dobni, D. and G.M. Zinkhan (1990), "In Search of Brand Image: A Foundation Analysis," in *Advances in Consumer Research*, Marvin E. Goldberg, Gerald Gorn, and Richard W. Pollay, eds., New Orleans: Association for Consumer Research, 110–118.

Else, Gerard Frank (1986), *Plato and Aristotle on Poetry*, Peter Burian, ed., Chapel Hill: The University of North Carolina Press.

Fergusson, Francis (1961), *Aristotle's Poetics*, S.H. Butcher, trans. New York: Hill and Wang.

Firat, A. Fuat and Alladi Venkatesh (1995), "Liberatory Postmodernism and the Reenchantment of Consumption," *Journal of Consumer Research*, 22 (December), 239–267.

Fodor, Jerry A. (1981), "Imagistic Representation," in *Imagery*, Ned Block, ed., Cambridge, MA: MIT Press, 63–86.

Friedman, Norman (1953), "Imagery: From Sensation to Symbol," *Journal of Aesthetics and Art Criticism*, 12 (Winter), 25–37.

Gage, John T. (1981), *In the Arresting Eye: The Rhetoric of Imagism*, Baton Rouge: Louisiana State University Press.

Golden, Leon, and O.B. Hardison Jr. (1981), *Aristotle's Poetics: A Translation and Commentary for Students of Literature*, Gainesville: University Press of Florida.

Hayakawa, Samuel Ichiey (1946 [1964]), *Language in Thought and Action*, 2d ed., New York: Harcourt, Brace, and World.

Hempel, Carl G. (1970), "Fundamentals of Concept Formation in Empirical Science," in *Foundations of the Unity of Science: Toward an International Encyclopedia of Unified Science*, Vol. II, Nos. 1–9, Otto Neurath, Rudolph Carnap, and Charles Morris, eds., Chicago: University of Chicago Press, 653–740.

Herschlag, Miriam and Rami Zwick (2000), "Internet Auctions—Popular and Professional Literature Review," *Quarterly Journal of Electronic Commerce*, 1 (2).

Hoffman, Donna L. and Thomas P. Novak (1996), "Marketing in Hypermedia Computer-Mediated Environments: Conceptual Foundations," *Journal of Marketing*, 60 (3), 50–68.

Hulme, T.E. (1924), *Speculations: Essays on Humanism and the Philosophy of Art*, Herbert Read, ed., New York: Harcourt, Brace.

Journal of Interactive Advertising (2000), [www.//jiad.org/v011/n01/editors/index/html].

Jupiter Media Metrix (2001), "Online Marketers Misunderstand Branding," (June 26), [www.nua.id/surveys/index].

Kassarjian, Harold H. (1977), "Content Analysis in Consumer Research," *Journal of Consumer Research*, 4 (June), 8–18.

Kozinets, Robert V. (1997), "'I Want to Believe': A Netnography of the X-Philes Subculture of Consumption," in *Advances in Consumer Research*, Merrie Brucks and Deborah J. MacInnis, eds., Vol. 24, Provo, UT: Association for Consumer Research, 470–475.

——— (1999), "E-Tribalized Marketing?: The Strategic Implications of Virtual Communities of Consumption," *European Management Journal*, 17 (3), 252–264.

Krishnamurthy, Sandeep (2000), "Deciphering the Internet Advertising Puzzle," *Marketing Management*, 9 (3), 34–40.

Kuegler, Thomas J., Jr. (2000), *Advertising and Marketing*, 3d ed., Rocklin, CA: Prima Tech.

Kyburg, Henry E. (1968), *Philosophy of Science*, New York: Macmillan.

Leeabaert, Derek, ed. (1999), *The Future of the Electronic Marketplace*, Cambridge, MA: MIT Press.

Leigh, James H. (2000), "An Informal, Qualitative Analysis of Shortages and Abundances in Academic Advertising Research," in *Advertising Research: The Internet, Consumer Behavior, and Strategy*, George Zinkhan, ed., Chicago: American Marketing Association, 75–81.

Leiss, William, Stephen Kline, and Sut Jhally (1986), *Social Communication in Advertising: Persons, Products and Images of Well-Being*, Toronto: Methuen.

Lentricchia, Frank (1990), "In Place of an Afterword—Someone Reading," in *Critical Terms for Literary Study*, Frank Lentricchia and Thomas McLaughlin, eds., Chicago: University of Chicago Press, 321–338.

Lowell, Amy (1915 [1969]), "Preface," in *Some Imagist Poets: An Anthology*, Boston: Houghton Mifflin Company, v–viii.

Luce, Mary Frances, James R. Bettman, and John W. Payne (2001), *Emotional Decisions: Tradeoff Difficulty and Coping in Consumer Choice*, Monographs of the *Journal of Consumer Research*, Chicago: University of Chicago Press.

Lynch, John G., Jr. and Thomas K. Srull (1982), "Memory and Attentional Factors in Consumer Choice: Concepts and Research Methods," *Journal of Consumer Research*, 9 (June), 18–37.

MacInnis, Deborah J. and Linda L. Price (1987), "The Role of Imagery in Information Processing: Review and Extensions," *Journal of Consumer Research*, 13 (March), 473–491.

Marks, Ronald B. (1976), "Operationalizing the Concept of Store Image," *Journal of Retailing*, 52 (Fall), 37–46.

Meeker, Mary (1997), *The Internet Advertising Report*, New York: HarperBusiness.

Mick, David Glen (1986), "Consumer Research and Semiotics: Exploring the Morphology of Signs, Symbols, and Significance," *Journal of Consumer Research*, 13 (September), 196–213.

——— (1997), "Semiotics in Marketing and Consumer Research: Balderdash, Verity, Pleas," in *Consumer Research: Postcards from the Edge*, Stephen Brown and Darach Turley, eds., London: Routledge, 249–262.

———— and Claus Buhl (1992), "A Meaning-Based Model of Advertising Experiences," *Journal of Consumer Research*, 19 (December), 317–338.

Neisser, Ulric (1976), *Cognition and Reality: Principles and Implications of Cognitive Psychology*, San Francisco, CA: W.H. Freeman.

The Oxford English Dictionary (1933), 2d ed., Oxford, UK: Clarendon Press.

Papineau, David (1979), *Theory and Meaning*, Oxford, UK: Clarendon Press.

Percy, Larry (1988), "The Often Subtle Linguistic Cues in Advertising," in *Advances in Consumer Research*, Vol. 15, Michael J. Houston, ed., Provo, UT: Association for Consumer Research, 269–274.

Pound, Ezra (1916 [1970]), *Gaudier-Brzeska: A Memoir*, London, John Lane.

Pratt, William (1963), "Introduction," in *Modern Poetry in Miniature: The Imagist Poem*, New York: E.P. Dutton, 11–39.

Puto, Christopher and William D. Wells (1984), "Informational and Transformational Advertising: The Differential Effects of Time," in *Advances in Consumer Research*, Vol. 11, Thomas C. Kinnear, ed., Provo, UT: Association for Consumer Research, 638–643.

Ranchod, Ashok, Ray Hackney, and Calin Gurau (1999), "Electronic Commerce: From Virtual Transactions to Virtual Offers," Andy Bytheway, ed., *Proceedings of BITWorld'99*, [www.uwc.ac.za/ems/is/bw/bw-note.htm].

Rayport, Jeffrey E. and Bernard J. Jaworski (2001), *e-Commerce*, Boston: McGraw-Hill/Irwin.

Reidman, Patricia (2001), "Net Ad Sector Moderates," *Advertising Age*, 72 (January 1), 72–74.

Reynolds, W.H. (1965), "The Role of the Consumer in Image Building," *California Management Review*, 7 (Spring), 69–76.

Ritson, Mark and Richard Elliott (1999), "The Social Uses of Advertising: An Ethnographic Study of Adolescent Audiences," *Journal of Consumer Research*, 26 (December), 260–277.

Schmitt, Bernd H. (1999), *Experiential Marketing: How to Get Customers to SENSE, FEEL, THINK, ACT, and RELATE to Your Company and Brands*, New York: Free Press.

———— and Alex Simonson (1997), *Marketing Aesthetics. The Strategic Management of Brands, Identity, and Image*, New York: Free Press.

Shih, Eric Chuan Fong (1998), "Conceptualizing Consumer Experiences in Cyberspace," *European Journal of Marketing*, 32 (7/8), 665–663.

Stafford, Thomas S. and Marla Royne Stafford (2001), "Identifying Motivations for the Use of Commercial Web Sites," *Information Resources Management Journal*, 14 (January–March), 22–30.

Stamler, Bernard (2001), "If You Hate Web Ads, You Can 'Just Say No,'" *New York Times* (June 13), 15.

Stern, Barbara B. (1988), "How Does an Ad Mean? Language in Advertising," *Journal of Advertising*, 17 (Summer), 3–14.

———— (1989), "Literary Explication: A New Methodology for Consumer Research," in *Interpretive Consumer Research*, Elizabeth C. Hirschman, ed., Provo, UT: Association for Consumer Research, 48–59.

———— (1991), "Detailed Image Analysis: Poetic Methodology for Advertising Research," *International Journal of Advertising*, 10 (2), 161–180.

———— (2001), "Netvertising Track," in *2001 AMA Winter Educators' Conference: Marketing Theory and Applications*, Vol. 12, Ram Krishnan and Madhu Viswanathan, eds., Chicago: American Marketing Association, vi.

———, George Zinkhan, and Anupam Jaju (2001), "Marketing Images: Construct Definition, Measurement Issues, and Theory Development," *Marketing Theory*, 1 (December), 201–224.

Steuer, Jonathan (1992), "Defining Virtual Reality: Dimensions Determining Telepresence," *Journal of Communication*, 42 (4), 75–93.

Thompson, Craig J., William B. Locander, and Howard R. Pollio (1989), "Putting Consumer Experience Back into Consumer Research: The Philosophy and Method of Existential Phenomenology," *Journal of Consumer Research*, 16 (September), 133–146.

Underwood, Benton J. (1957), *Psychological Research*, New York: Appleton-Century-Crofts.

Unnava, H. Rao, Sanjeev Agarwal, and Curtis P. Haugtvedt (1996), "Interactive Effects of Presentation Modality and Message-Generated Imagery on Recall of Advertising Information," *Journal of Consumer Research*, 23 (June), 81–88.

Vanden Bergh, Bruce G. and Helen Katz (1999), *Advertising Principles: Choice, Challenge, Change*, Chicago: NTC Publishing.

Wells, William D. (1989), "Lectures and Dramas," in *Cognitive and Affective Responses to Advertising*, Patricia Cafferata and Alice M. Tybout, eds., Lexington, MA: Lexington Books, 13–20.

Wilcox, Ronald T. (2000), "Experts and Amateurs: The Role of Experience in Internet Auctions," *Marketing Letters*, 11 (September), 363–374.

Wind, Jerry and Arvid Rangaswamy (2001), "Customerization: The Next Revolution in Mass Customization," *Journal of Interactive Marketing*, 15 (February), 13–32.

Zeff, Robbin Lee and Brad Aronson (1999), *Advertising on the Internet*, New York: Wiley.

Zinkhan, George (2000), "Introduction to Advertising Research," in *Advertising Research: The Internet, Consumer Behavior, and Strategy*, George Zinkhan, ed., Chicago: American Marketing Association, 2–8.

3

Intermedia Effects for Appropriate/Inappropriate Print and Internet Stimuli

Shelly Rodgers

Intermedia effects have been of interest to advertising scholars and practitioners for many decades. An intermedia effect, also called a "vehicle source effect," is defined as a "measure of the increment to advertising response contributed by one vehicle rather than another" (Assmus 1977, 4). Intermedia effects have raised important issues for advertising practice and theory. Media planners incorporate differential intermedia weights for the various media options under consideration. The study of intermedia effects also raises fundamental theoretical questions about cognitive processes for advertising and marketing scholars.

A goal of experimental studies on intermedia effects is to determine whether a differential effect occurs if a person is exposed to the same ad in one medium versus another. This is done by manipulating the media context while holding the ad or content constant across media. Much research on intermedia effects has compared print and broadcast media. Stimulus materials are typically created either by having a talking head read a print ad on video (i.e., the broadcast condition) or by transcribing existing audiovisual content to produce a print ad (i.e., the print condition). The bulk of evidence suggests that, when content is held constant, print is superior to audiovisual presentations (Eveland and Dunwoody 2001).

The rapid growth of the Internet has turned recent attention to understanding intermedia effects online. Like broadcast studies, comparable content is created for Internet stimuli by creating a print stimulus and posting it online. Although such controls are necessary for validity purposes, manipulations such as these raise concerns about the selection of appropriate stimuli. Eveland

and Dunwoody (2001) have noted that television newscasts designed to look like print news provide an unrealistic comparison for the broadcast condition. Internet stimuli designed to look like print raise similar concerns.

The purpose of this research is to examine intermedia effects for appropriate/inappropriate Internet and print stimuli. This was accomplished with a series of three experiments. We begin with a review of the relevant literature.

Literature Review

Several advertising studies have examined intermedia effects for the Internet. For example, Sundar and his colleagues (1999) examined memory effects for print versus online ads. The independent variable, medium, was manipulated for the print and Internet conditions. Both conditions used comparable print ads to optimize treatment equivalence (826). Their findings revealed higher recall for subjects exposed to the print (versus Internet) advertisement.

Gallagher, Foster, and Parsons (2001) tested intermedia effects of advertising for print and Internet media. The stimulus materials consisted of a promotional brochure containing five ads for tourists visiting Newfoundland. A printed version of the brochure constituted the print condition and the Internet version was manipulated by posting the brochure online. Their findings revealed that the article and ads were evaluated more favorably for the print than the Internet condition. The authors noted that subjects exposed to the Internet condition were "consistently and significantly more critical than Print participants in their evaluation of exactly the same content presented exactly the same way, except for presentation medium" (69). The results were replicated with a student (but not the adult) sample in a follow-up study (Gallagher, Parsons and Foster 2001).

Bezjian-Avery, Calder, and Iacobucci (1998) conducted an experiment to explore the effectiveness of Internet advertising in a new platform. The platform allowed individuals to view ads in a linear or nonlinear fashion, the two conditions. According to the authors, the two conditions represented features of traditional (linear) and interactive (nonlinear) media, a comparison that is arguably germane to intermedia studies. Both conditions resembled a print display ad. Their findings revealed that users exposed to the traditional print condition spent less time viewing the ads and were less likely to indicate intent to purchase the advertised products than users exposed to the Internet condition.

The findings above indicate that when content is held constant, print is superior to Internet presentations. These effects were observed for memory (Sundar et al. 1999), attitudes (Gallagher, Foster, and Parsons 2001), purchase intentions (Bezjian-Avery, Calder, and Iacobucci 1998; Gallagher, Foster, and Parsons 2001) and viewing time (Bezjian-Avery, Calder, and Iacobucci 1998). However, the Internet stimuli in each study resembled a print medium and therefore may not be representative of Internet messages. Representativeness refers to the degree of realism in the independent variable. In the Sundar and colleagues (1999) study, the Internet condition resembled a print display ad; the Internet stimulus in the Gallagher studies (both 2001) was a print brochure that contained print display ads. The Bezjian-Avery and colleagues (1998) study compared traditional and interactive platforms that resembled print display ads. The question, then, is whether a print brochure or print display ad represents the kinds of ads and messages we see online. The answer is "no."

In effect, the approach taken in the above studies had an inherent advantage for one medium over the other because the print messages looked more realistic (and hence, more appropriate) than the Internet messages. The reality is that different media have different features that are unique to that medium. Television has greater visual capacity than radio, and magazines and newspapers have greater informational capacity than television (Rossiter and Danaher 1998). Different media are also organized differently, require different levels of control on the user's part, and contain varying amounts and kinds of content or information (Eveland 2003). The same is true of print and Internet messages.

Internet sites are perceived as being distinct from traditional media, as revealed by a survey of Web managers (Leong, Huang, and Stanners 1998). The Internet has features, such as interactivity, that are unique to that medium (Morris and Ogan 1996). Most Internet ads also look and are structured differently than print ads (Rodgers and Thorson 2000). Thus, Internet stimuli that look like print would not seem as appropriate to individuals as print stimuli that look like print.

Theoretically speaking, people have different schemas for different media. A schema is a cognitive structure that contains knowledge about a concept, its attributes, and relationships among attributes (Reeve 1997). Schemata provide default values that can be used to fill in gaps of knowledge (Abelson 1981). When individuals encounter a print medium, schema aid comprehension by evoking the features, forms, contents, and structures that make print a print medium and not the Internet. In addition, schema congruity is emotionally positive; whereas schema incongruity is emotionally negative (Mandler 1982). Thus, Internet messages designed to look like print will not match a user's Internet schema and may therefore be judged negatively on that basis.

In short, each medium takes into account different forms and features. Therefore, it is important to provide a "fair" comparison by testing forms and features of the appropriate medium. One way to accomplish this is to provide a series of tests that examine representative stimuli for *both* media being compared.

With this goal in mind, a series of three experiments was conducted. Study 1 compared media-appropriate print with media-inappropriate Internet stimuli; Study 2 compared media-inappropriate print with media-appropriate Internet stimuli; and Study 3 compared media-appropriate stimuli for both print and Internet conditions.

If the foregoing discussion is correct, Studies 1 and 2 should yield findings favoring the media-appropriate stimuli, whereas Study 3 should yield no differences because both stimuli were made to be appropriate for their respective media. Insofar as print media have served as the primary medium of comparison in previous studies, Study 1 will test the following hypothesis:

H1: Ad evaluations and purchase intentions will be higher for the medium-appropriate (print) versus medium-inappropriate (Internet) condition.

Method: Study 1

Subjects

The subjects for Study 1 were 218 journalism and advertising students enrolled at a major midwestern university. A total of 99 subjects viewed the Internet condition and 119 viewed the print condition. Three students from the Internet condition and two from the print condition left portions of the survey blank and were subsequently dropped from the study. This left a total sample of 213 participants (96 Internet, 117 print). Of these participants 137 were female (64 percent) and 76 were male (36 percent). Extra credit was offered for participation. Although student participants have been criticized in the literature, a student sample was deemed appropriate because their homogeneity relative to the general population reduces the impact of factors other than the manipulated independent variable (Schmidt and Hitchon 1999).

Design

Study 1 used a one-factor between-subjects design. The independent variable, media type, had two levels, print and Internet. Consistent with previous studies, media type was manipulated by varying the medium in which the ad appeared. A newspaper was selected as the medium because of its ease of manipulation and popularity among college students. A print newspaper constituted the print condition and the Internet condition was manipulated by posting the print newspaper online.

Stimulus Materials

The stimulus materials were designed to look like a print newspaper. One fictional newspaper name (*The Daily News*) appeared at the top of the page/ screen. Beneath that, the section heading was featured. A health section of the newspaper was selected for its general appeal to both males and fe- males. Typical of daily newspapers, the newspaper's flag appeared at the top of the page followed by the section heading, story headline, reporter byline, and news stories. The ad was placed in the newspaper just below the flag and above the story headline. The ad was formatted as a sponsor- ship and read, "Today's sponsor is . . ." followed by the sponsor's brand name and product. A sponsorship was selected because it represents one of the few ads that are media neutral. Having a media-neutral ad should pro- vide a conservative estimate of any effects attributed to the ad. That is, if we still find that the print condition outperformed the Internet condition in spite of having a media neutral ad, then we can place even greater confi- dence in the findings of this research. One fictional sponsor (Birele Vita- mins) was used for control purposes. The brand was selected from a group of fictional names that had been elaborately pretested for factors like cred- ibility, likability, and familiarity (see Rodgers 2000). The news story ap- peared below the ad.

One news story about health was taken from a real newspaper, edited for length and pretested for credibility, involvement, and ease of reading (see Rodgers 2000). The story was about the health benefits of vitamins. It was important to match the sponsor (vitamin brand) with a story about vitamins because mismatched sponsors/stories can create possible confusion (Rodgers 2003).

Both the print and Internet newspapers were designed to resemble a print newspaper. This was done by structuring the newspaper in a column format characteristic of the medium. The print condition was printed on 8½ x 11 sheets of paper and the same newspaper was posted to the researcher's Web site for the Internet condition. To increase authenticity, a professional graphic designer created the stimulus materials. Participants in both conditions filled out a paper-and-pencil survey.

Procedures

Participants in the print condition were handed copies of the print newspa- per and were asked to read it thoroughly. As the print newspapers were being handed out, participants were told "this is a print newspaper" to es- tablish the print condition. Participants in the Internet condition sat in front of a computer that featured the print newspaper posted online and were asked to read the newspaper story thoroughly. After sitting down in front of the computer screen, participants were told "this is an electronic newspaper" to establish the Internet condition. To increase motivation to read the stories, participants in both conditions were told that they would be asked to recall details about the stories once they finished. Subjects were given a maximum of seven minutes to read the stories—a time that had been determined by averaging the reading times of a fast and slow read prior to the experiment.

Dependent Measures

Study 1 had two dependent measures that are typical of advertising studies. These included attitude toward the ad and purchase intent. Scaled items were reverse coded where necessary so that a lower value indicated a negative attitude and a higher value indicated a positive attitude. The measures were taken in the following order. First, participants were asked to rate their attitude toward the ad (A_{ad}) on three, 5–point semantic differential scales: bad/good, disliked/liked, favorable/unfavorable ($\alpha = .92$) (Lutz, Mackenzie, and Belch 1983).

Next, purchase intent (*PI*) was measured using three, 5–point semantic differential scales, which included the brand name and product followed by the endpoints: I'm likely to make a purchase/I'm unlikely to make a purchase, I would like to have more information/I would not like to have more information, and I'm interested in it [the brand/product]/I'm not interested in it [the brand/product] ($\alpha = .80$) (Rodgers 2000).

Findings

The purpose of Study 1 was to replicate previous intermedia effects studies that compare print and Internet media. This was accomplished by comparing a printed version of a print-style newspaper to a print-style newspaper viewed on the Internet. If the prediction is correct, the findings should be strongest for the print condition (H1). To examine this possibility, an independent samples *t*-test was conducted using media type as the independent variable and A_{ad} and *PI* as the dependent variables.

The results supported Hypothesis 1. As shown in Table 3.1, participants indicated greater liking for the print than the Internet condition.

Purchase intentions were also higher for the print than Internet condition ($t = 8.85$, $df = 211$, $p < .001$).

Table 3.1

Study 1: Means and Standard Deviations for the Dependent Measures

Experimental condition	Attitude toward ad	Purchase intention
Realistic condition (print)	M = 11.79 SD = 2.13	M = 3.61 SD = 1.93
Unrealistic condition (Internet)	M = 9.00 SD = 2.48	M = 2.15 SD = 1.29

M = means; SD = standard deviation.

Discussion

Consistent with previous studies, Study 1 found that the ad in the print medium was more effective than the Internet ad for influencing attitude toward the ad and purchase intention. The findings offer some support for the argument presented here—that stimuli made to resemble one medium will not perform as well when placed in a different medium. However, a single study provides only an indication of what might exist and the results cannot be used to refute or support a theory or hypothesis (Babbie 2001). Therefore, a follow-up experiment was conducted to overcome some of the limitations inherent in a single study. In Study 1, the print and Internet stimuli resembled a print newspaper. To provide a "fair" test of intermedia effects it was important to create print and Internet stimuli that resembled an *Internet* newspaper. With this goal in mind, Study 2 tested the following hypothesis:

> H2: Attitude toward the ad and purchase intent will be higher for the medium-appropriate (Internet) versus medium-inappropriate (print) condition.

Method: Study 2

Subjects

The subjects for Study 2 were 227 undergraduates (different from Study 1) enrolled in advertising and journalism courses at a major midwestern university. One survey was filled out incorrectly and was subsequently dropped, leaving a total sample size of 226 (142 females, 84 males). Subjects were randomly assigned to the print ($N = 117$) and Internet ($N = 110$) conditions. Extra credit was offered for participation.

Design

Study 2 used a one-factor between-subjects design. The independent variable, media type, had two levels, print and Internet. Consistent with Study 1, media type was manipulated by varying the medium in which the ad appeared. A newspaper was again selected for its ease of manipulation and popularity among college students. An electronic newspaper (e-newspaper) constituted the Internet condition and the same newspaper was printed on paper to represent the print condition.

Stimulus Materials

The stimulus materials were designed to look like an e-newspaper (see Figure 3.1). Study 2 used the same stimuli as Study 1 including the newspaper's name (*The Daily News*), health section logo, news stories, fictional brand (Birele Vitamins), and ad. Using the same stimuli from Study 1 was important to maintain consistency across studies. Introducing a new brand could create an artifact that would make it difficult, if not impossible, to attribute any effects found in Study 2 to the manipulation of the independent variable. The only difference between the two studies was that the newspaper in Study 2 resembled an e-newspaper.

Typical of e-newspapers, the flag appeared at the top of the page followed by the section heading, story headline, reporter byline, and news stories. The story was structured with a single column down the middle of the screen. The print and Internet conditions looked exactly the same except for medium presentation. The print version of the e-newspaper was printed on 8½ x 11 sheets of paper. To increase authenticity, a professional graphic designer was paid to create the stimulus materials. Participants in both conditions filled out a pencil-and-paper survey.

Procedures

To maintain consistency across studies, the procedures used in Study 1 were also used in Study 2.

Dependent Measures

Study 2 used the same two dependent measures used in Study 1. These included attitude toward the ad ($\alpha = .88$) and purchase intent ($\alpha = .80$).

Findings

The purpose of Study 2 was to attempt to provide a "fair" test of intermedia effects. Because Study 1 compared two media designed to look like print,

Figure 3.1 **Example of Medium-Appropriate Internet Stimuli**

How Much Tea Is Too Much?
John Oslund, Staff Health Reporter

More health-conscious people are drinking tea these days in the hope that it will offer some protective effects against cancer and heart disease.

Researchers are trying to find out exactly what health benefits green and black tea provide. But even with the verdict out, consumers are asking two questions: How much tea? And what kind?

Some tea researchers say one cup is better than none, and two are better than one. Others say you may need to drink four or five cups a day to get many of the purported benefits. And they say freshly brewed is probably better than bottled.

Ronald Prior, chief of the Phytochemical Laboratory at the USDA Human Nutrition Research Center on Aging at Tufts University in Boston, has studied tea and its components. He says the most recent evidence suggests that people may want to drink five or more cups a day. Prior himself drinks the equivalent of six cups of iced tea daily.

But C.S. Yang, a professor of chemical biology at Rutgers University who drinks a couple of cups of tea each day—mostly green—cautions against downing too much tea. It can cause stomach upset and affect absorption of iron and other nutrients, he says. "Too much of a good thing can be toxic."

Then again, some people are more sensitive to caffeine than others, and they become too wired or hyper if they drink too much tea, experts say.

Tea contains polyphenols—antioxidants that neutralize free radicals, unstable molecules that damage cells. Scientists believe that polyphenols may be part of the explanation for tea's benefits. Exactly how much of the antioxidants a cup of tea contains depends on numerous variables, including the brand.

But tea drinkers shouldn't get too hung up with the antioxidant levels in tea because there may be components other than antioxidants in tea that are equally important—or maybe more important, says Allan Conney, director of the Laboratory for Cancer Research at the College of Pharmacy of Rutgers University.

Table 3.2

Study 2: Means and Standard Deviations for the Dependent Measures

Experimental condition	Attitude toward ad	Purchase intention
Realistic condition (Internet)	M = 8.85 SD = 2.50	M = 7.05 SD = 3.30
Unrealistic condition (print)	M = 11.52 SD = 3.92	M = 5.44 SD = 2.92

M = mean; SD = standard deviation.

Study 2 compared the effects of print and Internet media designed to look like an Internet newspaper. If the prediction is correct, the findings should be strongest for the Internet condition (H2). To examine this possibility, an independent samples t-test was conducted using media type as the independent variable and A_{ad} and PI as the dependent variables. The results partially supported Hypothesis 2. As predicted, purchase intentions were higher for the Internet than the print condition ($t = 3.92$, $df = 225$, $p < .001$). However, participants indicated greater liking for the print than the Internet ad, as measured by attitude toward the ad ($t = 6.09$, $df = 211$, $p < .001$). Table 3.2 displays the means and standard deviations.

Discussion

Study 2 was a replication of Study 1 with one exception. The stimuli were altered to resemble an Internet (versus print) newspaper. The findings showed that, when content is held constant, the Internet was superior to the print medium in terms of purchase intention. The findings were not consistent, however, for both dependent measures. Participants in the Internet condition did not like the ad as well as did participants in the print condition.

Given the inconsistent findings, a third experiment was conducted. Study 3 provided a further test of the hypothesis presented here. If media-appropriate stimuli generally outperform media-inappropriate stimuli, then comparing two appropriate media should result in no performance differences. In statistical terms this means that no significant differences should result when stimuli are designed to reflect their respective media. This thinking translates to the following hypothesis:

H3: Attitude toward the ad and purchase intent will be equal, statistically speaking, when comparing realistic print and realistic Internet stimuli in the appropriate media.

Method: Study 3

Subjects

The subjects for Study 3 were 34 undergraduates (different from Studies 1 and 2) enrolled in an advertising course at a major midwestern university. There were 24 females (72 percent) and 10 males (29 percent). Subjects were randomly assigned to the Internet ($N = 17$) and print ($N = 17$) conditions. Extra credit was offered for participation.

Design

Study 3 used a one-factor between-subjects design. The independent variable, media type, had two levels, print and Internet. Media type was manipulated by varying the medium in which the ad appeared. A print newspaper constituted the print condition and an e-newspaper constituted the Internet condition.

Stimulus Materials

The stimulus materials were structured to resemble their respective media. The print newspaper created in Study 1 served as the stimulus for the print condition and the e-newspaper created in Study 2 served as the stimulus for the Internet condition. This provided consistency across studies, a requisite for replications, and offered greater efficiency in terms of time and expense associated with creating and pretesting new stimuli.

Procedures

To maintain consistency across studies, the procedures used in Studies 1 and 2 were also used in Study 3.

Dependent Measures

Study 3 used the same two dependent measures used in Studies 1 and 2. These included attitude toward the ad ($\alpha = .80$) and purchase intent ($\alpha = .92$).

Findings

The purpose of Study 3 was to compare the effects of print and Internet contexts manipulated to look appropriate for their respective media. If the

Table 3.3

Study 3: Means and Standard Deviations for the Dependent Measures

Experimental condition	Attitude toward ad	Purchase intention
Realistic condition (Internet)	M = 9.88	M = 6.13
	SD = 2.18	SD = 3.70
Realistic condition (print)	M = 9.82	M = 8.18
	SD = 2.67	SD = 3.97

M = mean; SD = standard deviation.

prediction is correct, the results should be statistically equal for both media (H3). To examine this possibility, an independent samples t-test was conducted using media type as the independent variable and A_{ad} and PI as the dependent variables. The results supported Hypothesis 3. Participants indicated equal liking ($p = .94$) and purchase intentions ($p = .14$) for both the print and Internet contexts (see Table 3.3).

Discussion

Study 3 provides additional support for the arguments presented here. When comparing the effects of print and Internet media resembling their respective contexts, no significant differences were found. The reader should note, however, that the mean differences for purchase intent were notable for the two conditions, even though they did not reach the level of statistical significance. Purchase intentions for the ad that appeared in the print newspaper, for example, were greater than the same ad that appeared in the Internet newspaper. This may be an example of how media schemas influence media perceptions. In this case, it may be that people have a distrust or lack of credibility schema that they attach to Internet advertising and this may negatively affect their purchase intentions. This point notwithstanding, the findings of Study 3 indicate that the Internet and print conditions performed equally well (from a statistical standpoint) when they were structured to resemble their respective media.

General Discussion

The purpose of this research was to examine intermedia effects of ads placed in Internet and print media. The author argued that past studies did not provide a "fair" comparison for each medium in that the Internet stimuli resembled print media or ads and therefore were not appropriate for the Internet.

The current research tested this proposition by conducting a series of three experiments, each designed to compare appropriate/inappropriate stimuli for both print and Internet media.

Study 1 compared an ad placed in a print newspaper and an Internet newspaper, designed to look like print. The findings indicated that print was superior to the Internet in terms of attitude toward the ad and purchase intent. The findings suggest that media-appropriate stimuli can yield superior effects to media-inappropriate stimuli. The findings also suggest that individuals have media schemas and when these schemas do not match a given situation negative reactions can result.

Study 2 provided a replication of the findings in Study 1 with slight variations in the independent variable. This time, the e-newspaper was structured to resemble the style of an Internet newspaper and the print newspaper was designed to represent the inappropriate condition by printing the e-newspaper on paper. The findings showed that the Internet ad was superior to print but only for one of the dependent measures, purchase intent. Contrary to predictions, individuals in the Internet condition did not like the ad as well as the same ad in the print condition structured to resemble an e-newspaper. Why?

One explanation is that people have media schemas that they apply regardless of the context. If they see any ad in an Internet situation (whether it was designed to be one or not), they associate it with negative schemas related to Internet ads (i.e., interfering, annoying, unwanted, etc.). Individuals who saw the Internet condition may have evaluated the ad negatively because it matched their Internet schema. Thus, the findings from Study 2 suggest that attitudes toward ads are composed of many factors including elements of the ad itself and consumer expectations of what ads placed in certain media look like.

Study 3 provided an additional test of the study's hypothesis. The point of Study 3 was to essentially remove the controls in Studies 1 and 2 and compare media-appropriate print to media-appropriate Internet stimuli. The findings revealed that the effects found in Studies 1 and 2 "disappeared" and no significant differences were found. Thus, the findings suggest that when messages are structured to resemble their respective media, differences due to media type may disappear, statistically speaking.

Taken as a whole, this research demonstrates the importance of providing an appropriate test for *each* medium compared. When both media are structured to resemble one medium, we remove features that make the comparison medium unique. In reality, Internet newspapers are structured differently than print newspapers. For example, printed newspapers have multiple, narrow columns whereas a section in an e-newspaper is typically presented in a single, wider column (e.g., USAToday.com). The findings of this research reveal that when Internet contexts are designed to *look* like Internet contexts, the results generally favored the Internet condition. This finding is contrary to what previous intermedia studies have found, perhaps due in part to attempts to provide media-appropriate stimuli here. Thus, intermedia studies that create Internet stimuli by merely posting print messages online may underestimate Internet advertising effects.

The findings of the current study also suggest that individuals have media schemas that they apply when confronted with an ad in a given medium. In theoretical terms, this means that the representativeness of the stimuli can influence consumers' advertising schemas. Thus, stimuli that neglect to capture the essence of a medium will not match individuals' schema for that medium, which, according to the current study, will have a detrimental effect on the findings. From a methodological standpoint, intermedia studies that fail to provide an appropriate test will likely yield findings that while internally valid, will lack external validity so badly that they may serve little practical purpose (Eveland and Dunwoody 2001).

The question, then, is how to balance the need to have realistic stimuli (i.e., external validity) without sacrificing control of those stimuli (i.e., internal validity). One idea is to provide a series of tests that compares appropriate/inappropriate stimuli for each medium, as was done here. Creating stimuli that capture forms and features of each medium could provide a "fair" comparison and help establish the validity of the findings. The author acknowledges the difficulties involved in creating appropriate stimuli, particularly for new media such as the Internet. In the current study, the structure of news stories was controlled for its ease of manipulation. However, there are many other features that make Internet newspapers and Internet ads unique, such as hyperlinks, audio clips, searchable archives, and interactive maps, and these will need to be explored as well. Representative Internet stimuli may therefore be possible to the extent that the researcher knows technology or is able to hire people who know how to create technology-appropriate features.

The challenge to research on intermedia effects will be to select new technology features that can translate to print or broadcast equivalents. However, this task may become more difficult as more and more ad campaigns become "media-neutral" and the trend toward media convergence grows. Under these circumstances, Eveland's (2003) "mix of attributes" approach, which considers media attributes to be multidimensional, might be a more appropriate model.

Another suggestion is to move beyond the question of "which medium works best" to the question of "which *features* of a given medium work best *for what purposes*." Rephrasing the question in this way changes the focus from a comparison of two media to a focus on what makes each medium unique and the subsequent effects of those unique characteristics. Restructuring intermedia studies in this way also reduces the need to provide similar media contexts that disadvantage one of the comparison media/ads. This is not to suggest that the former question is without merit. Rather, rearticulating the question in this way helps move us from an "either/or" outcome to a better understanding of the combinations of media and features within media that work best under a given situation. This is arguably what guides media planners in making decisions about ad placements. Media planners rarely rely on a single medium for a given campaign. Rather, the best *combinations* of media (and nonmedia) are typically selected on the basis of what will help the brand accomplish its goals. Thus, there may be practical *and* theoretical advantages to expanding research on intermedia effects in this way.

Limitations and Future Research

The strength of the current research is that of replication. Each study replicated the next with slight variations in the independent variable. By controlling factors such as the name of the newspaper and the brand advertised, internal validity was increased and experimental artifacts were decreased. Using fictitious brand names also increased internal validity. Using students as subjects provided a more homogenous sample and presumably aided internal validity to some degree. Each of these steps helped provide a content equivalent, which researchers have deemed necessary for intermedia studies.

Inasmuch as these decisions represent strengths, they also pose limitations. Using the same stimuli across three studies may have produced effects that were design specific. In addition, fictional brands differ from real brands and these differences affect relationships between attitudes and behavior (Wells 2001). Students differ from each other and other members of the population and these differences also affect research findings (Peterson 2000).

Thus, future studies will need to overcome these deficiencies by creating different stimuli, using real brands, selecting different subjects, and sampling additional types of ads. If the results are to be of any use to other media, different print contexts, such as magazines, or broadcast contexts, such as television or radio, will need to be examined.

There are other factors that can undermine the representativeness of stimuli and these should be examined in future studies as well. For example, in determining the representativeness of a selected stimulus the representativeness of the number of levels of the stimuli and their intensity should be considered. Of course, the greatest weakness of any laboratory experiment is its artificiality. Social processes that occur in a laboratory setting might not occur in more natural social settings (Babbie 2001). Future studies will therefore need to investigate the hypotheses presented here from many different methodological perspectives before any significance can be attributed to the results.

Conclusion

It is important for intermedia studies to provide an appropriate test for each medium compared. One way to accomplish this is to provide a series of tests that create appropriate/inappropriate stimuli for the media and ads of comparison. This research has shown that medium-appropriateness can be as big a factor as content equivalence in assessing intermedia effects.

References

Abelson, R.P. (1981), "Psychological Status of the Script Concept," *American Psychologist*, 36, 715–729.

Assmus, Gert (1977), "An Empirical Investigation into the Perception of Vehicle Source Effects," *Journal of Advertising*, 7 (1), 4–10.

Babbie, Earl (2001), *The Practice of Social Research*, 9th ed., Belmont, CA: Wadsworth/Thomson Learning.

Bezjian-Avery, Alexa, Bobby Calder, and Dawn Iacobucci (1998), "New Media Interactive Advertising vs. Traditional Advertising," *Journal of Advertising Research*, 38 (4), 23–32.

Eveland, William P., Jr. (2003), "A 'Mix of Attributes' Approach to the Study of Media Effects and New Communication Technologies," *Journal of Communication*, 53 (3), 395–410.

——— and Sharon Dunwoody (2001), "User Control and Structural Isomorphism or Disorientation and Cognitive Load? Learning from the Web Versus Print," *Communication Research*, 28 (1), 48–78.

Gallagher, Katherine, K. Dale Foster, and Jeffrey Parsons (2001), "The Medium Is Not the Message: Advertising Effectiveness and Content Evaluation in Print and on the Web," *Journal of Advertising Research*, 41 (4), 57–70.

———, Jeffrey Parsons, and K. Dale Foster (2001), "A Tale of Two Studies: Replicating Advertising Effectiveness and Content Evaluation in Print and on the Web," *Journal of Advertising Research*, 41 (4), 71–81.

Leong, Elaine K.F., Xueli Huang, and Paul-John Stanners (1998), "Comparing the Effectiveness of the Web Site with Traditional Media," *Journal of Advertising Research*, 38 (5), 44–51.

Lutz, Richard J., Scott B. Mackenzie, and George E. Belch (1983), "Attitude Toward the Ad as a Mediator of Advertising Effectiveness," in *Advances in Consumer Research*, Vol. 10, R. Bagozzi and A. Tybout, eds., Ann Arbor, MI: Association for Consumer Research, 532–539.

Mandler, G. (1982), "The Structure of Value: Accounting for Taste," in *Affect and Cognition*, M.S. Clark and S.T. Fiske, eds., Hillsdale, NJ: Lawrence Erlbaum Associates, 3–36.

Morris, Merrill and Christine Ogan (1996), "The Internet as Mass Medium," *Journal of Communication*, 46 (1), 39–50.

Peterson, Robert A. (2000), "A Meta-Analysis of Variance Accounted for in Exploratory Factor Analysis," *Marketing Letters*, 11 (August), 261–275.

Reeve, Johnmarshall (1997), *Understanding Motivation and Emotion*, 2d ed., Orlando, FL: Holt, Rinehart and Winston.

Rodgers, Shelly (2000), "Predicting Sponsorship Effects in E-newspapers Using the Sponsorship Knowledge Inventory," Ph.D. dissertation, University of Missouri-Columbia, School of Journalism.

———— (2003), "The Effects of Sponsor Relevance on Consumer Reactions to Internet Sponsorships," *Journal of Advertising*, 32 (4), 69–79.

———— and Esther Thorson (2000), "The Interactive Advertising Model: How Users Perceive and Process Online Ads," *Journal of Interactive Advertising*, 1 (1), [www.jiad.org/vol1/no1/rodgers].

Rossiter, John R. and Peter J. Danaher (1998), *Advanced Media Planning*, Norwell, MA: Kluwer Academic.

Schmidt, Toni L. and Jacqueline C. Hitchon (1999), "When Advertising and Public Relations Converge: An Application of Schema Theory to the Persuasive Impact of Alignment Ads," *Journalism and Mass Communication Quarterly*, 76 (3), 433–455.

Sundar, S. Shyam, Sunetra Narayan, Rafael Obregon, and Charu Uappal (1999), "Does Web Advertising Work? Memory for Print vs. Online Media," *Journalism and Mass Communication Quarterly*, 75 (4), 822–835.

Wells, William D. (2001), "The Perils of N = 1," *Journal of Consumer Research*, 28 (December), 494–498.

4

A Survey of Measures Evaluating Advertising Effectiveness Based on Users' Web Activity

Subodh Bhat, Michael Bevans, and Sanjit Sengupta

Relative to traditional media like newspapers, radio, and television, advertising in such digital forms as the World Wide Web (www) and the mobile browser has been growing at a significantly more rapid rate. Most major for-profit and nonprofit organizations across the globe now have a Web site, which is emerging as an important medium of communication with consumers and others. They are also spending an ever-greater proportion of their communication budget on advertising on other Web sites through such varied ad elements as banner ads, pop-up ads, pop-under ads, Web site sponsorships, co-branded buttons, and click-through linkages. As a result, advertising on an organization's Web sites is becoming an important revenue stream for these organizations. Experts predict a substantial increase in Web advertising expenditure. Forrester Research predicts $42 billion in Web advertising by 2005, which eclipses spending on most traditional media (Forrester Research 2001). As this new medium becomes more mainstream, both in terms of consumer access and advertiser presence, the issue of evaluating and enhancing the effectiveness of Web advertising becomes ever-more crucial.

In modern organizations, the main purpose of advertising has been to convey information to and elicit a positive response from customers about the organizations' offerings. Within this overall purpose, each advertising campaign may have different objectives such as increasing sales, enhancing product or brand awareness, conveying information about the product or brand, developing a brand's image, stimulating emotions, or creating brand preference. Obviously, the best measures of advertising effectiveness are ones that directly assess whether specific objectives have been met. Unfortunately, it is often difficult, if not impossible, to establish direct correspondence between an advertising campaign and its objective, insofar as the effect typically occurs over a long period of time. Bendixen (1993) suggests potential problems when one popular objective, sales, is used as a measure of advertising effectiveness. For example, sales can be influenced by any number of factors, of which advertising is only one. The lack of a direct or one-to-one correspondence between advertising spending and the ultimate objectives is the major reason why advertisers have focused on more immediate and tangible objectives such as reach and frequency, which capture information at a point in time preceding purchase decisions or other consumer actions. Over the past few decades, a large number of measures have been developed to gauge the effectiveness of advertising in traditional media. However, despite the fact that traditional media have been with us a long time, evaluating the effectiveness of advertising in traditional media has never been easy and is still quite contentious.

There are several differences between traditional media and new digital media. In this chapter, the focus is on the www, currently the most popular digital medium. First, there are differences in the objective characteristics of the Web relative to traditional media. Following Steuer (1992), Hoffman and Novak (1996) suggest that unlike traditional media, a Web site reflects a medium in which communication exists not only between the sender and the receiver but also with the mediated environment. In other words, the sender and the receiver interact not only through the media but also with the media. Hoffman and Novak (1996) further observe that the Web has unique characteristics such as its many-to-many communication model and its use of text, image, audio, and video, which allow for multimedia and dynamic content. Other research suggests that the Web can also be distinguished by the potential for user interactivity (Hoffman, Novak, and Chatterjee 1995; Ghose and Dou 1998). Interactivity implies that users have much greater control over when and how they process information from Web sites (Gallagher, Foster, and Parsons 2001). Differences in objective characteristics and user processing are not the only differences between traditional media and the Web. Most advertisers do not own traditional media like magazines or radio stations and consequently cannot use media editorial content to promote themselves, but their Web sites can serve as direct advertising and communication channels with their customers. In this sense, Web advertising comprises not only advertisements on Web sites but also the Web sites themselves and is, therefore, broader in scope than advertising in traditional media. This is one reason why we use the word "advertiser" in this chapter to include operators of Web sites as well as those who advertise on others' Web sites. Empirical data from managers also confirms differences. Leong, Huang, and Stanners (1998) found that Web site managers believed that Web sites differed from traditional media in their advertising effectiveness. Managers reported that Web sites were relatively superior in communicating detailed information, triggering consumer action, and being cost effective in reaching a target audience, while, at the same time, being ineffective in arousing emotions. Thus, a number of perspectives suggest the existence of differences between traditional and new digital media. At the same time, for the Web to become well accepted for advertising purposes, advertisers need standardized measures for evaluating ad effectiveness (Dreze and Zufryden 1998). Such standardization would also permit comparison between the Web and traditional media. For all these reasons, we believe that there is a great need to examine Web advertising-effectiveness measures.

In order to make informed decisions about the effectiveness of a Web site or a Web-based ad campaign, it is important that Web advertisers be clear about what they are trying to measure and understand which sets of measures or metrics are best for their purpose. Similarly, academics need to understand these metrics for use in their research of the Web, especially when they are comparing the impact of different types of messages on user processing or comparing the Web to traditional media.

As compared to traditional media, advances in digital technology permit advertisers to more easily and, arguably, more precisely measure the effectiveness of their methods on the Web. In the digital realm, advertisers can more easily track an individual consumer's behavior on a Web site or across different Web sites. However, the ever-increasing ability to obtain data comes with its own set of problems. Perhaps the biggest problem is that technology has made it so easy to set up measurement tools on the Web that a number of measures have proliferated in the past few years, giving rise to confusion.

Another point to keep in mind is that despite the use of state-of-the art technology to collect different Web metrics, the resulting perception of precision may be rather illusory. Dreze and Zufryden (1998) computed one effectiveness measure, the Number of Web Visitors, based on the popular use of Internet Protocol (IP) addresses (one method of identifying a user's computer), and compared it to the same measure using both IP addresses and unique visitor identities (IDs), the latter usually available when a user registers on a Web site. They found that across the five Web sites they surveyed, the undercounting error was 39 percent, which is undisputedly large. This error led to errors in calculating popular, downstream Web metrics like Number of Visits (error of -35 percent), Number of Web Pages per Visit (+64 percent), Time Spent per Visit (+79 percent), Number of Repeat Visits (+9 percent), Reach (+25 percent), Frequency (–1 percent), and Impressions (+23 percent). It must be noted that the benchmark in this study, unique visitor IDs or registration, has its own biases, which we discuss later. These findings imply that advertisers and academics should pay more attention to how different Web metrics are calculated.

Despite the importance of this topic, we did not come across any comprehensive review of the range of Web metrics in either the academic or the practitioner literature. This chapter, with its objective of providing readers with some understanding of the different Web-measurement tools that exist, is intended to fill this void. Its focus is on how these tools or metrics are derived, what information they provide, what relative advantages and disadvantages they possess in evaluating their objective, and how they can be used in Web advertising decisions. In our discussion of these metrics, we are not necessarily prescriptive in approach because no one metric outshines others in measuring a certain objective. Rather, each metric has its specific strengths and weaknesses. Besides, the choice of a metric depends on such things as advertisers' measurement objectives and their technological, budgetary, and time limitations.

Because advertisers not only use others' Web sites to advertise but also use their own Web sites to advertise to and communicate directly with their audience, we review the tools or metrics that cover the gamut of user activity on Web sites. The discussion of measures is based upon a comprehensive review of industry practice, and academic and practitioner publications.

Background

Improvements in technology have led to advances in monitoring a host of consumer Web site-related activities to assess the effectiveness of Web advertising. Yet, advertisers still have trouble understanding how to determine the success or failure of a Web advertising program and what they can do to improve it. Much of this can be blamed on the multiplicity of measurement tools, each based on a different technology, that currently exist and the failure of the Web-measurement industry to agree upon measurement standards. "Advertisers and media buyers have learned to depend on measurement standards across traditional media, including TV (Nielsen), print (ABC and BPA International) and radio (Arbitron). However, the complex nature of audience measurement on the internet coupled with the wide array of vendors that provide measurement services have added to advertisers' confusion" (Ianni 1999, 7).

There have been attempts to standardize measurement. Two industry bodies, the Internet Advertising Bureau (IAB) and the Future of Advertising Stakeholders (FAST) committee, have published voluntary guidelines that were to be followed in deriving comparable measurements. Unfortunately, these guidelines were themselves vague and therefore open to different interpretation. In January 2002, the IAB for a second time published a set of guidelines for standardizing measurement of Web usage. However, a number of

Web-measurement companies were not involved in this process and continue to use their own methods. In the absence of a consensus on the definition and calculation of metrics, metrics cannot be easily compared across different Web-measurement companies. In any case, we believe the guidelines are still ambiguous enough that it may be difficult to achieve the desired standardization. For example, the IAB (2002) defines an ad impression as "a measurement of responses from an ad delivery system to an ad request from the user's browser, which is filtered from robotic activity and is recorded at a point as late as possible in the process of delivery of the creative material to the user's browser." Each aspect of this definition is vague enough for different measurement techniques to conform to these guidelines but still provide different counts. For instance, take "robotic activity." Filtering of robotic activity is based on lists of known robots, and because these are constantly evolving, different measurement services may use different lists. Further, there are no standard technical ways to eliminate the effect of these robotic activities.

As noted, a Web advertising-effectiveness measure can be derived using several different methodologies. Some major differences are discussed next to enable readers to understand the complexities in the measurement of individual metrics.

First, some metrics measure user activity at a Web site whereas others measure user reaction to an advertisement on a site. For the purpose of this chapter, we refer to the first set of measures as "metrics for Web sites." These metrics are useful to the operators of a Web site who wish to understand how effectively the messages on their Web site are being communicated. These measures are also useful to advertisers who wish to advertise on a specific Web site (e.g., Ameritrade may be interested in the Yahoo! Finance Web site's metrics to make decisions on whether to advertise there). We refer to the second set of metrics as "metrics for Web advertisements." These metrics are useful to advertisers interested in the effectiveness of an advertisement on a Web site. Our discussion of individual metrics is organized into two sections, each describing one of these two sets of metrics.

Second, some metrics measure users' Web site activity whereas other metrics capture other information about users such as their demographic profiles. Also, Web site activity itself can be measured at the aggregate level (where individual activity is pooled for counting purposes) or at the individual user level.

Another difference is that while most metrics can evaluate the effectiveness of past Web advertising, a few others such as "Observed Profiling," a measure of targeting efficiency, do not really evaluate past advertising but simply capture users' Web activity to help in planning future messages.

Yet another difference relates to the point in time and place that different methods capture individuals' Web activities: at the browser in the computer being used to access the Web, at the server associated with the Web site being visited, or over the wire that connects the individual's computer with the Web site.

Another difference has to do with whether the measure is based on all Web activity or extrapolated from the activities of a selected panel of individuals. Census measurement is based on all activity associated with a Web site and involves methods like log file analysis, which is done at the Web site's server, and "packet sniffing," which is conducted during the exchange of information between the server and the user's computer. In contrast, panel measurement uses a sample of individuals to represent the Web-surfing population of interest. Panel members are required to install software on their computers that tracks all their Web-surfing activity for a given period. The panel companies use statistical models to extrapolate their panel members' activity to the population of interest based upon individual members' demographic or psychographic profiles. The population of interest, the sampling method used, and the profiles of the panel members vary for different panel companies. Advertisers must understand that they will have different results depending upon the panel used.

In addition to the commonly known advantages and disadvantages of census and panel data, such as a panel's small size or its representativeness relative to the audience of interest, there are some unique differences on the Web between the two methods. A technical issue peculiar to the Web is that census data do not capture cached activity, which can result in an undercount of the number of impressions made, because caching allows a user to download a Web page just once and access it multiple times without having to request it again from a Web site server. Another problem with census data is that it is not easy to associate individuals' Web site behavior with their demographic or psychographic profiles. On the other hand, one limitation of a panel is that it often ignores users surfing the Web from work or school or from international destinations because panel data are usually based upon counts from panel members' homes in a single country. Thus, there are many differences in the objectives and measurement of different metrics.

Additionally, Web advertisers have a number of different objectives. First, advertisers would like to know the overall popularity or exposure of their Web site or ad, or, in other words, how many users viewed or interacted with their site or ad. A measure of popularity or exposure is similar to the reach metric in traditional media. Among other uses, this information enables advertisers to compare the reach of their message with projections or with the reach of other Web pages, sites, or ads. Second, advertisers would be interested in evaluating the site's ability to attract and hold users' attention. The term "stickiness" has often been used to describe the idea of keeping users interested or involved in a site for the duration of their visit. The longer the duration of the visit, the more "sticky" the site, and the greater the opportunity to deliver messages or ads to users. While stickiness is a desirable objective, Web advertisers also want to develop long-term relationships with users. User relationship or loyalty reflects user involvement with a site over a period of time rather than during just one visit. In this sense, tracking stickiness and the quality of user relationships is similar. Third, because informing and influencing users with content or messages is a major purpose of a Web site, it is important to evaluate the site's usefulness with the objective of improving content or site navigation. Fourth, because co-marketing or cross-selling opportunities represent a popular revenue stream for Web sites, advertisers would want to evaluate the success or value of current co-marketing arrangements. Such evaluation would allow advertisers to alter co-marketing programs to be more effective. Finally, advertisers are interested in knowing about the efficiency of their targeting efforts. They can compare their users' profiles with desired profiles; knowledge of their users' profiles also allows them to be more effective in future targeting efforts. Thus, in Web advertising, the five major objectives may be: exposure or popularity; stickiness and quality of user relationships; usefulness; co-marketing success; and targeting efficiency. These objectives will be used to categorize the metrics in subsequent discussion. Different sets of metrics address these different objectives and in some cases, the same objective can be assessed with different metrics. To add to the confusion, the same metric can be derived using different methods or from different sources of data. For these reasons, a comprehensive review of commonly used metrics, which identifies the uses, strengths, weaknesses, and derivation of each metric, should be useful to advertising practitioners and academics in understanding how to use these different measures to assess and improve the effectiveness of Web advertising. Appendix Table 4.1 provides a summary of the objectives of Web advertising and the more popular Web metrics that help in evaluating these objectives.

It is important to point out that advertisers and researchers can obtain these metrics from a variety of sources. First, they can set up systems on their servers to capture information from their Web sites. Second, they can obtain these metrics from their application service providers or their Internet service providers. Third, there are a very large number of third-party providers of such information. The choice of a source depends on such factors as cost, scale of data needed, availability of technical resources, and need for customization.

Description of Metrics for User Activity at Web Sites

In this section, we will describe the common metrics for assessing user activity on Web sites. In the next section, we will describe the popular metrics for assessing user reaction to Web advertisements. Within each section, we have organized the discussion in terms of the metrics' overall objectives, which we have discussed earlier: exposure or popularity; stickiness and quality of user relationships; usefulness; co-marketing success; and targeting efficiency. In the case of metrics with multiple objectives, the strengths, weaknesses, and calculation details are provided in the section relating to their first objective (in the above order). Only information directly relevant to a second or third objective is discussed in the sections relating to those objectives.

Metrics for Evaluating Exposure or Popularity

Page Requests/Page Views/Page Impressions

All Web sites are a collection of electronic pages, with each page being a hypertext markup language (HTML) document that contains text, images, or media objects. A page impression (also called page request or page view) occurs when a user's browser requests a page from the Web site's server. Only one page may be counted per request according to the IAB's Media Measurement Task Force (IAB MMTF 1997, 3). A Web site's server logs the page request when it receives a status code that confirms delivery of the page to the user's browser. Page impressions are an estimate of the total number of pages served in a given period and thus a good indicator of a Web page's popularity or audience exposure. This metric can be compared with target figures to assess the effectiveness of the exposure. Please note that for advertisers, each page served also represents one or more opportunities to serve an advertisement. Comparisons of page impressions across competing Web sites, such as those of Yahoo! Finance and MSN Finance, are also possible—provided there is similarity of methodology. This information can then be used to compare the effectiveness of exposure across different Web sites and to persuade companies to advertise on a certain site. A weakness of this metric as a measure of a Web page's popularity is that it provides only a basic and limited perspective. For example, it does not disclose the number of individuals who viewed the page nor does it reveal what users actually did on the page, which may be more important for diagnostic purposes. If, in addition to total page impressions, advertisers desire information on the number of individuals visiting a page, they can use census data that use cookies or unique registration to identify unique visitors or turn to panel data. With census-based methods, the effect of automated activities, such as that caused by spiders, crawlers, or other robots that access Web pages, must be eliminated. In this context, spiders, crawlers, and robots are automated programs used to capture information on Web sites for various purposes such as categorization by search engines and the comparison of price data across e-commerce sites. The use of panel data eliminates the need to adjust for inflation caused by robotic activity. Panel data have an additional advantage in that panel companies can track the number of pages that actually loaded onto a panel member's browser. Of course, it is impossible to determine if the page was actually viewed by the user, just as it is impossible to be sure that a television viewer sitting in front of a television set actually watched a commercial.

While this seems like a simple metric, it can be very complicated to measure because of confounds in counting caused by pop-up ads, pop-under ads, interstitials, HTML newsletters, auto-refreshed pages, and frames. A pop-up is an ad that appears in a new browser window, a pop-under is an ad that appears in a new browser window behind a currently open browser window, and an interstitial is an ad that pops up a separate window as a Web page is loading. In this context, an HTML newsletter is an e-mail newsletter in the form of a hypertext document, an auto-refreshed page is one where the site refreshes content at certain intervals without the user requesting it, and a frame is part of a page with independently generated content. The IAB (2002) recommends that to standardize measurement of page impressions, ads such as pop-ups, pop-unders, and interstitials be counted as ad impressions rather than page impressions and that HTML newsletters be counted as page impressions unless they consist only of advertisements. It further advises that auto-refreshed pages be counted as page impressions unless the pages in question are in the background or are minimized. One problem with this recommendation is that page impressions are counted even when the user is away from the computer and has not requested the subsequent auto-refreshed pages, resulting in inflation of page impression counts. Frames pose another problem in that multiple frames may comprise a page and page counts may vary depending on whether advertisers count frames independently of pages. The IAB (2002) recommends that only frames that contain a majority of a page's content be counted as page impressions. Advertisers should adjust for these issues when using this metric to compare pages on different sites.

Top Pages Requested

This metric provides the pages most requested on a Web site by calculating the number of times a visitor accessed that page on a site. Advertisers can use this information to compare the actual exposure to desired or targeted exposure. A Web site's top pages can be compared with those of competing Web sites to attract external advertisers. These top pages can also be viewed as opportunities to target visitors with special offers to encourage them to visit less-heavily-trafficked areas. One disadvantage is that by highlighting top pages to advertisers, the importance to advertisers of other niche areas on the site may be inadvertently minimized because other pages that do not receive a lot of traffic may still be very useful to a specific user. For example, General Motors might be better off advertising in the Auto section of Yahoo! than in the top page (say, the home page) because they may reach an audience more interested in automotive products.

Peak Activity

Peak activity is a simple census-based metric that helps advertisers understand the times of the day and the days of the week during which the Web site records the most activity. Because it is possible to change Web content or ads easily, the information provided by this metric can help an advertiser target specific content or promotions at peak hours, thereby reaching the greatest number of visitors. Unfortunately, sites often use multiple server locations, which can create technical problems (discussion of which is outside the scope of this chapter) in implementing its measurement accurately.

Hits

A hit is a census-derived metric that, though not very popular today, is worth defining because of its widespread use in the infancy of the Web and the misunderstanding associated with the term. A hit is a very basic measurement of user activity at a Web site. A hit refers to an entry or a line in a server log file that records an action by a visitor, such as the request for a document, a file, an image, or even several requests for multiple elements that will eventually make up a Web page. Hits were the first thing measured on the Web, and the perception was that the number of hits a Web site received in a given time period indicated that site's success. Unfortunately, hits are not an accurate metric because one must aggregate hits to make up the page that users see when they click on a uniform resource locator (URL), which is the address or location of the Web page. For example, a Web page comprising seven design elements in the form of different text sections or images would count as seven hits but is really one page impression. By changing the number of elements comprising a page, the number of hits changes but the page impression count remains the same. Thus, hits do not provide any relevant information to an advertiser because the number of hits can change with a change in the number of design elements comprising a page. This is perhaps why the IAB (2002) does not address this metric. However, the number of hits may be useful to an engineer monitoring the "load" placed on the site's servers.

Visits

A visit refers to one user session at a Web site. A visit is one session attributable to a single browser in which page requests are made and during which thirty consecutive minutes of inactivity do not occur (adapted from IAB 2002). This metric provides an advertiser with an estimate of the frequency of visits to a particular site during a certain period of time. Thus, this metric is a proxy for a Web site's overall popularity among the Web-surfing population and is used to assess exposure against prior targets or to compare exposure across competing Web sites with similar methodology. Because each visit is an opportunity to serve one or more messages, a high visits figure is often used in marketing a Web site to external advertisers. However, this metric is just a simple indicator of a Web property's attractiveness: Advertisers may be more interested in visitors' profiles or why a certain site is popular. It must also be noted that some methods of calculating visits may include multiple visits by the same user. Another issue is that there may be wide variation in the frequency of visits by different users. Therefore, this metric should not be used as a proxy for the number of visits by *unique visitors*. The latter metric is termed frequency and is discussed in a later section.

While a visit is a basic metric, its calculation can be distorted by the presence of automated activity at a Web site such as that caused by spiders and other robots. It is therefore desirable to remove the effect of such automated activity before reporting this figure. One solution recommended by the IAB (2002) is the use of unique registration or cookies, both of which are discussed in the next section. Another option to deal with the automated activity problem is to calculate visits using a panel, where specific users are known.

Unique Users/Unique Visitors

The IAB (2002) defines unique visitors as the number of individuals with one or more visits to a Web site. The number of unique users or visitors indicates to advertisers the number of people they are reaching with their message, and is thus another indicator of a Web site's popularity. The number of unique visitors can be compared with the target to assess effectiveness in terms of exposure. Comparing a site's metric with those of competing sites can help evaluate the relative exposure of messages on the sites. Each visitor also represents an opportunity to serve one or more messages, and as such, a high unique visitors count can be used in marketing Web sites to external advertisers. This metric can overcome the problem of using the visits metric as a measure of popularity because some methods of calculating visits do not take into account multiple visits by the same user.

While simple to understand, the measurement of unique visitors can create confusion as there are many acceptable ways to implement it. Three popular methods are discussed below. Unfortunately, these metrics are not equivalent and can give rise to different counts for reasons we discuss below.

1. *Unique registration* refers to the method where users register themselves on the Web site during their first visit and then enter a unique user name and password on subsequent visits. This provides an easy way to track the activity of visitors. Sites that register visitors can easily determine page requests by the same visitor. In addition, if the site requires users to supply demographic or other information as part of the registration process, it can be used to relate Web activity to user profiles. Advertisers can benefit from this information because they know the reach of their message, and, in situations where demographic or other information is collected, whether their message is reaching the right audience. A major weakness with registration lies in the reluctance on the part of some users to spend time registering at a site. Another problem is that many people forget their user name or password and either register multiple times or stop visiting the site. Yet another weakness is that multiple users, such as roommates, may sometimes use the same registration, leading to an understatement of unique visitors. Nonetheless, this is one of the three acceptable methods noted by IAB (2002).

2. *Unique cookie* involves a method in which a Web server stores a cookie with a user's browser, with a cookie being information that identifies that browser. Each time a user returns to a site, the Web site recognizes the cookie and thus the unique user. Cookies provide a site with a good way to track users without requiring registration and are in fact one of the three methods acceptable to the IAB (2002). There are some problems with this method: Users can turn off cookies in a browser, they can erase cookies on a regular basis, they can use multiple browsers resulting in the association of several cookies to the same user, or multiple users may use one browser. These actions can distort the unique visitor count. Another problem with this method is the distortion caused by caching. Some online services cache cookies, which means that after the first user requests a page from a certain Web site, the online service will store that page on its own server for distribution to subsequent users, thus decreasing the measured visitor count for that page. Dreze and Zufryden's (1998) study found that an average of 30 percent of page requests were not recorded by servers. Another bias occurs in

undercounting visitors without cookies. A cookie can identify only a unique computer, not truly a unique individual. However, because inactivity over thirty minutes is a cutoff point in the calculation of visits, it should be relatively safe to use cookies to identify a unique visitor.

3. *Unique IP addresses* refers to a collection of hypertext transfer protocol (HTTP) requests from an IP address grouped together to form a visit. In this context, HTTP requests are requests for some action, such as those for a Web page, by a user's computer whereas an IP address is a unique number that identifies a user's computer. Visits are calculated by assuming that all page requests from one IP address are from one individual, unless the IP address has been identified as serving more than one visitor. In other words, one needs to ensure that an IP address does not belong to a gateway or proxy machine, which may serve multiple users, as is the case with Internet service providers, which use multiuser IP addresses. Otherwise, it deflates the actual number of unique visitors. Dreze and Zufryden (1998) list various scenarios for miscalculation when using this approach. In their empirical study assessing the accuracy of a few Web metrics, Dreze and Zufryden (1998) found that different IP addresses were assigned to the same visitor in about 16 percent of the address assignment cases. Additionally, they observed an average ratio of 2.1 visitors per IP address, implying that a given address is assigned on average to about two visitors. Overall, they noted that this method understated the figure computed using both IP addresses and unique IDs by about 39 percent. Thus, it seems that this method is not very accurate. However, because the extent of error in other methods is not known, it is not possible to comment on the relative accuracy of the three methods.

Metrics for Evaluating Stickiness and Quality of User Relationships

Unique Users/Unique Visitors

In addition to its role as an indicator of popularity, unique visitors is the first component of the stickiness of a site, that is, the ability of the site to attract and hold visitors' interest. The greater the number of visitors, the greater is the attraction of the site and, therefore, the aggregate user involvement, and this in turn makes the site more "sticky."

Average Time per Visit

This metric is the average time spent on a Web site during each visit or user session. Average time per visit is calculated by dividing the total time all visitors spend on a site by the total number of visits during a given period of time, and either a census or a panel approach can be used for this purpose. It is an indicator of the stickiness of a site. It helps an advertiser understand how long a potential customer may be exposed to an advertising opportunity so that they may use an appropriate message. For example, if average time per visit is short, advertisers should ensure that the advertisement not contain too much information, which may be hard to process in a short time, or contain excessive graphics, which can result in downloading delays. On the other hand, if average time per visit is long, advertisers might need to constantly update messages to keep their visitors engaged. A weakness of this method is the bias that arises when a user is not at the computer or is otherwise occupied during the entire duration of the "visit," thus inflating the time actually spent on the Web site. Of course, such bias is also present in measurement of traditional media, such as in television viewing. Another weakness of this measure is that a lengthy visit may also be the result of poorly presented content or poor site navigation rather than any involvement on the part of visitors (Novo 2001b). As a way of dealing with this weakness, Novo (2001b) recommends that this measure be considered together with unique visitors. If a large number of visitors are spending a lot of time, it is unlikely that they are all experiencing content or navigation problems. Another problem with this metric as a measure of effectiveness is that visitors may spend a lot of time on a site but not make purchases or take other action desired by the advertiser (Bannan 2001).

Average Time per Unique Visitor

This metric refers to the average time that a unique visitor spends on a site during a given period, usually a month. It is calculated by averaging the time spent on visits or sessions by all unique visitors during a certain period. This metric is one component in assessing the stickiness of a site and can be calculated with either a census or a panel. Web sites like Yahoo! keep adding new features and services to increase this metric. The logic behind this is to keep users involved so that they spend more time on the site, and consequently there is a greater opportunity to reach that visitor with messages. For this reason, Web sites use stickiness figures like average time per unique visitor to promote their Web sites to other advertisers as advertising vehicles. Additionally, sites with a high average time per visitor may be able to offer a visitor a series of messages or an entire advertising campaign comprised of different messages over a period of time. An obvious weakness of this method is that it is not possible to verify that users were actually interacting with the site during the time they ostensibly spent there. Also, visitors who spend a lot of time on a site may not make purchases or take other action desired by the advertiser (Bannan 2001).

Repeat Visitor Percentage

This metric is designed to capture the percentage of repeat visitors among all visitors who visited a site during a certain period of time. This is an aggregate-level and census-based measure. By tracking unique visitors, a Web advertiser can determine the proportion of repeat visitors among its total visitors. A high repeat percentage suggests high "stickiness" and implies greater opportunity to reach an audience. Web advertisers are always trying to build relationships with their users, and a higher proportion of repeat visitors is one way to demonstrate the existence of such relationships. An advertiser can use a site with a large proportion of repeat visitors to repeat the same message or serve a series of different messages. Conversely, a low repeat-visitor count implies that an advertiser must constantly attract new visitors to the site to get the same exposure (page or ad impressions) to a message. Assuming the same page impressions, advertisers can use this metric to decide whether to target messages repetitively to the same audience or to appeal to a broader one. This metric can be compared to those of competing sites, assuming similar methodology, to assess relative user loyalty. Insofar as this metric is derived from unique-visitor counts, all the strengths and weaknesses of the unique-visitor metric will also apply to this metric.

Frequency

The frequency metric is the average number of times a visitor returns to a Web site during a certain period of time and is equivalent to a similarly named metric in traditional media. It is also the same as the total number of visits by unique users and involves calculating visits using methods such as unique registration or cookies that identify unique visitors. In most situations, marketers covet loyal, regular customers rather than casual ones and the benefits of loyalty and long-term customer relationships is well understood. Frequency is a good measure of user loyalty in the Web context. Comparing frequency across competing sites gives some idea of relative user loyalty and a high relative frequency count can be the basis of an appeal to external advertisers to advertise on a site to reach this loyal audience. This metric may also be important to advertisers because some messages may need to be conveyed multiple times before they have the desired effect on an audience. Frequency is typically calculated by dividing visits by unique visitors, and the strengths and weaknesses of those basic metrics will transfer to this metric.

Recency

This metric is designed to capture the interval between visits to a Web site. Its measurement necessitates tracking unique visitors and measuring the time interval between the current and the previous visit of each visitor. An average of all visitors' recency figures is then calculated. Recency is one component of the stickiness of a site, with higher recency suggesting more user involvement. Recency is another indicator of visitors' loyalty toward a Web site, with a higher recency figure implying greater loyalty among visitors or a higher level of user relationships. Recent customers are more likely to repeat an action, such as viewing a page or clicking, and are more responsive to promotions associated with this action (Novo 2001a). For this reason, Novo (2001a) suggests that more recent users have a greater monetized value to the business than less recent users. Novo (2001b) suggests that recency is a better indicator of loyalty than frequency because the most frequent visitors may not have visited in a long time. High recency figures give sites the opportunity to update messages frequently. High recency, especially when compared to the corresponding figures of competing sites, can form the basis of an appeal to advertisers to buy ad space on that site.

Stickiness

Stickiness is a metric that is also unique to the Web and is a function of four separate metrics: the number of unique visitors, the frequency of visits, the recency of their visits, and the total amount of time they spend at the site (average time per visit or average time per unique visitor). By understanding all these metrics collectively, an advertiser can understand how "sticky" a Web site is to a visitor. A Web site with a high stickiness factor should appeal to Web advertisers because it demonstrates the ability of the site to capture and hold an audience, and in turn, suggests they have a much greater chance of conveying their message to their audience or spending more money at the site (Landon 2000). A sticky Web site also suggests that users find it very relevant. Advertisers should note that each of the unique visitor, frequency, recency, and average time metrics can be weighed differently to come up with a stickiness factor depending on the Web advertisers' objectives. In other words, there is no standardized measure for stickiness. For example, if the goal of the financial section of Yahoo! is to get users to return to a site often to check stock quotes, and, in the process, watch a series of promotional ads for an advertiser, Yahoo! should focus more on the frequency and recency of its users' visits than on the time metric when conveying its site's stickiness to potential advertisers. On the other hand, visitors use National Geographic for lengthy periods of time to view its special content and use features like map-making (Silber 2002). National Geographic should, therefore, highlight the number of visitors and the duration of time that they spend on its site to its advertisers more than the other factors in conveying its site's stickiness to potential advertisers. Thus, one or more of the components of stickiness can be highlighted depending upon the advertiser's objective.

Metrics for Evaluating Usefulness

Page Impressions

In addition to being an indicator of exposure or popularity, page impressions can be used to evaluate the usefulness of a page or the relative usefulness of different pages within a Web site or across different Web sites. This information can give advertisers diagnostic information about the relevance of content to users. For example, a higher page impressions for the "Check Flight Times" page than for the "Travel Newsletter" page on the Yahoo! travel site suggests that flight-time content may be more relevant to the broad audience than travel newsletters. Page impressions can also be tracked over time to understand the impact of changing a message (content or an ad).

Top Pages Requested

While this metric has already been discussed as a measure of exposure, it can also serve as an indicator of the usefulness of the top page. In this sense, it helps advertisers understand why that page is attracting visitors, and this information can help them plan future messages or redesign a site.

Visits

Apart from its use as a gauge of exposure, visits can serve as an indicator of a site's usefulness because with other things constant, a greater number of visits implies greater utility to visitors. Tracking visits over time during which content changes gives advertisers an idea about the relevance to users of different messages.

Unique Visitors

In addition to being an indicator of exposure, unique visitors can also serve as an indicator of a site's usefulness in the aggregate because a larger number of users is suggestive of greater usefulness to the Web-surfing community as a whole. Comparing unique visitors between different periods of time can help assess the impact of messages that have changed during that time, thus giving advertisers some idea of the relevance of different content.

Average Time per Visit

This metric, which is also a measure of stickiness, can be used to measure the usefulness of a site insofar as users would presumably spend time only if the site's content was beneficial to them. This metric can be used to examine the effect of changes in content or ads on visit duration, giving advertisers some idea about which features or ads are more interesting to visitors. Comparisons with figures at other sites can be an indicator of relative usefulness. One weakness of this measure is that users may spend more time on a site because of poor content or site navigation rather than because the content is useful to them (Novo 2001b). One way of dealing with this weakness is to consider this measure concurrently with unique visitors (Novo 2001b): The idea is that if a large number of visitors are spending a lot of time, it is unlikely that they are all experiencing content or navigation problems.

Average Time per Unique Visitor

In addition to its role as a measure of stickiness, this metric also serves as a good indicator of the overall usefulness of a site to its visitors, the assumption being that a user spends more time at a site only when he or she finds it beneficial. One problem with this metric as a measure of usefulness is that the value of the site to users may be inflated when poor content or navigation issues cause users to spend more time (Novo 2001b).

Also, visitors who spend a lot of time on a site may not make purchases or take other action desired by the advertiser (Bannan 2001).

Repeat Visitor Percentage

This metric, discussed earlier as a measure of user relationship quality, can also be a proxy for the usefulness of a site to users. A site with a high percentage of repeat visitors suggests that visitors are returning to the site and, as such, provides some evidence that visitors are obtaining the type of experience they want. A low repeat-visitor figure may suggest that content needs to be reviewed to attract and keep visitors.

Frequency

The frequency metric, an indicator of user relationship quality, can also provide diagnostic information about the usefulness of the site to its visitors. For example, a low frequency of return visits may suggest that the site did not meet visitors' needs or did not provide them with a reason to come back, and may suggest a need to improve content. Tracking frequency over time may give an early warning about the deteriorating interest in the site (Novo 2001b). The relative usefulness of competing sites can also be assessed by comparing frequency statistics.

Recency

This metric, discussed in an earlier section as a measure of the quality of relationships with the user, can also indicate usefulness of site content. High recency suggests that visitors are obtaining the information or experience they want, whereas low recency may suggest the need for messages to be changed to attract and keep visitors. A Web site may also have to constantly update messages to ensure freshness and maintain the high recency of its visitors. Recency figures can be compared across Web sites to assess which site has more relevant content.

Top Entry and Top Exit Pages

The top entry and top exit pages are the most popular pages through which a visitor enters and exits a Web site, respectively. This census-derived metric gives advertisers some insight about what draws visitors and why they leave, and helps them redesign the site or change content to attract and keep visitors. A major disadvantage is that capturing such data increases the load on the Web site's server and the vast amount of data that needs to be analyzed makes it time consuming and expensive. Another weakness is that, sometimes, what exactly draws visitors to a site may not be clear just by examining the top entry page. This might occur, for example, when different users who use the same entry page have different motivations or there are multiple message elements on a page that make it hard to diagnose a specific reason for the page's popularity. Similar weaknesses characterize top exit pages.

Path Analysis

Path analysis refers to the mapping of the paths navigated by visitors to a site. For example, a typical visitor path may start with the home page, then a channel page, then a registration page, and finally an exit page. This census-method metric, which provides the paths taken by different visitors, helps advertisers answer questions such as what visitors did on the Web site. Please note that this is an aggregate-level measure and does not identify individual users. This information is important to advertisers because understanding the behavior of visitors allows them to alter the site to provide visitors with a better experience and greater functionality. For example, with path analysis data, a Web store may find that certain paths are less likely to result in completed transactions, implying some problems with site navigation or with the content of certain pages. The strength of this metric is that it goes beyond broad measures of exposure or popularity to give some insight into the behavior of users on a Web site. For example, if a path analysis reveals that most visitors skipped an intermediate page, advertisers can decide to drop the page or change its content in an attempt to improve relevance to visitors. Such analysis seems unique to the Web and is unknown in traditional media. A major problem, however, is that it is difficult and time-intensive to capture.

Metrics for Evaluating Co-Marketing Success

Clicks

The IAB MMTF (1997) defines a click as "an interaction with an advertisement" (1997, 2). This means that an ad was served to a visitor's browser and then clicked on by that visitor. This click is recorded in the log files of the Web site's servers as a request by a visitor to be transferred to another location or browser window to learn more about the product or promotion advertised. The IAB (2002) suggests that a click can be one of three types of user interactions: click-throughs, in-unit clicks, and mouse-overs. Click-throughs are instances where users click on an advertisement, which results in their being redirected to another Web site. In-unit clicks are instances when users click on an advertisement, which results in new content being served. Mouse-overs arise when users pass their computer mouse over the ad, which also leads to new content being served.

While clicks are useful as a measure of the popularity of a Web advertisement (see discussion in the next section), they can also be used to evaluate current co-marketing campaigns (e.g., which Web site generated the greatest number of clicks to the advertiser's site?), giving advertisers information to plan more successful co-marketing strategies by partnering with Web sites that drive more business to them.

Duplication

Duplication refers to the number of unique visitors common to two or more different Web sites. This metric gives an advertiser information on the other sites a visitor visited during the month that they visited a specific site or clicked on a specific ad. This metric is unique to panels. This information can be used to determine potential affiliate relationships or co-marketing opportunities with sites that attract a similar audience. It also gives advertisers some information on the number of people who view specific ads on two or more Web sites, and can serve as another measure of the overall exposure of the ad. This metric is unfortunately difficult to implement and has all the inherent weaknesses of panel data.

Metrics for Measuring Targeting Efficiency

Composition

Composition is a panel-based metric of the percentage of a Web site's visitors that belong to specific demographic or other groups. The strength of this metric is that it goes beyond the aggregate or average Web metrics such as visits or ad impressions to provide richer data about users. Advertisers can use this metric to assess whether their site's visitors met the targeted demographic or other profiles, and make decisions for future targeting. However, as with use of group information in traditional media, it is useful only if the group is reasonably homogeneous and group membership is highly correlated with actual attitudes and behaviors.

Global Geographic Overview

This is a census-based metric derived by looking up the domain for a visitor's IP address. This lookup will provide the countries of origin of a Web site's visitors, from which one can determine the number of visitors from any given country. This metric also answers the question that advertisers may ask about where their visitors come from and may be valuable to an advertiser in assessing whether the desired international audience was reached or to make decisions about the means of reaching such an audience. Its weakness is that the information is often too broad to be actionable. Another caveat is that while domain lookup databases are fairly accurate in the United States, that is not the case for the rest of the world, which leads to bias.

Observed Profiling

Observed profiling refers to a census-based method where a Web site captures the usage patterns of its visitors. Through the use of a cookie, a site can track a user's actions on the Web, but, unlike a panel, individuals are not identified by any personal information but rather by their behavior on a given site. This information can then be compiled into an observed profile report, which describes the behavior of each of that site's visitors. It thus answers a question Web advertisers often ask: What are visitors doing on the site? Knowing users' observed profiles helps advertisers in the planning of advertising campaigns. For example, if an observed profile of a unique (but unknown) visitor shows that the visitor typically spends a lot of time in the financial section of Yahoo!, finance companies can then target this person with ads. While conceptually simple, capturing this data in practice has proved to be technically very challenging. Another major problem with observed profiling is the privacy concerns of users, most of whom do not like being watched as they use the Web. Some Web access providers, such as Comcast, have recently stopped monitoring their subscriber's Web surfing behavior as a result of such concerns. These reasons have prevented this metric from becoming popular.

Description of Metrics for User Reaction to Advertisements on Web Sites

In this section, we describe the popular metrics used to measure users' reactions to Web advertisements on sites.

Metrics for Evaluating Exposure/Popularity of an Ad

Ad Requests/Ad Views/Ad Impressions

The IAB MMTF (1997, 2) defined an ad request as "an opportunity to deliver an advertising element to a Web site visitor." The vagueness of this definition resulted in much confusion due to variation in counting. The IAB MMTF (1997) chose the term "ad request" over the prevailing industry terms "ad impression" or "ad view" to emphasize that one cannot be certain that the ad was viewed by the user or that an impression was actually made on the user. In an about-face, the IAB (2002) uses the term "ad impression" instead of "ad request" or "ad view" and defines it as a measurement of the response of an ad delivery system to an ad request from a user's browser. The IAB recommends the use of filtration techniques to remove the effect of robotic activity such as that of spiders. Ad impressions is a broad indicator of the overall exposure of an advertisement on the Web. As such, it gives advertisers a sense of the ad's success in reaching an audience, where success is conceived in terms of visibility or brand recognition. It is, however, not a good indicator of user involvement with the ad because it does not track whether users interacted with the ad. This metric can be captured through a census or in panels. One weakness of the census method is that there is no guarantee that the ads were actually viewed by users. In contrast, because panels are able to track the actual receipt of an ad by a member's browser, there is a stronger assumption that the ad was actually viewed. However, as with traditional media, it is not easy to ascertain whether users actually paid any attention to the ads they received. Another weakness is that auto-refreshed pages may inflate the number of ad impressions, just as with page impressions.

Clicks

Besides being an indicator of co-marketing success as discussed in an earlier section, the total number of clicks provides advertisers with the knowledge that someone acted on their advertisement by clicking on it. As a measure of ad effectiveness, it is better than ad impressions because a click goes beyond mere exposure to some form of user interaction with the ad. Advertising objectives are not limited to gaining brand or message exposure but may sometimes involve more complex issues such as stimulating audience interest or offering more information. In such situations, clicks may be a better metric than ad impressions. Clicks have another important function: They can be used to transfer users to another Web site or another browser window where more information can be provided to them. A weakness of this measure is that it may underestimate effectiveness because there is evidence that mere exposure to an ad can lead people to go directly to the site referenced or look up the Web site or product later on, whether or not they click on it (Engage AdKnowledge 2000).

Click-Through Rate

The click-through rate is the number of clicks divided by the number of ads requested and served to users during a certain period of time. This metric has been broadly used to determine the effectiveness of an advertisement in terms of actual response to the ad in contrast to mere exposure to it. Certain advertising objectives, such as delivering more information or getting more audience involvement, go beyond simply gaining brand recognition or visibility. In such situations, click-through rates may be a better metric than ad impressions. Also, click-through rate may indicate effectiveness of an ad's message insofar as it is the proportion of ads with which users interact to the total number of ads they receive. The assumption is that the better the message, the more likely users are to click on the ad. Therefore, more effective ads have higher click-through rates. However, one weakness of this method in measuring advertising effectiveness is that clicks by themselves may understate actual user action with respect to an ad. This is because people who were exposed to an ad several times but never clicked on it often went directly to the Web site mentioned in the ad or looked up the Web site later (Engage AdKnowledge 2000).

Conclusion

While some of the basic ideas of measurement are common to both traditional media and new media such as the World Wide Web, the relative ease of measuring activities on the Web has resulted in a plethora of metrics, each different in its derivation, the information it provides, and its usefulness in Web advertising decisions. While Web advertisers have more data at their disposal than have been available to any advertiser in history, the challenge is how to use this information effectively to facilitate decision-making.

Advertisers must start first with their objectives, which may be different depending on a number of issues, the most important of which are the specific strategic decisions that are under consideration (e.g., a co-marketing arrangement), the nature of the Web site, the nature of the targeted audience, and the type of message. In this chapter, we show that there are five broad objectives of Web advertising: exposure or popularity, stickiness and quality of user relationships, usefulness, co-marketing success, and targeting efficiency. Advertisers can then use the various metrics we have discussed individually or in any combination. Appendix Table 4.1 summarizes our discussion of these broad objectives and the metrics that can help to achieve these objectives.

We have enumerated only the major advantages and disadvantages of each metric. It should be obvious that there is no one best way to measure Web effectiveness. Rather, for each objective, an advertiser would be well advised not to rely on any single metric but to use multiple ones, where possible, to obtain more insight. The most important thing for an advertiser to keep in mind is the objective of the measurement. For example, an advertiser who wishes to understand the exposure of an ad can study either ad impressions, the number of times the ad was requested by a user's browser, or clicks, the number of times users interacted with an ad. Each of these two metrics has its specific advantages and disadvantages, as discussed earlier. For a branding campaign, ad impressions is probably more relevant than clicks as a good measure of the overall visibility of the ad. For campaigns that are trying to convey a lot of product information, clicks would be more relevant in that they provide an opportunity to take users to a Web site or a window that can contain more product information. For a promotion-focused campaign, advertisers can use both measures to obtain a richer and hopefully consistent understanding of the ad's exposure. To give another example, both visits and unique visitors give distinctive views of a Web site's overall popularity. Visits, which is the total number of user sessions at a Web site during a given period, is indicative of the total user activity at a Web site whereas unique visitors, which is the total number of visitors during a certain period, is indicative of the number of users who find the site useful. It may also be useful to integrate information from census and panel data and from Web server-based and browser-based methods, where available, to obtain convergent validity of the information. We recommend that for Web advertising to earn greater legitimacy and grow even faster, Web advertisers need to take steps to construct more rigorous and standardized measurement methodology.

We expect this review of current Web-measurement practices to be a first phase of more research in this area. Very few academic studies concerning Web advertising have used the numerous metrics that we discuss in this chapter. We believe that our review of the available metrics will be useful to academics in designing future empirical research such as comparing the effect of different types of messages on user processing. It would also be profitable for academics to focus their attention on assessing the reliability and validity of the various metrics and methods. Dreze and Zufryden's (1998) pioneering empirical work is a step in the right direction. By empirically comparing the figures derived from different methods, it may be possible to identify an optimal metric or method for a specific objective. The relative popularity of certain tools among practitioners and the reasons for it need to be studied. Both approaches will enable us to understand the seriousness of the concerns or weaknesses of the metrics that we have identified in this chapter. While we are aware that the debate about the relationship between immediate and long-term advertising objectives in traditional media has not ended, we suggest the need for research to understand this relationship on the Web. Examining how measures that reflect immediate advertising objectives such as ad impressions, which are the focus of this chapter, relate to measures of longer-term advertising effectiveness such as sales or brand image is very important. Such research will enable us to understand how users process information on the Web and whether the effect is truly long term. Empirical research comparing the short- and long-term effectiveness of Web advertising and that of more traditional media is also necessary.

Both advertisers and academics know that measurement is very crucial in determining the efficacy of an advertising message or campaign. Advertisers are also interested in testing different advertising messages, which is easier on the Web. By shedding some light on the objectives, uses, strengths, weaknesses, and derivation of the commonly used Web-measurement tools, we believe this chapter contributes to a better understanding of these measures.

Appendix

Table 4.1

Web Advertisers' Objectives and the Metrics That Address These Objectives

Objectives and metrics	Metrics for User Activity at Web Sites		
	What does it measure?	How is it used?	For what is it used?
Measures of exposure/popularity			
Page impressions	No. of users exposed to a page	Measure of page exposure	Evaluation of message singly or comparatively
		Comparison with target	Opportunity to serve messages
		Comparison with other pages at same or other sites	
Top pages requested	No. of users exposed to most popular page	Measure of page exposure	Evaluation of message exposure singly or comparatively
		Comparison with target	Opportunity to serve messages
		Comparison with other sites	Opportunity to attract visitors to other parts of site
			Obtain higher prices for ads (compared with other pages)
Peak activity	Period during which there is maximum user activity	Exposure of maximum no. of users	Opportunity to reach largest audience
Hits	Records of user actions	Measure of load on Web site servers	Not directly relevant to advertisers
Visits	No. of user sessions	Measure of site exposure	Evaluation of message exposure (no. of times exposed) singly or comparatively
		Comparison with target	Each visit is an opportunity to serve messages

(continued)

94

(Table 4.1 continued)

Metrics for User Activity at Web Sites

Objectives and metrics	What does it measure?	How is it used?	For what is it used?
Unique visitors	No. of unique users	Measure of site exposure	Evaluation of message exposure (no. of people) singly or comparatively
		Comparison with target	Each visitor represents an opportunity to serve messages
		Comparison with competing sites	

Measures of stickiness/user relationship quality

Unique visitors	No. of unique users	First component of stickiness	Helps in evaluating stickiness
		Comparison with competing sites	No. of visitors an indicator of aggregate involvement
Average time per visit	Average duration of visit	Component of stickiness	Helps in evaluating stickiness
		Comparison with competing sites	Decisions on appropriate message length and type (graphics, etc.)
Average time per unique visitor	Average time visitor spends on site	Component of stickiness	Helps in evaluating stickiness
		Comparison with competing sites	Many opportunities to deliver messages to a visitor
			Opportunity to offer series of messages/advertising campaign comprised of different messages to a visitor over time
Repeat visitor percentage	No. of repeat visitors as % of total visitors	Measure of user loyalty and relationship quality (how many visitors are repeat visitors)	Evaluation of loyalty and relationship quality, singly or comparatively

		Comparison with competing sites	Opportunity to reach a loyal audience
			Opportunity to serve series of messages/advertising campaign comprised of different messages to a certain audience (loyal users)
Frequency	No. of visits by unique users	Component of stickiness	Evaluation of stickiness, singly or comparatively
		Measure of loyalty/relationship quality (frequency of visits)	Evaluation of loyalty and relationship quality, singly or comparatively
		Comparison with competing sites	Opportunity to reach most frequent visitors
			Facilitates execution of advertising strategy requiring repeating messages
Recency	Average interval between user visits	Component of stickiness	Evaluation of loyalty and relationship quality, singly or comparatively
		Measure of loyalty/relationship quality (recency of visits)	Opportunity to reach most recent users; recent users most likely to respond to messages
		Comparison with competing sites	Opportunity to update messages frequently
Stickiness	Composite no. of users, frequency, recency, average time per visit/visitors	Composite measure of stickiness	Evaluation of stickiness; basis of appeals to advertisers
			Opportunity to reach one or more of the following: large no. of frequent and recent visitors who spend a lot of time on site
Measures of usefulness			
Page impressions	Relevance of page's content	Measure of page's usefulness	Evaluation of usefulness (no. of impressions), singly or comparatively

(continued)

(Table 4.1 continued)

Metrics for User Activity at Web Sites

Objectives and metrics	What does it measure?	How is it used?	For what is it used?
Top pages requested	Relevance of most popular page's content	Comparison with other pages	Analysis of why content is useful; planning of future messages
		Track usefulness over time	Assessment of impact of changing message
		Measure of page's usefulness	Evaluation of usefulness (no. of impressions)
			Understanding why page attracts users; planning of future messages
Visits	Usefulness of site (no. of visits)	Measure of usefulness	Evaluation of usefulness (how many times), singly or comparatively
		Comparison over time with other sites	Assess impact of changing message
Unique visitors	Usefulness of site (no. of visitors)	Measure of usefulness	Evaluation of usefulness (how many people), singly or comparatively
		Comparison over time with other sites	Assess impact of changing message
Average time per visit	Usefulness of site (duration of visit)	Measure of usefulness	Evaluation of usefulness (time per visit), singly or comparatively
		Comparison over time with other sites	Assess impact of changing message
Average time per unique visitor	Usefulness of site (time spent on site)	Measure of usefulness	Evaluation of usefulness (total time spent), singly or comparatively
		Comparison over time with other sites	Assess impact of changing message

Repeat visitor percentage	Usefulness of site (large proportion of repeat visitors)	Measure of usefulness	Evaluation of usefulness (repeat visitors), singly or comparatively
		Comparison over time with other sites	Assess impact of changing message
Frequency	Usefulness of site (frequency of visits)	Measure of usefulness	Evaluation of usefulness (frequent visitors), singly or comparatively
		Comparison over time with other sites	Assess impact of changing message
			Decisions about improving content
Recency	Usefulness of site (recency of visits)	Measure of usefulness	Evaluation of usefulness (recent visitors) singly or comparatively
		Comparison over time with other sites	Assess impact of changing message
			Decisions about updating content
Top entry page	Usefulness of page (most popular entry page)	Indicates which page attracts most visitors	Planning content changes at this page or other pages
Top exit page	Usefulness of page (most popular final page on site)	Indicates the final page on the site for most visitors	Review and change of content or site navigation
Path analysis	Paths taken through site by visitors	Indicates most popular paths in site	Change content or site navigation

Measure of co-marketing success

Clicks	No. of clicks from originating buttons/links	Measure of success of co-marketing with originating and destination link sites	Evaluate co-market partners' improve co-marketing programs
Duplication	Other sites visitors visit	Measure of commonality with other sites (shared users)	Evaluate exposure to ads on multiple sites
			Design co-marketing program with sites that have high commonality

(continued)

(Table 4.1 continued)

Metrics for User Activity at Web Sites

Objectives and metrics	What does it measure?	How is it used?	For what is it used?
Measures of targeting efficiency			
Composition	Visitors' profile	Assess exposure within certain groups	Evaluate and improve targeting of groups
		Comparison with target	
Global geographic overview	Visitors' country	Assess exposure by country	Evaluate and improve targeting of message by country
		Comparison with target	
Observed profiling	Visitors' past site behavior	Understanding what visitors are doing on the site	Improve targeting of messages by studying visitors' behavioral patterns
Measures of exposure popularity			
Ad impressions	No. of users exposed to an ad	Measure of exposure	Evaluation of visibility of message or brand recognition
		Comparison with target	
Clicks	No. of user interactions with an ad	Measure of exposure	Evaluation of response to an ad (because it tracks actual user action)
		Comparison with target	Can transfer user to other sites or browser windows to convey more messages
Click-through rate	Percent of ads exposed that users click (clicks divided by ad impressions)	Measure of ad effectiveness	Evaluation of response to an ad (because it tracks actual user action)
			Evaluation of ad messages' effectiveness (because better messages would lead to more clicks as a percentage of impressions)

References

Bannan, Karen (2001), "Measure for Measure," cfoAsia [www.cfoasia.com/archives/200107–22.htm].

Bendixen, Mike T. (1993), "Advertising Effects and Effectiveness," *European Journal of Marketing*, 27 (10), 19–32.

Dreze, Xavier and Fred Zufryden (1998), "Is Internet Advertising Ready for Prime Time," *Journal of Advertising Research* (May/June), 7–18.

Engage AdKnowledge (2000), "Online Advertising Report, Third Quarter 2000," [www.engage.com/company/oar_docs/oar_3rdqtr00.pdf].

Forrester Research (2001), "Tech Strategy Report June 2001," [www.forrester.com].

Gallagher, Katherine, K. Dale Foster, and Jeffrey Parsons (2000) "The Medium Is Not the Message: Advertising Effectiveness and Content Evaluation in Print Ads and on the Web," *Journal of Advertising Research*, 41 (4) (July/August), 57–70.

Ghose, Sanjay and Wendy Dou (1998), "Interactive Functions and Their Impacts on the Appeal of Internet Presence Sites," *Journal of Advertising Research* (March/April), 29–43.

Hoffman, Donna L. and Thomas P. Novak (1996), "Marketing in Hypermedia Computer-Mediated Contexts," *Journal of Marketing*, 60 (July), 50–68.

———, ———, and P. Chatterjee (1995), "Commercial Scenarios for the Web: Opportunities and Challenges," *Journal of Computer-Mediated Communication*, Special Issue on Electronic Commerce, 1, 3.

Ianni, Drew (1999), "Audience Measurement—Stressing Accuracy Over Ease of Use," Jupiter Communications Report. Private report available to author.

Internet Advertising Bureau (1997), Media Measurement Task Force, "Metrics and Methodology," September 15, [www.iab.net/advertise/content/mmtf3.html].

——— (2002), "Interactive Audience Measurement and Advertising Campaign Reporting and Audit Guidelines [www.iab.net]."

Landon, Lyle (2000), "Measuring Stickiness to the Highest Degree Possible," [www.digitrends.net/marketing/13637–12397.htm].

Leong, Elaine K. F., Xueli Huang, and Paul-John Stanners (1998), "Comparing the Effectiveness of the Web Site with Traditional Media," *Journal of Advertising Research* (September/October), 44–51.

Novo, Jim (2001a), [www.jimnovo.com/recencymodel.htm].

——— (2001b), "Drilling Down—Turning Customer Data into Profits with a Spreadsheet," [www.drilling-down.com/measure-loyalty.htm#frequency].

Silber, Debra Judge (2002), "Sizing Up Internet Benchmarking Tools," *Magazine for Magazine Management*, 2 (1) (Winter), 29–32.

Steuer, Jonathan (1992), "Defining Virtual Reality: Dimensions Determining Telepresence," *Journal of Communication*, 42 (4), 73–93.

Part II

Important Elements of Internet Advertising

5

Rethinking Interactivity

What It Means and Why It May Not Always Be Beneficial

Yuping Liu and L.J. Shrum

Everyone seems excited about the "interactive revolution" that is apparently upon us. In its May 31, 1993, issue, *Newsweek* proclaimed the virtues of an "interactive life" and explained how interactivity would change the way we "shop, play, and learn" (Jensen 1998, 185). Colleges and universities are on the fast track to providing the latest in interactive courses, and academic researchers are similarly anxious to explore the nuances of interactivity. Moreover, nary a negative word can be heard about interactivity, or at least so it seems.

Yet, in reading across the rapidly growing literature in both the academic and lay press, it is unclear that anyone really knows what interactivity is. Or, perhaps better put, people have their own ideas about what interactivity is, but these ideas seldom appear to be consistent across people. There are at least two relatively innocuous and interrelated reasons for these inconsistencies. First, the word is a fairly common one that has taken on a technical definition. Second, the construct is a complex and (we argue) multidimensional one. Consequently, the inconsistencies across definitions may result from two people simply talking about different aspects of interactivity. In other words, both may be accurate.

In this chapter, we argue that a thorough understanding of the complexities of interactivity and a precise, concrete conceptualization and definition of the construct are crucial to advancing research in the area. In the first part of the chapter, we make this argument by reviewing the many definitions of interactivity that have appeared in the literature. We then integrate this literature into a precise but multidimensional definition of interactivity, and conclude with a review of selected research on interactivity effects and the implications of our definition of interactivity for reconciling disparate findings. In the second part of the chapter, we address the consequences of our conceptualization of interactivity for the effectiveness of Internet advertising. In particular, we explore the processes that likely underlie interactivity and show that these processes have implications for both enhancing and inhibiting the effectiveness of persuasive communications. In doing so, we offer a program of research in the form of a series of testable propositions.

What Is Interactivity?

Interactivity has been defined in many ways. For example, Blattberg and Deighton (1991) define interactivity as the facility for persons and organizations to communicate directly with one another regardless of distance or time. Deighton (1996) considers interactivity to have two primary features: the ability to address a person and to gather and remember the response of that person. Steuer (1992, 84) suggests that interactivity is "the extent to which users can participate in modifying the format and content of a mediated environment in real time."

On closer examination, these different definitions can be classified by whether they focus on user–machine interaction, user–user interaction, or user–message interaction (Cho and Leckenby 1997). User–machine interaction was the focus of early definitions of interactivity, in which the emphasis was on human interaction with computers. To be interactive, a computer system must be responsive to users' actions. However, though user–machine interaction is an important aspect of interactivity, it alone is not adequate to capture the concept of interactivity since the emergence of more advanced technology such as the Internet. As a result, researchers have turned to two other types of interaction: user–user interaction and user–message interaction.

User–user interaction is most often discussed from an interpersonal communication perspective. The more that communication in a computer-mediated environment resembles interpersonal communication, the more interactive the communication is (Ha and James 1998). However, one problem with looking at interactivity from the angle of interpersonal communication is that it ignores the ability of a medium such as the Internet to break the boundaries of traditional interpersonal communication. Not only do people no longer need to be at the same place, they do not even need to be communicating at the same time. With online translation service, people also do not need to understand each other's language to be able to communicate. Furthermore, research has shown that computer-mediated communication and face-to-face communication are not functional alternatives (Flaherty, Pearce, and Rubin 1998).

From a user–message interaction perspective, interactivity is defined as the ability of the user to control and modify messages (Steuer 1992). Whereas people have little control over messages in traditional media, the Internet gives users much more freedom in controlling the messages they receive and allows users to customize messages according to their own needs.

Although attempts to define interactivity abound, research on the effects of interactivity has been sparse and relatively inconclusive. Some researchers have found that interactivity has a positive impact on user attitudes (Cho and Leckenby 1999; Wu 1999), whereas others have concluded that it has no significant effect on customer satisfaction (Shankar, Smith, and Rangaswamy 2000) and that it may even be detrimental to advertising effectiveness (Bczjian-Avery, Calder, and Iacobucci 1998). These conflicting results may be partly due to the lack of a clear definition of interactivity and the resulting very different operationalizations of the construct. To advance our understanding of the new media and how marketing communications should evolve in the new environment, a clarification of the construct and formal programmatic research on its influence is needed.

Defining Interactivity

Although each of the three aspects of interaction just mentioned (user–machine, user–user, and user–message) is an important component of interactivity, few definitions have incorporated all of them. Here we propose a three-dimensional construct of interactivity that captures all three types of interaction. The emphasis of the current definition is on providing a concrete picture of consumers' online experiences. In doing so, we can identify the potential benefits and limitations of interactivity in online communication. We define interactivity as follows:

> the degree to which two or more communication parties can act on each other, on the communication medium, and on the messages and the degree to which such influences are synchronized

In addition, we specify three dimensions of interactivity: active control, two-way communication, and synchronicity.

Active Control

Active control is characterized by voluntary and instrumental action that directly influences the controller's experience. The Internet features a network of linked contents (Hoffman and Novak 1996), which is a parallel, nonlinear structure. In controlling such a nonlinear structure, users are able to customize the information flow and jump from one location in the network to another. In contrast, the linearity of a medium such as television makes it possible for a person to watch television without taking any action except to switch channels once in a while. Although he or she still has some control, the control is not absolutely necessary and does not effectively change his or her viewing experience.

The control an Internet user exerts is voluntary. While surfing the Internet, the user acts according to his or her own goals and wills. This is best illustrated by looking at banner advertising versus advertising on television. Because television commercials forcibly interrupt viewing, viewers must involuntarily switch channels to avoid commercials. Even for magazine advertising, where readers have more control over whether they read an ad or not, most times readers still must turn an ad page to go to the content they want to read. This behavior is totally different from banner advertising. Because banner ads are put on the page being viewed, Web surfers do not need to do anything to avoid advertising. If surfers are interested in an ad, they can click on the ad to obtain more information. If not, they can simply ignore the ad without doing anything special. Therefore, Web surfers control their experience on the basis of their own preferences and volition.

Two-Way Communication

Two-way communication refers to the ability for reciprocal communication between companies and users and users and users. Traditional media are somewhat effective in transmitting company messages to consumers but can hardly pass on messages in the other direction, from consumers to companies (Hoffman and Novak 1996). To gather information from consumers, a company must rely on other tools. The Internet changes this old way of marketing communication and makes instant feedback possible. Consumers can now give instant feedback to companies implicitly or explicitly while on the Internet. Implicit feedback is facilitated by techniques that track consumers' online behavior. By recording a banner ad's click-through rate or tracking the time a visitor stays at a Web site, companies can effectively gauge consumers' interest in their messages and products. Consumers can also provide explicit feedback to a company by sending an e-mail or filling out a form on the company's Web site. Internet technology makes both giving and collecting feedback very easy, which further encourages two-way communication.

Another important aspect of two-way communication is the ability to make transactions directly online. Although they have long been used to sell products, none of the traditional media can fulfill transactions alone. Consumers must either mail or telephone in their orders. The Internet is the only medium that can be used for transactions without the help of other tools. Necessary activities in a transaction, such as product display, order placing, and payment, can all be done on the Web. For digital products, even delivery can be made online. The ability to conduct transactions online greatly enhances the two-way communication between companies and consumers and makes it easier for companies to understand consumer purchase behavior.

Synchronicity

Synchronicity refers to the degree to which users' input into a communication and the response they receive from the communication are simultaneous. Traditional media provide few channels for audience input. Even when they do (e.g., through readers' letters or telephone calls), the time elapsed between sending the input and receiving a response is usually quite long. In contrast, the Internet is able to make the communication much more synchronized. It takes only seconds from inputting a piece of information on the Internet (such as typing in a search keyword on a search engine) to getting a response (such as the search results based on the keyword). Many Web sites also allow users to customize pages. Users can indicate what content and layout they like and immediately be able to see the page exactly as they want it.

System responsiveness is essential to this dimension of interactivity. To achieve synchronicity, the system, whether it is a Web site or an e-mail server, must be able to respond to user actions and requests in a timely matter. Because of technology limitations and the pitfalls of human fulfillment of technology, there are occasions when synchronicity cannot be achieved even on the Internet. For example, a user may click on a link and receive nothing more than a "Page Not Found" error message. Another example would be a significant delay in e-mail communication because of a server error. Therefore, maintaining a responsive system is important to create a synchronous and interactive online experience.

Structural Versus Experiential Aspects of Interactivity

In defining interactivity, it is necessary to distinguish between structural and experiential aspects of the construct. The structural aspect of interactivity refers to the hardwired opportunity of interactivity provided during an interaction, whereas the experiential aspect of interactivity is the interactivity of the communication process as perceived by the communication parties. For example, from a structural perspective, synchronicity may involve maintaining appropriate server structure, providing adequate bandwidth, and ensuring correct linkage between documents. Felt synchronicity, in contrast, is how synchronized users feel the communication is. This may be influenced by the speed of the users' Internet connection or the users' expectations, which cannot be controlled by the company.

Similar distinctions exist for active control and two-way communication. On one hand, companies can offer consumers more control opportunities by making the structure of their Web sites more flexible and avoiding annoying pop-up ads; on the other hand, consumers may not always be motivated to exert control efforts and thus do not feel a higher level of control. Similarly, not all consumers will take advantage of online feedback mechanisms made available to them. This may be because they do not feel the need to communicate with the companies or because they are concerned about privacy. By distinguishing between the two aspects of interactivity, companies can better utilize the controllable elements of interactivity and understand the uncontrollable elements, which may produce effects different from company expectations.

Applying the Definition of Interactivity to Theory and Practice

Although important, merely providing a definition of interactivity is limited in its contribution to knowledge. In the following sections, we demonstrate the usefulness of our conceptualization of interactivity by relating it to current practice. In the first section, we provide a comparison of different Internet marketing tools in terms of the degree to which they differ on the three dimensions of interactivity we have proposed. In the second section, we review selected scholarly research on the effects of interactivity, with an eye toward studies that appear to produce conflicting findings. We then use the different dimensions of interactivity to attempt to reconcile these findings by showing how the various studies differ in their focus on the interactivity dimensions.

Comparing Popular Online Marketing Tools on Interactivity

Not only is interactivity a fundamental difference between traditional media and online media, but the various online tools also differ in their degree of interactivity. To illustrate the dimensions of interactivity better, we compare the seven most popular forms of online marketing tools on their degree of interactivity as defined by the three dimensions. These seven most popular tools are Internet presence sites (company Web sites), Web communities (Web sites that serve as a channel for information exchange between people with similar interests or beliefs), online stores, banner ads, pop-up ads, e-mail

Figure 5.1 **Comparison of Popular Online Marketing Tools on Interactivity**

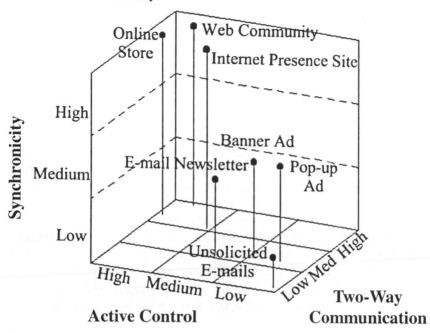

Note: The three dimensions are shown to be orthogonal for ease of representation. In reality, they can be correlated with one another.

newsletters, and unsolicited e-mails (spam). Figure 5.1 provides a graphical representation of the seven tools on the three dimensions of interactivity.

Active Control

Web sites, including Internet presence sites (IPSs), online stores, and Web communities, feature the highest levels of active control. Users choose to go to a Web site in which they are interested, and while surfing the site, they are constantly controlling their experiences. Among different Web sites, online stores offer the most active control. Compared with merely surfing a Web site, shopping tends to be more focused and demanding. Users need to pay closer attention and make comparisons and choices all the time. E-mail newsletters also provide users with some degree of active control, though not as much as that offered by Web sites. A major advantage of e-mail newsletters is that users decide whether to subscribe. Those who subscribe are usually interested in the company's products and services. Banner or pop-up ads, in contrast, use forced exposure. Worse yet, pop-up ads directly inter-fere with users' online activities. To avoid a pop-up ad, users must manually close the pop-up window. Therefore, from an active control point of view, pop-up ads are less interactive than are banner ads. Finally, unsolicited e-mail provides the least amount of active control and is probably the most unwelcome type of online marketing, as users have little control over such junk e-mails.

Two-Way Communication

On the two-way communication dimension, Web communities rank the high-est. An essential property of Web communities is interaction (Kozinets 1999). Community members can interact with one other through chat rooms and discussion groups. Although such communication often occurs among cus-tomers, it offers companies great insight into their customers' attitudes and preferences. Other types of Web sites can also foster two-way communica-tion, as they carry customer feedback forms, company contact information, or a customer satisfaction survey. With the ease of use of these feedback tools, two-way communication tends to be encouraged. The emergence of Web tracking techniques further enables companies to gather implicit feed-back from site visitors.

Similar tracking techniques can also be used with banner and pop-up ads. By recording click-throughs, companies can obtain information on customer interests. However, banner and pop-up ads usually need to be combined with Web sites to respond to users' actions, making them rank lower on the two-way communication dimension than do Web sites. E-mail newsletters offer similar levels of two-way communication as banner and pop-up ads. Compa-nies can track user responses to these promotional e-mails by embedding links in the messages, and users can offer explicit feedback by choosing the kind of newsletters to which they want to subscribe. Conversely, unsolicited e-mails offer virtually no two-way communication, as the recipient can rarely have input through such devices.

Synchronicity

As for synchronicity, e-mail newsletters do not perform as well as Web sites and online ads because of the delay inherent in e-mail communication. Ban-ner and pop-up ads are also less synchronous than Web sites, as users must click on a banner ad to obtain detailed information. Well-designed and well-maintained Web sites, however, offer seamless communication with users. Although the company usually puts the materials on a Web site onto the Web well in advance, by designing a responsive system, the company can promote a sense of real-time communication.

Implications for Research and Practice

As should be clear from the previous discussion and Figure 5.1, Web sites can differ drastically not only in terms of the *level* of interactivity they offer (i.e., quantity of features), but also in the *nature* of the interactivity (i.e., quality of features as a function of the different dimensions of interactivity). The distinction is an important one. For example, in terms of trying to improve "interactivity" (however defined), a company might focus on simply adding more features. However, some features may be more interactive than others or may at least be perceived as such by the user. Moreover, among features perceived to be equal in interactivity, some features may be valued more highly than others. Consequently, it is important for companies to determine which features are more highly valued and which are perceived as dispensable.

This is also true in terms of research on the effects of interactivity. As we discuss in more detail in the next section, it is tempting to operationalize the degree of interactivity of a stimulus Web site as the presence or absence of particular features or the quantity of features present. However, without valid manipulation checks, it is impossible to determine what the participants in the study actually think. It may be that certain dimensions of interactivity are weighted more heavily than others, and thus, the features associated with these dimensions may be perceived as not only more interactive but also more useful. Without an understanding of how participants perceive the actual interactive features, researchers run the risk of creating an invalid operationalization of interactivity.

Examining Conflicting Research Findings

To date, research findings on the effects of interactivity on various measures of marketing and advertising effectiveness (e.g., attitudes, purchase behavior, recall) have been remarkable for their lack of consistency across studies. As always, there are several possible explanations for these inconsistencies. However, we focus on the key independent variable, interactivity, and examine how different conceptualizations of the construct, particularly within the scope of the three dimensions of interactivity that we have described, may contribute to the disparate findings. In addition, we note how the structural and experiential aspects within each dimension have produced differences in research findings.

Active Control

The active control dimension of interactivity has received by far the most attention among the three dimensions. Researchers have studied the effects of active control on end variables such as attitudes and decision-making accuracy (e.g., Ariely 2000; Bezjian-Avery, Calder, and Iacobucci 1998), as well as intermediary variables such as telepresence (e.g., Coyle and Thorson 2001; see also Shih 1998). In experimental studies, active control has been manipulated mainly in two ways. The first method creates high control by allowing study participants to choose the path they take when going through the information, whereas the second method manipulates control by offering more or less choice availability in the form of the number of clickable links.

Ariely's (2000) work clearly falls into the first category. The author used a computer simulation of an interactive home shopping experience for a camera to approximate the online experience and manipulated the control that participants had over the information to which they had access. In the low-control condition, participants had no freedom in determining the sequence of the information they received; in the high-control condition, they had complete freedom to choose which information to access. The task for the participants was to rate the quality of a set of cameras. Over five experiments, Ariely (2000) observed that greater control of information was generally associated with better memory and learning. However, this advantage disappeared (and in fact was reversed), at least initially, when demands on processing resources were high (e.g., a novel or difficult task).

Bezjian-Avery, Calder, and Iacobucci (1998) investigated interactivity by manipulating whether participants had control over the ads they viewed ("interactive," by clicking on icons, which simulated a Web site) or did not have control ("linear," simulating advertising through traditional media such as television). The results showed that interactivity actually had a detrimental effect. Those in the interactive condition spent less time viewing the ads and indicated less of an intention to purchase the advertised product than did those in the linear condition.

At first glance, it would appear that the Ariely (2000) and Bezjian-Avery, Calder, and Iacobucci (1998) studies provide conflicting results on the dimension of active control. However, there is an important difference between the two studies. Whereas participants in Ariely's (2000) experiments were clearly informed prior to accessing product information that they would be making decisions about the cameras, participants in Bezjian-Avery, Calder, and Iacobucci's (1998) study were merely asked to go through the information provided and then rate their attitudes and purchase intention. Thus, the two studies likely differed in goal orientation. Not unexpectedly, active control does not work independently of other variables.

Sundar, Brown, and Kalyanaraman's (1999) study is an example of the second method of control manipulation. They manipulated interactivity as the type of interactive feature: no extra links (low interactivity), a "more information" link (moderate interactivity), and two additional information links that were "layered" (i.e., the participant could get to the second link only via the first one). Only partial support for the benefits of interactivity was found. Results showed that participants in the moderate-interactivity condition judged the political candidate to be more caring and more qualified than did participants in the low-interactivity condition but that those in the high-interactivity condition judged the candidate as less caring and less qualified than did those in either the moderate- or low-interactivity condition. This may be due to the extra effort needed to navigate too many layers of information without the actual benefit of obtaining more information. No significant differences were found for judgments of charisma or appeal.

Coyle and Thorson (2001) also manipulated interactivity by varying the number of clickable links on the first page of a Web site. Although interactivity led to a heightened sense of telepresence, it had no impact on attitude toward the site. The lack of support for interactivity effects in this second method of control manipulation suggests that different ways of implementing active control may have different effects on users. Although active control can satisfy heterogeneity in information needs (Ariely 2000), it may be contingent on the users' goals and the extra effort sometimes needed to manage the enhanced control.

Two-Way Communication

Although two-way communication is frequently mentioned as a component of interactivity, research focusing on its effects has been surprisingly sparse. The only research that has explicitly studied the effect of two-way communication is that of Sundar and his colleagues (1998). They conducted their study on the effects of interactivity in the context of attitudes toward a political candidate. They manipulated two-way communication through the presence or absence of an e-mail link. No overall effect of two-way communication was found. However, when the effects of interactivity were considered as a function of participant apathy, a different pattern emerged. Apathetic participants were positively affected by level of two-way communication, but nonapathetic participants were either not or somewhat negatively affected. The authors posit that interactivity serves as a peripheral cue and, as such, has an effect only on those who are relatively less involved.

Two questions are relevant for further research on two-way communication. First, what techniques will users perceive as facilitating two-way communication? Obviously, the mere presence of an e-mail link is not enough, though from a structural perspective, an e-mail link provides more opportunities for two-way communication. This calls for the extrication of experiential interactivity from the mere opportunity of interaction and an accurate measure of two-way communication (or interactivity in general) as perceived by the user. Second, what are the conditions in which users are likely to utilize the two-way communication opportunities provided to them? This may include users' privacy concerns and technical fluency at using the two-way communication tools.

Synchronicity

Research on synchronicity has been less ambiguous compared with the other two dimensions. Sears, Jacko, and Borella (1997) simulated Internet delay by a trace-driven simulation technique. In the short-delay condition, downloading was delayed for an average of 575 milliseconds; and in the long-delay condition, the delay averaged 6,750 milliseconds. They found that, for documents with both text and graphics, a longer delay resulted in less favorable attitudes. For text-only documents, however, a longer delay generated more positive attitudes toward the document. The authors attributed this finding to users' appreciation of the use of plain text when substantial delay is involved. Because most Web sites now have graphics, the negative influence of delays is probably more relevant to companies. However, when significant delay is unavoidable because of a speed bottleneck at the users' end, using plain text may be helpful.

Dellaert and Kahn (1999) also investigated the effect of synchronicity by adding a waiting time to information downloading. In four experiments, participants viewed and evaluated an Internet magazine. The results are particularly revealing of the difference between actual synchronicity and perceived synchronicity. For participants not informed of possible delays, delay had a negative influence on their evaluation of their experience. For participants told in advance of the possible delays, however, waiting had a less-salient effect. Moreover, negative affect generated from the waiting was transferred to the evaluation of the magazine itself, but only for participants who were not informed of possible delays. In the informed-delay condition, participants had expectations of delay. Therefore, the actual lack of synchronicity became less salient perceptually, in contrast with the uncertainty uninformed participants felt.

Experiential Interactivity

Several researchers have looked at the effects of interactivity purely from an experiential point of view. In these studies, interactivity is usually measured rather than manipulated. For example, Wu (1999) measured participants' attitudes toward and their perceived interactivity of particular Web sites. Results showed a strong correlation between the two ($r = .64$ and $.73$ for two different sites). Similarly, Cho and Leckenby (1999) measured participants' intention to interact with a target (banner) ad and found positive relations (correlation coefficients ranged between $.30$ and $.75$) between intention to interact with the ad and attitudes toward the ad, attitudes toward the brand, and purchase intention. Yoo and Stout (2001) also observed this general pattern of results. Although this body of research has shown encouraging signs of the usefulness of perceived interactivity, the results should be treated with caution, because the studies all used different measures of interactivity and the measures tended to be confounded with affect or behavioral intentions. It seems likely that a better understanding of the nature of perceived interactivity, and thus what interactivity means to users, might be accomplished through qualitative research methods that investigate the user's point of view.

Integrating the Results

Is there a discernible pattern to the results just discussed? One of our stated goals for this review was to reconcile apparent conflicting findings in terms of the three dimensions of interactivity that we have proposed. Some conclusions, however tentative, can be reached. On the one hand, active control seems to be useful, but only in certain conditions such as goal-directed searches (Ariely 2000) and not while surfing for pleasure (Bezjian-Avery, Calder, and Iacobucci 1998). Moreover, there seems to be a limit to the positive effects of active control. Sundar and colleagues (1998) found that moderate levels of interactivity (in the form of the active control dimension) were more effective than either low or high levels. On the other hand, synchronicity seems generally to enhance users' experiences with such things as downloading, but forewarning can lessen this advantage (Dellaert and Kahn 1999). Finally, it seems clear that, regardless of how researchers manipulate interactivity in an objective way, the *perception* of increased interactivity (whatever that may mean to users) has a positive effect on users' attitudes and behavior (cf. Cho and Leckenby 1999; Wu 1999; Yoo and Stout 2001).

Is Interactivity Always a Good Thing?

As a central characteristic of online media, interactivity has important implications for Internet users' behavior. It is usually assumed that interactivity is a good thing to have, it can make surfing a more satisfying experience to users, and the more of it the better. As we argue in the following discussion (and as is suggested by the reviewed studies), though this may often be true, there are exceptions to this notion. These exceptions represent boundary conditions that involve aspects of the person (user) and the situation.

We consider the effects of interactivity and these boundary conditions by examining the individual dimensions of interactivity we previously proposed. As we show, whereas some of the dimensions may have a positive influence on a particular variable, other dimensions may have no relationship with the variable at all. This is a potentially important concept that has implications for the measurement, operationalization, and interpretation of interactivity. For example, if interactivity is treated as a sum of the three dimensions, important relations between a variable and a particular dimension may be obscured simply because the other two dimensions showed no relation with that variable. Similarly, when effects are noted, they may be attributed to a global concept of interactivity when only one or two dimensions of interactivity are driving the relations. For these reasons, it is important to isolate and investigate the effects of individual dimensions of interactivity.

In the following section, we present a framework of interactivity effects that is derived from theory and research in cognitive, social, and personality psychology. As shown in Figure 5.2, the framework deals with processes that occur during the interaction and consequences resulting from the interaction. In particular, we consider one process variable (cognitive involvement) and two outcome variables (user learning and satisfaction). Although there are other aspects of the interaction that may be influenced by interactivity, we chose these three variables because of their importance in the communication process. Not only do these variables represent the essential process of a communication, they also play a pivotal role in persuasion and attitude formation (Eagly and Chaiken 1993; MacKenzie and Lutz 1989; Petty, Wegener, and Fabrigar 1997). Furthermore, these variables have been largely ignored in previous interactivity effects research.

User Cognitive Involvement

The term "involvement" has been given diverse meanings in psychological and consumer behavior research and has often caused confusion (Cohen 1983). Therefore, it is necessary to clarify first what we mean by cognitive

Figure 5.2 **A Theoretical Framework of Interactivity Effects**

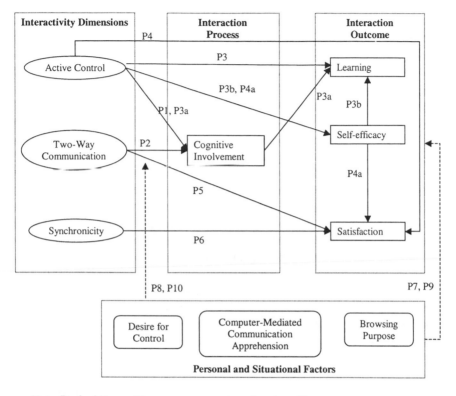

Note: Dashed lines with arrows represent moderating effects.

involvement in the present context. For our purposes, cognitive involvement refers to the extent of cognitive elaboration that occurs in a communication process. It is different from the enduring involvement people have with an object, which is the popular concept of product involvement. Rather, it is a situational construct that starts and ends with the communication process and is more in line with Batra and Ray's (1985) conceptualization of involvement as an elaboration process.

Interactivity creates cognitively involving experiences through active control and two-way communication. Active control requires users to be cognitively active and make choices. A highly interactive online experience requires users' closer attention and more cognitive processing than is needed for traditional media or low interactive online experiences. Furthermore, two-way, synchronized communication is potentially more engaging than one-way, unsynchronized communication. On the one hand, in traditional media, the communicator encodes the message and sends the encoded message to the audience. The audience then receives and decodes the message. In this one-way communication, the audience consists of passive message receivers. The Internet, on the other hand, engages the audience in the communication process. Internet users are not only message receivers but also active message creators. By engaging users in an active dialog, higher interactivity should lead to higher user involvement. This leads to our first two propositions:

P1: Active control is positively related to user cognitive involvement.
P2: Two-way communication is positively related to user cognitive involvement.

User Learning

A direct result of the more cognitively involving experience induced by higher interactivity is better user learning. It invites users to engage in deeper cognitive processing. Through such deeper cognitive processing, messages are likely to be better understood and remembered. Furthermore, being in control enables users to obtain information in a way most suitable to them. This satisfies heterogeneity in information needs across consumers and across time, making information acquisition more effective for a consumer (Ariely 2000). Finally, higher interactivity can lead to better learning by enhancing users' self-efficacy. Self-efficacy is an important motivational factor in learning and has been found to contribute to better learning performance (Mitchell et al. 1994; Zimmerman 2000). The active control dimension of interactivity enables users to control their own communication experiences, which potentially leads to higher self-efficacy beliefs (Gist and Mitchell 1992; Tafarodi, Milne, and Smith 1999). With increased self-efficacy beliefs, users will be more likely to be confident in themselves and more motivated to learn, which will result in better learning. These provide the basis for the following propositions:

P3: Active control is positively related to user learning.
P3a: The relationship between active control and user learning is at least partially mediated by cognitive involvement.
P3b: The relationship between active control and user learning is at least partially mediated by self-efficacy.

User Satisfaction

Interactivity can enhance user satisfaction through active control. Controllability, or the feeling of being in control, has been considered a desirable psychological state. The feeling of being in control has been found to lead to increased self-efficacy beliefs (Gist and Mitchell 1992; Tafarodi, Milne, and Smith 1999), less stress (Amirkhan 1998), and higher satisfaction (Judge, Bono, and Locke 2000). Lack of control, however, produces stress and lower perceived competency (Amirkhan 1998; Judge, Bono, and Locke 2000). By giving users the power to control their online experiences actively, interactivity can enhance users' self-efficacy beliefs and lead to higher satisfaction. Thus, our next two propositions are as follows:

P4: Active control is positively related to user satisfaction.
P4a: The relationship between active control and user satisfaction is at least partially mediated by self-efficacy.

In addition to the benefits provided by active control, two-way communication and synchronicity can result in higher user satisfaction (Dellaert and Kahn 1999). A highly interactive online experience responds quickly to users' actions and requests, treats users as active participants in the communication, and ensures that their opinions are heard. This reduces the frustration associated with waiting and feeling ignored and manipulated by the company, potentially resulting in a more satisfying communication experience. This leads to the next two propositions:

P5: Two-way communication is positively related to user satisfaction.
P6: Synchronicity is positively related to user satisfaction.

Interactivity May Not Always Be Beneficial

The first six propositions suggest advantages for interactivity. However, there are aspects of both the person and the situation that may circumscribe these advantages.

Personal Factors

The relationship between interactivity and user satisfaction is likely to be constrained by user idiosyncratic characteristics. In other words, not all users will prefer high levels of interactivity. It is impossible to exhaust all factors that can play a role in this process. Here, we focus on two enduring personal variables that reflect a person's motivation and affective state in communication, which are important moderators of communication effectiveness.

One relevant motivational factor is a user's desire for control (Burger and Cooper 1979). Desire for control refers to "the extent to which people generally are motivated to see themselves in control of the events in their lives" (Burger 1992, 6). People with high desire for control often ask themselves how much control they have over a situation. They attend to control-relevant information closely, process the information in great detail, and tend to seek to obtain control actively during an interaction (Burger 1992). When unable to control their life events, people with high desire for control are likely to feel depressed (Burger 1984). As a result, the active control dimension of interactivity is likely to have a significant effect on these people's communication experiences and on their satisfaction. Conversely, people with low desire for control do not attend to and process control-relevant information as diligently as people with high desire for control (Burger 1992), and thus, active control is not likely to make such a salient difference. They may even feel uncomfortable with exerting too much control. This interaction between desire for control and active control forms our next proposition:

P7: Higher active control will produce more satisfaction for people with high desire for control than for people with low desire for control.

Computer-mediated communication apprehension (CMCA) is another relevant user variable that may moderate the relationship between interactivity and satisfaction. It refers to the level of anxiety associated with communicating with others via a computer (Clarke 1991). People with high levels of CMCA can be novice computer users who are anxious about using computers, or they may simply have high levels of general communication anxiety (Flaherty, Pearce, and Rubin 1998). These people tend to avoid interaction in a computer-mediated environment and are less likely to enjoy the two-way communication on the Internet (Clarke 1991). Therefore, people with high levels of CMCA may be less satisfied with highly interactive online experiences that involve a lot of two-way communication than are people with low levels of CMCA, and they may be more likely to enjoy less interactive online experiences than their counterparts. This reasoning suggests an interaction between two-way communication and CMCA that forms the basis of our eighth proposition:

P8: More two-way communication will produce more satisfaction for people with low levels of CMCA than for people with high levels of CMCA.

Situational Factors

The purpose for which a user is surfing the Internet is a situational factor that can influence the user's preference for interactivity. We can broadly categorize browsing into two types: task-oriented browsing and hedonic browsing. In task-oriented browsing, users usually have a very clear utilitarian purpose in mind, such as obtaining information on a product they are planning to buy (Hoffman and Novak 1996). With such information needs, the ability to control the way they obtain information becomes important. The active control offered by interactivity can satisfy heterogeneity in information needs both across users and within users over time, thereby helping them better fulfill their purpose (Ariely 2000). Other cosmetic features of a Web site, however, will not be as attractive. Sometimes such cosmetic features may even be distracting to users. Consider Google's Web site, for example. Compared with other Web sites, Google features a seemingly too simplistic user interface. However, it still draws heavy traffic because users go to Google to search for specific information. The users presumably appreciate the ease of control and ability to fulfill their goals on Google.

When users browse for hedonic purposes, however, they tend to seek enjoyment and experiential surfing experiences (Hoffman and Novak 1996). In such conditions, the ability to look around and experience the features of a Web site may be important, much as people derive excitement from window shopping. Interactions facilitated by two-way communication can increase the fun and excitement during this process. Users browsing for hedonic reasons are more likely to experience and enjoy such fun to a fuller degree than when they surf the Web for utilitarian reasons. As a result, they are likely to derive more satisfaction from a highly interactive surfing experience that facilitates two-way communication than from one that has less two-way communication. This suggests an interaction between interactivity and motivation for Web site use:

> P9: Higher active control will produce more satisfaction in task-oriented browsing than in hedonic browsing.
> P10: More two-way communication will produce more satisfaction in hedonic browsing than in task-oriented browsing.

Conclusion

In this chapter, we argue that a clear definition of interactivity is crucial to valid operationalizations of the construct. We provide a multidimensional definition of interactivity and attempt to demonstrate its utility by reviewing previous work on interactivity effects within a marketing context. We argue that at least one important explanation for the disparate results regarding interactivity effects can be traced directly to how the construct is defined and operationalized.

We also propose a research program that makes use of the concepts we delineate in the first part of the chapter. In particular, we were interested in understanding both the benefits and the limitations of using interactivity in a marketing and advertising context. We admit, however, that this proposed program of research is a limited one and by no means encompasses any more than a small portion of potential areas of investigation. As just one example, we propose two individual difference variables (desire for control and CMCA). Clearly, there are many other potential individual difference moderators of interactivity effects. In fact, two of the studies we reviewed included such individual difference moderators (visual versus verbal style of processing, Bezjian-Avery, Calder, and Iacobucci 1998; apathy, Sundar et al. 1998). Likewise, there are likely many other situational variables that might moderate interactivity effects.

In conclusion, we reiterate our initial claim that the rush to implement interactivity features into a marketing situation must be tempered, or at least mediated, by consideration and understanding of precisely what interactivity is, what it can do well, and, just as important, what it cannot do. Such consideration is often absent from marketing strategies, as companies rush ahead for fear of being left behind. This situation reminds us of a television ad that appeared a few years ago. We share this ad to illustrate our point about rushing blindly toward the latest technological fad without understanding both its advantages and limitations. In the ad, two executives are shown talking to each other about company strategy, and one says to the other, "We *have* to get a company Web site." The other asks "Why?" at which point the first says, "I don't know."

References

Amirkhan, James H. (1998), "Attributions as Predictors of Coping and Distress," *Personality and Social Psychology Bulletin,* 24 (September), 1006–1018.

Ariely, Dan (2000), "Controlling the Information Flow: Effects on Consumers' Decision Making and Preferences," *Journal of Consumer Research,* 27 (September), 233–248.

Batra, Rajeev and Michael L. Ray (1985), "How Advertising Works at Contact," in *Psychological Processes and Advertising Effects,* Linda F. Alwitt and Andrew A. Mitchell, eds., Hillsdale, NJ: Lawrence Erlbaum Associates, 13–43.

Bezjian-Avery, Alexa, Bobby Calder, and Dawn Iacobucci (1998), "New Media Interactive Advertising vs. Traditional Advertising," *Journal of Advertising Research,* 38 (July/August), 23–32.

Blattberg, Robert and John Deighton (1991), "Interactive Marketing: Exploiting the Age of Addressability," *Sloan Management Review,* 33 (1), 5–14.

Burger, Jerry M. (1984), "Desire for Control, Locus of Control, and Proneness to Depression," *Journal of Personality,* 52 (March), 71–89.

———— (1992), *Desire for Control: Personality, Social and Clinical Perspectives,* New York: Plenum.

———— and Harris M. Cooper (1979), "The Desirability of Control," *Motivation and Emotion,* 3 (December), 381–393.

Cho, Chang-Hoan and John D. Leckenby (1997), "Internet-Related Programming Technology and Advertising," in *Proceedings of the 1997 Conference of the American Academy of Advertising,* M. Carole Macklin, ed., Cincinnati, OH: American Academy of Advertising, 69.

———— and ———— (1999), "Interactivity as a Measure of Advertising Effectiveness: Antecedents and Consequences of Interactivity in Web Advertising," in *Proceedings of the 1999 Conference of the American Academy of Advertising,* Marilyn S. Roberts, ed., Gainesville, FL: American Academy of Advertising, 162–179.

Clarke, C.T. (1991), "Rationale and Development of a Scale to Measure Computer-Mediated Communication Apprehension," Ph.D. dissertation, Kent State University, *Dissertation Abstract International,* 52–04, A1129.

Cohen, Joel B. (1983), "Involvement and You: 1000 Great Ideas," in *Advances in Consumer Research,* Richard Bagozzi and Alice Tybout, eds., Vol. 10, Provo, UT: Association for Consumer Research, 325–328.

Coyle, James E. and Esther Thorson (2001), "The Effects of Progressive Levels of Interactivity and Vividness in Web Marketing Sites," *Journal of Advertising,* 30 (Fall), 65–77.

Deighton, John (1996), "The Future of Interactive Marketing," *Harvard Business Review,* 74 (6), 151–162.

Dellaert, Benedict C.T. and Barbara E. Kahn (1999), "How Tolerable Is Delay?: Consumers' Evaluation of Internet Web Sites after Waiting," *Journal of Interactive Marketing,* 13 (Winter), 41–54.

Eagly, Alice H. and Shelly Chaiken (1993), *The Psychology of Attitudes,* Fort Worth, TX: Harcourt Brace Jovanovich.

Flaherty, Lisa M., Kevin J. Pearce, and Rebecca B. Rubin (1998), "Internet and Face-to-Face Communication: Not Functional Alternatives," *Communication Quarterly,* 46 (3), 250–268.

Gist, Marilyn E. and Terence R. Mitchell (1992), "Self-Efficacy: A Theoretical Analysis of Its Determinants and Malleability," *Academy of Management Review,* 17 (April), 183–211.

Ha, Louisa and E. Lincoln James (1998), "Interactivity Reexamined: A Baseline Analysis of Early Business Web Sites," *Journal of Broadcasting and Electronic Media,* 42 (Fall), 457–474.

Hoffman, Donna L. and Thomas P. Novak (1996), "Marketing in Hypermedia Computer-Mediated Environments: Conceptual Foundations," *Journal of Marketing,* 60 (3), 50–68.

Jensen, Jens F. (1998), "Interactivity: Tracing a New Concept in Media and Communication Studies," *Nordicom Review,* 19 (1), 185–204.

Judge, Timothy A., Joyce E. Bono, and Edwin A. Locke (2000), "Personality and Job Satisfaction: The Mediating Role of Job Characteristics," *Journal of Applied Psychology,* 85 (April), 237–249.

Kozinets, Robert V. (1999), "E-Tribalized Marketing?: The Strategic Implications of Virtual Communities of Consumption," *European Management Journal,* 17 (June), 252–264.

MacKenzie, Scott B. and Richard J. Lutz (1989), "An Empirical Examination of the Structural Antecedents of Attitude Toward the Ad in an Advertising Pretesting Context," *Journal of Marketing*, 53 (April), 48–65.

Mitchell, Terence R., Heidi Hopper, Denise Daniels, and Jane George-Falvy (1994), "Predicting Self-Efficacy and Performance During Skill Acquisition," *Journal of Applied Psychology*, 79 (August), 506–517.

Petty, Richard E., Duane T. Wegener, and Leandre R. Fabrigar (1997), "Attitudes and Attitude Change," *Annual Review of Psychology*, 48, 609–647.

Sears, Andrew, Julie A. Jacko, and Michael S. Borella (1997), "Internet Delay Effects: How Users Perceive Quality, Organization, and Ease of Use of Information," in *CHI97: Late-Breaking/Short Talks*, Steven Pemberton, ed., New York: Association for Computing Machinery, 353–354.

Shankar, Venkatesh, Amy K. Smith, and Arvind Rangaswamy (2000), "Customer Satisfaction and Loyalty in Online and Offline Environments," eBusiness Research Center Working Paper 02–2000, Penn State University.

Shih, Chuan-Fong (1998), "Conceptualizing Consumer Experiences in Cyberspace," *European Journal of Marketing*, 32 (7/8), 655–663.

Steuer, Jonathan (1992), "Defining Virtual Reality: Dimensions Determining Telepresence," *Journal of Communication*, 42 (4), 73–93.

Sundar, Shyam S., Justin Brown, and Sriram Kalyanaraman (1999), "Reactivity vs. Interactivity," paper presented at the meeting of the International Communication Association, San Francisco, May 27–31.

———, Kenneth M. Hesser, Sriram Kalyanaraman, and Justin Brown (1998), "The Effect of Web Site Interactivity on Political Persuasion," paper presented at the meeting of the International Association for Media and Communication Research, Glasgow, UK, July 26–30.

Tafarodi, Romin W., Alan B. Milne, and Alyson J. Smith (1999), "The Confidence of Choice: Evidence for an Augmentation Effect on Self-Perceived Performance," *Personality and Social Psychology Bulletin*, 25 (November), 1405–1416.

Wu, Guohua (1999), "Perceived Interactivity and Attitude Toward Web Sites," in *Proceedings of the 1999 Conference of the American Academy of Advertising*, Marilyn S. Roberts, ed., Gainesville, FL: American Academy of Advertising, 254–262.

Yoo, Chan Y. and Patricia A. Stout (2001), "Factors Affecting Users' Interactivity with the Web Site and the Consequences of Users' Interactivity," in *Proceedings of the 2001 Conference of the American Academy of Advertising*, Charles R. Taylor, ed., Villanova, PA: American Academy of Advertising, 53–61.

Zimmerman, Barry J. (2000), "Self-Efficacy: An Essential Motive to Learn," *Contemporary Educational Psychology*, 25 (January), 82–91.

6

Measures of Perceived Interactivity

An Exploration of the Role of Direction of Communication, User Control, and Time in Shaping Perceptions of Interactivity

Sally J. McMillan and Jang-Sun Hwang

The word "interactive" is often used as a synonym for new media such as the World Wide Web. Advertising practitioners and researchers use the phrase "interactive advertising" to describe Internet or Web-based advertising. However, despite the widespread use of such terms, scholars have noted that interactivity is often either undefined or underdefined (Hanssen, Jankowski, and Etienne 1996; Heeter 1989, 2000; Huhtamo 1999; Miller, Katovich, and Saxton 1997; Schultz 2000; Smethers 1998).

A better understanding of interactivity is of critical importance for those who want to analyze and/or develop Web-based advertising. Bezjian-Avery, Calder, and Iacobucci (1998) indicate that new media fundamentally change relationships between consumers and producers by opening up the potential for new forms of dialogue. However, their study also indicates that "the consumer can still simply buzz right through the interactive media, paying so little attention to the advertisements, that the message cannot function persuasively" (Bezjian-Avery, Calder, and Iacobucci 1998, 30). If advertising is to be persuasive in environments such as the Web, advertisers need to understand interactivity better so that they can more effectively engage and interact with consumers.

A central focus of advertising research is consumer perception. Researchers have begun to develop perceptual measures for the Web, such as attitude toward the Web site (Chen and Wells 1999). To date, research on perceived interactivity of the Web has been primarily conceptual rather than operational or has used measures that were not fully tested and sometimes had low reliability (Cho and Leckenby 1999; Heeter 2000; Lee 2000; McMillan 2000a; Sundar et al. 1998; Wu 1999). The purpose of this study is to operationalize measures of perceived interactivity in the context of the World Wide Web using the rigorous scale development process applied to many marketing scales. Scales for perceived interactivity are needed to help researchers understand the role of interactivity and advertisers benefit from the potential of Web-based interactivity.

Literature

For the past twenty years, interactivity has been widely discussed in fields such as advertising, marketing, communication, information science, computer science, and education. Table 6.1 summarizes some key definitions of interactivity, with emphasis on advertising, marketing, and communication literature. Several examples of pre-Web definitions of interactivity are also included.

Definitions of interactivity can be categorized on the basis of the primary focus of the authors on process, features, perception, or combined approaches. In the process perspective, scholars focus on activities, such as interchange and responsiveness, that are key to interactivity. Scholars who focus on features seek to identify either general characteristics (such as user control and two-way communication) or specific characteristics of Web sites (such as search engines and chat rooms) that define interactivity. Lee (2000) suggests that interactivity should not be measured by analyzing processes or counting features. Rather, researchers should investigate how users perceive and/or experience interactivity. The focus on perception is consistent with marketing, advertising, and communication traditions. As Reeves and Nass (1996, 253) note, "*Perceptions* are far more influential than reality defined more objectively." Little work has been done to operationalize perceived interactivity. This study seeks to fill that gap.

As illustrated in Table 6.1, interactivity has been defined using multiple processes, functions, and perceptions. However, three elements appear frequently in the interactivity literature: direction of communication, user control, and time. These elements hold promise for the exploration of perceived interactivity on the Web because they serve as umbrellas for many of the elements identified in Table 6.1. For example, direction of communication encompasses the concepts of responsiveness and exchange, user control includes functions such as participation and features such as search engines, and the concept of time embraces issues such as timely feedback and time required for information retrieval.

Table 6.1

Definitions of Interactivity

Study	Definition/description of interactivity	Key elements
Definitions that focus on process		
Bezjian-Avery, Calder, and Iacobucci 1998	"In interactive systems, a customer controls the content of the interaction requesting or giving information. . . . The hallmark of these new media is their *interactivity*—the consumer and the manufacturer enter into dialogue in a way not previously possible" (23).	User control and dialogue between consumer and manufacturer
Cho and Leckenby 1999	"The degree to which a person actively engages in advertising processing by interacting with advertising messages and advertisers" (163).	Interchange between individuals and advertisers
Guedj et al. 1980	"A style of control" (69).	User control
Ha and James 1998	"Interactivity should be defined in terms of *the extent to which the communicator and the audience respond to, or are willing to facilitate, each other's communication needs*" (461).	Responsiveness
Haeckel 1998	"The essence of interactivity is exchange" (63).	Exchange
Heeter 2000	"An interaction is an episode or series of episodes of physical actions and reactions of an embodied human with the world, including the environment and objects and beings in the world."	Action and reaction
Miles 1992	"An interactive communication involves responsiveness of the displayed message to the message receiver" (150).	Responsiveness
Pavlik 1998	"Interactivity means two-way communication between source and receiver, or, more broadly multidirectional communication between any number of sources and receivers" (137).	Two-way communication
Rafaeli 1988	"Interactivity is an expression of the extent that in a given series of communication exchanges, any third (or later) transmission (or message) is related to the degree to which previous exchanges referred to even earlier transmissions" (111).	Responsiveness

(continued)

(Table 6.1 continued)

Study	Definition/description of interactivity	Key elements
Steuer 1992	"Interactivity is the extent to which users can participate in modifying the form and content of a mediated environment in real time" (84).	Real-time participation
Definitions that focus on features		
Ahren, Stromer-Galley, and Neuman 2000	Media interactivity was defined in terms of features such as audio and video. Human interaction was defined in terms of features such as bulletin boards and chat rooms.	Multimedia, features for two-way communication
Carey 1989	Interactive media are "technologies that provide person-to-person communications mediated by a telecommunications channel (e.g. a telephone call) and person-to-machine interactions that simulate interpersonal exchange (e.g. an electronic banking transaction)" (328).	Channels for human-to-human or human-to-computer exchange
Ha and James 1998	Identified five characteristics of interactivity: playfulness, choice, connectedness, information collection, and reciprocal communication.	Five characteristics that constitute interactivity
Jensen 1998	"Interactivity may be defined as: a measure of a media's potential ability to let the user exert an influence on the content and/or form of the mediated communication" (201).	Features that enable user control
Lombard and Snyder-Dutch 2001	"We define interactivity as a characteristic of a medium in which the user can influence the form and/or content of the mediated presentation or experience."	Features that enable user control
McMillan 2000a	Identified thirteen features that, based on literature about interactivity, might suggest that a Web site is interactive, including e-mail links, registration forms, survey/comment forms, chat rooms, search engines, and games.	Web site features that facilitate two-way communication and control
Novak, Hoffman, and Yung 2000	Interactive speed is a construct that contributes to flow and is based on measures such as waiting time, loading time, and degree to which interacting with the Web is "slow and tedious" (29).	Time required for interaction

Straubhaar and LaRose 1996	"We will use the term *interactive* to refer to situations where real-time feedback is collected from the receivers of a communications channel and is used by the source to continually modify the message as it is being delivered to the receiver" (12).	Functions that enable customized and timely feedback

Definitions that focus on perception

Day 1998	"The essence of interactive marketing is the use of information *from* the customer rather than *about* the customer." (47).	Consumer involvement
Kiousis 1999	"With regard to human users, it [interactivity] . . . refers to the ability of users to *perceive* the experience to be a simulation of interpersonal communication and increase their awareness of telepresence" (18).	Simulation of interpersonal communication
McMillan 2000b	Individuals rated interactivity of sites on the basis of their perceptions of two-way communication, level of control, user activity, sense of place, and time sensitivity.	Perception of two-way communication, control, activity, sense of place, and time sensitivity
Newhagen, Cordes, and Levy 1996	Conceptualize interactivity on the basis of "the psychological sense message senders have of their own and the receivers' interactivity" (165).	Perception of interaction by self and others
Schumann, Artis, and Rivera 2001	"Ultimately it is the consumer's choice to interact, thus interactivity is a characteristic of the consumer, and not a characteristic of the medium. The medium simply serves to facilitate the interaction."	Consumer's choice to interact
Wu 1999	"Perceived interactivity can be defined as a two-component construct consisting of navigation and responsiveness" (6).	Perceptions of navigation and responsiveness

Definitions that combine process, features, and/or perception

Coyle and Thorson 2001	"A Web site that is described as interactive should have good mapping, quick transitions between a user's input and resulting actions, and a range of ways to manipulate the content" (67).	Mapping, speed, and user control

(continued)

(Table 6.1 continued)

Study	Definition/description of interactivity	Key elements
Hanssen, Jankowski, and Etienne 1996	"Aspects of interactivity were clustered around three terms: *equality* (containing aspects such as participants, mutual activity, role exchange, control), *responsiveness* (e.g., mutual discourse, nature of feedback, response time) and *functional communicative environment* (e.g., bandwidth, transparency, social presence, artificial intelligence)" (71).	Equality, responsiveness, and functional environment
Heeter 1989	Interactivity is a multidimensional concept that includes complexity of choice available, effort users must exert, responsiveness to the user, monitoring information use, ease of adding information, and facilitation of interpersonal communication.	Complexity, effort, responsiveness, monitoring, participation, interpersonal communication
Lieb 1998	Interactivity is seen as having two primary definitions. The first is a kind of personalization. The second type is community building.	User control, interpersonal communication
McMillan 2002	Identifies four types of interactivity based on intersection of user control and direction of communication: monologue, feedback, responsive dialogue, and mutual discourse.	Monologue, feedback, responsive dialogue, and mutual discourse
Zack 1993	Suggests that the following key factors emerge from the literature as elements of interactivity: the simultaneous and continuous exchange of information; the use of multiple nonverbal cues; the potentially spontaneous, unpredictable, and emergent progression of remarks; the ability to interrupt or preempt; mutuality; patterns of turn-taking; and the use of adjacency pairs.	Exchange, nonverbal cues, spontaneity, unpredictability, progression of remarks, ability to interrupt, mutuality, turn-taking, and adjacency

Direction of Communication

Researchers who examine ways that computers facilitate human interaction often focus on the importance of enabling two-way communication (Beniger 1987; Bretz 1983; Chesebro 1985; S. Duncan 1989; Durlak 1987; Garramone, Harris, and Anderson 1986; Kirsh 1997; Rafaeli and Sudweeks 1997; Zack 1993). In some of the literature, two-way communication is characterized as mutual discourse (Ball-Rokeach and Reardon 1988; Burgoon et al. 2000; Hanssen, Jankowski, and Etienne 1996; Williams, Rice, and Rogers 1988), whereas other scholars focus on the capability for providing feedback (Day 1998; Duncan and Moriarty 1998; Ha and James 1998; Newhagen, Cordes, and Levy 1996).

Massey and Levy (1999) note that the Web provides for "interpersonal interactivity" because persons can communicate with one another through tools such as chat rooms and bulletin boards. By making their Web sites friendly to users, marketers can facilitate this kind of interpersonal interactivity and generate positive word of mouth for their companies (Hoffman and Novak 2000). Interpersonal two-way communication through the Web also facilitates other kinds of business relationships, such as customer service and supply-chain management (Berthon, Holbrook, and Hulbert 2000; Peltier, Schibrowsky, and Davis 1998).

User Control

The Web often provides users with more content and navigational tools than do traditional media. Much of the literature that focuses on human-to-computer interaction (HCI) examines the ways humans control computers and other new media, such as DVDs and video games (Burgoon et al. 2000; Hanssen, Jankowski, and Etienne 1996; Huhtamo 1999; Milheim 1996; Murray 1997; Preece 1993; Tan and Nguyen 1993; Trevino and Webster 1992).

Reeves and Nass (2000) note that some HCI studies focus on human perception and others on computer design. Studies with a human focus examine how persons interpret computer personality (Moon and Nass 1996), the level of agency that persons perceive they have in working with computers (Huhtamo 1999; Murray 1997), individual decision styles (Vasarhelyi 1977), and the goals that persons bring to the system (Belkin, Marchetti, and Cool 1993; Xie 2000). Computer-focused studies examine issues such as interfaces and input devices (Baecker 1980; Biocca 1993; Laurel 1990; Naimark 1990; Nielsen 2000; Schneiderman 1998), navigation tools (Heeter 2000; Nielsen 2000), features for user choice and input (Belkin, Marchetti, and Cool 1993; Daft, Lengel, and Trevino 1987; Durlak 1987; Hanssen, Jankowski, and Etienne 1996; Looms

1993; Mahood, Kalyanaraman, and Sundar 2000; Steuer 1992; Zeltzer 1992), and system activity (Milheim 1996; Valacich et al. 1993).

Time

The perception of Web-based interactivity is influenced by the speeds at which messages can be delivered and at which persons can process messages. Crawford (1990, 105) notes that, for interactive systems, "The ideal is to have the computer moving at a speed that doesn't inhibit the user." Speed of response is a central concern of both developers and users of interactive media (Dellaert and Kahn 1999; Kay 1990; Nielsen 2000; Vora 1998).

Another time element important to interactivity is the ability of users to navigate through a wealth of information quickly and easily find what they are seeking (Mahood, Kalyanaraman, and Sundar 2000; Nielsen 2000; Wu 1999). One study (Latchem, Williamson, and Henderson-Lancett 1993, 23) notes that a benefit of interactive systems is that users "can work in their own time and at their own pace, choose their preferred navigational pathways and delivery systems and develop their own mental models and schemata."

Overlapping Dimensions

Each of the three dimensions is central to the concept of interactivity, but in much of the literature, these concepts overlap and are interrelated. Communication and control overlap in that higher levels of control lead to more active participation in communication. As Naimark (1990, 455) notes, interactivity is often defined at the intersection of these two concepts: "Though interactivity always requires information flowing in both directions, it is our input and its effect that distinguishes it from non-interactivity."

The intersection of time and communication is often viewed in the framework of whether interactive communication occurs in real time. Some have suggested that real-time, synchronous communication is central to the concept of interactivity (Kiousis 1999; Murray 1997; Steuer 1992; Straubhaar and LaRose 1996). Others have suggested that asynchronous communication, characterized by tools such as e-mail and newsgroups, is a key benefit of interactivity (Rheingold 1993; Williams, Rice, and Rogers 1988). Some studies have compared synchronous and asynchronous communication in the context of interactivity (Hesse, Werner, and Altman 1988; McGrath 1990; McMillan and Downes 2000; Morris and Ogan 1996; Walther 1992).

Time and control also overlap in that the complexity of control systems (e.g., navigation tools) affects the time required to access content. But time spent controlling the system is not always related to complexity; increased

Figure 6.1 **Key Dimensions of Interactivity.**

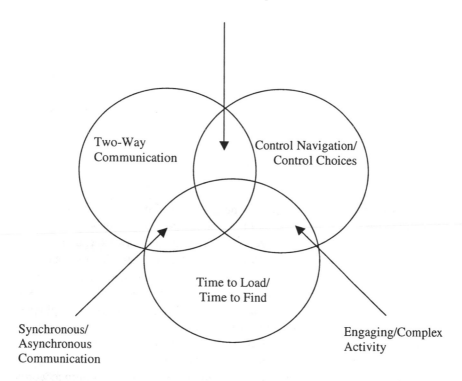

time can also be a result of intense engagement. Literature on the concept of "flow" (Csikszentmihalyi 1975; Ghani and Deshpande 1994; Hoffman and Novak 1996; Novak, Hoffman, and Yung 2000; Trevino and Webster 1992) focuses on how users can become absorbed in new media and lose track of time. Ghani and Deshpande (1994) define flow as the activities that result from both the exploratory, and often time-consuming, use of the computer and the person's sense of being in control of the computer.

Figure 6.1 illustrates the overlapping of the three dimensions of perceived interactivity that are central to this study. Web-based interactivity involves communication among persons, the ability those persons have to control information and participate in active communication, and time—to load the message, to find information, to communicate with others, and the loss of time as the user gets caught in the flow of computer-mediated communication. Users' perceptions of the direction of communication, control, and time are central to how interactive they perceive Web sites to be.

Scale Development

Churchill's (1979) paradigm for scale development serves as the primary guideline for developing a scale for measuring perceived interactivity. Other updated guidelines (e.g., DeVellis 1991; Gerbing and Anderson 1988) were also considered. A multimethod approach is used to specify the domain of interactivity and generate an initial pool of items designed to measure perceived interactivity. In addition, two pretests, as well as two data collection stages, are used to generate and refine a set of scale items. This multistage process ensures construct validity by enabling the researchers to identify, purify, and assess potential scale items on the basis of multiple types of qualitative and quantitative feedback.

Item Generation

Three sources were used to specify the domain of interactivity and generate the initial item pool. First, the literature on interactivity suggested a conceptual model that identified three overlapping constructs that underlie interactivity (see Figure 6.1). Second, in-depth interviews with ten subjects who produce and teach interactive communication were used to probe for understanding of the concept of interactivity (McMillan and Downes 2000). Transcripts of those interviews were reviewed, and all words and phrases used in conjunction with interactivity were identified. Third, two focus groups were conducted. In these focus groups, subjects identified and discussed words and concepts that they associated with interactivity.

From the literature, expert interviews, and focus groups, 157 unique words and phrases emerged. Upon examination, some words and phrases were eliminated because they addressed concepts related, but not central, to interactivity (e.g., words for specific technologies such as computers and digital television). Other terms were closely related and could be summarized with two to three synonyms rather than the ten to fifteen different terms on the original list. In addition, the researchers identified antonyms for each core concept. The purpose of these antonyms was to ensure that study participants were actually reading all items rather than simply selecting one rating and applying it to all items. Correlations between the antonyms and related terms in each step of the analysis yielded strong negative correlations. This indicates that respondents differentiated antonyms from words positively associated with interactivity.

The list of 157 words and phrases was reduced to twenty-six core concepts. Five core concepts were associated with communication, five with control, and six with time. Ten additional core concepts addressed areas of overlap between dimensions. Although some concepts in the original list were eliminated, these twenty-six core concepts were most central to the literature and the experts and were frequently mentioned in focus groups.

Data Collection

On the basis of a pretest with sixty undergraduate students, computers were chosen as the topic for exploration of interactivity because they scored well on three criteria: likelihood of seeking information, likelihood of communicating with others about the topic, and likelihood of online purchase. Two Web sites were developed to provide an environment in which to evaluate perceptions of interactivity. Laptop computers were the subject of both Web sites; the sites contained virtually identical information. However, one site was designed to have fewer interactive features and fewer opportunities for interactive exchange, thus making it likely to generate lower scores on a scale of perceived interactivity than the other site that included features such as chat rooms, bulletin boards, a site map, and enhanced navigation bars. The purpose for creating these two environments was to generate variance in response to measures.

Participants were randomly assigned to review either the high- or low-interactivity Web site. Both Web sites included a menu item that led users to an online survey. Participants were instructed to spend about fifteen minutes reviewing a site before selecting the survey option. All participants were issued a unique identification number that they provided when answering the survey. These numbers were used to track which of the two sites each participant had viewed, as well as to ensure that each subject completed the survey only once.

Participants used a seven-point scale, anchored by the phrases "not at all descriptive" and "very descriptive," to indicate how well scale items described the Web site they had viewed. Participants were also asked five factual questions to ensure they had reviewed the site. Finally, three measures of attitude toward the Web site were adapted from the Chen and Wells (1999) A_{ST} scale for testing the predictive validity of perceived interactivity. Data collection tools (Web sites and survey) were pretested by eleven faculty members and eight doctoral students.

A total of 126 subjects from various backgrounds evaluated one of the Web sites and completed the survey in the two rounds of data collection. Many participants (72%) were nonstudents (e.g., business consultant, politician, retired). Ages ranged from twenty-one to seventy-four years (mean = 31.7). In the first round of data collection, sixty-one participants evaluated the sites. On the basis of their feedback, the scale items were refined and purified. In the second round of data collection, sixty-five participants evaluated the sites using the revised list of scale items.

Round 1: Data Collection and Initial Purification of Measures

The primary purpose of the Round 1 data collection was to purify measures. The authors focused on improving problematic items and concepts. The primary statistical tool for purification at this stage was reliability analysis. Data collected in Round 1 supported the construct validity of the overall scale and subscales for key dimensions of interactivity. The alpha coefficient for the original twenty-six items was 0.8926. Reliability analysis for the communication subdimension was good, with an alpha of 0.8442, and reliability for the scale could not be significantly improved by removing any communication items.

Both the control and time subdimensions were somewhat problematic in terms of their reliabilities (coefficient alphas were 0.6463 and 0.6814 for control and time, respectively); removal of individual items could not significantly improve the reliability of either scale. After a reexamination of the literature, the researchers concluded that both the control and time subdimensions needed to be conceptually subdivided. Control includes both control of navigation and control of choices. Time includes both time to load and time to find information. Some items were also reworded for clarity.

Reliability analyses for items that were designed to measure overlapping aspects of the conceptual model in Figure 6.1 (e.g., control/time) yielded coefficient alphas ranging from 0.4794 to 0.7317. These relatively low alphas were to be expected because these items might group together with one or more of the primary dimensions. However, minor wording changes were made to items that seemed most problematic in reliability analyses to ensure that they were not misinterpreted.

Round 2: Data Collection, Repurification, and Assessment of Measures

A revised list of twenty-eight items was used in Round 2 of data collection. A series of exploratory factor analyses was conducted to determine how well these scale items group together to measure underlying concepts related to interactivity. The factors were extracted by principal components analysis with the direct oblimin rotation method. In the factor analysis, the authors removed items with factor loadings lower than 0.45 and those that crossloaded on two or more factors. The authors also examined scree plots and the eigenvalue of each factor in the exploratory factor stage.

Table 6.2

Factor Loadings of Perceived Interactivity

Items[a]	Item number[b]	Real-time conversation	No delay	Engaging
Enables two-way communication (com)	I_1	0.879		
Enables concurrent communication (t/com)	I_2	0.833		
Nonconcurrent communication (t/com)[c]	I_3	0.826		
Is interactive (all)	I_4	0.807		
Primarily one-way communication (com)[c]	I_5	0.760		
Is interpersonal (com)	I_6	0.758		
Enables conversation (com)	I_7	0.721		
Loads fast (t1)	I_8		0.936	
Loads slow (t1)[c]	I_9		0.931	
Operates at high speed (t1)	I_{10}		0.924	
Variety of content (con2)	I_{11}			0.745
Keeps my attention (t/con)	I_{12}			0.745
Easy to find my way through the site (con1)	I_{13}			0.713
Unmanageable (con1)[c]	I_{14}			0.640
Doesn't keep my attention (t/con)[c]	I_{15}			0.621
Passive (com/con)[c]	I_{16}			0.597
Immediate answers to questions (t2)	I_{17}			0.578
Lacks content (con2)[c]	I_{18}			0.534
Eigenvalue		6.205	2.635	1.975
% of variance		34.471	14.640	10.970

Notes: Extraction method was principal component analysis. Rotation method was direct oblimin with kaiser normalization (pattern matrix). Only loadings of 0.45 or higher are shown.

[a]Phrases are coded to indicate which dimension they were designed to measure: com = communication, con1 = control of navigation, con2 = control of choices, t1 = time to load, t2 = time to find information, com/con = overlap of communication and control, t/com = overlap of time and communication, t/con = overlap of time and control, and all = overlap of all items.

[b]Item numbers are assigned to coordinate with Figure 6.2.

[c]Phrase recoded for analysis.

These analyses yielded a reduced scale of eighteen items that loaded on three factors. Table 6.2 provides the pattern matrix from the principal components analysis with oblique rotation for data from Round 2. The origins of the 18 items in this analysis are widely distributed to include all of the subdimensions identified in the literature (communication, control, and time), as well as all of the overlapping dimensions (e.g., control/time). Although the three factors correspond roughly to the three dimensions identified in the literature, the overlapping nature of concepts led to slight rewording. For example, the real-time conversation factor clearly shows the overlap of the time and communication dimensions.

A confirmatory factor analysis (CFA) using Amos assessed unidimensionality and factorial structure, convergent validity, and discriminant validity. This measurement model CFA examines whether the scale's structure is internally consistent, as explicated by the theoretical model proposed in Figure 6.1. The measurement items that are purported to load on a particular factor must load on it. The overall goodness of fit is evaluated according to the similarity of the predicted and actual correlation (Gerbing and Anderson 1988). Figure 6.2 presents the structure of the scale with the three factors and individual items. The fit for this model was excellent (chi-square = 212.116 at $df = 132$; normed fit index = 0.935; relative fit index = 0.915; incremental fit index = 0.974; Tucker-Lewis index= 0.966; confirmatory fit index = 0.974). As illustrated in Figure 6.2, the real-time conversation factor and the engaging factor show high covariance, and the no delay factor shows moderate covariance with the other two factors. Although these three factors do not correspond exactly to the three dimensions predicted in the theoretical model, the factors exhibit the predicted overlapping nature of communication, control, and time and are conceptually consistent with the theoretical model. Thus, the final structural model confirms the model proposed in Figure 6.1.

Scales were created on the basis of these three factors, and reliability of all three scales was strong, as indicated by the high alpha coefficients (0.9034 for real-time conversation, 0.9195 for no delay, and 0.7889 for engaging).

Measures of Perceived Interactivity

On the basis of the findings of this study, the authors propose three measures of perceived interactivity (MPI) scales. The first scale for real-time conversation includes seven items that focus on communication and the overlap of time and communication. The "is interactive" item also loaded on this scale. Although this item was designed to represent all three aspects of perceived interactivity, it seems to be most closely associated with the concept of real-time conversation.

The no delay scale includes three items that relate to the time to load concept and highlight the importance of speed in interactivity. The engaging scale includes eight items that focus primarily on control but also include time-related concepts, especially time to find, which suggests a strong overlap between these two dimensions, as is indicated in the literature about the concept of flow.

Figure 6.2 Perceived Interactivity: Three Primary Dimensions and Their Measurement Items

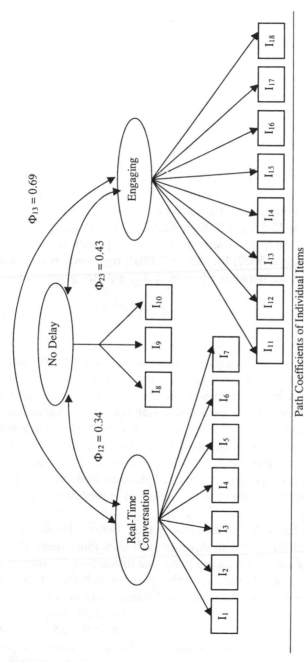

Path Coefficients of Individual Items

Real-time conversation	$\lambda(I_1) = 1.00$	$\lambda(I_2) = 0.97$	$\lambda(I_3) = 0.85$	$\lambda(I_4) = .87$	$\lambda(I_5) = 0.85$	$\lambda(I_6) = 0.82$	$\lambda(I_7) = 0.71$
No delay	$\lambda(I_8) = 1.00$	$\lambda(I_9) = 0.99$	$\lambda(I_{10}) = 0.89$			
Engaging	$\lambda(I_{11}) = 1.00$	$\lambda(I_{12}) = 0.90$	$\lambda(I_{13}) = 0.97$	$\lambda(I_{14}) = 1.17$	$\lambda(I_{15}) = 1.05$	$\lambda(I_{16}) = 0.78$	$\lambda(I_{17}) = 0.86$	$\lambda(I_{18}) = 0.71$

Notes: Coefficient alphas: 0.9034 for real-time conversation, 0.9195 for no delay, and 0.7889 for engaging.

Test of the Scale Validity Based on Attitude Toward the Site

Attitude toward the Web site (A_{ST}) is a scale that has been developed specifically for measuring advertising constructs in new media (Chen and Wells 1999). Researchers are coming to support the A_{ST} as one of the major indicators of the effectiveness of Web advertising (e.g., Pavlou and Stewart 2000). Several researchers have suggested that interactivity might help predict attitude toward a Web site (Ahren, Stromer-Galley, and Neuman 2000; McMillan 2000a; Wu 1999). However, prior to development of the MPI, there has not been an effective scale for examining the relationship between perceived interactivity and A_{ST}.

To evaluate predictive validity, the authors examined whether the MPI scales predict A_{ST}. Multiple regression with three predictors, the three MPI scales, showed that perceived interactivity explained much of the variance in A_{ST} ($R = 0.740$, $F = 22.57$, $p = 0.000$). Although the literature suggests that other predictors, such as involvement, cannot be ignored in assessing A_{ST} (Hwang and McMillan 2002; McMillan 2000a), regression results indicate that the MPI scales are strong predictors of A_{ST} and thus good indicators of Web site effectiveness.

Discussion

The MPI items can enable researchers to examine relationships among perceptions of interactivity and other key new media variables, such as attitude toward the Web site, involvement with the site topic, and site characteristics. For example, if a researcher wants to understand effects of changes in a Web site design, the MPI could be an important measure to determine whether design changes are perceived as changing the interactivity of the site. Furthermore, researchers can use the MPI to determine appropriate levels of interactivity for specific situations. For example, increased interactivity might not benefit corporate Web sites that are designed to present a controlled image of a company.

The MPI also has value to advertising practitioners. By understanding perceived interactivity, they can develop Web sites that effectively utilize interactivity. They can also measure perceived interactivity of sites at which they may wish to place banner advertising and match the interactivity of their advertising with users' experiences of interactivity at Web sites.

Each of the three MPI scales has potential for explaining some of the differences between Web-based communication and traditional media. Whereas traditional media have utilized some forms of two-way communication, such as 800 telephone numbers for direct response, the capacity for two-way communication is dramatically enhanced on the Web. Even though Web-based communications are still mediated, it seems that consumers expect interactive advertising content to be more like the real-time, face-to-face interaction that occurs in personal selling than like the asynchronous, one-way communication associated with mass advertising. Advertisers who want to take full advantage of interactive media must be willing to invest the time and money to develop a dialogue with their consumers. This suggests the need for very careful training of those who represent the advertiser in online dialogue. A mistake or incorrect impression given in face-to-face conversation with a consumer often goes no farther and can be corrected. The same mistake made in e-mail correspondence can, with a few keystrokes, be sent around the world.

Advertisers must be attentive to the Web users' need for speed. If advertising messages make a site slow to load, consumers will simply leave before the message is seen. This applies to slow-loading banners as well as corporate Web sites. Advertisers may need to rethink their presentation strategies. Whereas graphics-heavy brochures might traditionally be a good medium for relaying product information, the same format on a Web site could be disastrous. Consumers expect to access interactive media content with no delays. As technology advances, multimedia files may load faster, but consumer expectations of speed will accelerate as well.

A basic advantage of advertising in traditional media is that advertisers have maintained control over both the content and the timing of messages. The findings from this study suggest that advertisers who want to develop interactive marketing communication messages must share some of that control with consumers, who expect to engage with the Web rather than simply be exposed to it. The construction of interactive advertising messages requires the development of new forms. The task for interactive advertisers is to make messages interesting and attention-holding in a multimedia environment while maintaining navigational ease.

This study suggests that a new aesthetic will emerge by which we judge interactive advertising messages. Traditional criteria such as "attracting attention" and "simple, orderly layout" have limited application to interactive media. The form must develop an aesthetic that incorporates such concepts as real-time conversation, loading speed, and ability to engage the consumer. Thus, a final, very practical use of the MPI is as a tool for pretesting messages that have been developed for the Web. The MPI, in conjunction with A_{ST} measures, might be a very good indicator of the potential success of a Web site or Web-based advertisement.

As illustrated in Figure 6.2, the overlap between communication and control is much stronger than the overlap between time and either of the other two dimensions. Nevertheless, as revealed in the literature, time is an important subdimension of interactivity. Furthermore, time-related factors, such as concurrent communication and immediacy, loaded on both the real-time conversation and engaging factors. Time-related findings may have been affected by the design of the Web site that was used in this study. Time to load the two sites was manipulated with larger graphic and text files in the low-interactivity site, but the time to load may not have been slowed enough to make the site recognizably slow. Further research is needed that more carefully controls the time dimension.

This study is a step forward in defining the often elusive concept of interactivity. Whereas it acknowledges the importance of both process- and feature-based approaches to interactivity, the primary focus is on perceived interactivity. Perceived interactivity is particularly important to advertising researchers whose goal is often to "get inside the head" of consumers and understand how and why they respond to commercial messages. On the World Wide Web, which is often characterized by interactivity, perceived interactivity is likely to be an important influence on consumer perception and behavior.

The MPI offers researchers a tool for measuring perceived interactivity that is consistent with the literature on interactivity, recognizes the reality that interactivity is a multidimensional construct, and allows for the overlapping of each of the three dimensions that are central to interactivity. The rigor reflected in the multiple methods for generating scale items and the multiple stages in the scale development process result in a scale that should be useful to both researchers and practitioners.

References

Ahren, R. Kirkland, Jennifer Stromer-Galley, and W. Russell Neuman (2000), "Interactivity and Structured Issue Comparisons on the Political Web: An Experimental Study of the 2000 New Hampshire Presidential Primary," paper presented at International Communication Association, June 1–5, Acapulco, MX.

Baecker, Ronald (1980), "Towards an Effective Characterization of Graphical Interaction," in *Methodology of Interaction*, R.A. Guedj, P.J.W. tenHagen, F.R. Hopgood, H.A. Tucker, and D.A. Duce, eds., Amsterdam: North Holland, 127–147.

Ball-Rokeach, Sandra J. and Kathleen Reardon (1988), "Monologue, Dialogue, and Telelog: Comparing an Emergent Form of Communication with Traditional Forms," in *Advancing Communication Science: Merging Mass and Interpersonal Process*, R.P. Hawkins, J.M. Wiemann, and S. Pingree, eds., Newbury Park, CA: Sage, 135–161.

Belkin, N.J., P.G. Marchetti, and C. Cool (1993), "Braque: Design of an Interface to Support User's Interaction in Information Retrieval," *Information Processing & Management*, 29 (3), 325–344.

Beniger, James R. (1987), "Personalization of Mass Media and the Growth of Pseudo-Community," *Communication Research*, 14 (3), 352–371.

Berthon, Pierre, Morris B. Holbrook, and James M. Hulbert (2000), "Brand Market Orientation: A Conceptualization of Market Evolution," *Journal of Interactive Marketing*, 14 (3), 50–66.

Bezjian-Avery, Alexa, Bobby Calder, and Dawn Iacobucci (1998), "New Media Interactive Advertising vs. Traditional Advertising," *Journal of Advertising Research*, 38 (4), 23–32.

Biocca, Frank (1993), "Communication Research in the Design of Communication Interfaces and Systems," *Journal of Communication*, 43 (4), 59–68.

Bretz, R. (1983), *Media for Interactive Communication*, Beverly Hills, CA: Sage.

Burgoon, Judee K., Joseph A. Bonito, Bjorn Bengtsson, Artemio Ramirez Jr., Norah E. Dunbar, and Nathan Miczo (2000), "Testing the Interactivity Model: Communication Processes, Partner Assessments, and the Quality of Collaborative Work," *Journal of Management Information Systems*, 16 (3), 33–56.

Carey, John (1989), "Interactive Media," in *International Encyclopedia of Communications*, E. Barnouw, ed., New York: Oxford University Press, 328–330.

Chen, Qimei and William D. Wells (1999), "Attitude Toward the Site," *Journal of Advertising Research*, 39 (5), 27–37.

Chesebro, James W. (1985), "Computer Mediated Interpersonal Communication," in *Information and Behavior*, B.D. Ruben, ed., New Brunswick, NJ: Transaction Books, 202–222.

Cho, Chang-Hoan and John D. Leckenby (1999), "Interactivity as a Measure of Advertising Effectiveness," in *Proceedings of the American Academy of Advertising*, M.S. Roberts, ed., Gainesville: University of Florida, 162–179.

Churchill, Gilbert A. (1979), "A Paradigm for Developing Better Measures for Marketing Constructs," *Journal of Marketing Research*, 16 (February), 64–73.

Coyle, James R. and Esther Thorson (2001), "The Effects of Progressive Levels of Interactivity and Vividness in Web Marketing Sites," *Journal of Advertising*, 30 (3), 65–77.

Crawford, Chris (1990), "Lessons from Computer Game Design," in *The Art of Human-Computer Interface Design*, B. Laurel, ed., Reading, MA: Addison-Wesley, 103–111.

Csikszentmihalyi, M. (1975), *Beyond Boredom and Anxiety*, San Francisco: Jossey-Bass.

Daft, Richard L., Robert H. Lengel, and Linda Klebe Trevino (1987), "Message Equivocality, Media Selection, and Manager Performance: Implications for Information Systems," *MIS Quarterly*, 11 (2), 355–366.

Day, George S. (1998), "Organizing for Interactivity," *Journal of Interactive Marketing*, 12 (1), 47–53.

Dellaert, Benedict G.C. and Barbara E. Kahn (1999), "How Tolerable Is Delay?: Consumers' Evaluations of Internet Web Sites after Waiting," *Journal of Interactive Marketing*, 13 (1), 41–54.

DeVellis, Robert F. (1991), *Scale Development: Theory and Applications*, Newbury Park, CA: Sage.

Duncan, Jr., Starkey (1989), "Interaction, Face-to-Face," in *International Encyclopedia of Communications*, E. Barnouw, ed., New York: Oxford University Press, 325–327.

Duncan, Tom and Sandra E. Moriarty (1998), "A Communication-Based Marketing Model for Managing Relationships," *Journal of Marketing*, 62 (April), 1–13.

Durlak, Jerome T. (1987), "A Typology for Interactive Media," in *Communication Yearbook 10*, M.L. McLaughlin, ed., Newbury Park, CA: Sage, 743–757.

Garramone, Gina M., Allen C. Harris, and Ronald Anderson (1986), "Uses of Political Computer Bulletin Boards," *Journal of Broadcasting and Electronic Media*, 30 (3), 325–339.

Gerbing, David W. and James C. Anderson (1988), "An Updated Paradigm for Scale Development Incorporating Unidimensionality and Its Assessment," *Journal of Marketing Research*, 25 (May), 186–192.

Ghani, Jawaid A. and Satish P. Deshpande (1994), "Task Characteristics and the Experience of Optimal Flow in Human-Computer Interaction," *Journal of Psychology*, 128 (4), 381–391.

Guedj, Richard A., Paul J.W. tenHagen, F. Robert Hopgood, Hugh A. Tucker, and David A. Duce, eds. (1980), *Methodology of Interaction*, Amsterdam: North Holland.

Ha, Louisa and Lincoln James (1998), "Interactivity Reexamined: A Baseline Analysis of Early Business Web Sites," *Journal of Broadcasting and Electronic Media*, 42 (4), 457–474.

Haeckel, Stephan H. (1998), "About the Nature and Future of Interactive Marketing," *Journal of Interactive Marketing*, 12 (1), 63–71.

Hanssen, Lucien, Nicholas W. Jankowski, and Reinier Etienne (1996), "Interactivity from the Perspective of Communication Studies," in *Contours of Multimedia: Recent Technological, Theoretical, and Empirical Developments*, N.W. Jankowski and L. Hanssen, eds., Luton, UK: University of Luton Press, 61–73.

Heeter, Carrie (1989), "Implications of New Interactive Technologies for Conceptualizing Communication," in *Media Use in the Information Age: Emerging Patterns of Adoption and Computer Use*, J.L. Salvaggio and J. Bryant, eds., Hillsdale, NJ: Lawrence Erlbaum Associates, 217–235.

——— (2000), "Interactivity in the Context of Designed Experiences," *Journal of Interactive Advertising*, 1 (1), [www.jiad.org].

Hesse, Bradford W., Carol M. Werner, and Irwin Altman (1988), "Temporal Aspects of Computer-Mediated Communication," *Computers in Human Behavior*, 4, 147–165.

Hoffman, Donna L. and Thomas P. Novak (1996), "Marketing in Hypermedia Computer-Mediated Environments: Conceptual Foundations," *Journal of Marketing*, 60 (3), 50–68.

——— and ——— (2000), "How to Acquire Customers on the Web," *Harvard Business Review*, 78 (3), 179–200.

Huhtamo, Erkki (1999), "From Cybernation to Interaction: A Contribution to an Archaeology of Interactivity," in *The Digital Dialectic: New Essays on New Media*, P. Lunenfeld, ed., Cambridge, MA: MIT Press, 96–110.

Hwang, Jang-Sun and Sally J. McMillan (2002), "The Role of Interactivity and Involvement in Attitude toward the Web Site," in *Proceedings of the American Academy of Advertising*, A. Abernethy, ed. Auburn, AL: Auburn University, 10–17.

Jensen, Jens F. (1998), "Interactivity: Tracing a New Concept in Media and Communication Studies," *Nordicom Review*, 19 (1), 185–204.

Kay, Alan (1990), "User Interface: A Personal View," in *The Art of Human-Computer Interface Design*, B. Laurel, ed., Reading, MA: Addison-Wesley, 191–207.

Kiousis, S. (1999), "Broadening the Boundaries of Interactivity: A Concept Explication," paper presented at Association for Education in Journalism and Mass Communication Annual Conference, August, New Orleans.

Kirsh, David (1997), "Interactivity and Multimedia Interfaces," *Instructional Science*, 25 (2), 79–96.

Latchem, Colin, John Williamson, and Lexie Henderson-Lancett, eds. (1993), *Interactive Multimedia: Practice and Purpose*, London: Kogan Page Limited.

Laurel, Brenda (1990), "Users and Contexts," in *The Art of Human-Computer Interface Design*, B. Laurel, ed., Reading, MA: Addison-Wesley, 91–93.

Lee, Jae-Shin (2000), "Interactivity: A New Approach," paper presented at Association for Education in Journalism and Mass Communication, August 9–12, Phoenix.

Lieb, Thom (1998), "Inactivity on Interactivity," *Journal of Electronic Publishing*, 3 (3), [www.press.umich.edu/jep/03-03/lieb0303.html].

Lombard, Matthew and Jennifer Snyder-Dutch (2001), "Interactive Advertising and Presence: A Framework," *Journal of Interactive Advertising*, 1 (2), [www.jiad.org].

Looms, Peter Olaf (1993), "Interactive Multimedia in Education," in *Interactive Multimedia: Practice and Purpose*, C. Latchem, J. Williamson, and L. Henderson-Lancett, eds., London: Kogan Page Limited, 115–134.

Mahood, Chad, Sriram Kalyanaraman, and S. Shyam Sundar (2000), "The Effects of Erotica and Dehumanizing Pornography in an Online Interactive Environment," paper presented at Association for Education in Journalism and Mass Communication, August 9–12, Phoenix.

Massey, Brian L. and Mark R. Levy (1999), "Interactivity, Online Journalism, and English-Language Web Newspapers in Asia," *Journalism and Mass Communication Quarterly*, 76 (1), 138–151.

McGrath, Joseph E. (1990), "Time Matters in Groups," in *Intellectual Teamwork: Social and Technical Foundations of Cooperative Work*, J. Galegher, R.E. Kraut, and C. Egido, eds., Hillsdale, NJ: Lawrence Erlbaum Associates, 23–61.

McMillan, Sally J. (2000a), "Interactivity Is in the Eye of the Beholder: Function, Perception, Involvement, and Attitude toward the Web Site," in *Proceedings of the American Academy of Advertising*, M.A. Shaver, ed., East Lansing: Michigan State University, 71–78.

——— (2000b), "What Is Interactivity and What Does It Do?" paper presented at Association of Education in Journalism and Mass Communication Conference, August 9–12, Phoenix.

——— (2002), "A Four-Part Model of Cyber-Interactivity: Some Cyber-Places Are More Interactive Than Others," *New Media and Society*, 4 (2), 271–291.

——— and Edward J. Downes (2000), "Defining Interactivity: A Qualitative Identification of Key Dimensions," *New Media and Society*, 2 (2), 157–179.

Miles, Ian (1992), "When Mediation Is the Message: How Suppliers Envisage New Markets," in *Contexts of Computer-Mediated Communication*, M. Lea, ed., New York: Harvester-Wheatsheaf, 145–167.

Milheim, William D. (1996), "Interactivity and Computer-Based Instruction," *Journal of Educational Technology Systems*, 24 (3), 225–233.

Miller, Dan E., Michael A. Katovich, and Stanley L. Saxton (1997), *Constructing Complexity: Symbolic Interaction and Social Forms*, Vol. 3, *Studies in Symbolic Interaction*, N.K. Denzin, ed., Greenwich, CT: JAI Press.

Moon, Youngme and Clifford Nass (1996), "How 'Real' Are Computer Personalities? Psychological Responses to Personality Types in Human-Computer Interaction," *Communication Research*, 23 (6), 651–674.

Morris, Merrill and Christine Ogan (1996), "The Internet as Mass Medium," *Journal of Computer Mediated Communication*, 1 (4), [www.ascusc.org/jcmc/v011/issue4/morris.html].

Murray, Janet H. (1997), *Hamlet on the Holodeck: The Future of Narrative in Cyberspace*, New York: Free Press.

Naimark, Michael (1990), "Realness and Interactivity," in *The Art of Human-Computer Interface Design*, B. Laurel, ed., Reading, MA: Addison-Wesley, 455–459.

Newhagen, John E., John W. Cordes, and Mark R. Levy (1996), "Nightly@NBC.Com: Audience Scope and the Perception of Interactivity in Viewer Mail on the Internet," *Journal of Communication*, 45 (3), 164–175.

Nielsen, Jakob (2000), *Designing Web Usability*, Indianapolis: New Riders.

Novak, Thomas P., Donna L. Hoffman, and Yiu-Fai Yung (2000), "Measuring the Customer Experience in Online Environments: A Structural Modeling Approach," *Marketing Science*, 19 (1), 22–42.

Pavlik, John V. (1998), *New Media Technology: Cultural and Commercial Perspectives*, 2d ed, Boston: Allyn and Bacon.

Pavlou, Paul A. and David W. Stewart (2000), "Measuring the Effects and Effectiveness of Interactive Advertising: A Research Agenda," *Journal of Interactive Advertising*, 1 (1), [http://jiad.org/v011/n01/pavlou].

Peltier, James W., John A. Schibrowsky, and John Davis (1998), "Using Attitudinal and Descriptive Database Information to Understand Interactive Buyer-Seller Relationships," *Journal of Interactive Marketing*, 12 (3), 32–45.

Preece, Jenny (1993), "Hypermedia, Multimedia and Human Factors," in *Interactive Multimedia: Practice and Purpose*, C. Latchem, J. Williamson, and L. Henderson-Lancett, eds., London: Kogan Page Limited, 135–150.

Rafaeli, Sheizaf (1988), "Interactivity: From New Media to Communication," in *Advancing Communication Science: Merging Mass and Interpersonal Process*, R.P. Hawkins, J.M. Wiemann, and S. Pingree, eds., Newbury Park, CA: Sage, 110–134.

―――― and Fay Sudweeks (1997), "Networked Interactivity," *Journal of Computer Mediated Communication*, 2 (4), [www.usc.edu/dept/annenberg/v012/issue4/rafaeli.sudweeks.html].

Reeves, Byron and Clifford Nass (1996), *The Media Equation: How People Treat Computers, Television, and New Media Like Real People and Places*, New York: Cambridge University Press/CSLI.

―――― and ―――― (2000), "Perceptual Bandwidth," *Communications of the ACM*, 43 (3), 65–70.

Rheingold, H. (1993), *The Virtual Community: Homesteading on the Electronic Frontier*, Reading, MA: Addison-Wesley.

Schneiderman, Ben (1998), *Designing the User Interface: Strategies for Effective Human-Computer Interaction*, 3d ed, Reading, MA: Addison-Wesley.

Schultz, Tanjev (2000), "Mass Media and the Concept of Interactivity: An Exploratory Study of Online Forums and Reader E-Mail," *Media, Culture & Society*, 22 (2), 205–221.

Schumann, David W., Andy Artis, and Rachael Rivera (2001), "The Future of Interactive Advertising Viewed through an IMC Lens," *Journal of Interactive Advertising*, 1 (2), [www.jiad.org].

Smethers, Steven (1998), "Cyberspace in the Curricula: New Legal and Ethical Issues," *Journalism and Mass Communication Educator*, 53 (4), 15–23.

Steuer, Jonathan (1992), "Defining Virtual Reality: Dimensions Determining Telepresence," *Journal of Communication*, 42 (4), 73–93.

Straubhaar, Joseph and Robert LaRose (1996), *Communications Media in the Information Society*, Belmont, CA: Wadsworth Press.

Sundar, S. Shyam, Kenneth M. Hesser, Sriram Kalyanaraman, and Justin Brown (1998), "The Effect of Website Interactivity on Political Persuasion," paper presented at Sociology and Social Psychology section at the Twenty-first General Assembly and Scientific Conference of the International Association for Media and Communication Research, July 26–30, Glasgow, UK.

Tan, William and Ann Nguyen (1993), "Lifecycle Costing Models for Interactive Multimedia Systems," in *Interactive Multimedia: Practice and Purpose*, C. Latchem, J. Williamson, and L. Henderson-Lancett, eds., London: Kogan Page Limited, 151–164.

Trevino, Linda Klebe and Jane Webster (1992), "Flow in Computer-Mediated Communication: Electronic Mail and Voice Mail Evaluation and Impacts," *Communication Research*, 19 (5), 539–573.

Valacich, Joseph S., David Paranka, Joey F. George, and J.F. Nunamaker Jr. (1993), "Communication Concurrency and the New Media: A New Dimension for Media Richness," *Communication Research*, 20 (2), 249–276.

Vasarhelyi, Miklos Antal (1977), "Man-Machine Planning Systems: A Cognitive Style Examination of Interactive Decision Making," *Journal of Accounting Research*, 15 (1), 138–153.

Vora, Pawan (1998), "Human Factors Methodology for Designing Web Sites," in *Human Factors and Web Development*, C. Forsythe, E. Grose, and J. Ratner, eds., Mahwah, NJ: Lawrence Erlbaum Associates, 153–172.

Walther, Jospeh B. (1992), "Interpersonal Effects in Computer-Mediated Interaction: A Relational Perspective," *Communication Research*, 19 (1), 52–90.

Williams, Frederick, Ronald E. Rice, and Everett M. Rogers (1988), *Research Methods and the New Media*, New York: Free Press.

Wu, Guohua (1999), "Perceived Interactivity and Attitude toward Website," in *Proceedings of the American Academy of Advertising*, M.S. Roberts, ed., Gainesville: University of Florida, 254–262.

Xie, Hong (2000), "Shifts of Interactive Intentions and Information-Seeking Strategies in Interactive Information Retrieval," *Journal of the American Society for Information Science*, 51 (9), 841–857.

Zack, Michael H. (1993), "Interactivity and Communication Mode Choice in Ongoing Management Groups," *Information Systems Research*, 4 (3), 207–239.

Zeltzer, David (1992), "Autonomy, Interaction, and Presence," *Teleoperators and Virtual Environments*, 1 (1), 127–132.

7

Impact of 3-D Advertising on Product Knowledge, Brand Attitude, and Purchase Intention

The Mediating Role of Presence

Hairong Li, Terry Daugherty, and Frank Biocca

Internet advertising has evolved dramatically since its inception in 1994 when the first banner ads appeared on the Hotwired site (Adams 1995). Although banner ads are still a dominant type of Internet advertising, their share decreased from 56 percent of the total $4.6 billion Internet advertising revenue in 1999 to 48 percent of the $8.2 billion in 2000. Furthermore, 2000 marked the first year in the United States that revenue from rich media advertising was listed separately, accounting for 2 percent of the total ad revenue (Interactive Advertising Bureau 2001). Rich media advertising is different from conventional banner ads, in that it generally incorporates high-impact sound with video and is often more interactive (Rewick 2001). More recently, three-dimensional (3-D) advertising has emerged as a new form of rich media advertising (Mirapaul 2000) that enables consumers to inspect products on the Web, much like they can in a retail store, for certain types of products. More important, 3-D advertising can simulate a new consumption experience—virtual experience.

Although the concept of virtual experience had been used in previous research (Klein 1998), Li, Daugherty, and Biocca (2001) defined it as psychological states that consumers undergo while interacting with 3-D products in a computer-mediated environment. McLuhan and McLuhan (1988) suggest that, within any medium, there is a connection among the human mind, the technology, and the environment that serves to immerse users. On the Internet, consumers are able to experience psychological states because the medium creates a sense of presence that results in augmented learning, altered behaviors, and a perceived sense of control (Hoffman and Novak 1996).

A sense of presence is an important mediator in the formation of virtual experience from 3-D advertising (Biocca, Li, and Daugherty 2001). Presence is defined as the illusion of "being there" (Lombard and Ditton 1997; Steuer 1992) or an experience of being in an environment while physically situated in another location (Witmer and Singer 1998). Researchers (Coyle and Thorson 2001; Klein 2001) have recognized the relationship between presence and virtual experience and attempted to test it empirically. However, the role of presence in generating virtual product experiences from 3-D advertising remains unclear. Therefore, the purpose of this study is three-fold. First, we explore the properties of 3-D advertising and its impact on consumers through an elevated sense of presence. Second, we explain how presence mediates the formation of virtual experience. Third, we test a set of hypotheses derived from the conceptualization to advance the knowledge of 3-D advertising in the area of electronic commerce.

Literature Review

Three-dimensional advertising is a new and innovative form of interactive advertising that provides prepurchase product inspection on the Internet using 3-D visualization technology to simulate real products. A simulated 3-D product may have many interface properties. For example, shoppers may rotate it, zoom in and out for inspection, animate features and functions of the product, and even change the color or contextualization with other products in different settings (for a review of interface properties of 3-D products, see Li, Daugherty, and Biocca 2001). Furthermore, marketers have the ability to utilize these properties within banner ads, pop-ups, and product Web sites to influence how consumers think and feel about a product when interacting with it on the Internet. The potential psychological impact of 3-D advertising can be better understood with the theories of presence and virtual experience.

Presence

Although presence is often explored in the literature of virtual reality, few media theorists would argue that the sense of presence suddenly emerged with the debut of virtual reality. The illusion of presence is a product of all media (Reeves and Nass 1996), and virtual reality is a medium that can generate the most compelling sense of presence (Biocca 1997). Presence, also known as telepresence, is an illusion of "being there" in a mediated environment. Biocca (1997, 5.3) wrote,

> When we experience our everyday sense of presence in the physical world, we automatically generate a mental model of an external space from patterns of energy on the sensory organs. In virtual environments, patterns of energy that stimulate the structure to those experienced in the physical environment are used to stimulate the same automatic perceptual processes that generate our stable perception of the physical world.

Previous research indicates that consumers feel a sense of presence while interacting with 3-D products in a nonimmersive, mediated environment (Biocca et al. 2001; Li, Daugherty, and Biocca 2001). Presence can be established for consumers when they are interacting with either a virtual product or a virtual environment. For example, when consumers surf through the aisles of a virtual store, they may feel as if they are walking in a conventional store and can pick up a brand from a virtual shelf to take a closer look by zooming in or rotating it as if they were examining the brand in a real store. Shoppers are likely to gain a unique experience when they feel physically present, because a virtual e-commerce environment is able to simulate many of the same experiences as a real store, with presence mediating the persuasive impact.

In a study designed to manipulate the sensory saturation of a consumer's visual perception, Kim and Biocca (1997) were able to detect significant differences in confidence levels regarding brand preferences when viewers were watching television. More specifically, the sense of presence resulted in a stronger experience; viewers became more confident in their attitudes toward the product information presented. Kim and Biocca (1997) concluded that the virtual experience created by presence simulated a direct experience, which resulted in increased persuasion. Li, Daugherty, and Biocca (2001) reported from an exploratory study that participants expressed a natural and physical sense of presence when they examined virtual product representations in e-commerce settings.

Interactivity and Richness

Two media characteristics that have been identified as antecedents of presence are interactivity and richness (Steuer 1992), which are core characteristics of 3-D advertising. The concept of interactivity has been explored in studies of computer-mediated communications (Heeter 1986; Rafaeli 1985, 1988; Rice 1984, 1987; Rogers and Rafaeli 1985), the Internet and virtual reality (Biocca 1992; Ku 1992; Newhagen and Rafaeli 1996; Steuer 1992), and Internet marketing and advertising (Alba et al. 1997; Deighton 1996; Ghose and Dou 1998; Hoffman and Novak 1996; Peterson, Balasubramanian, and Bronnenberg 1997). The construct of interactivity is considered a multidimensional concept (Heeter 1986). Rafaeli (1985, 1988) defined interactivity in terms of the responsiveness of participants and the degree to which a communication process resembles human discourse. The high relevance of later messages to earlier messages is referred to as "response contingency" (Alba et al. 1997), "message tailoring" (Rimal and Flora 1997), and "mapping" (Steuer 1992). Immediacy of response is considered another dimension of interactivity (Ku 1992; Rice 1987), though it is an intrinsic attribute of responsiveness itself. A communication process is perceived to be interactive when responses are exchanged in real time (Newhagen and Rafaeli 1996). Interactivity is also defined by the ability to select the timing, content, and sequence of a communication act within a mediated environment, which is a form of user control. Steuer (1992, 84) simply defines interactivity as "the extent to which users can participate in modifying the form and content of a mediated environment in real time." Three-dimensional advertising is able to provide nonimmersive user control over many aspects of a simulated product.

Another intrinsic property of 3-D advertising is media richness, which tends to enhance a sense of presence. Media richness also is referred to as media vividness (Steuer 1992). It means the intensity with which a mediated environment is able to present information to the senses. Two aspects of media richness are sensory breadth, which is the number of sensory dimensions simultaneously presented, and sensory depth, which is the resolution of each perceptual channel (Steuer 1992). Breadth is a function of the ability of a communication medium to present information across the senses. For example, television addresses both the audio and visual systems, whereas radio addresses only the audio system. Thus, television has greater sensory breadth. Depth refers to the quality of information; an image with greater depth is generally perceived as being of higher quality than one with less depth for both auditory and visual representation. The premise of media richness lies in the assumption that messages appealing to multiple perceptual systems are better perceived than are those that call on single perceptual systems and that high-quality messages are more effective than low-quality messages. Although this assumption should be true in most cases, we cannot always assume that a richer mediated environment is better. Therefore, it is reasonable to speculate that adequate richness for a given cognitive task is more important than excessively low or high richness in 3-D advertising.

Figure 7.1 **A Basic Model of Virtual Experience**

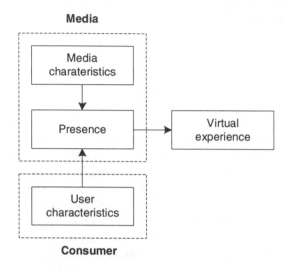

Virtual Experience

Three-dimensional advertising is able to generate a virtual experience. Tra-ditionally, product experiences have been dichotomized as direct or indirect. Direct product experience is the unmediated interaction between consumers and products in full sensory capacity, including visual, auditory, taste and smell, haptic, and orienting (Gibson 1966). Indirect experience can occur from various sources (e.g., word of mouth, *Consumer Reports*), yet the most prevalent form explored in consumer psychology is advertising. Indirect ex-perience offers a limited amount of sensory stimuli, and consumers gener-ally have very little control over the content of any type of indirect experience from marketers, other than to change the channel, flip the page, or visit an-other Web site.

A virtual experience is a form of indirect experience, because both are mediated experiences (Heeter 2000). However, virtual experience tends to be richer than indirect experience rendered by print ads, television com-mercials, or even two-dimensional (2-D) images on the Web. Li, Daugherty, and Biocca's research (2001) indicates that virtual experience, as simu-lated in 3-D advertising, consists of more active cognitive and affective activities than 2-D marketing messages. They attribute these psychological and emotional effects to the interface properties of 3-D advertising, as well as to the psychological sensation of presence. The relationship between presence and virtual experience is presented in Figure 7.1. Two antecedents of presence are media characteristics and user characteristics, and presence has one consequence, virtual experience. These relationships are reviewed in the next section (user characteristics are not addressed in this study).

Impact of 3-D Advertising

The impact of 3-D advertising can be ascertained from cognitive, affective, and conative dimensions (Hutchinson and Alba 1991; Lutz 1975; Wright 1980). As with traditional advertising, it is logical to assume that the effectiveness of 3-D advertising should be measured along these elements. Cognitive measures are used to determine the ability of an advertisement, physical product, or other marketing stimulus to attract attention and ultimately generate product knowledge. This element is fundamental in determining the amount of knowledge a consumer has for a product and can be measured from actual knowledge (recall) or perceived knowledge (self-reported) (Bettman and Park 1980). Affective measures are used to identify either established or created attitudes from marketing or advertising stimuli, and attitude toward the brand serves as a commonly used effectiveness measure (Fazio, Powell, and Williams 1989; MacKenzie and Lutz 1989). Conative measures are used to anticipate a response behavior resulting from a marketing or advertising stimulus. They generally involve some type of behavior intention, such as searching for additional information or purchase (Brucks 1985; Hoch and Ha 1986). The most widely used conative measure in advertising effectiveness research is intention to purchase (Andrews et al. 1992; Beerli and Santana 1999).

Hypotheses

Assuming personal preferences are held constant, the research proposition is that consumers interacting with products in 3-D advertising are more likely to perceive a sense of presence, which results in a positive consumer response as measured by increases in product knowledge, brand attitude, and purchase intention. Therefore, we propose the following hypotheses:

H1: Three-dimensional advertising will result in a greater sense of presence than will 2-D advertising.

H2: Three-dimensional advertising will result in (a) greater product knowledge, (b) more favorable brand attitude, and (c) increased purchase intent than will 2-D advertising.

Study 1

Research Design

To test the hypotheses, an experiment was conducted in a laboratory setting in which each participant accessed a product Web site via the computer. Each Web site represents an experience type: 3-D advertising for virtual experience and 2-D advertising for indirect experience. Three-dimensional advertising was operationally defined as a user-controlled product Web site in which consumers may rotate, zoom in or zoom out, and move the product for detailed inspection. In contrast, 2-D advertising was operationally defined as a noninteractive, static product Web site in which a photograph of a product is presented for inspection, thus representing a standard indirect experience portrayed on countless e-commerce sites.

Participants

A total of sixty undergraduate students enrolled at a major midwestern U.S. university participated in the experiment and were randomly assigned to the experimental conditions. The use of a student sample was deemed acceptable because of the nature of the study and students' literacy for the computer and Internet. The sample consisted of thirty-four women (56.7 percent) and twenty-six men (43.3 percent) with an average age of 21.6 years ($SD = 1.84$).

Stimulus

To investigate the relative impact of both virtual and indirect experience, the test product needed to (1) be effectively represented in each type of experience, (2) require participants to engage in information processing, and (3) stand for a brand of moderate interest. The first parameter stems from the need to minimize the differences between the stimulus materials to isolate the type of experience properly as the influencing variable. The second parameter was necessary to engage the participants in active processing for evaluation of the test product. This is commonly achieved in consumer behavior research by informing participants that they will be asked to report their opinions and thoughts upon completion of the study (Kempf and Smith 1998). The final requirement was important to minimize any preconceived response bias.

Several products were evaluated and considered (i.e., ring, watch, bedding material, computer, cellular telephone, headphones) prior to the selection of a digital video camera as the test product. A digital video camera was judged appropriate because it represents a high-involvement purchase item that can be evaluated using both experience attributes (e.g., weight, size, visual clarity) and search attributes (e.g., price, warranty, special effect features). In addition, to increase the legitimacy of the study, a reputable digital video camcorder company (Panasonic) was identified in a pretest ($n = 76$) as a neutral brand against four major manufacturers (Sony, JVC, Canon, and Sharp). Participants were asked to rate the perceived quality of each of the digital video camcorder brands using a seven-point scale (low quality/high quality). Results showed that Sony ($M = 6.04$, $SD = 1.03$) and Canon ($M = 5.16$, $SD = 1.06$) were perceived as the two highest quality brands and Sharp ($M = 4.59$, $SD = 1.40$) and JVC ($M = 4.33$, $SD = 1.41$) as the two lowest quality brands, with Panasonic ($M = 4.88$, $SD = 1.18$) between these two sets of brands.

Another step in developing the stimulus material was to identify salient product attributes using a free elicitation technique recommended by Fishbein and Ajzen (1975) and commonly used in consumer research (Kempf and Smith 1998; Smith 1993). During a pretest, participants from the student population at the same university were asked to write down the most important product attributes they would consider when buying a digital video camcorder. A total of twenty-seven different attributes were identified, and the five most salient were selected (price, size/weight, special effects, quality, and ease of use) and combined with the company logo and slogan to construct the product Web site.

Two versions of the product Web site were created: one representing 3-D advertising followed by an identical version that substituted 2-D advertising. The 3-D advertisement contained specific interactive features (move, rotate, and zoom in or out) previously identified by research as creating an effective virtual experience (Li, Daugherty, and Biocca 2001). Finally, the message appeal was held constant across each condition using an informative approach that framed the identified salient attributes positively, such as "crystal-clear detail" and "easy-to-use functionality."

Procedures

The experiment began with a short survey designed to collect background information on each participant. Once the survey was completed, participants were escorted into a large laboratory and seated at a computer station corresponding to the assigned experimental condition. Participants were instructed that the purpose of the study was to collect their evaluation of the product, so they should thoroughly examine the Web site to determine how they think and feel about the product. For the virtual experience condition, brief navigation instructions were given to explain how to rotate and zoom in or out to examine the product. In addition, evaluation times were held constant at five minutes for each condition to prevent overexposure. Finally, participants were told that, on conclusion of their evaluation, they would be asked to complete a survey. This served to prime participants to engage in cognitive processing and is consistent with previous consumer experience studies (Kempf and Smith 1998).

Dependent Measures

The dependent variables of the study (presence, product knowledge, brand attitude, and purchase intention) were measured using semantic differential and Likert-type items. Presence was measured using a shortened version of the Independent Television Commission-Sense of Presence Inventory (ITC-SOPI; Lessiter et al. 2000). The ITC-SOPI is a self-reported, forty-four-item Likert scale (strongly disagree/strongly agree) designed to measure four dimensions of presence (physical, engagement, naturalness, and negative effects). The scale is used to measure presence across multiple types of media and focuses on participant experiences within the mediated environment. The first dimension, experiencing a sense of physical space, corresponds to the traditional definition of "being there" in the mediated environment. Usually, this dimension is measured using twenty items, but only fourteen were considered relevant for this study. The six excluded items dealt with either social interaction or olfactory sensory experiences. The second dimension, engagement, measures the intensity and enjoyment experienced in the mediated environment (thirteen items). The third dimension, naturalness, taps into the sense that characters or objects are perceived as life-like and real (five items). Finally, the fourth dimension, negative effects, explores the adverse physiological reactions sometimes associated with the feeling of presence, such as dizziness and nausea (six items). However, due to the absence of high-speed motion and the limited range of sensory immersion when examining a standard computer display, it was determined from previous research (Biocca et al. 2001) that no negative effects are experienced in these experimental conditions, so these items were excluded.

An established three-item scale was used to assess self-reported product knowledge (Smith and Park 1992). Participants were asked to indicate their agreement (strongly disagree/strongly agree) with statements regarding how knowledgeable they felt about the product and the amount of additional information they would need to make a purchase decision or a quality judgment of the product. Although Smith and Park's (1992) original scale included a fourth item, previous research has indicated low reliability, resulting in the exclusion of the item in this study (Biocca et al. 2001).

Overall brand attitude was assessed using a published scale (Bruner 1998) that asks participants to indicate how they feel about the product using six-point semantic differential items (bad/good, unappealing/appealing, unpleasant/pleasant, unattractive/attractive, boring/interesting, and dislike/like).

Purchase intention is a common effectiveness measure and often used to anticipate a response behavior. The method of asking participants to evaluate an advertisement or product and then indicate an intention is prevalent throughout the literature (Andrews et al. 1992; Beerli and Santana 1999). Thus, an established four-item (unlikely/likely, improbable/probable, uncertain/certain, and definitely not/definitely), seven-point semantic differential scale was used to measure the likelihood that participants would purchase the evaluated product (Bearden, Lichtenstein, and Teel 1984).

Results

Data Analysis

All the scales were tested for internal consistency and a specified factor structure based on theory-driven indicators using confirmatory factor analysis and found to be unidimensional (Hunter and Gerbing 1982). Furthermore, reliability assessment was conducted using Cronbach's alpha for each scale (presence-physical $M = 2.52$, $SD = .82$, $\alpha = .90$; presence-engagement $M = 2.59$, $SD = .62$, $\alpha = .87$; presence-naturalness $M = 3.33$, $SD = .64$, $\alpha = .71$; product knowledge $M = 4.10$, $SD = 1.23$, $\alpha = .78$; brand attitude $M = 5.13$, $SD = 1.01$, $\alpha = .91$; purchase intention $M = 3.11$, $SD = 1.33$, $\alpha = .90$), and all exceeded the generally accepted guideline of .70 (Hair et al. 1998). Composite measures for each of the scales were then constructed to represent the multiple items and used in the subsequent analysis to reduce measurement error.

Hypotheses Testing

To test the hypotheses, independent sample t-tests were conducted that compared the mean differences between the 3-D and 2-D conditions for each of the dependent variables (see Table 7.1). Hypothesis 1 predicted that participants evaluating the 3-D interactive product would experience a greater sense of presence than would those evaluating the 2-D static product. The effects of user-controlled interactivity and media richness from 3-D advertising showed significant differences across all three dimensions of presence, in support of the hypothesis. Specifically, physical presence ($M = 2.92$), engagement ($M = 2.81$), and naturalness ($M = 3.51$) were consistently higher

Table 7.1

Dependent Measures Across Experimental Conditions

Measure	3-D	2-D	t	Degrees of freedom	p <
Presence					
Physical	2.92	2.12	4.31	59	0.01
Engagement	2.81	2.37	2.87	59	0.01
Naturalness	3.51	3.15	2.20	59	0.05
Product knowledge	4.57	3.63	3.15	59	0.01
Brand attitude	5.40	4.85	2.18	59	0.05
Purchase intention	3.39	2.83	1.66	59	0.10

for participants evaluating the product in 3-D advertising compared with the reported levels of physical presence ($M = 2.12$, $t(59) = 4.31$, $p < .01$), engagement ($M = 2.37$, $t(59) = 2.87$, $p < .01$), and naturalness ($M = 3.15$, $t(59) = 2.20$, $p < .05$) in 2-D advertising.

The second hypothesis predicted that an increase in presence would result in greater product knowledge, brand attitude, and purchase intent. The results largely support this assertion; participants report significantly higher values for product knowledge ($M = 4.57$) in the 3-D advertising condition compared with in the 2-D advertising condition ($M = 3.63$, $t(59) = 3.15$, $p < .01$). Likewise, participants indicated more favorable brand attitudes for 3-D advertising ($M = 5.40$) than for 2-D advertising ($M = 4.85$, $t(59) = 2.18$, $p < .05$). However, purchase intention was not significantly greater for the 3-D ($M = 3.39$) than the 2-D condition ($M = 2.83$, $t(59) = 1.66$, $p > .05$).

Mediation Analysis

To determine whether presence mediates the relationship between the type of Internet advertising experience and reported product knowledge, brand attitude, and purchase intention, a mediation analysis was conducted as specified by Baron and Kenny (1986). To establish mediation, the following must hold: (1) the type of experience (3-D versus 2-D) must positively affect the mediator (physical, engagement, and naturalness), (2) the type of experience must positively affect the dependent variable (product knowledge, brand attitude, and purchase intention), and (3) the mediator must positively affect the dependent variable when regressed in conjunction with the independent variable. Providing these conditions are met, the effect of the independent variable on the dependent variable must be less in the third step than in the second step (Baron and Kenny 1986).

The first set of analyses indicated that the type of experience positively influenced perceived physical ($\beta = .49$, $t(58) = 4.31$, $p < .01$, $R^2 = .24$), engagement ($\beta = .35$, $t(58) = 2.87$, $p < .01$, $R^2 = .12$), and naturalness ($\beta = .28$, $t(58) = 2.20$, $p < .05$, $R^2 = .08$) dimensions of presence. Furthermore, the second set of analyses demonstrated that the type of experience positively influenced product knowledge ($\beta = .38$, $t(58) = 3.15$, $p < .01$, $R^2 = .13$) and brand attitude ($\beta = .28$, $t(58) = 2.18$, $p < .05$, $R^2 = .08$) but did not yield significant results for purchase intention ($\beta = .21$, $t(58) = 1.65$, $p > .05$). This lack of significance excluded purchase intention from the mediation analysis. Finally, the third set of analyses supported presence as a mediating variable along the physical and engagement dimensions for product knowledge ($\beta = .30$, $t(2,57) = 2.19$, $p < .05$, $R^2 = .21$; $\beta = .34$, $t(2,57) = 2.77$, $p < .01$, $R^2 = .25$, respectively) and brand attitude ($\beta = .53$, $t(2,57) = 4.15$, $p < .01$, $R^2 = .29$; $\beta = .43$, $t = 3.44$, $p < .01$, $R^2 = .23$, respectively). Accordingly, the effect of advertising experience on product knowledge diminished when included in the analysis with the physical ($\beta = .24$, $t(2,57) = 1.75$, $p > .05$) or engagement ($\beta = .26$, $t(2,57) = 2.14$, $p < .05$) dimensions, and the effect on brand attitude was also reduced when regressed along with the physical ($\beta = .01$, $t(2,57) = .10$, $p > .05$) or engagement ($\beta = .13$, $t(2,57) = 1.02$, $p > .05$) dimensions. However, the naturalness dimension was not supported as a mediating variable for either product knowledge ($\beta = .15$, $t(2,57) = 1.17$, $p > .05$) or brand attitude ($\beta = .16$, $t(2,57) = 1.26$, $p > .21$). Thus, the results indicate that the physical and engagement dimensions of presence served as mediators in the relationship between the type of advertising experience and product knowledge, as well as brand attitude, for this study.

Discussion

Results of this study support the proposition that consumers interacting with 3-D advertising rather than 2-D advertising are more likely to experience an elevated sense of presence. The mediation analysis confirms the role of presence in affecting online consumers. These findings establish an important relationship among virtual experience, presence, and marketing effectiveness measures that several scholars have suggested exists (Hoffman and Novak 1996; Kim and Biocca 1997; Klein 1998; Li, Daugherty, and Biocca 2001). However, after testing only a single product, it remains uncertain if a sensation of presence can be created across different products by utilizing 3-D advertising to enhance a virtual experience. To extend the external validity of this causality, it is necessary to confirm it with different types of products, because previous research has indicated that different types of products often affect how consumers evaluate these products (Klatzky, Lederman, and Matula 1991; Norman 1998).

Study 2

Product Types

Product attributes play a significant role in determining how consumers evaluate products (Deighton 1997; Klein 1998; Smith 1993; Smith and Swinyard 1982; Wright and Lynch 1995), and different product classifications have been conceptualized on the basis of product attributes. Nelson (1976, 1981) made distinctions between search and experience products, which he subsequently refined as search and experience attributes because a product can have both types of attributes. Search attributes are those features of a product that consumers can assess without actual use of the product, such as size, color, and price. Experience attributes are those that consumers can assess only through actual use or direct contact, such as taste, softness, or fit. McCabe and Nowlis (2001) examined the influence of different product attributes on the consumer's information search and purchases in e-commerce. They adopted the definition of geometric and material attributes from Klatzky, Lederman, and Matula (1991), who observed that people explore everyday objects through two sensory dimensions: vision and touch. Objects with attributes that can be fully understood through vision are called geometric objects. Objects with attributes that require touching for understanding are called material products. According to McCabe and Nowlis (2001), examples of material products would be a sweater and a towel. A candy bar, a compact disc, or a bag of potato chips would be examples of geometric products, because it is possible for consumers to get sufficient information about them without touching them. McCabe and Nowlis (2001) found that the consumer's preference for either online or offline information search largely depends on different product attributes. Li, Daugherty, and Biocca (2003) extended McCabe and Nowlis's (2001) classification by adding a third product type: mechanical products. This new type of product includes those products that consumers prefer to interact with in prepurchase inspection, such as a laptop computer, camcorder, or personal digital assistant (PDA).

Product Affordances

With these different product classifications, the issue becomes what type of dominant product attribute is more likely influenced by virtual experience and presence. It is helpful to review the concept of product affordances for this exploration. In consumer psychology, product affordances are perceptual cues that guide consumers interacting with products during prepurchase inspection. Li, Daugherty, and Biocca (2003) expand Norman's (1998) concept of

Figure 7.2 **Expanded Model of Virtual Experience**

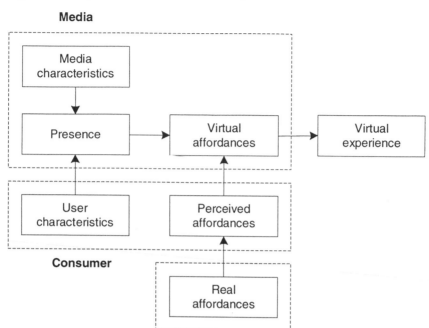

affordances to include virtual affordances in addition to real and perceived affordances. Real affordances are physical attributes of a product, perceived affordances are perceptual cues a consumer possesses and uses in assessing a product prior to purchase, and virtual affordances are perceptual cues a consumer forms from 3-D advertising that could differ from perceived affordances. An important point is that perceived affordances vary by consumers, because two people examining the same product can formulate completely different perceptions of what a product can offer. For example, perceived affordances of the same camera are quite different for a professional photographer and an amateur. In turn, virtual affordances can be restricted, equal, or exceed real and perceived affordances (Li, Daugherty, and Biocca 2003). The relationships among real, perceived, and virtual affordances, presence, and virtual experience are presented in a model of virtual experience (Figure 7.2).

Hypotheses

The sensation of presence is stimulated in a mediated environment from the intensity of sensory information presented and the degree of interactivity with the content (Steuer 1992). Because 3-D advertising provides enhanced visual sensory information and user control over how to inspect a product, elevated levels of presence are expected compared with 2-D advertising, regardless of product types. Thus, the following hypothesis is proposed to extend the findings from Study 1 to geometric and material products:

> H3: Three-dimensional advertising will result in a greater sense of presence than will 2-D advertising for both geometric and material products.

When consumers inspect a geometric product, visual inspection is usually sufficient for them to make a confident purchase decision. However, when consumers examine a material product prior to purchase, they normally prefer to touch and feel the product to gain further information that is not available by merely viewing the product. Therefore, it is reasonable to assume that 3-D advertising is limited in its capacity of simulating tactile affordances to meet such a need in consumers. On the basis of the concepts of product types and affordances, the following hypotheses are proposed:

> H4: Three-dimensional advertising will result in (a) greater product knowledge, (b) more favorable brand attitude, and (c) increased purchase intent than will 2-D advertising when evaluating a geometric product.

> H5: Three-dimensional advertising will result in no differences for (a) product knowledge, (b) brand attitude, or (c) purchase intent compared with 2-D advertising when evaluating a material product.

Method

Experimental Design

The experiment was conducted in a laboratory setting in which each participant accessed a Web site for one of two products through the computer. A between-subjects 2×2 design was used with ad type (3-D versus 2-D) and product type (geometric versus material) serving as the two factors. Cell sizes ranged from twenty to twenty-six subjects each. The construction of the stimulus materials, dependent variables, and experimental procedures followed Study 1, with the only difference stemming from the additional factor of product type.

Participants

A total of ninety-three undergraduate students enrolled at a major midwestern U.S. university participated in the experiment and were randomly assigned to the experimental conditions. Of those who participated, 76.3 percent were women with a mean age of 20.9 years ($SD = 1.76$).

Stimulus

Several products were evaluated, and the goal was to select alternatives on the basis of different product affordances. Therefore, using the classifications from previous research (Klatzky, Lederman, and Matula 1991; Li, Daugherty, and Biocca 2001; McCabe and Nowlis 2001), a watch and jacket were identified as suitable alternative test products. The watch was judged as appropriate because it represents a product that is primarily evaluated using the visual senses (i.e., a geometric classification). In turn, a jacket is examined, for the most part, using tactile feedback to evaluate the feel and texture or the comfort and fit against the body (i.e., a material classification).

Results

Data Analysis

As in Study 1, all scales were tested for internal consistency using confirmatory factor analysis and found to be unidimensional. The Cronbach's alpha for each scale (presence-physical $M = 2.28$, $SD = .85$, $\alpha = .93$; presence-engagement $M = 2.39$, $SD = .78$, $\alpha = .90$; presence-naturalness $M = 2.92$, $SD = .79$, $\alpha = .74$; product knowledge $M = 4.08$, $SD = 1.61$, $\alpha = .90$; brand attitude $M = 4.86$, $SD = 1.25$, $\alpha = .89$; purchase intention $M = 2.97$, $SD = 1.70$, $\alpha = .79$) was again acceptable, with composite measures constructed and used in the subsequent analyses.

Hypotheses Testing

Study 1 established empirically that 3-D advertising evokes higher levels of reported presence. Hypothesis 3 stated this relationship with both geometric and material products. The results of Study 2 support H3, in that participants again reported experiencing higher levels of physical presence ($M = 2.79$), engagement ($M = 2.75$), and naturalness ($M = 3.27$) when evaluating 3-D advertising compared with the reported levels of physical presence ($M = 1.82$, $F(89) = 45.62$, $p < .01$), engagement ($M = 2.08$, $F(89) = 20.80$, $p <$

.01), and naturalness ($M = 2.56$, $F(89) = 22.84$, $p < .01$) for 2-D advertising. A significant main effect was also discovered for product type, with participants indicating higher levels of physical presence ($M = 2.15$) and engagement ($M = 2.60$) after examining the material product compared with reported levels of physical presence ($M = 2.45$, $F(89) = 4.48$, $p < .05$) and engagement ($M = 2.24$, $F(89) = 6.13$, $p < .01$) for the geometric product. However, no significant effect was detected for naturalness between the material ($M = 2.85$) and the geometric product ($M = 2.98$, $F(89) = .79$, $p > .05$). As was expected, there were no significant interactions between ad type and product type for physical presence ($F(89) = .79$, $p > .05$), engagement ($F(89) = .02$, $p > .05$), or naturalness ($F(89) = .24$, $p > .05$).

The significant main effects for product type on two dimensions of presence (physical and engagement) are unexpected because presence is a mediated experience rather than a product classification phenomenon. Therefore, contrast comparisons were tested to ensure the hypothesized effect for 3-D advertising was not a consequence of product type. The results again support H3, in that participants reported experiencing higher levels of physical presence ($M = 2.58$), engagement ($M = 2.56$), and naturalness ($M = 3.30$) when evaluating the watch in the 3-D advertising compared with the reported levels of physical presence ($M = 1.75$, $F(89) = 4.58$, $p < .01$), engagement ($M = 1.91$, $F(89) = 3.73$, $p < .01$), and naturalness ($M = 2.66$, $F(89) = 3.21$, $p < .01$) for the 2-D version. Similarly, physical presence ($M = 3.00$), engagement ($M = 2.94$), and naturalness ($M = 3.24$) were elevated when evaluating the jacket in 3-D compared with the reported levels of physical presence ($M = 1.90$, $t(40) = 4.89$, $p < .01$), engagement ($M = 2.25$, $t(40) = 2.80$, $p < .01$), and naturalness ($M = 2.46$, $t(40) = 3.55$, $p < .01$) for the same product in 2-D. These findings clearly indicate that the user-controlled 3-D advertising in this study induced a significantly higher level of perceived presence than 2-D advertising.

To test H4 and H5, an examination of the interaction between the ad type and product type was first conducted. The results show significant main effects in support of ad type, with participants indicating higher levels of product knowledge ($M = 4.67$), brand attitude ($M = 5.34$), and purchase intention ($M = 3.46$) after evaluating 3-D advertising compared with reported product knowledge ($M = 3.43$, $F(89) = 16.23$, $p < .01$), brand attitude ($M = 4.41$, $F(89) = 14.19$, $p < .01$), and purchase intention ($M = 2.54$, $F(89) = 7.19$, $p < .01$) for 2-D advertising. As was expected, there were no main effects across product type for product knowledge ($M = 4.31$), brand attitude ($M = 4.76$), or purchase intention ($M = 2.79$) when examining the geometric product versus the product knowledge ($M = 3.80$, $F(89) = 2.72$, $p > .05$), brand attitude ($M = 4.99$, $F(89) = .84$, $p > .05$), or purchase intention ($M = 3.19$, $F(89) = 1.46$,

Table 7.2

Dependent Measures Across Experience and Product Category

Product	Measure	3-D	2-D	t	Degrees of freedom	p<
Watch	Presence					
	Physical	2.58	1.75	4.58	51	0.01
	Engagement	2.56	1.91	3.73	51	0.01
	Naturalness	3.30	2.66	3.21	51	0.01
	Product knowledge	4.73	3.88	2.10	51	0.05
	Brand attitude	5.25	4.26	2.92	51	0.01
	Purchase intention	3.27	2.31	2.05	51	0.05
Jacket	Presence					
	Physical	3.00	1.90	4.89	40	0.01
	Engagement	2.94	2.25	2.80	40	0.01
	Naturalness	3.24	2.46	3.55	40	0.01
	Product knowledge	4.62	2.98	3.48	40	0.01
	Brand attitude	5.42	4.55	2.46	40	0.05
	Purchase intention	3.65	2.76	1.77	40	0.08

$p > .05$) for the material product. In addition, no significant interaction was detected between ad type and product type for product knowledge ($F(89) = 1.63$, $p > .05$), brand attitude ($F(89) = .06$, $p > .05$), or purchase intention ($F(89) = .01$, $p > .05$). The lack of an interaction obviously indicates that any further analyses should proceed with caution. However, because the planned contrasts correspond with the significant main effect of ad type, H4 and H5 can be confidently tested (Iacobucci 2001; Winer, Brown, and Michels 1991, 141).

In testing the hypotheses, planned comparisons were conducted to examine the mean differences between 3-D and 2-D advertising for each of the dependent variables (see Table 7.2). Hypothesis 4 predicted that 3-D advertising would be more effective than 2-D advertising for the geometric product (watch). The results support the hypothesis. Participants reported a significantly higher level of product knowledge ($M = 4.73$) after examining the 3-D interactive watch than the 2-D static representation ($M = 3.88$, $t(51) = 2.10$, $p < .05$). Likewise, brand attitude ($M = 5.25$) was significantly greater for the 3-D interactive version compared with the 2-D static product ($M = 4.26$, $t(51) = 2.92$, $p < .01$). Finally, purchase intention ($M = 3.27$) was significantly higher for the watch in 3-D advertising than in the 2-D advertising counterpart ($M = 2.31$, $t(51) = 2.05$, $p < .05$).

Hypothesis 5 anticipated that 3-D advertising would result in no significant differences from 2-D advertising when evaluating a tactile product (jacket). However, significant differences were detected in favor of the 3-D condition over the 2-D condition for reported product knowledge and brand attitude when evaluating the jacket, resulting in the rejection of H5. Surprisingly, participants reported a significantly higher level of product knowledge (M = 4.62) after examining the jacket in 3-D than in 2-D (M = 2.98, $t(40)$ = 3.48, $p < .01$). In addition, brand attitude (M = 5.42) was significantly greater for 3-D advertising compared with 2-D advertising (M = 4.55, $t(40)$ = 2.46, $p < .05$). The mean scores for purchase intention (M = 3.65) in the 3-D condition followed the same pattern but were not significantly different than in the 2-D condition (M = 2.76, $t(40)$ = 1.77, $p > .05$). One possible explanation for these findings is that consumers in the 3-D advertising condition were able to experience a limited haptic sensation by zooming, rotating, and moving the product. This enhanced virtual experience when evaluating a material product is unexpected yet interesting and warrants further discussion.

Mediation Analysis

A mediation analysis was again conducted to determine whether presence mediates the relationship between the type of Internet advertising and reported product knowledge, brand attitude, and purchase intention for each test product. The first set of analyses for the geometric product indicated that the type of advertising positively influenced the perceived physical (β = .55, $t(50)$ = 4.58, $p < .01$, R^2 = .30), engagement (β = .47, $t(50)$ = 3.73, $p < .01$, R^2 = .22), and naturalness (β = .41, $t(50)$ = 3.21, $p < .01$, R^2 = .17) dimensions of presence. Similarly, the second set of analyses for the watch demonstrated that the type of experience positively influenced product knowledge (β = .29, $t(50)$ = 2.10, $p < .05$, R^2 = .08), brand attitude (β = .38, $t(50)$ = 2.92, $p < .01$, R^2 = .15), and purchase intention (β = .28, $t(50)$ = 2.05, $p < .05$, R^2 = .08). However, the third set of analyses rejected presence as a mediating variable for the geometric product along the physical, engagement, and naturalness dimensions for product knowledge (β = .19, $t(2,49)$ = 1.19, $p > .05$; β = .03, $t(2,49)$ = .21, $p > .05$; β = .02, $t(2,49)$ = .10, $p > .05$, respectively) and brand attitude (β = .03, $t(2,49)$ = .20, $p > .05$; β = .17, $t(2,49)$ = 1.17, $p > .05$; β = -.22, $t(2,49)$ = 1.58, $p > .05$, respectively). Nevertheless, presence was supported as a mediating variable for purchase intention along the physical (β = .48, $t(2,49)$ = 3.19, $p < .01$, R^2 = .24) and engagement (β = .49, $t(2,49)$ = 3.55, $p < .01$, R^2 = .2) dimensions, with naturalness resulting in no effect (β = .12, $t(2,49)$ = .77, $p > .05$). The effect of advertising on purchase intention for the watch diminished when included in the analysis with the physical (β = .02, $t(2,49)$ = .14, $p > .05$) or engagement (β = .05, $t(2,49)$ = .36, $p > .05$) dimensions.

For the material product, the first set of analyses indicated that the type of advertising positively influenced the perceived physical (β = .62, $t(39)$ = 4.89, $p < .01$, R^2 = .38), engagement (β = .41, $t(39)$ = 2.80, $p < .01$, R^2 = .18), and naturalness (β = .49, $t(39)$ = 3.55, $p < .01$, R^2 = .24) dimensions of presence. In addition, the second set of analyses for the jacket demonstrated that the type of advertising positively influenced product knowledge (β = .49, $t(39)$ = 3.48, $p < .05$, R^2 = .24) and brand attitude (β = .37, $t(39)$ = 2.46, $p < .01$, R^2 = .14) but did not result in a significant effect for purchase intention (β = .27, $t(39)$ = 1.77, $p > .05$), which caused the variable to be excluded from the remaining analyses. Finally, the third set of analyses for the material product supported presence as a mediating variable along the physical, engagement, and naturalness dimensions for product knowledge (β = .44, $t(2,38)$ = 2.69, $p < .01$, R^2 = .36; β = .29, $t(2,38)$ = 1.97, $p < .05$, R^2 = .31; β = .30, $t(2,38)$ = 1.96, $p < .05$, R^2 = .31, respectively) and brand attitude (β = .73, $t(2,38)$ = 4.83, $p < .01$, R^2 = .47; β = .58, $t(2,38)$ = 4.26, $p < .01$, R^2 = .41; β = .51, $t(2,38)$ = 3.36, $p < .01$, R^2 = .33, respectively). Appropriately, the effect of advertising on product knowledge diminished when included in the analysis with physical (β = .21, $t(2,38)$ = 1.29, $p > .05$), engagement (β = .37, $t(2,38)$ = 2.49, $p < .01$), or naturalness (β = .34, $t(2,38)$ = 2.17, $p < .05$) dimensions. Likewise, the effect of experience on brand attitude for the jacket was also weakened when regressed along with the physical (β = -.08, $t(2,38)$ = .55, $p > .05$), engagement (β = .13, $t(2,38)$ = .95, $p > .05$), or naturalness (β = .11, $t(2,38)$ = .75, $p > .05$) dimensions.

In summary, the results of the mediation analysis for Study 2 indicate that the physical and engagement dimensions of presence mediated the relationship between the type of advertising and purchase intention for the geometric product. Furthermore, all three dimensions of presence served to mediate the association between product knowledge and the type of advertising for the material product. This relationship was also supported for brand attitude.

Discussion

The most interesting finding of Study 2 is that 3-D advertising results in better knowledge and more positive brand attitude than 2-D advertising for a material product (jacket). This is contradictory to the belief that perceived affordances would propel consumers to feel and touch such an item in a prepurchase inspection. Thus, we need to seek alternative explanations for these findings.

We speculate that perceived affordances may have been altered by the illusion of presence, which resulted in a new set of virtual affordances rather than the perceptual cues that normally regulate a consumer's assessment of a product. For example, when consumers interact with a product, their perceived affordances will initially guide them in terms of what to see, feel, and try. However, because they are interacting with a 3-D product, they will soon take advantage of the interface properties offered by the virtual experience. For example, a virtual experience may enable them to engrave their name on the inner band of a ring or customize the color of bed linens. Thus, they feel as if they are dealing with a real product, and a sense of presence emerges. As a result, presence may transform their perceived affordances by weighting aspects of a product differently. Shoppers may always believe the texture of a jacket is important; however, when they see bright colors or fashionable designs, combined with user-controlled interactivity, they may think these attributes are more important than the feel of the jacket for their product evaluation within the context of e-commerce. These new perceptual cues that guide a shopper's assessment of a product in a 3-D environment are what we call virtual affordances.

Presence is the bridge between perceived affordances and virtual affordances. Precisely, presence can transform perceived affordances into virtual affordances through imagery association in 3-D advertising. In a seminal review, Klein (1998) suggests that virtual experience may occur in each of three scenarios. First, information about a product's specific attributes is easily accessible on the Internet. Second, the format of information presented can alter the weight that consumers give to different attributes, especially when experience attributes are absent. For example, the history or personality of a wine product may be sufficient for a consumer in the absence of direct contact with the packaging or display information. Third, Internet advertising may provide experience from expert sources to assist consumer learning. As a result, such a virtual experience is able to "transform" experience attributes into search attributes and thereby reduce perceived risk prior to purchase in e-commerce.

The notion of virtual experience evolves as advances in 3-D visualization technologies emerge. If Klein's (1998) concept of virtual experience is based on "semantic associations," interactive 3-D advertising is more likely to generate a virtual experience through "imagery associations." Both spontaneous and voluntary imagery can facilitate the simulation of an experience (Richardson 1984). Imagery-based virtual experience is likely to be richer than semantic-based virtual experience, though both types may be interwoven in a consumer's interaction with a product in a virtual environment. As a result of the imagery association, perceived affordances may be altered. It is our belief that the perceived product affordances (touch and feel) that normally dominate the evaluation of a material product were transformed because of presence. Subsequently, participant evaluations were based on the virtual affordances offered by 3-D advertising, such as the ability to control the content of the media, because the heightened sense of presence served to simulate consumption.

Limitations

Inherent within any study are potential limitations that affect the overall validity and reliability of the results. With regard to this research, a few limitations should be considered when interpreting the findings. One limitation is the use of a student sample in combination with a laboratory experiment. This type of experiment restricts the external validity, which should be kept in mind when interpreting the results. Although strong consideration and planning took part in the selection of appropriate test products, the selection of different product categories that incorporate more search or experience attributes could affect the results. Another limitation is that Internet access and computer performance were optimized in this study, so participants were not exposed to any effect of slow download time or poor computer performance. As a result, the findings of this study should be more pertinent to e-commerce when consumers can experience 3-D product visualization through broadband Internet connections. Finally, product evaluation times were restricted in length and held constant across both studies. Although this provides adequate control for comparison purposes, additional research should explore consumers in a browsing frame of mind by removing this restraint.

Conclusion

The purpose of this study was to expand the knowledge of consumer experience by testing the relationship between 3-D advertising and presence. These frameworks are important to both scholars and practitioners because the Internet has the ability to serve as a more powerful medium than traditional media, in the sense that consumers are able to interact with products in multimedia environments. The managerial implications are immediate, because the ability to establish a virtual experience is not beyond the current capabilities of marketers. By creating compelling online virtual experiences with products, advertisers potentially can enhance the value of the product information presented, engage consumers in an active shopping experience, increase the number of unique and repeat traffic visitors for a site, and ultimately establish an online competitive advantage. The underlying reason for this is that virtual experiences allow for vicarious consumption because consumers are actively engaged in the inspection and control of a product in 3-D advertising rather than relegated to be being a passive observer, as is common in more traditional media. Furthermore, the findings of this study consistently show that 3-D advertising outperforms the 2-D advertising commonly used today to display and present product information online.

The conceptualization of a virtual experience has emerged because advancements in computer technology have led to a movement toward more multisensory online experiences. Similar to traditional forms of indirect experience, 3-D advertising enables consumers to form prior hypotheses by framing the information presented. However, in contrast with indirect experience, 3-D advertising is able to offer user control over the inspection of a product. This is an important advantage because high information control in e-commerce environments has been found to improve consumer decision quality and knowledge (Ariely 2000). This level of control is not a representation of an actual product but rather a simulation of the consumption experience, which has become increasingly important as society moves toward an experience economy (Pine and Gilmore 1998).

This study represents two laboratory experiments in this new and unexplored area. Therefore, replications and extensions of this work are needed to verify and validate the results and to fully understand the impact of a virtual experience in the form of 3-D advertising. Although increased sensory information enhances the sense of presence, future research should explore at what point cognitive resources are overloaded and the effectiveness of 3-D advertising diminishes. In addition, the use of avatars and virtual shopping worlds in e-commerce warrants further investigation. Another area often neglected in research that explores presence and 3-D advertising is the impact of individual user characteristics. For example, consumer information processing style (i.e., utilitarian versus hedonic) could provide valuable insight into the design and customization of e-commerce sites to achieve maximum effectiveness. Through continued research, the key is to develop and explore fully the psychological and emotional states created in a virtual experience.

References

Adams, Mark (1995), "Brands of Gold," *Mediaweek*, (November 13), 30–32.

Alba, Joseph, John Lynch, Barton Weitz, Chris Janiszewski, Richard Lutz, Alan Sawyer, and Stacy Wood (1997), "Interactive Home Shopping: Consumer, Retailer, and Manufacturer Incentives to Participate in Electronic Marketplaces," *Journal of Marketing*, 61 (3), 38–53.

Andrews, J. Craig, Syed H. Akhter, Srinivas Durvasula, and Darrel Muehling (1992), "The Effects of Advertising Distinctiveness and Message Content Involvement on Cognitive and Affective Responses to Advertising," *Journal of Current Issues and Research in Advertising*, 14 (Spring), 45–58.

Ariely, Dan (2000), "Controlling the Information Flow: Effects on Consumers' Decision Making and Preferences," *Journal of Consumer Research*, 27 (2), 233–249.

Baron, Reuben M. and David A. Kenny (1986), "The Moderator-Mediator Variable Distinction in Social Psychological Research: Conceptual, Strategic, and Statistical Considerations," *Journal of Personality and Social Psychology*, 51 (6), 1173–1182.

Bearden, William O., Donald R. Lichtenstein, and Jesse E. Teel (1984), "Comparison Price, Coupon, and Brand Effects on Consumer Reactions to Retail Newspaper Advertisements," *Journal of Retailing*, 60 (2), 11–34.

Beerli, Asuncion and Josefa D. Martin Santana (1999), "Design and Validation of an Instrument for Measuring Advertising Effectiveness in the Printed Media," *Journal of Current Issues and Research in Advertising*, 21 (2), 11–30.

Bettman, James A. and Whan C. Park (1980), "Effects of Prior Knowledge and Experience and Phase of the Choice Process on Consumer Decision Making Processes: A Protocol Analysis," *Journal of Consumer Research*, 7 (December), 234–248.

Biocca, Frank (1992), "Virtual Reality Technology: A Tutorial," *Journal of Communication*, 42 (4), 23–72.

——— (1997), "Cyborg's Dilemma: Progressive Embodiment in Virtual Environments," *Journal of Computer Mediated-Communication*, 3 (2), [www.ascusc.org/jcmc/v013/issue2/biocca2.html].

———, Terry M. Daugherty, Hairong Li, and Zoo-Hyun Chae (2001), "Effect of Visual Sensory Immersion on Product Knowledge, Attitude toward the Product and Purchase Intention," in *Proceedings of the Experiential E-Commerce Conference*, Frank Biocca, ed. [CD-ROM], East Lansing: Michigan State University.

———, Hairong Li, and Terry M. Daugherty (2001), "Experiential E-Commerce: Relationship of Physical and Social Presence to Consumer Learning, Attitudes, and Decision-Making," paper presented at the Presence Conference, May 21–23, Philadelphia.

Brucks, Merrie (1985), "The Effects of Product Class Knowledge on Information Search Behavior," *Journal of Consumer Research*, 12 (June), 1–16.

Bruner, Gordon C. (1998), "Standardization and Justification: Do Ad Scales Measure Up?" *Journal of Current Issues and Research in Advertising*, 20 (1), 1–18.

Coyle, James R. and Esther Thorson (2001), "The Effects of Progressive Levels of Interactivity and Vividness in Web Marketing Sites," *Journal of Advertising*, 30 (3), 65–77.

Deighton, John (1996), "The Future of Interactive Marketing," *Harvard Business Review*, 76 (2), 151–160.

——— (1997), "Commentary on 'Exploring the Implications of the Internet for Consumer Marketing,'" *Journal of Academy of Marketing Science*, 25 (4), 347–351.

Fazio, Russell H., Martha C. Powell, and Carol J. Williams (1989), "The Role of Attitude Accessibility in the Attitude-to-Behavior Process," *Journal of Consumer Research*, 16 (December), 280–288.

Fishbein, Martin and Icek Ajzen (1975), *Belief, Attitude, Intention and Behavior: An Introduction to Theory and Research*, Reading, MA: Addison-Wesley.

Ghose, Sanjoy and Wenyu Dou (1998), "Interactive Functions and Their Impacts on the Appeal of Internet Presence Sites," *Journal of Advertising Research*, 38 (2), 29–43.

Gibson, J. J. (1966), *The Senses Considered as Perceptual Systems*, Boston: Houghton Mifflin.

Hair, Joseph F., Rolph E. Anderson, Ronald L. Tatham, and William C. Black (1998), *Multivariate Data Analysis*, 5th ed., Upper Saddle River, NJ: Prentice Hall.

Heeter, Carrie (1986), "Perspectives for the Development of Research on Media Systems," Ph.D. dissertation, Michigan State University, East Lansing.

——— (2000), "Interactivity in the Context of Designed Experience," *Journal of Interactive Advertising*, 1 (1) [www.jiad.org/v011/n01/heeter/index.html].

Hoch, Stephen J. and Young-Won Ha (1986), "Consumer Learning: Advertising and the Ambiguity of Product Experience," *Journal of Consumer Research*, 13 (September), 221–233.

Hoffman, Donna L. and Thomas P. Novak (1996), "Marketing in Hypermedia Computer-Mediated Environments: Conceptual Foundations," *Journal of Marketing*, 60 (3), 50–68.

Hunter, John E. and David W. Gerbing (1982), "Unidimensional Measurement, Second Order Factor Analysis, and Causal Models," *Research in Organizational Behavior*, 4, 267–320.

Hutchinson, J. Wesley and Joseph W. Alba (1991), "Ignoring Irrelevant Information: Situational Determinants of Consumer Learning," *Journal of Consumer Research*, 18 (December), 325–345.

Iacobucci, Dawn (2001), "Can I Test for Simple Effects in the Presence of an Insignificant Interaction?" *Journal of Consumer Psychology*, 10 (1& 2), 5–9.

Interactive Advertising Bureau (2001), *IAB Internet Advertising Revenue Report: 2000 Fourth-Quarter Results and Full-Year Hightlights*, New York: PricewaterhouseCoopers.

Kempf, DeAnna S. and Robert E. Smith (1998), "Consumer Processing of Product Trial and the Influence of Prior Advertising: A Structural Modeling Approach," *Journal of Marketing Research*, 35 (August), 325–338.

Kim, Taeyoung and Frank Biocca (1997), "Telepresence via Television: Two Dimensions of Telepresence May Have Different Connections to Memory and Persuasion," *Journal of Computer-Mediated Communication*, 3 (2), [www.ascusc.org/jcmc/v013/issue2/kim.html].

Klatzky, Roberta L., Susan J. Lederman, and Dana E. Matula (1991), "Imagined Haptic Exploration in Judgments of Object Properties," *Journal of Experimental Psychology: Learning, Memory and Cognition*, 17 (March), 314–322.

Klein, Lisa R. (1998), "Evaluating the Potential of Interactive Media Through a New Lens: Search versus Experience Goods," *Journal of Business Research*, 41 (3), 195–203.

——— (2001), "Creating Virtual Experiences: The Role of Telepresence," in *Proceedings of the Experiential E-commerce Conference*, Frank Biocca, ed. [CD-ROM], East Lansing: Michigan State University.

Ku, Linlin (1992), "Impacts of Interactivity from Computer-Mediated Communication in an Organizational Setting: A Study of Electronic Mail," Ph.D. dissertation, Michigan State University.

Lessiter, Jane, Jonathon Freeman, Edmun Keogh, and Jules Davidoff (2000), "Development of a New Cross-Media Presence Questionnaire: The ITC-Sense of Presence Inventory," paper presented at the Third International Workshop on Presence, March 27–28, Technical University of Delft, Netherlands.

Li, Hairong, Terry Daugherty, and Frank Biocca (2001), "Characteristics of Virtual Experience in Electronic Commerce: A Protocol Analysis," *Journal of Interactive Marketing*, 15 (3), 13–30.

———, ———, and ——— (2003), "The Role of Virtual Experience in Consumer Learning," *Journal of Consumer Psychology*, 13, 4, 395–407.

Lombard, Matthew and Theresa Ditton (1997), "At the Heart of It All: The Concept of Presence," *Journal of Computer-Mediated Communication*, 3 (2), [www.ascusc.org/jcmc/vol3/issue2/lombard.html].

Lutz, Richard J. (1975), "Changing Brand Attitudes Through Modification of Cognitive Structure," *Journal of Consumer Research*, 1 (March), 49–59.

MacKenzie, Scott B. and Richard J. Lutz (1989), "An Empirical Examination of the Structural Antecedents of Attitude Toward the Ad in an Advertising Pretesting Context," *Journal of Marketing*, 53 (April), 48–65.

McCabe, Deborah Brown and Stephen M. Nowlis (2001), "Information Integration across Online and Offline Shopping Environments and Its Effects on Consumers' Purchase Decisions," in *Proceedings of the Experiential E-commerce Conference*, Frank Biocca, ed., [CD-ROM], East Lansing: Michigan State University.

McLuhan, Marshall and Eric McLuhan (1988), *Laws of Media: The New Science*, Toronto: University of Toronto Press.

Mirapaul, Matthew (2000), "3-D Space as New Frontier," *New York Times on the Web* (October 5), [www.nytimes.com/2000/10/05/technology/05SPAC.html].

Nelson, Phillip (1976), "Economic Value of Advertising," in *Advertising and Society*, Yale Brozen, ed., New York: New York University Press.

——— (1981), "Consumer Information and Advertising," in *Economics of Information*, Malcolm Galatin and Robert D. Leiter, eds., Boston: M. Nijhoff.

Newhagen, John E. and Sheizaf Rafaeli (1996), "Why Communication Researchers Should Study the Internet: A Dialogue," *Journal of Communication*, 46 (1), 4–13.

Norman, Donald (1998), *The Invisible Computer: Why Good Products Can Fail, the Personal Computer Is So Complex and Information Appliances Are the Solution*, Cambridge, MA: MIT Press.

Peterson, Robert A., Sridhar Balasubramanian, and Bart J. Bronnenberg (1997), "Exploring the Implications of the Internet for Consumer Marketing," *Journal of the Academy of Marketing Science*, 25 (4), 329–346.

Pine, B. Joseph and James H. Gilmore (1998), "Welcome to the Experience Economy," *Harvard Business Review*, 76 (4), 97–105.

Rafaeli, Sheizaf (1985), "If the Computer Is a Medium, What Is the Message: Explicating Interactivity," paper presented at the International Communication Association convention, May, Honolulu.

——— (1988), "Interactivity: From New Media to Communication," in *Advancing Communication Science: Merging Mass and Interpersonal*, R. Hawkins, J.M. Wieman, and S. Pingree, eds., Beverly Hills, CA: Sage, 110–134.

Reeves, Byron and Clifford Nass (1996), *The Media Equation*, Palo Alto, CA: CSLI Publications.

Rewick, Jennifer (2001), "Choices, Choices: A Look at the Pros and Cons of Various Types of Web Advertising," *Wall Street Journal* (April 23), R12.

Rice, Ronald (1984), *The New Media: Communication, Research, and Technology*, Beverly Hills, CA: Sage.

——— (1987), "Computer-Mediated Communication and Organizational Innovation," *Journal of Communication*, 37 (4), 65–94.

Richardson, Alan (1984), *The Experiential Dimension of Psychology*, Queensland, Australia: University of Queensland Press.

Rimal, Rajiv N. and June A. Flora (1997), "Interactive Technology Attributes in Health Promotion: Practical and Theoretical Issues," in *Health Promotion and Interactive Technology: Theoretical Applications and Future Directions*, Richard L. Street,

William R. Gold, and Timothy R. Manning, eds., Mahwah, NJ: Lawrence Erlbaum Associates, 19–38.

Rogers, Everett M. and Sheizaf Rafaeli (1985), "Computers and Communication," in *Information and Behavior*, Vol. 1, Brent D. Ruben, ed., New Brunswick, NJ: Transaction Books.

Smith, Daniel C. and C. Whan Park (1992), "The Effects of Brand Extensions on Market Share and Advertising Efficiency," *Journal of Marketing Research*, 29 (August), 296–313.

Smith, Robert E. (1993), "Integrating Information from Advertising and Trial: Processes and Effects on Consumer Response to Product Information," *Journal of Marketing Research*, 30 (May), 204–219.

———— and William R. Swinyard (1982), "Information Response Models: An Integrated Approach," *Journal of Marketing*, 46 (Winter), 81–93.

Steuer, Jonathan (1992), "Defining Virtual Reality: Dimensions Determining Telepresence," *Journal of Communication*, 42 (4), 73–93.

Winer, Benjamin J., Donald R. Brown, and Kenneth M. Michels (1991), *Statistical Principles in Experimental Design*, 3d ed., New York: McGraw-Hill.

Witmer, Bob G. and Michael J. Singer (1998), "Measuring Presence in Virtual Environments: A Presence Questionnaire," *Presence*, 7 (3), 225–240.

Wright, Alice A. and John G. Lynch Jr. (1995), "Communication Effects of Advertising versus Direct Experience When Both Search and Experience Attributes Are Present," *Journal of Consumer Research*, 21 (March), 708–718.

Wright, Peter (1980), "Message-Evoked Thoughts: Persuasion Research Using Thought Verbalization," *Journal of Consumer Research*, 7 (September), 151–175.

8

Managing the Power of Curiosity for Effective Web Advertising Strategies

Satya Menon and Dilip Soman

A primary challenge in creating effective advertising is to ensure that the advertisement not only attracts the target consumer's attention, but also generates interest and educates the consumer about product benefits and positioning (cf. Aaker, Batra, and Myers 1992). Various suggestions have been made previously to achieve these objectives (e.g., teaser headlines, Fazio, Herr, and Powell 1992; repetition of message, Maynard 1995; provision of detailed information, Olson 1983). However, most of these suggestions are tactical in nature and applicable to an individual advertisement but do not speak to the strategic development of an entire campaign.

The challenges of generating interest and educating consumers become especially relevant in the domain of Internet advertising. Unlike a television commercial or print advertisement, most Internet advertising is in a form (e.g., banners, buttons) that requires sufficient interest and motivation on the part of the consumers to interact with the advertisement and access appropriate information rather than be passive recipients of the message (Hanson 2000; Kirsner 1997; Ries and Ries 2000). Consequently, Web advertisers are concerned that they have limited, if any, control over the exposure of the content of the advertising and, hence, the education of consumers (Briggs and Hollis 1997; Maddox 2001). Whereas some advertisers and managers believe that Internet ads have a role in creating brand awareness and image (Frankel 2000), many others have questioned the effectiveness of Internet advertising and argued that advertising off the Internet will always be bigger than advertising on the Internet (Ries and Ries 2000; see McKillen 2001 for a discussion). These fears are consistent with very low "click-through" rates that are registered for most Internet advertising (Hanson 2000).

The Internet as a communication medium is uniquely different from other media on several dimensions, such as interactivity, control, dynamic content, and depth of content accessible to the consumer (Hoffman and Novak 1996). Researchers have recently proposed that consumer behavior in this medium is greatly shaped by consumers' holistic experiences with this new medium. These researchers have proposed different constructs, such as the state of flow (Csikszentmihalyi 1990; Hoffman and Novak 1996) and cognitive absorption (Agarwal and Karahanna 2000), to capture the unique dimensions of holistic experiences in technology-based interactions. A common thread underlying these different constructs is the suggestion that consumer experiences in a medium such as the Internet may often be characterized by a state of deep attention, engagement, and fun, such that "nothing else seems to matter" (Csikszentmihalyi 1990, 4). This perspective points to both the challenge and the opportunity for those seeking to advertise on the Internet. It explains why advertisers find it difficult to divert the attention of persons who are deeply engrossed in other activities, either experiential (e.g., net surfing) or goal-directed (e.g., online shopping; Hoffman and Novak 1996). It also suggests that, if appropriately designed using a suitable "creative hook," Internet advertisements would be able to leverage the same optimal experience of flow or cognitive absorption that the medium is capable of delivering to consumers.

This chapter addresses concerns about the effectiveness of Internet advertising by prescribing a solution that can increase consumer motivation and experienced enjoyment of the interaction with Internet ads. Previous research has shown that consumers' motivation and ability to process new information is enhanced by generating curiosity and encouraging curiosity-based elaboration about the new information (cf. Berlyne 1960; Loewenstein 1994). Specifically, Loewenstein (1994) proposes that curiosity or "the desire to know" arises when persons become alerted to the existence of an information gap in a particular knowledge domain. In this chapter, we argue that this power of curiosity can be harnessed to design an effective advertising strategy that results in greater information acquisition, enhanced learning, and better evaluation of the advertised product.

We have three specific objectives. First, we seek to demonstrate that an Internet advertising campaign in which curiosity-generating ads precede product information ads will be significantly more effective than a campaign that uses only product information ads. Second, we build a theory of curiosity generation and curiosity resolution to suggest general guidelines for executing an effective curiosity strategy. Third, we track information acquisition patterns and other process measures related to gauging Internet advertising effectiveness and study the relationship between these measures and the hypothesized product-related learning and evaluation.

The Importance of Motivating and Facilitating Consumer Learning

Internet advertising is done in a variety of forms, including banners, buttons, interstitials, hot corners, and portals (Hanson 2000). However, all forms of Internet advertising share the common characteristic that the consumer must initiate some action (e.g., click on a small graphic) to be exposed to the communication. Although banner ads on the Internet could be designed to enhance awareness and build brand image, most advertisers use them mainly as drivers of Web traffic (Hanson 2000). However, even for this objective, Internet ads are only effective when they can motivate consumers to transport themselves to the advertisers' Web sites (Briggs and Hollis 1997; Hanson 2000; O'Brien 1998). In particular, Ries and Ries (2000) claim that, due to consumer control over the information flow in cyberspace, Internet advertising can never match off-line advertising in terms of its ability to motivate and enable consumer learning, liking, and brand building. Others (Hanson 2000; O'Brien 1998) suggest that, to be successful, banner advertisements must incorporate some mechanisms that motivate consumers to interact with the medium and reach detailed product information (see also Frankel 2000). Furthermore, to encourage consumers to take immediate behavioral action with respect to the product (such as requesting a brochure or purchasing online), the advertisements must effectively educate consumers about both the target product and the purchasing process. Motivating consumers to search for information and facilitating learning seem to be basic requirements of an Internet-based advertising strategy.

In addition to presenting these challenges, however, the Internet also provides opportunities to develop and execute interactive marketing strategies (Deighton 1996). Interactivity allows consumers to attend selectively to the information of their choice and has been shown to facilitate learning of new information (Ariely 2000). This suggests that the Internet could be used as an effective medium for disseminating new product information. However, sufficient consumer interest and motivation to search for information are essential for the benefits of interactivity to accrue (Alba et al. 1997; Ariely 2000). Recent work in the information technology domain suggests that it may be possible to utilize the characteristics of the Internet to motivate and engage consumers actively in their interactions on the Internet. Building on prior work in psychology, many researchers have suggested that, in certain antecedent conditions, consumers may feel a heightened degree of intrinsic motivation, intense concentration, and enjoyment while engaging in technology interactions (such as behavior on the Internet). This experience (conceptualized variously as a state of flow, cognitive absorption, and so on) could lead to many positive outcomes, such as positive attitudes, increased learning, and more participation (Agarwal and Karahanna 2000; Ghani and Deshpande 1994; Hoffman and Novak 1996). However, for consumers to experience such a state of flow or cognitive absorption, they must first experience a heightened sense of curiosity, intrinsic interest, challenge, perceived control, and a narrowed focus of attention (Ghani and Deshpande 1994; Hoffman and Novak 1996). We suggest that an ad strategy based on the psychology of curiosity could actively engage the consumer in processing the ad information, searching for more information, and, ultimately, learning more about the advertised product.

In this chapter, we focus on Internet advertising for new products and innovations (sometimes referred to as "really new products," Lehmann 1994). To appreciate new products, consumers typically have to learn new benefits, new attributes, and new levels of existing attributes or new technologies (Lehmann 1994; Urban, Weinberg, and Hauser 1996). Therefore, an important goal during product launch is to facilitate consumer learning of key benefits and attributes. A second objective is to influence the categorization of the new product concurrently (Fusco 1994). This entails learning how the attribute–benefit relationships that characterize the new product are different from those of existing products. For successful positioning, consumers must perceive the new brand as the pioneer of a new and distinct product category so that it can gain the advantages associated with being the first entrant (cf. Carpenter and Nakamoto 1989). For example, the marketer of a new brand of digital camera would like consumers to categorize it as a new product type (i.e., digital camera) with distinctive benefits and attributes rather than as a modified version of an existing category (e.g., a filmless 35mm camera).

The Psychology of Curiosity and Implications for Advertising

Philosophers and psychologists have written extensively about curiosity and the role that it plays in human behavior across various domains (e.g., child development, education, scientific discovery, behavioral disorders; see Loewenstein 1994 for an extensive review). However, the literature on the subject has focused primarily on the sources and effects of curiosity and the measurement of curiosity traits. Little empirical work has studied the situational determinants of curiosity and the cognitive processes underlying curiosity resolution.

One recent theoretical treatment of curiosity is the "knowledge gap" perspective (also referred to as the "information gap," Loewenstein 1994). A knowledge gap can be defined as the difference between two quantities: what a person knows and what he or she would like to know. Curiosity arises when people become aware of the existence of a knowledge gap in a particular domain or when they encounter novel or inconsistent stimuli (Berlyne 1954, 1960), stimulus ambiguity or incongruity (Hebb 1949), or stimuli that violate their expectations (Hunt 1963). These situations highlight their knowledge deficiencies (Loewenstein 1994). Awareness of a knowledge gap produces an aversive feeling of deprivation or discomfort that can be alleviated only by obtaining the information needed to close the gap, which consequently produces an intense desire to modify the existing knowledge structure (Berlyne 1960).

Does the presence of a knowledge gap always result in elaboration and information search? Consider advertising for digital cameras from 1997, when they were first introduced. As one example of a knowledge gap, a "teaser" advertisement (Enrico 1995) for a product called QV might promise consumers that the QV "changes the ways in which you capture, create, and communicate pictures." Although this advertisement would be likely to attract attention, it might not translate into curiosity and active elaboration because the reader has no clues to interpret the presented information. In particular, though the consumer may realize that the advertised product is new, he or she may have neither the motivation nor the ability to elaborate further about the product. We refer to such advertising, which presents a high knowledge gap, as "no-cue curiosity." Now consider a second advertisement that also hints that the new product is a camera and uses digital technology. A reader of this second type of advertisement (which presents a moderate knowledge gap and will be referred to as "cued curiosity" hereafter) can use this additional information (cue) to generate focused and meaningful hypotheses about the QV by linking the new information with existing knowledge about both cameras and digital technology. In addition, by increasing interest in gathering information that can verify these self-generated hypotheses, the cue also facilitates search, processing, and integration of information.

Thus, curiosity—manifested as the desire to seek knowledge—is generated only when the gap in knowledge is perceived as manageable or moderate (Loewenstein 1994) and consumers have some "cue" that helps link the missing information with preexisting knowledge in that domain. Several theoretical perspectives in psychology are consistent with such an inverted-U relationship between curiosity and the size of the knowledge gap (Berlyne 1960; Hebb 1949; Hunt 1963). We therefore hypothesize that

> H1: The extent of curiosity will be stronger when the knowledge gap is moderate than when the knowledge gap is either very low or very high. A moderate knowledge gap can be created by advertising that provides a cue to help consumers elaborate about the missing information.

Curiosity prompts people to elaborate and generate hypotheses about the knowledge gap and thus motivates them to seek information to confirm or disconfirm these hypotheses (Klayman and Ha 1987), which result in a greater longing for knowledge (Loewenstein 1994). In addition, when curiosity-resolving information becomes available, the person implicitly reviews it to examine its degree of fit with self-generated hypotheses. This type of review, or "reprocessing," of a message will result in better recall and comprehension of the new information (Fazio, Herr, and Powell 1992; O'Brien and Myers 1985).

Prior research shows that people expose themselves voluntarily to curiosity-arousing stimuli such as crossword puzzles and mystery novels (Loewenstein 1994) because of the anticipated pleasure from satisfying the curiosity. In situations in which curiosity resolution results in the revelation of extant knowledge, Loewenstein (1994) suggests that the person generally feels disappointed with the actual information. For example, for mystery ads, Fazio, Herr, and Powell (1992) suggest that consumers may feel a sense of anticlimax (a "big deal!" response, Fazio, Herr, and Powell 1992, 10) when curiosity is resolved for familiar brands. We propose that this anticlimax might occur when the curiosity-resolving information is itself not very new, but for novel and truly innovative brands, an "Aha" response and positive affect is more likely to result. In an advertising context, this suggests that the affective reactions from curiosity resolution may carry over to the new product in terms of general brand affect (see Mitchell and Olson 1981). More formally, we hypothesize that

> H2: Generating more curiosity about a product will result in (a) greater elaboration, (b) greater information search, (c) better learning of the information, and (d) enhanced brand affect.

Early treatments of curiosity (e.g., Berlyne 1960) are consistent with H2b, in that they show greater information acquisition by curious persons. However, they do not study the direction of this information acquisition. The knowledge-gap perspective suggests that a salient aspect of curiosity-based processing is that it provides persons with a goal to discover the information needed to close the gap and prompts them to generate specific questions and hypotheses regarding the object of curiosity. Goals help people determine the relevance of incoming information, which results in knowledge being encoded, interpreted, and organized in memory around the underlying theme or goal (Bransford and Johnson 1972; Huffman and Houston 1993; Wyer et al. 1982). This suggests that the specific trigger used to generate curiosity (e.g., an unexpected new benefit) will act as a node for processing and organizing further product information (see Huffman and Houston 1993). In a product advertising context, for example, it may be possible to generate curiosity in an advertisement by focusing on a single new benefit or feature (the curiosity "trigger") that is inconsistent with expectations about the product. We expect that the hypotheses generated by consumers would be focused on the inconsistent benefit, and consequently, the information search and elaboration would be directed toward the testing of those specific hypotheses (Klayman and Ha 1987). Thus, an advertisement could direct learning toward a particular feature or benefit by using it as the curiosity trigger. These predictions are formally captured in the following hypothesis:

> H3: The generation of curiosity about a specific product feature will direct elaboration and information search toward this feature. Consequently, there will be better learning of information about this product feature.

We note that curiosity is different from other message strategies designed to elevate motivation or involvement (e.g., increasing personal relevance), because it directs attention to specific information rather than causes a generalized tendency toward more effortful processing. We next describe two experiments designed to test these hypotheses. The first experiment enabled us to test H1, that the extent of curiosity would be highest for a moderate knowledge gap. We designed two sets of ads, each with a three-level, knowledge-gap manipulation, and each set used a different product feature as the curiosity trigger. In the second experiment, we embedded the same ads within a simulated Internet environment and studied the effects of the knowledge gap and curiosity trigger manipulations on information search, elaboration, and learning (H2 and H3). The second study enabled us to provide a real-world context in which subjects could choose to ignore the ad or, alternatively, link to more information about the advertised product.

In both experiments, we used digital cameras as the new product featured in the test advertisements. These studies were conducted in 1997 when the product was new to the market and consumers were relatively unfamiliar with its features and benefits. For our research, we designed advertisements for a fictitious brand of digital camera called the "Sony QV." This product allowed consumers to take filmless photographs that were stored digitally and could be handled like any computer files. Therefore, the consumer could edit photographs for content, enrich the quality of images, and change backgrounds or other art of their choice. They could also transmit photographs using the Internet and other digital technology, such as into remote computers or through a video camera onto a television screen. The device thus used two technologies (digital information processing and the Internet) to deliver two unique benefits: the ability to create images by manipulation (create benefit) and the ability to communicate them in clever ways (communicate benefit). Two sets of ads were created that featured each of these benefits as the main theme in the ad.

Experiment 1

Stimuli, Design, and Procedure

The study used a 3 (knowledge gap) × 2 (curiosity trigger) full-factorial, between-subjects design. The curiosity trigger was either the create benefit or the communicate benefit of the digital camera and was prominent in the headline of the ad. Within each curiosity trigger, three ads using the same headline and visual but differing in the size of the knowledge gap were developed. The low-knowledge-gap ad (labeled control) revealed that the Sony QV was a digital camera and provided detailed information about the product benefits in the headline and other features. The moderate-knowledge-gap ad (labeled cued curiosity) had no details about the product, but the tagline provided a cue that Sony QV was a camera. The high-knowledge-gap ad (labeled the no-cue curiosity) provided neither product details nor a cue about the product category of Sony QV.

One hundred eight undergraduate students at a large state university were recruited as subjects and compensated for their participation with a token gift. Subjects were told to view a print version of an advertisement for a new product and respond to a short questionnaire. Subjects were randomly assigned to one of the six versions of the test advertisement.

Manipulation Checks

To check our manipulation of the knowledge gap, we asked subjects two questions, both of which were measured on nine-point scales. First, the variable ADEQ was the response to "In your opinion, how complete (or adequate) is the information that the ad provides about the product?" Second, KNOW was measured as a response to "How knowledgeable did you feel about this product after reading the ad?" Because ADEQ and KNOW were highly correlated (.83), we used their mean as a manipulation check for knowledge gap. A 3 × 2 analysis of variance (ANOVA) yielded only a significant main effect of knowledge gap ($p < .001$, other $ps > .55$). The control ad was perceived as providing the highest knowledge ($X = 6.33$) followed by the cued curiosity ad ($X = 4.92$) and the no-cue curiosity ($X = 3.89$, $ps < .05$ in the Student-Newman-Keuls test for multiple comparison of means). Our knowledge gap manipulation appeared to be successful.

Results and Analysis

We collected four measures that were designed to measure the amount of the generated curiosity in response to the print ad. Each of the following measures were collected on nine-point scales, with nine indicating the highest degree of curiosity:

CURIOUS: How curious do you feel about this product?
READ: How interested would you be in reading more about this product?
INVOLVE: How involved did you feel in reading the advertisement about the product?
STORE: How interested would you be in checking out this product at a store?

These variables correlated highly (Cronbach's alpha = .80), so we used their mean as a measure of generated curiosity. A 3 × 2 ANOVA showed a significant main effect only of the knowledge gap ($p < .001$, other $ps > .35$). As predicted, the mean CURIOSITY score was the highest for the cued condition ($X = 6.50$), lower for the no-cue condition ($X = 4.03$), and lowest for the control condition ($X = 3.67$). We note that the difference between the no-cue curiosity and the control conditions was small and barely approached significance ($p = .11$).

The results of Experiment 1 support H1 by showing that a higher degree of curiosity is generated when the knowledge gap about a new stimulus is moderate rather than when it is low or high. Furthermore, subjects perceived the digital camera as a novel product ($X = 7.12$), and their self-rated prior knowledge about digital cameras was low ($X = 3.1$). Therefore, we used the same stimuli in Experiment 2, which employed a simulated Internet context to study the consequences of curiosity on elaboration, information search, and (directed) learning about the new product.

Experiment 2

Stimuli, Design, and Procedure

Subjects were 131 undergraduate students at a large state university who earned course credit for participation. They were randomly assigned to one of the six experimental conditions, which represented the same 3 (knowledge gap) × 2 (curiosity trigger) manipulations used in Experiment 1. Subjects were asked to evaluate a cyber magazine on the basis of two successive sample issues. Each issue had eight pages of editorial articles interspersed with four ads (one test ad, three filler ads). The first issue included the test ad (referred to hereafter as AD1; it was one of the six ads used to manipulate curiosity), which was placed at the same location within the magazine for all subjects. The second issue carried an ad (referred to hereafter as AD2) that provided full information about the curiosity trigger in AD1, as well as links to access more information about the product features. AD2 was identical to the control advertisement for the corresponding curiosity trigger. Subjects went through the first issue of the magazine, came across AD1, subsequently saw other editorial sites and filler ads, and then rated the magazine on various aspects. Next, they went through the second issue of the magazine, in which they came across AD2, as well as other editorial sites and filler ads. Opinions on the magazine were collected first, followed by a distraction task and an on-screen questionnaire that was administered to measure the dependent variables. We note that the advertising across the three knowledge-gap conditions is identical in terms of total information made available and the total number of exposures but differs in the temporal dissemination of information. In the control condition, all the information is available at the first exposure, whereas in the curiosity conditions, some of the information is withheld until the second exposure.

All the ads in the cyber magazine provided clickable buttons that linked to additional Web sites that provided more related information. Of particular relevance to our analysis, AD1 included a link to a product home page. If this link was accessed, it led to a product homepage that was ostensibly "under construction" to provide answers to frequently asked questions (FAQs) and prompted visitors to submit questions that they wanted answered after seeing the product ad. This enabled us to get two process measures without giving any additional information to visitors. First, we can observe click-through to this link as an immediate response measure to curiosity, thereby capturing the desire to get more product information. Second, we can analyze the nature of questions submitted on this page as a measure of ad-generated elaboration.

The full information ad (AD1 in the control condition and AD2 in all conditions) included additional links to various features of the product, including the curiosity trigger feature that was highlighted in the test ad. We measure click-through on these links as an indication of the extent of information search in response to curiosity. Subjects could browse the magazine as long as they wanted while the computer tracked their click-through pattern, the time spent reading each ad-related link, and the time spent on the entire task.

An on-screen questionnaire was presented at the end of the magazine browsing task to elicit unaided and aided recall of ads and brands featured in the magazines. In addition, subjects were asked to recall thoughts that went through their minds while reading the test ads and specific questions or goals that they may have pursued while processing information in the test ads, as well as to list features and benefits they remembered from the digital camera ads. Specific ratings on product attributes and purchase interest were also collected. Two researchers who were blind to the experimental manipulations coded all open-ended responses, and their codes were tallied for interrater reliability. Coding conflicts were resolved by discussion between the coders.

Description of Variables, Analysis, and Results of Experiment 2

We obtained three kinds of data from Experiment 2. First, we obtained clickstream data (e.g., a record of screens visited and time spent) recorded by the computer. Second, we collected attitude and behavioral intention data. Third, we collected open-ended protocol data. We use a combination of these data in the analysis presented. Because we use click-through rates on test ads as a key dependent variable to measure search, we analyzed overall click-through rates on nontest ad links embedded in the magazine and filler ads to ensure that there were no differences in the overall propensity to click across conditions. The average number of nontest links accessed ($X = 3.21$ out of 6) did not significantly differ across the experimental conditions ($F_{5, 125} = 1.50, p > .19$).

For the purpose of discussion, results are grouped by the hypotheses (H1, H2, and H3) tested in this experiment. In each category, we use variables analyzed by a 3 (knowledge gap) × 2 (curiosity trigger) ANOVA. Comparison of means across the three knowledge gap conditions was conducted using the Student-Newman-Keuls test to adjust for error terms for multiple comparisons. We also tested for the inverted-U prediction (with highest effects in the moderate knowledge gap or cued condition) using a quadratic contrast. As per H1 and H2, we expected to find a higher level of curiosity, information search, elaboration, and learning in the cued condition relative to both the no-cue and the control conditions. We did not predict any differences across the curiosity trigger conditions in terms of the overall levels of search, elaboration, and learning; any differences found in these measures are not particularly interesting from a conceptual perspective and therefore will not be discussed at length. Theoretically, the curiosity trigger manipulation is predicted to affect only the direction of search, elaboration, and learning (H3).

Degree of Curiosity

Several variables were used to measure the level of curiosity and interest generated by exposure to the first advertisement (see Table 8.1 for means). First, we consider retrospective self-rated curiosity motivation to find out

Table 8.1

Effects of Knowledge Gap in Ad Processing and Consequences

Knowledge gap Curiosity condition	Low control ($n = 44$)	Moderate cued ($n = 47$)	High no-cue ($n = 40$)	F (2, 125) (p-value)
Degree of curiosity:				
Curiosity motivation (scale 1–9)	3.36[a]	6.09[a,b]	3.69 [b]	35.19 (.00)
% Visiting FAQ site (FAQ1)	9[a]	53[a,b]	33 [b]	10.63 (.00)
Information search:				
Number of links visited	1.92	2.45	2.05	0.82 (.40)
(NUMLINKS range: 0–6)				
Time on AD1 & AD2	59.89[a]	122.99[a]	99.65	5.41 (.00)
(ADTIME in seconds)				
Extent of elaboration:				
Number of queries on	n.a.	2.31[b]	0.92[b]	10.92 (.00)
FAQ site ($n = 38$)				
Total number of questions	0.88[a]	2.97[a,b]	1.14[b]	27.99 (.00)
Total number of thoughts	1.18	1.89	1.33	3.24 (.04)
Curiosity thoughts	0.11[a]	1.28[a,b]	0.62[b]	17.04 (.00)
Memory and learning:				
% Unaided brand recall	29[a]	80[a,b]	44[b]	14.74 (.00)
% Unaided recall of category	11[a]	48[a,b]	5[b]	16.69 (.00)
(digital camera)				
Total number of benefits/features	2.04[a]	4.16[a,b]	2.52[b]	23.50 (.00)
recalled				
Product evaluation (scale 1–9)				
Product AFFECT	4.68[a]	6.88[a,b]	4.83[b]	43.30 (.00)
Product NOVELTY	5.38[a]	7.26[a,b]	5.83[b]	48.27 (.00)
Product INTEREST	4.98[a]	7.22[a,b]	5.01[b]	26.15 (.00)
Product KNOWLEDGE	3.89[a]	5.64[a,b]	3.97[b]	13.75 (.00)

[a]Difference between control and cued curiosity is significant at $p = 0.05$ level.
[b]Difference between cued and no-cue curiosity is significant at $p = 0.05$ level.

more about the product featured in the advertisement, which is measured as the mean of three scale items (product relevance, interest, and involvement in reading about the product). A 3 × 2 ANOVA for the self-rated curiosity motivation showed a significant main effect of the knowledge gap ($F_{2, 125}$ = 35.19; $p < .001$), with the other effects not approaching significance ($p > .37$). Comparison of means showed that the curiosity motivation was significantly higher in the cued condition ($X = 6.09$) relative to both the no-cue condition ($X = 3.69$) and the control condition ($X = 3.36$) at $p < .05$, but the means in the latter two conditions were not significantly different from each other. A test for the inverted-U prediction in H1 using a quadratic contrast for the three knowledge-gap conditions showed a significant curvilinear effect ($F_{1, 125} = 69.25$; $p < .001$).

A second variable, FAQ1, represents the proportion of subjects that accessed the product home page (i.e., the FAQ page) from AD1. This measures the behavioral response to curiosity by capturing the desire to get more information immediately after exposure to the curiosity manipulation in AD1. ANOVA results for FAQ1 yielded a significant main effect of knowledge gap $(F_{2, 125} = 10.63, p < .01)$, with other effects not being significant $(p > .70)$. A comparison of means indicated that all three conditions were significantly different from one another $(p < .05)$. As Table 8.1 indicates, FAQ1 in the cued condition $(X = 53\%)$ is significantly greater than FAQ1 in the no-cue condition $(X = 33\%)$ and in the control condition $(X = 9\%)$.

Again, the quadratic contrast for testing the curvilinear prediction is significant $(F_{1, 125} = 14.99; p < .001)$. This result is in line with our prediction that subjects in the cued condition, which represents a moderate knowledge gap, would exhibit the greatest degree of curiosity and desire to get more information.

Information Search

We also examined two variables that represented the degree of information search during exposure to the test ads. The variable NUMLINKS captured the breadth of search by tracking the number of different links that were accessed. NUMLINKS could range from zero to six. The level of interest and the extent of attention paid to the accessed information could be captured by the time spent browsing the test ads and embedded links (other than the FAQ link) across the two exposures (ADTIME). The overall ANOVA model did not approach significance for NUMLINKS $(F_{5,125} = 1.10; p > .36)$, though the extent of search was in the predicted direction, with higher scores in the cued curiosity condition relative to the other two conditions (see Table 8.1). As predicted, ADTIME showed a significant main effect of knowledge gap $(F_{2, 125} = 5.41; p < .01)$, with $p > .30$ for other effects, and a significant curvilinear effect in the quadratic contrast, as predicted $(F_{1, 125} = 6.88; p < .01)$. Browsing time was highest in the cued condition $(X = 125$ seconds) but not significantly different from the no-cue condition $(X = 100$ seconds, $p > .05)$. Browsing time was the lowest in the control condition $(X = 60$ seconds; $p < .05$ relative to the other two conditions).

In summary, there was an inverted-U–shaped relationship between the level of information provided in the first advertisement and the degree of interest generated in subsequent processing of the ad. Specifically, a moderate knowledge gap (cued condition) was the most effective in motivating search behavior. Although the average number of links accessed by subjects did not vary dramatically across the knowledge gap conditions, the total time spent on information search and self-reported curiosity motivation were significantly different. This suggests that the primary impact of curiosity might have been on the level of attention paid to the information that was accessed (i.e., quality of search), not merely the quantity of search.

Extent of Elaboration

Two sources of data were used to test for the differences in the extent of elaboration (see Table 8.1 for means). The first set of evidence comes from the open-ended questions that subjects entered on the product home page (FAQ page). These data were available for only those subjects who accessed this homepage link. Because only four subjects in the control condition visited this screen, we confined our analysis to the two curiosity conditions, in which a total of thirty-eight subjects accessed the product home page. The number of questions submitted indicates the degree of elaboration on the test ad. ANOVA results on the number of questions indicated a significant main effect of knowledge gap ($F_{1, 34} = 10.92, p < .002$). The main effect of curiosity trigger and the interaction were not significant ($p > .44$). Subjects in the cued condition submitted an average of 2.31 questions relating to the product, significantly higher than the average of .92 questions in the no-cue condition ($p < .002$).

In the online questionnaire, the second set of evidence, subjects were asked to list any specific goals, questions, or hypotheses they tried to confirm while they read the digital camera ads. A content analysis of this data replicated the previous findings. Subjects in the cued condition listed a significantly higher number of questions or goals ($X = 2.97; p < .05$) than did those in the other two conditions, and this variable conformed to the curvilinear prediction (quadratic contrast $F_{1,125} = 54.86; p < .001$) . The mean number of thoughts listed by subjects was not significantly different across conditions ($p > .05$), though there is a significant effect for the quadratic contrast ($F_{1, 125} = 6.14; p < .01$; see Table 8.1 for means). In a further analysis, these thoughts were coded to capture specific elaboration related to curiosity generation or resolution ("curiosity thoughts"). The highest number of curiosity thoughts were in the cued condition ($X = 1.28$), followed by the no-cue condition ($X = .62$) and the control condition ($X = .11$, all pairwise comparisons $p < .05$, and quadratic contrast $F_{1, 125} = 26.84; p < .001$). As was expected, none of these variables (measuring the degree of curiosity experienced by subjects) was affected by the curiosity trigger manipulation or the interaction ($p > .2$).

We conclude that subjects engaged in a greater degree of elaboration in the cued condition than in the control or no-cue conditions. The pattern of results is very consistent with our reasoning that providing an initial cue with the curiosity manipulation facilitates greater elaboration and leads to richer hypotheses generation about the product.

Product Memory and Learning

Several product-related measures were used to examine the consequences of a curiosity strategy on memory for product details, extent of learning, and evaluation of the product (see Table 8.1). Product memory was assessed using unaided recall of brand name and product category association. After a distraction task that lasted approximately six minutes, subjects were asked to recall brand names and category descriptions of products they saw advertised in the cyber magazine. In this unaided recall task, 53 percent of the subjects mentioned the brand name featured in the test ad for the digital camera. As was predicted, the knowledge gap manipulation had a significant impact on unaided brand recall ($F_{2,\ 125} = 14.74; p < .001$). There was no impact due to the curiosity trigger manipulation ($p > .15$) and no interaction effect ($p > .69$). Unaided brand recall in the cued condition ($X = 80\%$) was significantly greater than that in the no-cue condition ($X = 44\%, p < .001$), as well as in the control condition ($X = 29\%, p < .001$), and conformed to the inverted-U prediction (quadratic contrast $F_{1,\ 125} = 26.81; p < .001$).

Although 53 percent of the subjects remembered the brand name spontaneously, only 22 percent were able to recall the product category correctly as digital camera. An ANOVA of the unaided category recall showed a significant main effect of the knowledge gap manipulation ($F_{2,\ 125} = 16.69; p < .001$) and a significant quadratic contrast ($F_{1,\ 125} = 33.03; p < .001$). As many as 48 percent of the subjects in the cued condition were able to recall the category specifically as digital camera, substantially higher than the levels of 5 percent and 11 percent in the no-cue and control conditions, respectively ($p < .001$). In the control condition, approximately 39 percent specified the category more generally as a camera product, relative to 15 percent in the cued and 23 percent in the no-cue conditions. Paradoxically, the control subjects who saw an AD1 specifying the product as a digital camera were able to recall the product only generally as a camera at the end of the campaign. In contrast, the cued condition subjects who saw an AD1 suggesting that the product was a camera were able to recall the product category more distinctly as a digital camera. The no-cue curiosity subjects who had no initial clue about the product category in AD1 associated the test product with the general category of cameras rather than with digital cameras. We believe that this finding encapsulates the real difference in the quality of processing the ad message between the control and curiosity formats and reflects the outcome of the differences in search, elaboration, and learning shown by the subjects in the different conditions.

The extent of learning about the test product was also assessed by collecting an unaided listing of benefits and features that subjects associated with the brand. We predicted a significant impact of cued curiosity on product learning due to the overall motivation and elaboration provided by the curiosity cue. As was predicted, a significantly higher number of product benefits and features were recalled in the cued condition ($X = 4.16$) than in either the control condition ($X = 2.04$; $p < .01$) or the no-cue condition ($X = 2.52$; $p < .01$), which conforms to the curvilinear prediction (quadratic contrast $F_{1, 125} = 44.30$; $p < .001$).

Product Evaluation

To test for the effect on product evaluation, subjects provided ratings of the test brand on several dimensions that were presented as 1–9 semantic scale items. We grouped these dimensions into four measures relating to affective reactions to the product, perceived newness of the product, purchase interest of the subject, and the subjective feeling of knowledge about the product. Product AFFECT is the mean of five items (overall opinion, liking, ease of use, value, and quality; Cronbach's alpha = .89). Product NOVELTY is the mean of four items (perceived newness, unusual, significance of benefits, and pioneer of a new category; Cronbach's alpha = .7). Product INTEREST comprises three items (interest in knowing product price, interest in checking product at a store, and interest in buying the product; Cronbach's alpha = .84). Product KNOWLEDGE is the mean of two items (extent of product knowledge and extent of confidence in beliefs about the product; correlation = .80).

For these four measures, we find a significant effect of knowledge gap ($p < .001$) with the means being higher in the cued condition relative to the other two conditions (see Table 8.1). The curiosity trigger manipulation had no main effect or an interaction effect with knowledge gap on these product ratings with one exception. Product NOVELTY was significantly affected by curiosity trigger; perceived novelty was higher in the communicate condition ($X = 6.33$) than in the create condition ($X = 5.98$; $p < .04$). All four variables showed a significant effect for the quadratic contrast ($p < .001$), indicating that they support the inverted-U prediction for the knowledge gap effect.

Processing Goals

We predicted that the trigger used to generate curiosity (create or communicate benefit) would serve as the goal around which information processing is centered. Our test ad (AD2) was designed to track benefit-specific processing. Specifically, this ad revealed product identity and provided some basic information about the product. However, additional details that completely resolved the curiosity were available in Web pages linked to AD2, such that there was an information Web page dedicated to each benefit in the test ad (i.e., create and communicate benefits), as well as other links. Subjects could choose to access any of these pages by clicking on the appropriate button in AD2. We expected to see a main effect of the curiosity trigger manipulation on all benefit-specific information processing. For example, we expected that when the create benefit was highlighted, as in the create condition, subjects might be more likely to visit the create information page and recall more details related to the create benefit. However, our interest was in testing whether such benefit-specific processing would be more prevalent when more curiosity is generated about it, such as in the cued condition when the benefit is used as the curiosity trigger rather than in the corresponding no-cue condition, as predicted by the goal orientation of curiosity. Thus, our test of H3 involves finding an interaction effect between knowledge gap and curiosity trigger, with the relevant comparison being between the cued and no-cue conditions.

We examined two sets of data, the click-stream data relating to the access of create and communicate benefit links and the time spent on these links and the coding of open-ended responses to examine benefit-specific content (see Table 8.2 for means). We defined all variables as relative differences between the subject's focus on the create benefit and the communicate benefit. For example, relative number of visits refers to the difference between the number of visits to the create link and the communicate link. Hypothesis 3 predicted that these variables would show a higher difference between the create and communicate curiosity trigger conditions when the cued curiosity ad was used relative to the no-cue ad. As expected, the relative number of visits favored the create link more when the create benefit was used to trigger curiosity, but this was true only in the cued curiosity condition, not in the no-cue condition ($F_{3, 83} = 6.84$; $p < .01$). Similarly, relative time (in seconds) spent on the create information screen (compared with the communicate screen) also showed differences in means in the predicted direction, though this was not significant ($p > .11$).

We also looked at benefit-specific content in the open-ended listing of processing goals or questions that subjects pursued while reading the ads. In this case, we found a significant interaction effect for relative number of questions ($F_{3, 83} = 38.64$; $p < .001$). Specifically, the results reveal that the tendency to focus on create-related questions in the create condition and communicate-related questions in the communicate condition was far greater in the cued condition than in the no-cue condition. We also inves-

Table 8.2

Effects of Knowledge Gap and Curiosity Trigger

Variables[a]	Moderate cued (n = 47)		High no-cue (n = 40)		Interaction $F_{1,83}$ (p-value)
	Create	Communicate	Create	Communicate	
Direction of information search					
Relative number of visits	0.44[b]	−0.03	−0.17[b]	−0.05	6.84 (.01)
Relative time spent	7.89	3.48	4.28	9.00	2.68 (.11)
Direction of elaboration					
Relative number of questions	1.61[b]	−1.62[b]	0.00[b]	−0.09[b]	38.64 (.00)
Direction of learning					
Relative number of recalls	3.11[b]	−2.72[b]	0.06[b]	−0.09[b]	159.17 (.00)

[a]Variables are defined as the difference between the means for create site (or feature) and communicate site (or feature).
[b]Difference between cued and no-cue conditions is significant at $p = 0.05$ level.

tigated whether the benefit used to trigger curiosity had a greater impact on the learning of that benefit when more curiosity was aroused (i.e., in the cued condition relative to the no-cue condition). To do this, the unaided listing of product benefits was coded to obtain the variable, relative number of recalls, or the difference between the number of benefits recalled related to the create and communicate features. Here also, we found support for the predicted interaction between the featured benefits and knowledge gap ($F_{3, 83} = 159.17; p < .001$). A comparison of the difference in means for create-related and communicate-related recalls shows that benefit-specific learning was higher in the cued condition than the no-cue condition (see Table 8.2).

In summary, we find substantial support for the goal directedness of the curiosity trigger when we examine the information acquisition pattern of subjects, retrospective elaboration protocols, and eventual recall of the product features. We find that subjects showed a greater tendency to focus on the featured product benefit in the advertisement when the ad aroused curiosity to a greater extent, as in the cued curiosity condition relative to the no-cue condition. This is consistent with our prediction that curiosity will influence ad processing more effectively if it is linked to a product class cue than if no initial product cues are provided.

General Discussion and Conclusions

Summary of Research

Research reported in this chapter studied the effects of curiosity generation on advertising effectiveness in the context of Internet advertising. Using a data set that included process tracking click-stream variables, traditional attitude and behavioral intention ratings, and open-ended protocols, we showed that ads that present a knowledge gap about a new product influence both the amount and the direction of elaboration and hypothesis generation about the stimulus. We also showed that curiosity resulted in more extensive and goal-directed elaboration, as well as greater learning of product information about the curiosity trigger. Finally, curiosity-based processing of advertising resulted in better product evaluation and greater perceived novelty. We find support for the theoretical framework we propose and conclude that the power of curiosity can be harnessed to enhance consumer motivation and learning.

Implications for Theory and Internet Advertising Strategy

Our work builds on prior research in psychology (Loewenstein 1994) and marketing (Fazio, Herr, and Powell 1992) that showed that curiosity enhances the desire for information and learning. Although this effect has been documented in various contexts (e.g., incomplete photographs, mystery novels, teaser ads), there has been no effort to study systematically the situational determinants and cognitive processes underlying curiosity. Our research suggests that, though curiosity may not dramatically increase the quantity of search (e.g., number of data sources consulted), it might substantially improve the quality of search (time spent and attention devoted to each data source). Curious persons seem to not expend their energies in looking at many sources of data, but may rather focus on more efficient processing and comprehension of data.

Prior researchers have concluded that the primary effect of curiosity is to motivate search and exploratory behavior (Loewenstein 1994). Our results suggest that the effects of curiosity may go beyond the mere search for information. In particular, we find that appropriately cued curiosity also serves to direct the nature of elaboration and may result in more goal-oriented information search.

These two sets of findings enable us to address an important debate in Internet advertising. Specifically, a few Internet marketers pay media bills only on the basis of proven click-through, or those persons who click and get transported to the advertisers' Web site. However, marketers traditionally pay on the basis of the total number of exposures to the banner ad. The latter group might be paying for the many exposures its banners generate without click-through (Briggs and Hollis 1997; Sterne 1997). Our results show that significant increases in advertising effectiveness (e.g., in product recall and evaluation) accrued without proportionately large effects on the click-stream data. Measures of elaboration quality and direction (i.e., thought protocols) account for our results better than do the behavioral data (i.e., click-streams). Thus, our research questions the use of click-streams and click-through rates as the primary measures of advertising effectiveness on the Web.

Our results also suggest implications for the role of the time gap between curiosity generation and resolution. According to our findings, a moderate time gap is optimal for curiosity generation, elaboration, and learning. Too short a time gap between curiosity generation and provision of curiosity-resolving information (e.g., as in our control ad or mystery ads in general) may not provide consumers with the opportunity to elaborate and generate hypothesis. However, if the time gap is too long (e.g., teaser billboards), consumers may not be motivated to elaborate because of the uncertainty of timely curiosity resolution. Our research thus predicts an inverted-U relationship between learning and the time gap.

How should the Internet advertiser use our results in developing an effective campaign? On the basis of the preceding results, we recommend four elements to a successful strategy. First, the campaign should develop curiosity by creating or highlighting a knowledge gap. This can be done in several ways (e.g., presenting surprising or incongruous information, violating expectations, posing questions). In the case of familiar brands, curiosity may be evoked by alluding to a new feature or using elements of the usage situation. Second, the knowledge gap should be created for the feature that represents the unique positioning of the brand and be accompanied by a cue that guides curiosity resolution. This will help focus elaboration and subsequent learning on the unique aspects of the product and thereby aid in the objective of building a unique positioning. Third, consumers should be assured of receiving information that will help them resolve curiosity, but this information should not be provided immediately. Fourth, we encourage advertisers to move beyond click-stream data and use measures of consumer elaboration and learning to test for advertising effectiveness.

Limitations and Future Research

Although we believe the present research has filled an important gap in our knowledge about the psychology of curiosity, our research had some limitations and opened several avenues of research. First, our stimuli used only one technology product. Although this was not a concern from a theoretical standpoint, the pattern of results we obtained might not hold for other types of categories. More generally, it would be useful to replicate the results in other product categories to ascertain their generalizability or determine product features that moderate our findings. Second, there were differences between the experimental environment and a real Internet environment. Most notably, our stimulus used full-screen ads, whereas most Internet advertising is smaller in size and therefore must compete more for attention. Although these differences pose no threats to the validity of our results, the sizes of the effects we obtain are likely to be tempered in a real Internet environment.

In addition, three potential moderators of the effectiveness of curiosity deserve further investigation. First, the effects of time separation between curiosity generation and resolution merit research. Second, it would be instructive to understand whether the novelty of the underlying product influences the effect. In contrast to our experimental results, Loewenstein (1994) argues that the resolution of curiosity often brings a sense of disappointment or anticlimax, but we predict that this occurs only when the curiosity-resolving information is mundane. Third, future research should explore the effects of expertise. Intuition suggests that moderately expert consumers would be the most likely to respond to curiosity strategies, with highly expert consumers already knowing too much and novice consumers not knowing enough to organize their information search and elaboration.

References

Aaker, David, Rajeev Batra, and John G. Myers (1992), *Advertising Management*, London: Prentice Hall International.

Agarwal, Ritu and Elena Karahanna (2000), "Time Flies When You're Having Fun: Cognitive Absorption and Beliefs About Information Technology Usage," *MIS Quarterly*, 24 (December), 665–694.

Alba, Joseph, John Lynch, Barton Weitz, Chris Janiszewski, Richard Lutz, Alan Sawyer, and Stacy Wood (1997), "Interactive Home Shopping: Incentives for Consumers, Retailers, and Manufacturers to Participate in Electronic Marketplaces," *Journal of Marketing*, 61 (July), 38–53.

Ariely, Dan (2000), "Controlling the Information Flow: Effects on Consumers' Decision Making and Preferences," *Journal of Consumer Research*, 27 (September), 233–248.

Berlyne, Daniel (1954), "An Experimental Study of Human Curiosity, " *British Journal of Psychology*, 45 (1), 256–265.

——— (1960), *Conflict, Arousal and Curiosity*, New York: McGraw-Hill.

Bransford, John D. and Marcia K. Johnson (1972), "Contextual Pre-requisites for Understanding: Some Investigations of Comprehension and Recall," *Journal of Verbal Learning and Verbal Behavior*, 11 (6), 717–726.

Briggs, Rex and Nigel Hollis (1997), "Advertising on the Web: Is There Response Before Click-Through?" *Journal of Advertising Research*, 37 (2), 33–45.

Carpenter, Gregory S. and Kent Nakamoto (1989), "Consumer Preference Formation and Pioneering Advantage," *Journal of Marketing Research*, 26 (August), 285–298.

Csikszentmihalyi, Mihaly (1990), *Flow: The Psychology of Optimal Experience*, New York: Harper and Row.

Deighton, John (1996), "The Future of Interactive Marketing," *Harvard Business Review*, 74 (6), 51–162.

Enrico, Dottie (1995), "Teaser Ads Grab Spotlight on Madison Ave.," *USA Today* (July 6), 01B.

Fazio, R.H., M. Herr, and M. C. Powell (1992), "On the Development and Strength of Category-Brand Associations in Memory: The Case of Mystery Ads," *Journal of Consumer Psychology*, 1 (1), 1–13.

Frankel, Rob (2000), *The Revenge of Brand X: How to Build a Big Time Brand—on the Web or Anywhere Else*, United States: Frankel & Anderson, Inc.

Fusco, Carl (1994), "New Product Introduction: Challenges in Researching Customer Acceptance," in *And Now for Something Completely Different: "Really" New Products*, Conference Summary, Marjorie Adams and Joseph LaCugna, eds., Marketing Science Institute Report No. 94–124 (December), 29–31.

Ghani, Jawaid A. and Satish P. Deshpande (1994), "Task Characteristics and the Experience of Optimal Flow in Human-Computer Interaction," *Journal of Psychology*, 128 (4), 381–91.

Hanson, Ward (2000), *Principles of Internet Marketing*, Cincinnati, OH: South-Western College Publishing.

Hebb, D.O. (1949), *The Organization of Behavior*, New York: Wiley.

Hoffman, Donna L. and Thomas P. Novak (1996), "Marketing in Hypermedia Computer-Mediated Environments: Conceptual Foundations," *Journal of Marketing*, 60 (July), 50–68.

Huffman, Cynthia and Michael J. Houston (1993), "Goal-Oriented Experiences and the Development of Knowledge," *Journal of Consumer Research*, 20 (September), 190–207.

Hunt, James M. (1963), "Motivation Inherent in Information Processing and Action," in *Motivation and Social Interaction*, O.J. Harvey, ed., New York: Ronald Press, 35–94.

Kirsner, Scott (1997), "Jack's Hearing a Word from Sponsors: Sold," *Wired News*, (September 29), [www.wired.com/news/news/business/story/7223.html].

Klayman, Joshua and Young-Wong Ha (1987), "Confirmation, Disconfirmation and Information in Hypothesis Testing," *Psychological Review*, 94 (2), 221–228.

Lehmann, Donald (1994), "Characteristics of 'Really' New Products," in *And Now for Something Completely Different: "Really" New Products*, Conference Summary, Marjorie Adams and Joseph LaCugna, eds., Marketing Science Institute Report Number 94–124, (December), 1.

Loewenstein, George (1994), "The Psychology of Curiosity: A Review and Reinterpretation," in *Psychological Bulletin*, 116 (1), 75–98.

Maddox, Kate (2001), "Outlook Brightens for Web Ads," *B to B*, 86 (15), 10.

Maynard, Roberta (1995), "Setting Your Product Apart from the Others," *Nation's Business*, 83 (11), 10.

McKillen, Dan (2001), "Online Branding—Beyond the Clicks," *Medical Marketing and Media*, 36 (8), 12–14.

Mitchell, Andrew and David Olson (1981), "Are Product Attribute Beliefs the Only

Mediator of Advertising Effects on Brand Attitude?" *Journal of Marketing Research*, 18 (3), 318–332.

O'Brien, Edward J. and Jerome L. Myers (1985), "When Comprehension Difficulty Improves Memory for Text," *Journal of Experimental Psychology: Learning, Memory and Cognition*, 11 (1), 12–21.

O'Brien, Jeffrey (1998), "Web Advertising and the Branding Mission," *Upside*, 10 (September), 90–94.

Olson, David (1983), "New Product Advertising: Guideline for Improvement," *Journal of Consumer Marketing*, 1 (1), 28–35.

Ries, Al and Laura Ries (2000), *The 11 Immutable Laws of Internet Branding*, New York: HarperBusiness.

Sterne, Jim (1997), *What Makes People Click? Advertising on the Web*, Indianapolis: Que Corporation.

Urban, Glen L., Bruce D. Weinberg, and John R. Hauser (1996), "Premarket Forecasting of Really-New Products," *Journal of Marketing*, 60 (January), 47–60.

Wyer, Robert S., Thomas K. Srull, Sallie E. Gordon, and Jon Hartwick (1982), "Effects of Processing Objectives on the Recall of Prose Material," *Journal of Personality and Social Psychology*, 43 (4), 674–688.

Part III

Banners, Pop-Ups, and Online Sponsorship

9

Banner Advertisement Pricing, Measurement, and Pretesting Practices

Perspectives from Interactive Agencies

Fuyuan Shen

Introduction

Within a short span of six years, the Internet has evolved into an important medium for advertisers and marketers for both branding and direct-selling purposes. As a central part of the fast-expanding digital economy, the Internet has attracted an enormous amount of advertising revenues. According to an industry report, Internet advertising revenue reached $4.62 billion in 1999 (Internet Advertising Bureau 1999). Although this is a small portion of overall advertising spending (estimated to be over $200 billion in 1999), total spending on the Internet has now exceeded that of outdoor advertising. Some predict that, by 2003, Internet advertising spending in the United States could grow to more than $13 billion (Internet Advertising Bureau 1999; Krishnamurthy 2000). Driving this rapid growth is the fact that the Internet has been drawing sizable audiences from other media. The number of Americans using the Internet has grown exponentially in the past few years, from fewer than 5 million in 1993 to as many as 110 million in 1999 (Department of Commerce 1999).

Technological innovations also have made the Internet an attractive medium for advertisers. Today, server-based technologies enable advertisers to display banner ads according to user profiles and interests and in ways that were not possible before. As an advertising medium, the Internet offers all the elements of other media and much more. Banner ads can now include not only graphics and text, but also streaming audio and video. Java and Shockwave technologies can be used to deliver highly dynamic and interactive banner ads. Such interactive and personalization technologies have made the Internet an effective and accountable medium with unlimited creativity.

Despite the Internet's phenomenal growth, measurement and pricing practices on the Web are far from being standardized. Most advertisers recognize that, for the Internet to become a fully viable advertising medium, there must be uniform measures so that they can make apple-to-apple comparisons with other media in campaign planning and evaluations (Coffey 2001; McFarland 1998). Because the Internet enables advertisers to track responses to online ads, some reason that advertisers should pay for their Internet ads on the basis of responses or performances (Ephron 1997; Parsons 1997). Others argue that such pricing and measurement methods would dismiss banner advertising's brand-building value and force Web publishers to assume accountability for the creativity and effectiveness of messages, because the role of the media has traditionally been to offer access to an audience, not to share in the responsibility for the quality of the advertisement itself (Parsons 1997; Zeff and Aronson 1999).

But how do agencies handle Internet banner advertising pricing and measurement now? And what do they perceive as challenges facing banner advertising measurement? How and to what extent do they pretest banner ads? Although many of the current discussions have focused on the merits and demerits of metrics and measures, there has been no research on what interactive advertising agencies are using to buy, measure, and pretest online ads. To fill this void and obtain some preliminary insights into these issues, this study reports findings from a national sample of interactive advertising agencies. These findings may provide advertising professionals with a better understanding of the current practices of interactive agencies and help facilitate the ongoing discussions of measurement standardization.

Background Review

One of the principal elements that drives advertising in all media is ratings. Each medium, be it print, television, radio, or the Internet, may use different names, but the concept is the same. Ratings point to the percentage of people that have the opportunity to be exposed to the advertising messages. As advertising on the Web has exploded in recent years, the need for accurate information and tracking of site traffic, advertisement delivery, and user response has grown increasingly important for both Web publishers and advertisers (Krishnamurthy 2000). Publishers need a simple way to understand and communicate the results of ad delivery on their sites. Advertisers and media buyers need reliable and standardized reports to plan their buys (Zeff and Aronson 1999).

A set of universal measures will make advertising on the Web easier and more efficient for both advertisers and publishers. Today, the Internet measurement—from terminology to technology—is still being developed and perfected. Part of the difficulty of developing universally acceptable standards is that the Web is a highly fragmented medium, with millions of sites and Web pages that accept advertising. Complicating this difficulty is the existence of myriad ways of advertising, from banner ads, text links, and sponsorships to affiliate programs. The lack of standardized measures has prompted online publishers and interactive advertising networks to come up with many homegrown measures. Unlike television, for which Nielsen dominates the program ratings, the Internet has many players and proprietary measurement programs. The lack of standards in measurement extends from terminology to pricing models (Novak and Hoffman 1996; Zeff and Aronson 1999).

In an effort to provide standardized guides, leading Web publishers formed the Internet Advertising Bureau (IAB) in 1994. Two years later, the IAB issued guidelines on banner ad sizes. Today, virtually all the banner ads on the Internet use one of the eight sizes recommended in the IAB guidelines. However, Internet advertising measurement and pricing standardization has not been as successful. In 1997, the Coalition for Advertising Supported Information and Entertainment (CASIE) and Future of Advertising Stakeholders (FAST) both published voluntary guidelines for the measurement of online advertising, including standard definitions of metrics (see CASIE 1997; FAST 2000). Their hope was that agencies and publishers would gradually adopt these measurement guidelines as the medium matures.

Internet Measurement and Pricing Models

In the past, researchers have identified several Web pricing and measurement models (see Ephron 1997; Hoffman and Novak 2000). This study considers three banner ad pricing and measurement models on the basis of how the user interacts with ads: (1) the exposure-based model assumes that advertisers pay for impressions or opportunities to see, much like they pay for ads on television and in other media; (2) the interaction-based model assumes that advertisers pay each time a user interacts with or clicks the ad; and (3) the outcome-based model assumes that advertisers pay for performances, such as inquiries and purchases.

The exposure-based pricing method includes flat fee and cost per thousand (CPM). Flat-fee pricing, the earliest form of Web pricing, consists of a fixed price for a given period of time. Alternatively, CPM is popular because it is a traditional media term that is readily comparable to other media. Several studies have reported, for example, that the average CPM of banner ads ranged from $20 to $40, substantially higher than that of television and magazine ads (Hoffman and Novak 2000; Meeker 1997; Zeff and Aronson 1999). Although it enables advertisers to make easier cross-media comparisons, CPM is nevertheless considered less accurate and less accountable than other measures (Ephron 1997).

The interaction-based model includes clicks or click-throughs, which are often considered more accountable ways of charging for Web advertising. A pricing model based on clicks guarantees not only exposure, but also interaction with the banner. The major problem is that only a small percentage of online visitors actually click on banner ads (Sweeney 2000; Zeff and Aronson 1999).

The ultimate goal of advertising is the outcome. For most banner ads, the outcome could be lead generation, online inquiry, registration, order, or purchase. Payment based on outcomes is considered more accurate than mere exposures or banner clicks, but not all banner ads are designed to generate immediate behavioral changes. Using outcomes alone disregards the branding objective of advertising and, at the same time, forces Web publishers to rely on the quality of the advertisers' creatives to generate revenues. Traditionally, publishers and broadcasters have been loath to take on such risk-sharing pricing practices (Parsons 1997). Therefore, it is unclear how agencies and online publishers will accept performance-based models for compensation purposes. Part of the objective of this chapter is to find out how frequently interactive advertising agencies use any of the three models to price and measure banner ads.

Measurement Problems

As a new medium, the Internet has its share of problems in measurement. One of the current problems is the lack of standardization, as has been recognized by several authors (see Dreze and Zufryden 1998; Ephron 1997; Krishnamurthy 2000; Novak and Hoffman 1996; Zeff and Aronson 1999). Despite the voluntary guidelines developed by industry groups, disagreements abound. For example, just the term "impression" can be measured and interpreted in different ways. Some count an impression as each time a page is loaded, whereas others count it as each time an ad is loaded. Compounding this problem is the lack of third-party auditing of Web site traffic. Traditionally, media such as newspapers and magazines can be audited to verify publications' circulation and readership (Ames, Lindberg, and Razaki 1999; Krishnamurthy 2000).

Caching and proxy servers are two other problems that researchers have identified as major hurdles for Internet measurement (Krishnamurthy 2000; Zeff and Aronson 1999). Caching, when used in relation to Web pages and ads, refers to the process of storing Web pages on a hard disk or server to speed downloading. Although it eliminates the need to download the same pages each time they are requested, caching can prevent publishers from receiving an accurate count of the Web traffic or ad impressions. Although companies such as MatchLogic have come up with software solutions to the problems of caching, for most advertisers it remains an issue. Proxy servers act as gateways from inside firewalls to the outside world. When proxy servers download Web pages, a publisher's log file may identify only one user with one Internet protocol (IP) address (or the proxy server) when hundreds of computers within a company or organization could have requested information from the site.

A cookie refers to a text file on the user's hard drive that can be written to and from which information can be retrieved. In most cases, cookies are considered useful for marketers to identify visitors to a Web site. Some use cookies to engage in intelligent targeting, matching ads with prior behaviors gathered from cookie files. Beyond the clear benefits, cookies can have potential problems. In most situations, a cookie can only identify computers rather than users. If several people use a computer, any cookies placed on it can lead to distorted profiles of the users. Part of the purpose of this study is to find out what agencies perceive as the major problems facing Internet advertising measurement and pricing. Identifying and addressing these problems could be the key to wide and fast adoption of standardized measures.

Pretesting Banner Advertisements

Pretesting advertisements, or copy testing, is a common practice in advertising. Although the Internet has been considered an ideal and efficient medium to pretest advertisements, there is little information about how interactive agencies conduct pretesting. The history of pretesting can be traced back to the turn of the twentieth century, when recall and memory were measured to test the effectiveness of print advertisements. Today, television commercials are often pretested. For example, King, Pehrson, and Reid (1993) find that more than 80 percent of surveyed agencies pretested television commercials. However, no parallel research exists for Internet advertising. This study therefore seeks to determine the extent to which agencies pretest banner ads using Internet measures, such as click-throughs, outcomes/actions, banner exposures, and ad-viewing duration, as well as conventional measures, such as brand attitude, ad memory, brand awareness, and purchase intention. These conventional measures have been used in the past by agencies to pretest ads for traditional media such as print and television (see Boyd and Ray 1971; King, Pehrson, and Reid 1993).

Research Questions

As previously stated, the overall purpose of this study is to investigate what interactive agencies are currently using to price, measure, and pretest banner ads. There is little available research to support the framing of any hypotheses. Therefore, this study was designed to address the following research questions: (1) What methods and measures are used most frequently by interactive agencies to price banner advertisements? (2) What methods and measures are used most frequently by interactive agencies to gauge the effectiveness of banner advertisements? (3) What do agencies perceive as major problems facing banner advertisement measurement? (4) How often do agencies pretest banner ads? What measures do they use to pretest them?

Methodology

Questionnaire

The questionnaire was organized around four major sections that correspond to the study's research questions. A majority of the questions were derived and developed from previous research and relevant literature (Hoffman and Novak 2000; Jobber and Kilbride 1986; King, Pehrson, and Reid 1993; Uyenco and Katz 1996; Zeff and Aronson 1999). The first section contained questions regarding the frequency with which agencies used five different pricing methods (Hoffman and Novak 2000; Zeff and Aronson 1999). An open-ended question was added to allow respondents to describe any additional pricing methods they may have been using.

The next section of the questionnaire included nine questions about how frequently agencies used different measures to gauge the effectiveness of banner ads (Jobber and Kilbride 1986; Zeff and Aronson 1999). The third section asked respondents to indicate what they saw as the major problems facing banner ad measurement (Krishnamurthy 2000; Zeff and Aronson 1999). In the final section, respondents were asked how often they pretested banner ads and what measures they used in pretesting (Jobber and Kilbride 1986; King, Pehrson, and Reid 1993). The questionnaire also included a series of questions about the nature and size of the agencies and respondents' positions at the agencies.

Sample and Procedure

The mail survey was sent to the top 164 interactive agencies in the United States. The agency sample was drawn from lists of top interactive agencies compiled by two leading industry publications, *Adweek* and *Advertising Age*. In addition, names and addresses of media directors of interactive advertising agencies were searched from *Adweek*'s online agency directory. After overlapping addresses and titles were merged, a total of 164 agencies was obtained for the survey sample. When the names and titles were not available, the correspondence was addressed to the "Media Director."

Each questionnaire was accompanied by a cover letter and a postage-paid return envelope. Four weeks after the initial mailing of the survey, a second questionnaire was mailed to the nonrespondents. All questionnaires analyzed for this study were received before the end of February 2000, four weeks after mailing the final questionnaires. A total of fifty-one completed and usable questionnaires was returned. This resulted in an overall response rate of 31.1 percent.

Findings

Of the agencies that responded to the survey, thirty were full-service interactive agencies, six were ad networks, fourteen were interactive divisions of traditional full-service advertising agencies, and one was an interactive creative shop (see Table 9.1). Although the sample size and response rate were relatively small, it appears that respondents represented a diverse sample of agencies involved in interactive advertising. Approximately half the agencies had more than 100 employees, which is a good size for an interactive advertising agency. Approximately 55 percent of the respondents were media directors, and the remainder of the respondents held positions of various responsibilities in their respective agencies.

The first section of the questionnaire asked agencies how often they had been using different banner pricing methods. Results showed that more than 90 percent of the respondents always or frequently used CPM in pricing (see Table 9.2). The other frequently used pricing method was click-throughs. Approximately 33.4 percent always or frequently used click-throughs. As Table 9.2 further indicates, flat fees, unique visitor information, and cost per action were less frequently used. A ranking of the pricing methods based on respondents' mean scores shows that CPM (Mean = 3.94) was the favorite pricing method used (see Table 9.2). Click-through (Mean= 3.06) was the second most frequently used measure, whereas cost per action and unique visitor were the least frequently used methods.

Table 9.1

Respondent Profiles

	Frequency	Percentage
Types of agencies		
Full-service interactive agency	30	58.8
Advertising network	6	11.8
Interactive creative shop	1	2.0
Interactive service of traditional full-service agency	14	27.5
	$N = 51$	
Number of employees		
Less than 50	13	25.5
51–100	12	23.5
101–200	18	35.3
201 and over	8	15.7
	$N = 51$	
Job position		
Vice president-media/media director	28	54.9
President/partner	4	7.8
Senior media planner/specialist	11	21.6
Marketing director	4	7.8
Other	4	7.8
	$N = 51$	

Table 9.2

Frequency of Pricing Methods ($N = 51$)

Pricing methods	Frequently/always (%)	Sometimes (%)	Seldom/never (%)	Means[a]
Cost per thousand	90.2	7.8	2.0	3.94
Click-through	33.4	45.1	21.5	3.06
Flat fee	19.6	21.6	58.8	2.45
Unique visitor	13.8	29.4	56.9	2.22
Cost per action/outcome	5.9	49.0	45.1	2.45

[a]Means are on a five-point scale, with "Never" = 1 and "Always" = 5.

To summarize, the survey reveals that CPM is the favorite pricing method for banner advertisement buying and selling. Click-through remains a distant second pricing method despite the Internet's unique ability to track reactions to banner ads.

The second section of the questionnaire asked agencies how often they used various measures to gauge the effectiveness of banner advertising. It is clear from Table 9.3 that an overwhelming majority of the agencies (86.3%) indicated that they always or frequently used click-throughs. Approximately

Table 9.3

Frequency of Measures to Gauge the Effectiveness of Banner Ads (*N* = 51)

Pricing methods	Frequently/ always (%)	Sometimes (%)	Seldom/never (%)	Means[a]
Banner ad click-through	86.3	9.8	3.9	4.17
Outcomes/action	72.6	17.6	9.8	3.82
Banner ad exposure	53.0	19.6	27.4	3.39
Brand awareness	35.3	33.3	31.4	2.88
Ad awareness	35.3	23.5	41.2	2.76
Brand attitude change	25.5	29.4	45.1	2.61
Memory of ad message	25.5	23.5	51.0	2.51
Purchase intention	21.6	37.2	41.2	2.61
Banner ad duration time	15.6	25.5	58.8	2.18

[a]Means are on a five-point scale with "Never" = 1 and "Always" = 5.

10 percent used it sometimes, and only a few agencies (3.9%) seldom or never used it. The next most often used measure was outcomes such as inquiries or purchases of products. More than 72 percent of the respondents indicated they used this method frequently. Banner ad exposure is the third most often used method, with 53 percent using it frequently. It is worth noting that approximately 27 percent of the agencies seldom or never used exposure to measure banner ad effectiveness.

The other measures—brand awareness, ad awareness, brand attitude, memory, and purchase intention—were less popular, used by only 35 percent or fewer of the agencies surveyed. The least used measure was banner ad viewing duration, with a mere 15.6 percent using it frequently. Table 9.3 also presents the ranking of these measures. It shows that click-through (Mean = 4.17) was the most popular measure, and outcomes/action (Mean = 3.82) was the second most popular measure.

It therefore appears that an overwhelming majority of agencies considered click-throughs and actions as the best benchmarks of banner ad effectiveness. This makes intuitive sense, because the Internet offers the unique ability to track the behaviors of visitors. However, this conflicts with the results from the previous section, which showed that click-throughs and actions were used less often than CPM in pricing. Clearly, a disparity exists in what agencies pay for and what they consider good measures of advertising effectiveness on the Internet.

The next section of the questionnaire asked respondents, "In your opinion, what are the major problems currently facing banner ad measurement?" Re-

Table 9.4

Perceived Problems Facing Banner Ad Measurement ($N = 51$)

Problems	Frequency	Percentage
Lack of measurement standards	31	60.8
Lack of independent auditing of sites	23	45.1
Cache/caching	22	43.1
Proxy servers	21	41.2
Cookies	6	11.8
Cost of services and analysis time	1	1.9

spondents were given five potential major problems or issues that many in the industry have discussed (Ott 1999; Uyenco and Katz 1996; Zeff and Aronson 1999). Approximately 60 percent of the agencies revealed that lack of standards in measuring banner ads was a major problem (see Table 9.4). This finding is consistent with industry reports from both agencies and advertisers (Mottl 1999; Krishnamurthy 2000). Approximately 45 percent of the agencies considered the lack of independent auditing as the next major concern.

Forty-three percent of the respondents indicated cache/caching, and 41 percent indicated proxy servers as other measurement problems. However, only 11 percent indicated that cookies were a problem. This is because, in most cases, a cookie serves as a unique identification for a computer user, and many see it as a useful tool for targeting and profiling rather than as a potential problem. In response to the open-ended question, one agency indicated that the cost of measurement services and the time for analysis were also measurement problems.

In short, despite efforts by various industry groups to provide voluntary measurement and pricing guidelines, many still see the lack of standards as the major problem. Caching, proxy servers, and a lack of site traffic auditing were the next three major problems according to the respondents. The challenge for the industry in the near future is to continue to explore the development of viable measurement and auditing standards. At the same time, technology-based solutions to proxy servers and caching will have an impact and ease some concerns in the future.

Banner ad pretesting was not widely used among the surveyed agencies. Although more than half of the agencies indicated that they pretested banner ads at least occasionally, only about one-third (37%) always or frequently pretested ads (see Table 9.5). Nearly 45 percent of the agencies never or seldom pretested banner ads. Overall, compared with television advertising, the frequency of pretesting banner ads is relatively low. Prior research, for example, found that 82 percent of the surveyed advertising agencies pre-

Table 9.5

How Often Agencies Pretest Banner Ads ($N = 51$)

	Frequency	Percentage
Always	8	15.7
Frequently	11	21.6
Sometimes	9	17.6
Seldom	15	29.4
Never	8	15.7

Table 9.6

Measures Used to Pretest Internet Banner Ads ($N = 51$)

Pretest measures	Frequency	Percentage
Banner ad click-through	33	64.7
Outcomes or action	23	45.1
Banner ad exposure	11	21.6
Memory of ad message	11	21.6
Brand awareness	9	17.6
Brand attitude change	7	13.7
Ad awareness	7	13.7
Purchase intention	6	11.8
Banner ad duration time	5	9.8

tested television commercials (King, Pehrson, and Reid 1993). This difference can be attributed to the fact that the Internet is still a relatively young medium, and advertising spending on the Internet is still a fraction of that for television. As the Web matures and grows, it will be interesting to see whether pretesting advertisements on the Web becomes more common.

Those that pretested banner ads at least occasionally were asked to indicate what measures they had used in pretesting. Results indicated that approximately 64 percent used click-throughs and 45 percent used outcomes/actions in pretesting (see Table 9.6). Approximately 21 percent of the respondents used exposure and memory to pretest banner ads. Less than 18 percent of the agencies used awareness, purchase intention, attitudes, or ad duration as pretest measures. Traditionally, behavioral measures such as product choices and purchases have been considered highly valuable (Boyd and Ray 1971), but they were rarely used in pretesting (King, Pehrson, and Reid 1993). The Internet offers the technical ability for advertisers to track immediate responses to their ads, which could be the reason interaction and performance-based measures were more popular in pretesting banner ads than were traditional communication measures.

Summary and Conclusions

The results of this survey have provided some initial insights on how agencies price, measure, and pretest Internet banner ads, as well as what they perceive as the problems in measurement. Although the findings are preliminary, they nevertheless raise several major points that deserve the attention of both professionals and academics.

- An overwhelming number of the agencies surveyed frequently use CPM to price banner advertisements. Approximately one-third of the agencies use click-throughs. Cost per outcome/action is the least used pricing method. This shows that, despite the technical ability of the Internet to track more precise user responses and actions, CPM remains a favorite pricing method.
- When using measures to gauge advertising effectiveness, most agencies indicate using click-throughs and outcomes/actions rather than exposures or impressions. This indicates that, when it is feasible, interaction and performance-based benchmarks are favored as measures of advertising effectiveness.
- Despite industry efforts to provide voluntary measurement metrics and guidelines, many agencies still consider the lack of standardization and auditing as major problems facing Internet banner advertising.
- Generally speaking, pretesting banner ads is not common practice among interactive agencies. For those using pretests, the measures commonly used are click-throughs and outcomes. Traditional measures such as awareness, attitude, and memory are less popular.

The most intriguing finding of the study is that impression- or exposure-based pricing models are more widely used in pricing banner advertising than are interaction- and performance-based models. However, advertisers often pay high CPMs for banner advertising on the premise that it offers a higher degree of accountability than does traditional advertising (Hoffman and Novak 2000; Zeff and Aronson 1999). Several reasons could explain this contradiction. First, a lack of uniform measurement and auditing standards could hamper agencies from using performance measures. Second, publishers might resist the use of performance measures because exposures are more readily comparable to television and print media's buying and selling practices. Moreover, the responsibility of publishers has been delivering the opportunity to see. Charging by exposures may be more in alignment with traditional media buying practices (Zeff and Aronson 1999).

The findings indicate that interaction and performance metrics are favored by agencies in measuring and pretesting advertising. This is most likely due to the metrics' ability to assess the impact of advertising spending in a more precise and efficient manner. The need for accountability is especially important for clients and agencies that pay relatively higher CPMs to employ banner ads in promotional and direct response campaigns. However, for ads that are designed for branding purposes, CPM will likely remain the primary unit for media buying and planning. Compared with traditional media, such as television, the Internet is unique in that it enables advertisers to use banner ads to pursue different marketing objectives within the same medium. It also has the technology to track consumers' various responses. To maximize the economics for both advertisers and Web publishers, the advertising industry clearly needs a multitiered pricing structure that incorporates interaction, performance, and exposure measures. A system that ties multiple pricing mechanisms to marketing objectives could propel the Internet to realize its full potential as a truly unique and more attractive advertising medium.

It should be noted that this study describes what agencies have been using to price, measure, and pretest banner ads rather than nonbanner promotional techniques, such as affiliate programs, referrals, or classifieds. Therefore, the reported findings do not necessarily apply to many nonbanner techniques that are more likely to use performance-based pricing measures. Industry reports indicate that the use of nonbanner advertising has been gaining increasing popularity in recent years (Hyland 2001; Sweeney 2000). In light of that, future research should study the changes in pricing and measurement practices regarding both banner and nonbanner advertising. For example, as the use of nonbanner advertising grows, it will be important to determine whether performance-based measures, such as cost per action or per lead, will take over exposure-based impressions and become the predominant pricing model in the future. In addition, this study does not directly address why certain measures are favored by agencies. More research is needed to identify factors influencing such practices. Finally, researchers should explore the extent to which the views and perceptions of the interactive agencies are shared by advertisers and online publishers. Future research efforts in these directions can be key steps toward narrowing the differences among the major players and helping develop optimal Internet advertising pricing and measurement mechanisms.

References

Ames, Gary Adna, Deborah L. Lindberg, and Khalid A. Razaki (1999), "Web Advertising Exposures," *Internal Auditor*, 56 (5), 51–54.

Boyd, Harper W. and Michael L. Ray (1971), "What Big Agency Men in Europe

Think of Copy Testing Methods," *Journal of Marketing Research*, 8, 218–133.

CASIE (1997), *Glossary of Internet Advertising Terms and Interactive Media Measurement Guidelines*, New York: Association of National Advertisers.

Coffey, Steve (2001), "Internet Audience Measurement: A Practitioner's View," *Journal of Interactive Advertising*, 1 (2), [www.jiad.org/].

Department of Commerce (1999), *The Emerging Digital Economy*, Washington, DC.

Dreze, Xavier and Fred Zufryden (1998), "Is Internet Advertising Ready for Prime Time," *Journal of Advertising Research*, 38 (3), 7–18.

Ephron, Erwin (1997), "Or Is It an Elephant? Stretching Our Minds for a New Web Pricing Model," *Journal of Advertising Research*, 37 (2), 96–98.

FAST (2000), "Principles of Online Media Audience Measurement," [www.fastinfo.org/measurement].

Hoffman, Donna L. and Thomas P. Novak (2000), "Advertising Pricing Models for the World Web," in *Internet Publishing and Beyond*, D. Hurley, B. Kahin, and H. Varian, eds. Cambridge, MA: MIT Press, 45–61.

Hyland, Tom (2001), "Web Advertising a Year of Growth," [www.iab.net/].

Internet Advertising Bureau (1999), "Metrics and Methodology," [www.iab.net/].

Jobber, David and Anthony Kilbride (1986), "How Major Agencies Evaluate TV Advertising in Britain," *International Journal of Advertising*, 5, 187–195.

King, Karen W., John D. Pehrson, and Leonard N. Reid (1993), "Pretesting TV Commercials: Methods, Measures and Changing Agency Roles," *Journal of Advertising*, 22 (3), 86–98.

Krishnamurthy, Sandeep (2000), "Deciphering the Internet Advertising Puzzle," *Marketing Management*, 9 (3), 34–40.

McFarland, Doug (1998), "Web Measurement Needs Standards, But Whose?" *Advertising Age*, (May 11), 48.

Meeker, Mary (1997), *The Internet Advertising Report*, New York: HarperCollins.

Mottl, Judith (1999), "The Trouble with Online Ads," *Information Week* (October 11), 90–93.

Novak, Thomas P. and Donna L. Hoffman (1996), "New Metrics for New Media: Toward the Development of Web Measurement Standards," [www.2000.0gsm.vanderbilt.edu/].

Ott, Karalynn (1999), "Seeking Ad Measurement Standards: Internet Ad Community Trying to Agree on Terms for Comparison," *Advertising Age's Business Marketing*, 84 (September), 24–25.

Parsons, Andrew J. (1997), "The Impact of Internet Advertising: New Medium or New Marketing Paradigm?" in *Understanding the Medium and Its Measurement: ARF Interactive Media Research Summit III*, New York: Advertising Research Foundation, 5–16.

Sweeney, Terry (2000), "Web Advertising: Money to Burn—Click-Through Rates on Online Ads Are Declining, But True Believers Say There's No Place Like the Web to Build the Brand," *Internet Week* (October), 57–58.

Uyenco, Beth and Helen Katz (1996), "Mastering the Web: What We Have Learned so Far?" in *Bringing Clarity to New Media: ARF Interactive Media Research Summit II* , New York: Advertising Research Foundation, 138–169.

Zeff, Robbin and Brad Aronson (1999), *Advertising on the Internet*, New York: Wiley.

10

Forced Exposure and Psychological Reactance

Antecedents and Consequences of the Perceived Intrusiveness of Pop-Up Ads

Steven M. Edwards, Hairong Li, and Joo-Hyun Lee

The idea that for every action there is an equal and opposite reaction has been termed reactance in psychology literature. Reactance theory is a social psychological theory that explains human behavior in response to the perceived loss of freedom in an environment (Brehm 1966). Reactance is postulated to be experienced in response to the environment and used to help persons reestablish freedom and control of a situation. When there is a threat to a person's freedom, that person will attempt to restore the freedom by exhibiting opposition or resisting pressures to conform (Brehm and Brehm 1981). Similarly, consumers have been shown to interpret commercial messages actively and react against threats of persuasion to further their own goals. This chapter explores Web surfers' reactions when they are forced to view advertising. Reactance may be especially important in light of new advertising delivery techniques developed for the Internet, such as pop-up ads.

The purpose of this research is twofold: First, we investigate what characteristics of pop-up ads are perceived as intrusive. Specifically, the study investigates four aspects of ads themselves that may moderate perceptions of pop-up advertisements as intrusive: timing of the display, duration of the ad, congruence with editorial content, and perceived informational and entertainment value. Second, we hope to understand better the relationship between the antecedents and consequences of ads being perceived as intrusive by examining reactions such as irritation and ad avoidance. We believe that, if the point at which advertising becomes intrusive can be identified, strategies for reducing irritation and the avoidance of advertising can be formulated.

Forcing Exposure to Internet Advertising

The declining click-through rates of conventional banner ads and rising doubts about Web sites' advertising business models are driving concerned advertisers beyond banner ads. As advertisers scramble to find alternatives, rich media are quickly becoming the standard by which the sophistication of Internet advertising is being judged. Rich media ads contain content created with new technologies (e.g., Java, JavaScript, Macromedia Flash, Macromedia Shockwave, (D)HTML, VRML) and are used to deliver high aural and visual impact. Use of rich media is growing at an annual rate of 53 percent, and is forecasted to reach $34 billion by 2004 (Bowen 2001). With the increase in the popularity of rich media ads, new delivery techniques have been developed to solve bandwidth problems associated with larger rich media file sizes.

Pop-ups are one of the popular techniques to deliver rich media ads that are able to contain more sophisticated messages on the Web (Milward Brown Interactive 1999a). According to Interactive Advertising Bureau's (2001) guidelines, pop-ups refer to a form of rich media ads that "automatically launch in a new browser window when a Web page is loaded." Pop-unders are another form of interstitials that load behind the users' Web browser so that they may be seen after users close the browser window (Taylor 2001). Although different forms of interstitials can be programmed, they are distinct from conventional banner ads in the manner in which they are displayed. Banner ads appear when viewing Web pages, usually at the top or along the sides of the page. Because banner ads are generally displayed on the periphery, they do not interrupt the activity of Web viewers. However, interstitials can be programmed to appear when entering or exiting a Web page, after a certain amount of time on a Web page, or when a link is selected. The window then can be programmed to remain for a predetermined length of time or until the user chooses to close the window.

When faced with interstitials, Web users are interrupted and forced to react to unrequested commercial messages. In some cases, viewers have the option to "zap" the advertisement by closing the pop-up window, but newer interstitial ad formats expand within a Web page and do not offer such an opportunity. Web surfers are forced to view a short commercial message if they wish to see the Web site. In either case, interruptions force users to respond cognitively, affectively, or behaviorally, possibly resulting in either positive or negative outcomes for the advertiser. This type of forced exposure may elicit a viewer's involuntary attention, as described by Kahneman (1973), which would result in positive effects such as greater processing and increased memory for the ad message. Industry studies have shown increases in ad recall, awareness, and purchase intention for interstitials compared with conventional banner ads (Milward Brown Interactive 1999b). However, forced exposure often interrupts a viewer's normal viewing process, and rich media content may cause a delay in downloading due to large file sizes. Both situations could lead to a negative perception of the advertising as intrusive. Although intrusive advertisements may enhance recall, they also may result in negative attitude formation (Ha 1996) or avoidance of the ads altogether (Abernethy 1991). Thus, an important theoretical and practical issue for pop-up ads online is how to minimize the negative perceptions while taking advantage of the potential effective benefits.

The Perceived Intrusiveness of Advertising

In a survey of U.S. consumers, Bauer and Greyser (1968) identify as the main reasons people criticize advertising the annoyance or irritation it causes, which is believed to lead to a general reduction in advertising effectiveness (Aaker and Bruzzone 1985). However, research also indicates that consumers' criticisms of advertising are generally directed at the tactics advertisers employ that make the experience of processing advertising negative, rather than at the institution of advertising itself (Bauer and Greyser 1968; Ducoffe 1996; Sandage and Leckenby 1980). Therefore, developing a better understanding of these "annoying" or "irritating" tactics should allow for the creation of more effective advertisements.

A few studies have identified aspects of advertising that lead to negative feelings. For example, some believe that irritation occurs as a function of the advertising content and level of stimulation. Content that talks down to consumers, is overly exaggerated, or makes confusing statements has been identified as irritating to consumers (Bauer and Greyser 1968). Advertisements that excessively stimulate consumers' senses can also elicit feelings of irritation. Consumers can become overwhelmed if the ads are too long, too loud, or too big (Aaker and Bruzzone 1985; Bauer and Greyser 1968). Consumers may also feel overstimulated when viewing many ads in a short time or seeing a single ad too frequently (Bauer and Greyser 1968). The likely result is a retreat away from the source of irritation, or ad avoidance (Kennedy 1971; Krugman 1983; Park and McClung 1985; Soldow and Principe 1981). Abernethy (1991) finds that consumers often leave the room or change channels to avoid advertising. Others have shown that television viewers simply ignore ads (Clancey 1994; Krugman and Johnson 1991). However, what is not clear is why the same advertising is annoying to some but not all consumers.

A possible explanation for why consumers view only some advertising as irritating is the concept of intrusiveness. Ha (1996) defines intrusiveness as the interruption of editorial content. Because the first objective of advertising is to get noticed, by definition, advertisements seek to interrupt editorial content. By interfering with the goals of consumers, advertising effectively limits the number of actions that consumers can take to attain their goals. Consumers must reevaluate their goals to include advertising (acquiesce), or negative reactions are likely to result in the avoidance of advertising in some way. Aaker and Bruzzone (1985) suggest that negative reactions to advertisements occur to the degree that they cause impatience. To the extent that advertisements are recognized as disturbing, negative outcomes such as irritation and avoidance may result (Kennedy 1971; Krugman 1983; Park and McClung 1985; Soldow and Principe 1981). Therefore, though irritation is a possible emotional reaction and avoidance is a potential behavioral outcome in response to intrusive advertising, the perception of an ad as intrusive is something different.

The perception of an advertisement as intrusive should be considered a cognitive evaluation of the degree to which the advertisement interrupts a person's goals. If we define what is intrusive according to the person, advertising itself is not intrusive. Rather, intrusiveness is defined by the degree to which a person deems the presentation of information as contrary to his or her goals (either functional or hedonic). As such, intrusiveness should be considered distinct from the emotional or behavioral outcomes that may result. Therefore, it becomes important to understand the means by which perceptions of intrusiveness can be limited to reduce the negative outcomes that are likely to result.

Pasadeos (1990) finds that, when ads are perceived as valuable (containing useful information), they elicit less irritation and avoidance. According to Ducoffe (1995), advertising value is best understood as an overall representation of the worth of advertising to consumers. Ducoffe's (1995, 1996) studies indicate that ad value is positively correlated with the informativeness and entertainment value of an ad and that both information and entertainment value are essential for communication exchanges between advertisers and consumers. Therefore, the perception of intrusiveness may be affected when an ad offers the viewer either utilitarian or aesthetic value or both. To the degree that advertising does not provide value, it may be perceived as coercive and unwelcome. It is this feeling of intrusiveness that may drive negative reactions toward ads that are recognized as trying to persuade.

Reactance

Brehm and Brehm (1981) describe attempts to change behavior as involving both persuasion and coercion and believe that the degree to which these attempts intrude on a person's freedom determines that consumer's response.

Brehm (1966) terms this feeling "reactance" and proposes that it occurs to the degree that (1) the behavior threatened is important, (2) the severity of the threat to the behavior increases, (3) the threat affects other freedoms, and (4) the person ever actually enjoyed the freedom. Clee and Wicklund (1980) describe reactance as a boomerang effect in which the perception of coercion is met with an equal but opposite influence, which is used by consumers to restore their freedom of choice. This effect can foster a desire to engage in the threatened behavior even more strongly (rebellion) or can be manifested as an attitude change in the person's belief that the activity is important (acquiescence).

Several studies demonstrate that hard-sell tactics are less persuasive than soft-sell tactics (Clee and Wicklund 1980; Reizenstine 1971), and Brehm and Brehm (1981) point out that hard-sell messages reveal the intent of the persuader and therefore should be met with greater resistance. Robertson and Rossiter (1974) find that perceptions of persuasion correlated with less favorable attitudes toward the product being sold. To the degree that advertisements are recognized as simply attempts at persuasion, they could evoke a mild form of reactance.

Although perhaps not as strong as other forms of direct coercion, advertisements may be perceived as an interruption and elicit a similar feeling. To the degree that radio listeners are enjoying music, the threat of advertising may result in channel surfing to regain the freedom to listen to music. To the degree that the option of changing stations is taken away or all stations are playing ads at the same time, increased psychological reactance should be manifest against the interruption (advertising) and perhaps radio stations themselves. Multiple theories of media interactions indicate that consumers are wary of persuasion. Consumers actively interpret the techniques that ads use to persuade (Friestad and Wright 1994) and form counterarguments against ad claims when they are highly involved (Petty and Cacioppo 1979), all in an effort to defend themselves or react against persuasive messages.

If consumers' reactions to advertising are defensive, it may not be an effective strategy to force them to view advertisements. Reactance theory would dictate that forced exposure will result in negative consequences for advertisers; however, not all forced advertising may be unwelcome. Discovery of the means by which reactance can be minimized may increase the efficacy of advertising that has the potential to threaten viewers' perceptions of freedom.

Hypotheses

As has been argued, intrusiveness can be thought of as a psychological consequence that occurs when an audience member's cognitive processes are interrupted and that may result in the avoidance of advertising. However, advertising may not always be perceived as equally intrusive. Perceived intrusiveness may be moderated by the intensity or focus of a cognitive process. By the intensity of a cognitive process, we mean the degree to which an audience is mentally engaged in an activity, not cognition itself. For example, a television commercial would be more intrusive when inserted in the middle of a highly involving show than at the end of a less arousing program. Similarly, the timing of exposure to rich media ads during normal surfing sessions on the Web may differentially affect perceptions of intrusiveness. For example, viewers' cognitive intensity is likely to be higher when they are viewing a content page than when taking a cognitive pause to switch pages. Similarly, cognitive intensity should be higher when taking a cognitive pause to switch pages than when finished surfing and closing the browser. Therefore, an ad displayed under different cognitive loads may be perceived as different in terms of intrusiveness. We hypothesize that

> H1a: Ads that interrupt content pages will be perceived as more intrusive than will ads displayed between breaks in content pages.
> H1b: Ads displayed between breaks in content pages will be perceived as more intrusive than will ads displayed upon closing the browser.

Similarly, the duration of the interruption may affect the perceived level of intrusiveness. The longer an interruption, the more intrusive it may be perceived to be. Theoretically, extended interruptions should be perceived as greater threats to freedom than should shorter interruptions, which should result in greater psychological discomfort and greater reactance. Therefore,

> H2: Longer ads will be perceived as more intrusive than will shorter ads in forced exposure situations.

Holding the intensity of cognition constant, there may be other aspects of advertisements that moderate the perception of intrusiveness. Persuasion attempts are not always perceived as intrusive and met with skepticism, counterarguments, or source derogations; they can be met with support arguments (Petty and Cacioppo 1979). Advertisements often provide relevant information and/or consumer gratifications, such as escapism, diversion, esthetic enjoyment, or emotional release (McQuail 1983). This psychological force, in opposition to reactance, has been termed positive social influence. Clee and Wicklund (1980) posit that persuasive communications elicit both reactance and positive social change and that the net result of any persuasive communication must take into account both forces. Given the existence of a positive social interpretation of persuasive communication, the degree to which viewers perceive benefits or gratifications from persuasion attempts should counter the perception of intrusiveness.

One possible positive social influence that may affect the perception of intrusiveness is the perceived value of an advertisement. More specifically, perceived intrusiveness may be lessened for ads that are deemed of high value. When faced with advertising online, users may regard the degree of congruity between the advertising content and the editorial content as valuable. For example, exposure to advertising for Chevrolet while surfing the Internet for information about a new car purchase would probably be perceived as less intrusive than would an ad for Microsoft in the same situation. Ads that are congruent with expectations and/or current cognitive activities could be perceived as positive social influences and thus not be considered threats to the consumer's freedom. In contrast, ads not congruent with expectations activate divergent knowledge structures and create added mental processing demands. These added demands threaten the freedom to continue with current processing activities and may result in considerable reactance. Therefore,

> H3: Ads that are congruent with the editorial content will be perceived as less intrusive than ads that are not congruent.
> H4: Ads that are congruent with the editorial content will be perceived as more informative than ads that are not congruent.
> H5: Ads that are perceived as more informative will be rated as less intrusive than ads that are perceived as less informative.

A second positive social influence identified by Bauer and Greyser (1968) and Ducoffe (1995) is entertainment. To the degree that advertisements are perceived as entertaining, they should provide value to the viewer. To the degree that the entertainment is welcome, it should not be perceived as interrupting the cognitive goals of the viewer, and therefore, it should garner less psychological reactance than advertising judged less entertaining. Thus, it is expected that

> H6: Ads that are perceived as more entertaining will be rated as less intrusive than ads that are perceived as less entertaining.

As reviewed previously, theories of psychological reactance suggest that, in response to a loss of freedom, viewers will feel uncomfortable and attempt to regain control of their experience. When advertising interrupts the goals of consumers, consumers are likely to seek their freedom either passively, by ignoring the interruption (Clancey 1994; Krugman and Johnson 1991), or actively, by dispensing with it (Abernethy 1991; Speck and Elliott 1997). The degree to which viewers seek freedom will be directly proportional to the perception of the ad as an intrusive threat to that freedom. The perception of the intrusiveness of an ad will likely result in feelings of irritation and ultimately the avoidance of that ad, if possible. Therefore, perceived intrusiveness, level of irritation experienced, and avoidance behaviors should all be related. On the basis of the reviewed literature, we believe that

> H7: The perception of intrusiveness will be positively related to feelings of irritation.
> H8: The perception of intrusiveness will be positively related to advertising avoidance.
> H9: Feelings of irritation will be positively related to advertising avoidance.

Methods

Participants

A total of 379 participants was recruited from undergraduate courses at a midwestern U.S. university to participate in the experiment. The courses were campuswide electives, so the participants represented a variety of majors and backgrounds. Women constituted 58 percent of the sample, men 42 percent.

Experimental Design

The experiment used a $2 \times 2 \times 3$ factorial design in which participants were asked to find out as much information as they could about either financial aid or current movies using a Web site provided. The three independent variables manipulated were editorial–ad congruence, duration of interruption, and intensity of cognition when faced with a pop-up ad. Two conditions of editorial–ad congruence were created by placing a pop-up ad for a movie on either a site that featured movie reviews or a site that featured financial aid information. When an interstitial was incongruent, it was assumed to be more intrusive than when the advertisement was congruent with the site content. Duration of interruption of the interstitial was manipulated by providing content that lasted either ten or twenty seconds. Although participants could close the interstitial at will, it was assumed that a longer interstitial would be more intrusive than a shorter one if watched entirely.

Cognitive intensity of the viewer when seeing the interstitial on a Web site was the third independent variable. In the first condition, an interstitial was programmed to pop up 20 seconds after the experimental page was opened. The experimental pages for either movie reviews or financial aid were pretested and took more than two minutes to read. This condition was designed to be the most intrusive, as it interrupted participants at a time they were actively processing information that was needed to complete the assigned task. In the second condition, the same content as appeared in the first condition was positioned on two Web pages with the interstitial placed between them. The ad opened only when the participants chose to move from the first to the second page. Providing participants the opportunity to take a "cognitive pause" from their reading was designed to reduce the level of intrusiveness felt in response to the advertisement. Participants had to request the second page of information, thereby giving them more control over the situation. The third condition was similar to the first condition, but the interstitial was shown only when the participants finished reading the articles and exited the experimental page. By placing the advertisement at the end of the task, participants were no longer actively processing the information at the Web site and therefore should not have experienced reactance.

Experimental Stimuli

Two Web sites were created for the experiment: One site contained movie reviews and the other financial aid information. The site themes were selected from a pretest in which sixteen topics were rated for student interest. The selected topics were rated as moderately interesting by a sample of both male and female students ($N = 35$) who did not participate in the main experiment. The content was adapted from existing Web sites. All experimental conditions were identical in structure, font size, color, and the number and length of the articles. The movie review site reviewed the movies *Beautiful* and *Cyberworld 3D*, and the financial aid site contained articles about "Stafford Loans" and "Loan Consolidation."

Two interstitials (created using Macromedia Flash) advertised a fictitious movie titled *The Good Days*. Both interstitials had identical format and content and varied only in length. The twenty-second interstitial used blank filler frames to maintain the same amount of information as the ten-second interstitial. Both interstitials were sized 350×350 pixels and set to pop up in the center of the computer screen. Specifically, the ads contained four still pictures representing the movie scenes, a soft piano as background music, and a listing of a fictitious title, director, and cast of the movie.

Procedure

Participants were randomly assigned to one of the twelve conditions (two levels of editorial–ad congruence, two levels of duration, and three levels of cognitive intensity) and asked to read an instruction page about the experiment. To stimulate interest in the Web content, participants were told they would be tested about the site content at the end of the viewing session and that the person who answered the most questions correctly would win a cash prize. Participants viewed the Web pages individually and were fitted with earphones to hear the music used in the ad. The ads were programmed to remain for either ten or twenty seconds, but participants were able to close the interstitials at will and continue with their assigned task. After the ten-minute viewing session was over, each participant was asked to quit the Web browser and fill out a questionnaire and then was debriefed.

Measures

A questionnaire was used to assess perceived intrusiveness, irritation, perceived informativeness and entertainment value of the movie ad, and the demographics of the participants. All items were answered using seven-point scales with response categories from strongly agree to strongly disagree. The intrusiveness measure consisted of seven items: distracting, disturbing, forced, interfering, intrusive, invasive, and obtrusive (Li, Edwards, and Lee 2001). Irritation was measured using five items: irritating, phony, ridiculous, stupid, and terrible (Wells, Leavitt, and McConville 1971). The perceived informativeness and entertainment value of the interstitial were measured using modified scales based on the work of Ducoffe (1996). Both informativeness (helpful, unimportant, uninformative, and useless) and entertainment value (attractive, enjoyable, entertaining, and fun to watch) were measured using four items. Finally, ad avoidance was measured using observational data. Participants' actual time spent viewing the ad was assessed using screen capture software and later coded for analysis. Although each of the measures had been used in previous studies, a confirmatory factor analysis of the items was conducted to investigate their validity in this context. Specifically, the measured constructs (intrusiveness, irritation, advertising entertainment, and advertising informativeness) were tested using first-order confirmatory factor models in which every item was confined to load on its specified factor. In all the models, the item-loading estimates on their prespecified factors were highly significant ($p < .001$), and goodness-of-fit indices demonstrated the quality of the measurement models (intrusiveness: goodness-of-fit index (GFI) = .984, adjusted goodness-of-fit index (AGFI) =

Table 10.1

Scale Reliabilities

Variable	Indicators	Alpha	N
When the ad popped up, I thought it was . . .			
Perceived intrusiveness	distracting, disturbing, forced, interfering, intrusive, invasive, and obtrusive	0.91	373
Perceived irritation	irritating, phony, ridiculous, stupid, and terrible	0.87	373
The movie ad I saw was . . .			
Informativeness	helpful, unimportant, uninformative, and useless	0.82	370
Entertainment	attractive, enjoyable, entertaining, and fun to watch	0.94	371

.965; irritation: GFI = .997, AGFI = .960; advertising entertainment: GFI = .998, AGFI = .990; advertising informativeness: GFI = .993, AGFI = .963). The questions asked and response items that make up each measure, along with reliability coefficients, are presented in Table 10.1.

Results

Manipulation Checks

To assess the validity of our manipulations, a third sample of sixty undergraduate students was randomly assigned to one of the twelve conditions in the main experiment and asked to assess the perceived congruence of the ad with the task, the perceived length of the ad, and the intensity of cognition at the moment the ad appeared. To check the manipulations of our independent variables, we first examined the degree to which participants recognized the editorial congruence of the ad. Participants were asked to agree or disagree with statements regarding the degree to which the ad helped them fulfill their task, provided useful information, and was relevant to their task on a seven-point scale. Those who saw a congruent ad reported significantly greater relevance ($\xi = 3.16$) than did those who saw a noncongruent ad ($\xi = 2.31$), $t_{(58)} = 2.49, p < .05$.

To assess if the length of the ads was recognized, participants were asked to agree or disagree with statements such as "the ad was short, seemed to play for a long time, and was over before I knew it." There was no significant difference between those who saw a ten-second ad ($\xi = 2.86$) and those who saw a twenty-second ad ($\xi = 2.68$), $p > .05$. Therefore, participants perceived the ads to be of similar length, which indicates the failure of our manipulation.

Finally, participants' levels of cognitive intensity at the moment the ads popped up were assessed. Participants reported that they were more involved with the article, more actively reading the information presented, and more focused on the article when an ad popped up while they were reading the text ($\xi = 5.20$) than if it appeared between pages ($\xi = 3.97$) or upon exiting the browser ($\xi = 3.87$), $F_{(2, 57)} = 4.71$, $p < .05$. Post hoc analyses revealed significant differences in cognitive intensity when participants were reading the text compared with when they were between pages or exiting the browser. There was no significant difference reported for between pages and exiting the browser. The manipulation resulted in only high and low levels of cognitive intensity, and therefore, no further distinction was made between the manipulations that resulted in similar levels of cognitive intensity.

To conduct an overall assessment of the degree to which these variables may have elicited reactance, we measured perceptions of the ad as threatening freedom. The sixty participants were asked to rate the degree to which they felt their freedom was threatened, that the ad infringed on their freedom, and that the ad forced them to respond. In contrast to expectations, those who saw a task-relevant ad reported a greater threat to freedom ($\xi = 3.07$) than did those who saw a nonrelevant ad ($\xi = 2.48$), $F_{(1, 48)} = 3.73$, $p < .05$. However, similar to the findings pertaining to the perceived duration of the ad, participants viewing a ten-second ad experienced a similar amount of reactance ($\xi = 2.64$) as did those viewing the twenty-second ad ($\xi = 2.90$), $p > .05$. Participants who saw an ad within a page reported greater reactance ($\xi = 3.32$) than did those who saw an ad between pages ($\xi = 2.83$), who reported greater reactance than did those who saw an ad when exiting the browser, $F_{(2, 48)} = 4.78$, $p < .05$. In summary, though the manipulations of editorial–ad congruence and cognitive intensity adequately distinguished between conditions, the strength of the reactance was only mild. That is, advertising may not warrant strong feelings about the loss of control. Editorial–ad congruence was recognized as congruent or not congruent to the assigned task, as anticipated, but ratings of the threat to freedom were opposite expectations. This finding may indicate that when ads are relevant they elicit greater attention and are perceived as greater threats to freedom than when not relevant. If true, the value that ads provide by being relevant must overcome the perceived threat to freedom to be perceived as unintrusive. Finally, the manipulation to change the perception of the duration of the interruption was unsuccessful and not expected to explain variance in the proposed model.

Figure 10.1 **A Conceptual Model of the Perceived Intrusiveness of Pop-Up Ads**

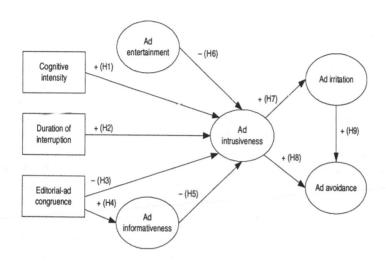

Model Testing

We tested the ten hypotheses using structural equation analysis with Amos 4.0. The promise of such an approach lies in that, when tested simultaneously, existing relationships between constructs may change and additional relationships may emerge. Structural equation modeling (SEM) captures these changes and thus provides a better description of the relationships among variables (Bollen 1989).

All constructs described in the hypotheses and shown in Figure 10.1 were specified in the initial model. Exogenous variables included cognitive intensity, duration of the interruption, and editorial congruence. Each was a manipulated variable and therefore categorical in nature. Although not ideal for SEM analysis, categorical variables can be successfully incorporated into such analysis (Jöreskog and Sörbom 1989). The variables were coded so that higher values reflect greater cognitive intensity, longer duration, and greater congruence. Five endogenous variables included ad informativeness, ad entertainment, ad intrusiveness, ad irritation, and ad avoidance. These are each observed, continuous measures. The maximum likelihood method was used in model estimation. The initial analysis indicated a poor fitting model, $\chi^2 =$ 668.09 (d.f. = 244), a GFI of .87, AGFI of .84, comparative fit index (CFI) of .92, and root mean squared error of approximation (RMSEA) of .07.

To improve the model, the significance of the regression weights was first examined for all variables. As expected on the basis of the nonsignificant findings of the manipulation check, the perceived duration of the interruption caused by the ad was not significantly related to perceived intrusiveness, $p > .05$. Unexpectedly, irritation did not significantly predict ad avoidance, $p > .05$. Instead, avoidance was driven by the perceived intrusiveness of the ad. Therefore, duration of the interruption was removed from the model, as was the link between irritation and ad avoidance. The revised model was further tested, and modification indices were used to identify any missed relationships in the original model. The degree to which an ad was rated as entertaining was shown to be related to the level of irritation experienced ($p < .01$) and therefore was added to the model. Although we expected this relationship to be moderated by intrusiveness, much of the literature on irritation points out that irritation occurs when ads contain untruthful or confusing content or are executed poorly (Aaker and Bruzzone 1985; Bauer and Greyser 1968). The model with the addition of the new causal path between entertainment and irritation was tested, and one item (irritation) from the irritation scale with excessive covariance was removed. The resulting model, presented in Figure 10.2, was found to fit the data well, $\chi^2 = 433.64$ (d.f. = 202), GFI = .91, AGFI = .89, CFI = .95, and RMSEA = .06. The significance of regression weights was examined for all remaining constructs, and their associated measures and all relationships were found to be significant at $p < .01$. A final model summary is presented in Table 10.2.

The final model provides support for seven of the ten hypotheses. In addition, a new causal relationship (ad entertainment $\rightarrow$ ad irritation) emerged and was added to the model. This addition is conceptually sound, in that previous studies have shown that entertaining ads are perceived as valuable by audiences (Alwitt and Prabhaker 1992; Biel and Bridgwater 1990; Ducoffe 1996). To the degree that viewers are entertained by ads, they are less likely to be irritated. All relationships in the final model seem reasonable and are in accordance with the literature reviewed.

Specifically, two manipulated variables—cognitive intensity and editorial–ad congruence—had a significant impact on perceived intrusiveness, whereas duration of the ad did not. That is, ads were found to be more intrusive by participants highly immersed in the content ($\xi = 4.42$, $S = 1.41$) than by those who were less cognitively engaged ($\xi = 3.70$, $S = 1.41$), $t_{(374)} = 4.70$, $p < .001$. The manipulation of cognitive intensity specified in H1b did not work and therefore could not be tested. However, evidence for H1a was found.

Table 10.2

Final Model Summary

	Independent variables	Dependent variables	Unstandardized parameters	Standard errors	Standardized parameters
H1	Cognitive intensity	Ad intrusiveness	−0.631	0.129	−0.233
H2ᵃ	Duration of interruption	Ad intrusiveness			
H3	Editorial–ad congruence	Ad intrusiveness	0.362	0.124	0.141
H4	Editorial–ad congruence	Ad informativeness	−0.470	0.131	−0.205
H5	Ad informativeness	Ad intrusiveness	−0.416	0.066	−0.373
H6	Ad entertainment	Ad intrusiveness	−0.305	0.057	−0.273
Added	Ad entertainment	Ad irritation	−0.324	0.041	−0.350
H7	Ad intrusiveness	Ad irritation	0.567	0.049	0.688
H8	Ad intrusiveness	Ad avoidance	−2.978	0.533	−0.297
H9ᵃ	Ad irritation	Ad avoidance			

Goodness-of-fit indices

χ^2 433.64 (df = 202), $p < 0.001$
Jöreskog-Sörbom goodness-of-fit index (GFI)   0.91
Adjusted goodness-of-fit index (AGFI)   0.89
Comparative fit index (CFI)   0.95
Root mean square error of approximation (RMSEA) 0.06

ᵃDropped in the final model.

Figure 10.2 **Antecedents and Consequences of Perceived Intrusiveness: The Final Model**

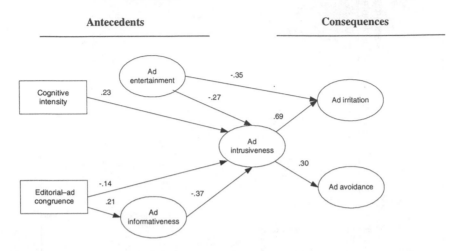

Unfortunately, H2 could not be supported. The duration of both ten- and twenty-second ads was perceived similarly, and thus, duration is not related to perceptions of intrusiveness, $p > .05$. Perhaps the existence of the interstitial itself triggered feelings of intrusiveness, and once a participant decided to watch the ad, the length might have not mattered. Editorial congruence was found to have a negative relationship with perceptions of intrusiveness, and therefore, H3 was supported. Ads were perceived as less intrusive when related to the participant's task ($\xi = 3.64$, $S = 1.42$) than when not related to the task ($\xi = 4.24$, $S = 1.43$), $t_{(374)} = 4.04$, $p < .001$. Editorial congruence also had a positive impact on the perception of the ad as informative, in support of H4. Those who saw the congruent ad reported it to be more informative ($\xi = 4.17$, $S = 1.32$) than did those who saw the noncongruent ad ($\xi = 3.77$, $S = 1.15$), $t_{(371)} = 3.14$, $p < .01$.

Hypotheses 5 and 6 were related to the degree to which ads that are perceived as informative and entertaining reduce perceptions of the ad as intrusive. Both variables were negatively related to perceptions of intrusiveness, indicating that the more value (information or entertainment) perceived in an ad, the less intrusive it is perceived. Both hypotheses are thus supported. Hypothesis 7 proposed a connection between perceptions of intrusiveness and feelings of irritation. A strong positive relationship was found in support of the relationship. However, the added relationship between the perception of an ad as entertaining and feelings of irritation now means that entertainment has both a direct and an indirect effect on irritation. Hypothesis 8 specified that perceptions of intrusiveness would be positively related to the avoidance of the ad. The model shows that avoidance is caused by the degree to which an ad is judged to be intrusive. Finally, the lack of support for H9 is interesting because feelings of irritation were not significantly related to ad avoidance. Similar to the findings of Cronin and Menelly (1992), this suggests that ad avoidance may take place upon recognition of the ad as intrusive, even though the viewer is not yet irritated.

Discussion

The current study provides evidence that when ads are perceived as intrusive, feelings of irritation are elicited and advertisements are avoided. Apparently, perceptions of interstitials as intrusive are related to the level of cognitive intensity with which viewers pursue their goals. When viewers are focused, they perceive interruptions as more severe than when they are not focused. However, through creative advertisement placement strategies, perceptions of intrusiveness may be moderated. When ads are requested or provide value, either in the form of information or entertainment, they are perceived as less of an interruption, are less irritating, and may be less likely to be dismissed as nuisances.

The variables found to limit perceptions of intrusiveness involve (1) targeting viewers when their cognitive effort is low, (2) increasing the relevancy of the advertising, and (3) providing value to viewers. First, strategies that seek to minimize the interruption of viewers' current activities are likely to meet with less resistance. Therefore, viewers should be exposed to pop-up ads only at breaks in content. In the current study, switching between pages offered such a break. However, Web pages could be designed with pictures or large banner ads separating sections of content, thereby providing the breaks needed to launch pop-up ads. Recent practices in the online advertising industry to use pop-unders or interstitials (ads that appear in the main Web browser when users attempt to move from one page to another) would be justified by the findings from the current study.

Second, another means of limiting perceptions of intrusiveness involves increasing the relevancy of pop-up advertisements by using content placement strategies. Although increasing relevance was found to increase reactance, participants actually reported feeling less intrusiveness. A possible explanation for this finding is that relevant ads could not be as easily discounted as meaningless. So, though they raised significantly greater reactance than nonrelevant ads, meaningful information tempered feelings of intrusiveness and irritation. This finding highlights the importance of content placement strategies, which have been used in print media (Janiszewski 1990; Yi 1990) and television (Murry, Lastovicka, and Singh 1992; Park and McClung 1985; Singh and Churchill 1987; Soldow and Principe 1981). The same rationale is being used online (Sherman and Deighton 2001). If consumers are surfing "cars.com" and an automobile ad is seen, it is likely to be more relevant than an ad for Budweiser and thus less likely to elicit feelings of intrusiveness and irritation.

Third, the final strategy to reduce intrusiveness is to increase the value viewers receive from ads. Information deemed important or interesting or an ad that is entertaining rewards the viewer, who is thereby less likely to feel irritated by the interruption. Through strategic use and placement of commercial messages, resistance of consumers can be lessened, which is likely to result in less irritation and greater message effectiveness.

However, there are several limitations to the current study that should be addressed. First, the manipulation of ad length was not perceived to differ among participants. Therefore, we cannot comment on previous claims that longer ads are more intrusive or irritating than shorter ads. Subjects had a modicum of control during the experiment, in that they could close the pop-up ad at will. Although participants exposed to the twenty-second ad left the ad open significantly longer than did those exposed to the ten-second ad, there was no perceived difference in the length of the ads. Perhaps the participants were not in a hurry to complete the task and therefore did not deem the length of the pop-up ad important. Alternative procedures could include providing an incentive for timely completion of the task or choosing very short and very long ads to maximize perceptions of ad length.

Second, the degree to which participants felt in control of the timing of the appearance of the ad may be a limitation. Participants in the "timed" cognitive intensity condition had no control over when the ad popped up, whereas participants in the second and third conditions were required to click a link (either to go to the next page or close the browser) before the ad popped up. Because of the importance of control in assessing perceived interactivity, teasing out the effects of control from cognitive intensity seems like an important next step in this line of research.

Third, the use of categorical exogenous variables in the tested SEM is unorthodox. Although acceptable analytically, cognitive intensity, duration of the interruption, and editorial congruence were manipulated to create experimental conditions and therefore limited the variation and explanatory power of the model. Future research should note this limitation and measure perceptions of such manipulations to facilitate greater explanation with continuous exogenous variables.

Conclusion

We have provided a framework for understanding negative responses to Internet advertising, such as feelings of irritation and ad avoidance. The proposed model is an initial step in understanding the relationships among intrusiveness, irritation, and ad avoidance in forced exposure situations. The proposed model offers several unique characteristics, in that it conceptualizes the role and nature of intrusiveness in understanding responses to advertising and demonstrates that perceptions of intrusiveness may be moderated by other factors. None of these issues has received explicit attention in previous literature. By bringing them together in a framework, we aim to guide future empirical research and theoretical work.

It must be noted that our findings cannot be generalized to all Web site viewing behaviors. This study examines the impact of perceived intrusiveness in the context of task-oriented, extrinsically motivated behavior. Participants were assigned to learn as much as possible about their given tasks, and thus, the motivation underlying the Web surfing task may limit the generalizability of the results. Intrinsically motivated, task-oriented surfing behaviors could be examined by providing participants with a range of topics from which to select. Intrinsically motivated behavior could result in more or less reactance, depending on the strength of the motivation. Therefore, it would be interesting to examine the relationship among motivation, cognitive intensity, and the perception of intrusiveness.

It should also be noted that not all Web site viewing behavior is task- or goal-oriented. Hoffman and Novak (1996) distinguish goal-directed behavior from experiential or ritual behavior on the Web. Whereas the former refers to activities such as information seeking and online shopping, the latter is less directed. Because intrusiveness has been defined as the interruption of cognitive processing, it would be worthwhile to investigate the effects of intrusiveness during experiential behavior. For example, when users are mindlessly surfing through various Web sites without any specific purposes, an interstitial may cause less intrusiveness than it does in a goal-directed context.

Unlike many Web sites with interstitials, only one interstitial popped up at the experimental Web site. Future studies may wish to examine multiple interstitials and vary the frequency with which ads pop up; their cumulative effects may exacerbate perceptions of intrusiveness. The type of message displayed in a pop-up ad may also interact with the act of popping up itself. Static banners may not provide the entertainment that rich media can offer. Alternatively, some consumers may be irritated by having to wait for rich media and prefer a simpler message.

In a similar vein, the method of placing ads in Web sites should be investigated in more depth. The current study manipulates cognitive intensity by placing the ad at different locations within the Web page: at the beginning, in the middle, and at the end. However, technological advances provide many more options for specifying ad placement. These different placements vary in the degree of forced exposure. For example, pop-unders can be loaded under the browser and be seen upon closing the browser. Ads can also be made to float on the browser window without disappearing, be full-screen ads that prevent people from viewing other content, or have the appearance of traditional banner ads but expand without leaving the current Web site. Other ads are programmed to appear only when users wait for the Web pages to load. These diverse tactics and new technologies are allowing for greater control over advertising placement, and it will be necessary to test how people perceive those new ad formats.

A third area that needs to be addressed in future research is the trade-off between good and bad exposure. The old saying that "any publicity is good publicity" illustrates this point. Even if viewers respond negatively to forced exposure advertisements, they are still exposed to the message. This exposure is likely to elicit increased levels of attention and should facilitate memory for the advertisement. Therefore, it becomes important to consider the goal of the campaign when studying about the effects of intrusiveness. For example, advertisers seeking positive attitude formation as a campaign objective may wish to avoid intrusive ads, which are likely to result in irritation. However, if recall or recognition is a goal, intrusive ads could be more effective than nonintrusive ads. Exploration of the relationship between intrusiveness and memory is needed to understand the benefits and drawbacks of using forced exposure ads.

Overall, the current research shows that judgments about ad interruptions may be changed by manipulating the antecedents of intrusiveness. These findings add to our understanding of how viewers come to define when an ad is intrusive. Furthermore, the research seeks to distinguish the intrusiveness of an advertisement from the consequences of the interruption itself. By demonstrating that intrusiveness is a precursor to feelings of irritation and avoidance behaviors, we have added to the understanding of the underlying mechanism by which negative reactions to advertising occur. By providing this evidence in a single model, we begin to understand how both the antecedents and consequences of forced exposure advertising are best understood by examining the construct of intrusiveness.

References

Aaker, David S. and Donald E. Bruzzone (1985), "Causes of Irritation in Advertising," *Journal of Marketing*, 49 (2), 47–57.

Abernethy, Avery M. (1991), "Physical and Mechanical Avoidance of Television Commercials: An Exploratory Study of Zipping, Zapping and Leaving," in *Proceedings of the American Academy of Advertising*, Rebecca Holman, ed., New York: American Academy of Advertising, 223–231.

Alwitt, Linda F. and Paul R. Prabhaker (1992), "Functional and Belief Dimensions of Attitudes to Television," *Journal of Advertising Research*, 32 (5), 30–42.

Bauer, Raymond A. and Stephen A. Greyser (1968), *Advertising in America: The Consumer View*, Cambridge: Harvard University Press.

Biel, Alexander L. and Carol A. Bridgwater (1990), "Attributes of Likable Television Commercials," *Journal of Advertising Research*, 30 (3), 38–44.

Bollen, Kenneth A. (1989), *Structural Equations with Latent Variables*, New York: Wiley.

Bowen, John (2001), "Analyst View: The Emergence of Rich Media," *Red Herring* (January 24), [www.redherring.com/index.asp?layout=story&channel= 20000002&doc_id=1210017521].

Brehm, Jack W. (1966), *A Theory of Psychological Reactance*, New York: Academic Press.

Brehm, Sharon S. and Jack W. Brehm (1981), *Psychological Reactance: A Theory of Freedom and Control*, New York: Academic Press.

Clancey, Maura (1994), "The Television Audience Examined," *Journal of Advertising Research*, 39 (5), 27–37.

Clee, Mona A. and Robert A. Wicklund (1980), "Consumer Behavior and Psychological Reactance," *Journal of Consumer Research*, 6 (4), 389.

Cronin, John J. and Nancy E. Menelly (1992), "Discrimination vs. Avoidance: 'Zipping' of Television Commercials," *Journal of Advertising*, 21 (Summer), 1–7.

Ducoffe, Robert H. (1995), "How Consumers Assess the Value of Advertising," *Journal of Current Issues and Research in Advertising*, 17 (1), 1–18.

——— (1996), "Advertising Value and Advertising on the Web," *Journal of Advertising Research*, 36 (5), 21–35.

Friestad, Marian and Peter Wright (1994), "The Persuasion Knowledge Model: How People Cope with Persuasion Attempts," *Journal of Consumer Research*, 21 (1), 1–31.

Ha, Louisa (1996), "Advertising Clutter in Consumer Magazines: Dimensions and Effects," *Journal of Advertising Research*, 36 (July/August), 76–83.

Hoffman, Donna L. and Thomas P. Novak (1996), "Marketing in Hypermedia Computer-Mediated Environments: Conceptual Foundations," *Journal of Marketing*, 60 (3), 50–68.

Interactive Advertising Bureau (2001), *Rich Media Ad Unit Guidelines*, Interactive Advertising Bureau (August 6), [www.iab.net/rich_content/index.html].

Janiszewski, Chris (1990), "The Influence of Nonattended Material on the Processing of Advertising Claims," *Journal of Marketing Research*, 27 (3), 263–278.

Jöreskog, Karl G. and Dag Sörbom (1989), *LISREL 7: A Guide to the Program and Applications*, 2d ed., Chicago: SPSS Inc.

Kahneman, Daniel (1973), *Attention and Effort*, Englewood Cliffs, NJ: Prentice Hall.

Kennedy, John R. (1971), "How Program Environment Affects TV Commercials," *Journal of Advertising Research*, 11 (1), 33–38.

Krugman, Dean M. and Keith F. Johnson (1991), "Differences in the Consumption of Traditional Broadcast and VCR Movie Rental," *Journal of Broadcasting & Electronic Media*, 35 (Spring), 213–232.

Krugman, Herbert E. (1983), "Television Program Interest and Commercial Interruption: Are Commercials on Interesting Programs Less Effective?" *Journal of Advertising Research*, 23 (1), 21–23.

Li, Hairong, Steven M. Edwards, and Joo-Hyun Lee (2001), "Measuring the Intrusiveness of Internet Advertising: Scale Development and Validation," in *Proceedings of the 2001 Conference of the American Academy of Advertising*, Charles R. Taylor, ed., Villanova, PA: American Academy of Advertising, 25–26.

McQuail, Dennis (1983), *Mass Communication Theory: An Introduction*, Thousand Oaks, CA: Sage.

Milward Brown Interactive (1999a), *The Wired Digital Rich Media Study*, San Francisco, CA: Millward Brown Interactive, [www.intelliquest.com/search/results.asp?vpath = /press/releases/mbi_release05.asp].

————— (1999b), *Evaluating the Effectiveness of the Superstitials*, Millward Brown Interactive, (October), [www.unicast.com/downloads/mbi.pdf].

Murry, John P., Jr., John L. Lastovicka, and Surendra N. Singh (1992), "Feeling and Liking Responses to Television Programs: An Examination of Two Explanations for Media Context Effects," *Journal of Consumer Research*, 18 (March), 441–451.

Park, C. Whan and Gordon W. McClung (1985), "The Effect of TV Program Involvement on Involvement with Commercials," in *Proceedings of the Association of Consumer Research*, Richard J. Lutz, ed., Las Vegas, NV: Association of Consumer Research, 544–547.

Pasadeos, Yorgo (1990), "Perceived Informativeness of and Irritation with Local Advertising," *Journalism Quarterly*, 67 (1), 35–39.

Petty, Richard E. and John T. Cacioppo (1979), "Issue Involvement Can Increase or Decrease Persuasion by Enhancing Message-Relevant Cognitive Responses," *Journal of Personality and Social Psychology*, 37 (10), 1915–1926.

Reizenstine, Richard C. (1971), "A Dissonance Approach to Measuring the Effectiveness of Two Personal Selling Techniques Through Decision Reversal," *Proceedings of the Conference of the American Marketing Association*, Chicago: American Marketing Association, 176–180.

Robertson, Thomas S. and John R. Rossiter (1974), "Children and Commercial Persuasion: An Attribution Theory Analysis," *Journal of Consumer Research*, 1 (1), 13.

Sandage, Charles H. and John Leckenby (1980), "Student Attitude toward Advertising: Institution vs. Instrument," *Journal of Advertising*, 9 (2), 29–33.

Sherman, Lee and John Deighton (2001), "Banner Advertising: Measuring Effectiveness and Optimizing Placement," *Journal of Interactive Marketing*, 15 (2), 60–64.

Singh, Surendra N. and Gilbert A. Churchill Jr. (1987), "Arousal and Advertising Effectiveness," *Journal of Advertising*, 16 (1), 4–10.

Soldow, Gary F. and Victor Principe (1981), "Response to Commercials as a Function of Program Context," *Journal of Advertising Research*, 21 (2), 59–65.

Speck, Paul Surgi and Michael T. Elliott (1997), "Predictors of Advertising Avoidance in Print and Broadcast Media," *Journal of Advertising*, 26 (3), 61–76.

Taylor, Catharine P. (2001), "The Crackle over 'Pop Unders,'" *Advertising Age*, 72 (July 16), 36.

Wells, William D., Clark Leavitt, and Maureen McConville (1971), "A Reaction Profile for TV Commercials," *Journal of Advertising Research*, 11 (December), 11–17.

Yi, Youjae (1990), "Cognitive and Affective Priming Effects of the Context for Print Advertising," *Journal of Advertising*, 19 (2), 40–48.

11

Category-Based Selection of Online Affiliates

Purushottam Papatla and Amit Bhatnagar

Introduction

Online commerce has experienced a downturn in the recent past. Forrester Research reports that, whereas total online sales were close to $4 billion in June 2000, they were only about $3 billion in June 2001 (Forrester Research 2001). Similarly, sales in July 2001 were flat and the same as in July 2000. This change in the fortunes of online retailing has stimulated businesses to analyze their approaches to online advertising in the hope of increasing their effectiveness. In particular, there is greater interest in understanding which formats work better and why.

Among the variety of advertising formats online, one format, namely, the banner ad, has perhaps gained the most widespread use. This is because banners are (1) relatively easy to develop compared with other formats and (2) quite inexpensive compared with traditional approaches to advertising. This extensive use of the format, however, has resulted in an erosion of its effectiveness because consumers have begun to view banners as the online equivalents of direct mail and ignore them. Some studies suggest that click-through rates, which measure how often a banner advertisement attracts a response, have fallen to as low as .36 percent (*San Francisco Chronicle* 2000). Some researchers therefore suggest that better targeting of banner ads may be the solution for improving their effectiveness (Hoffman and Novak 2000).

As Hoffman and Novak (2000) demonstrate with the case of the BuyWeb Network of CD Now, affiliate marketing offers an excellent way of targeting banner ads. In this format, pioneered by Amazon.com, an online retailer, the sponsor, places a hyperlink for its business at another online business's or host's site. The hope in this arrangement is that visitors to the host site will

237

notice the sponsor's link and click on to it to reach the sponsor site as well. If this happens and if the visitor makes a purchase at the sponsor site, a percentage of the sales revenue is paid to the host as a commission. For example, if a visitor clicks a banner at a host site, reaches CD Now, and purchases a CD, CD Now pays the host site a commission that can vary from 7 percent to 15 percent of the price of the CD (Hoffman and Novak 2000). The actual rate, however, depends on the overall volume generated by the host. Similarly, Amazon.com pays its affiliate partners up to 15 percent of the sale price on individually linked books that they feature on their site and 5 percent on anything else that is purchased through their links, including CDs, videos, DVDs, toys, consumer electronics, and so forth (Amazon 2001).

One interesting characteristic of affiliate advertising is that there are no up-front costs to either the host or the sponsor (Zeff and Aronson 1997). This means that, in principle, the number of hosts that a sponsor can use is virtually limitless. The sponsor, however, faces some hidden costs of entering into an affiliate relationship with too many partners. For example, such costs may include keeping track of all the hosts, identifying and crediting each host for the sales for which it is a source, and computing the commissions to be paid to each host. Added to this is the need for third-party auditing and certification of the analyses, which result in additional costs to the sponsor. Other expenses, such as affiliate training costs, would also increase with the number of affiliates. Finally, as the number of hosts increases, the sponsor may fail to maintain a strong relationship with any of the affiliates. Consequently, it may incur some long-term, nonmonetary costs as well. It is therefore important for sponsors to be selective in the number and variety of hosts with which they work.

The choice of a right affiliate is also important for hosts that need to generate revenue from a limited resource, that is, the space available on the typical computer screen. They therefore must identify, and enter into a relationship with, only those sponsors that are likely to be of interest to their visitors. Failure to do so will result in parts of the site being devoted to unprofitable affiliates.

Despite the importance of this problem for both sponsors and hosts, surprisingly, there are as yet few guidelines regarding the choice of the right hosts for a given sponsor. This is the issue that we address in this chapter. Specifically, we present an approach that online retailers can use to find appropriate hosts. Our approach is based on two assumptions. First, we assume that hosts that carry products that are related to those of the sponsor will be good affiliates. We operationalize the notion of relationship between two products in two dimensions. The first relates to the substitutability/complementarity of the products. The second dimension refers to the strength of the relationship, or whether the substitutability and/or complementarity are ongoing, strong, or occasional.

We label strong relationships as strict substitutability/complementarity, because two products with such a relationship can always be used as substitutes or complements. Weaker relationships, however, are labeled episode substitutability/complementarity, because when the relationship between two products is not strong, they may serve as substitutes or complements for each other on some occasions or episodes but not on others.

Second, we assume that the relationships between products are reflected in how consumers search for information. In particular, we assume that, if consumers search for information on a product, they are likely to do so for related products as well. We present a model to uncover relationships between products on the basis of this assumption.

In the next section, we present our conceptual framework for identifying affiliate partners. In the third section, we describe our empirical model and the methodological approach to calibrate the model on actual data. Next, we detail the data on which we calibrate the proposed model. Finally, we present our empirical results and discuss the findings.

A Conceptual Framework

As mentioned in the previous section, intuition suggests that the ideal host site for an affiliate sponsor would be one that attracts the same, or similar, customers in whom it is interested. This in turn implies that the host should be one that retails products that share some commonality with the products sold by the affiliate sponsor. The problem then is identifying the relationships among the different product categories. This is similar to the category management problem faced by traditional retailers and extensively explored in the retailing literature (Blattberg and Neslin 1990; Kahn and Lehmann 1991; Russell and Kamakura 1997; Walters 1991; Zenor 1994). In this case, the marketers' chief interest is studying demand substitutability (within product categories) and demand complementarity (across product categories) to guide decisions with respect to merchandising, store layout decisions, and so forth (Russell and Kamakura 1997). Advertisers interested in affiliate partnerships would therefore benefit by using a similar approach to investigate the issue of product substitution and complementarity. We next discuss briefly what constitutes a substitute and when a product would be a complement to another one.

Substitutes

Product substitutes are any two commodities that can satisfy the same need (Henderson and Quandt 1958). Substitutes in the context of retail assortments have been both theoretically (Katz 1984; Moorthy 1984; Oren, Smith, and Wilson 1984) and empirically (Kumar and Leone 1988; Moriarty 1985) studied extensively. In the context of identifying affiliates, sites carrying product substitutes are likely to be ideal hosts because they may attract similar consumers. For example, a site such as www.gateway.com, which carries computers and related products, would be the ideal affiliate for www.dell.com. Because they are competitors, such an arrangement is unlikely to materialize. The alternative for a business like Dell therefore would be to identify sites that carry products that are not substitutes but are likely to be of interest to consumers who buy computers online. These could be retailers of products that are part of the same purchase and/or consumption episode, that is, are co-consumed, and are therefore appropriate for forming affiliate partnerships.

Substitutability can be viewed as a continuum. Products can be strict substitutes for each other, in that they are very similar and perform the same functions. For example, in the preceding example of Dell and Gateway, the two brands of computers are strict substitutes. Similarly, two brands of detergents, such as Tide and Wisk, are strict substitutes. Whereas strict substitutes are interchangeable, episode substitutes are those that can substitute for another product only during certain consumption episodes. Thus, computers and televisions might be episode substitutes if they are used in entertainment consumption episodes but not if the television is used to watch news and the computer to perform analyses. Therefore, for identifying affiliate partners, both strict substitutes and episodic substitutes should be considered.

Complements

Products that are used in conjunction with other products to satisfy a particular need are known as complements (Henderson and Quandt 1958). Understanding the complementarity of products has been called the essence of merchandising, and yet the subject has not been sufficiently explored by researchers (Walters 1991). Complementarity of products is also likely to be a continuum, and consequently, for many product categories, identification of complements as a means of finding affiliate partners may be difficult. For example, products such as computer software and hardware restrict complements because they must be used together (Walters 1991). For other products, however, complementarity may depend on the specific consumption episode. Therefore, there might be some products that are complements in certain consumption episodes but independent in others. For example, milk and coffee can be used together or separately; they are complements on some

Figure 11.1   **Four Types of Category Relationships**

	Strict	Episode
Substitutes	Strict substitutes	Episode substitutes
Complements	Strict complements	Episode complements

occasions but not on others. Another example would be gas and milk, which are consumed during the same episode if a person is going on picnic (Betancourt and Gautschi 1990). We label products that must be used together strict complements and those that can be used jointly only on some occasions episode complements. Again, as in the case of substitutes, advertisers should look at not only strict complements but also episodic complements to identify affiliate partners.

Our discussion suggests that the relationships between products for identifying affiliate partners can be investigated in terms of whether they are substitutes, strict or episode, or complements, strict or episode. In all, there can be four types of product relationships, as illustrated in Figure 11.1.

In this classification, the ideal host affiliate would be a site that carries strict substitutes because such a site attracts the type of customers in which the sponsor is interested. However, this is not feasible because the sponsor and the host would be direct competitors. The next best alternative is sites that carry strict complements because, as the two products must be used together, those who buy one of the products should be interested in purchasing the other. Unfortunately, however, such affiliations may also be difficult to develop in that, given the natural relationship between strict complements, sites that carry one of the products may carry the other product as well. Thus, the two options that are more feasible for online retailers are to enter into affiliate relationships with sites that carry episode substitutes and complements. Sponsors therefore must identify what products and/or services might fit such categories and develop affiliations with retailers who carry them. We next discuss how the relationships between products may be identified.

Identifying the Relationships Between Products

Identifying strict substitutes and strict complements is not very difficult because, with knowledge of the principal function of the product, all products that provide the same function are strict substitutes, and those that are needed to obtain the principal function are strict complements. Products that might serve as episode substitutes and complements, however, may not be obvious, because different types of consumers may be aggregating their consumption functions at different levels (Betancourt and Gautschi 1991). For example, whereas some consumers might use a computer primarily as a device to undertake research on the Internet, others might use it mostly to obtain and play music. A third group might use it solely as a communication device to send and receive e-mail and engage in audio and/or video communications with friends and family. A fourth segment may use it exclusively for online trading of stocks and other financial instruments. For each of these consumption episodes, the set of substitutes and complements would be different. Thus, identifying episode substitutes and complements as a means of identifying affiliate partners may be difficult.

One approach to identifying episode substitutes and complements might be to undertake consumer surveys regarding how consumers use different products. The principal drawback of such an approach would be that it may not be comprehensive enough to reveal the variety of consumption experiences that different consumers derive from a product. An alternative approach to circumvent this problem would be to observe or survey consumers regarding where they search for information about different products. If consumers find episodic relationships between two products, where and how they search for information regarding them might be similar. This is the approach we suggest herein for identifying affiliate partners.

We argue that, if two products are seen as related on some episodic dimension, which may not always be known to the marketer, consumers may search similar sources for information regarding those products. In addition, the extent and patterns of search for the two products would be similar. Therefore, if researchers can observe the search behavior of consumers and use the patterns in that behavior to group products together, they should be able to identify clusters that contain products that are substitutes and/or complements, either strict or episodic.

Our methodology takes advantage of the research tradition of market structure studies (Russell and Kamakura 1997) to develop a consumer preference segmentation model and uses the model output to analyze patterns in brand preferences. Our research goal is to develop a marketing tool that can uncover patterns of preference correlation across product categories and provide us with a basis for profitably identifying partners for affiliate relationships.

A unique feature of our model is that it needs data only on whether a person browses in a product category. Marketing mix variables are not necessary for estimating the preference correlationships. Our approach makes excellent sense when marketing mix data are incomplete or missing altogether (Russell and Kamakura 1997). In the next section, we present our methodology to cluster products for identifying partners for affiliate relationships.

The Model

We assume that consumers browse the Internet for information about different product categories. We also assume that consumers derive some utility from obtaining information about a product. The utility might be due to the reduction in uncertainty regarding a product, more knowledge about the specific features of different brands of a product, or the ability to take a more informed decision regarding which brand to purchase.

Let U_{ij} be the utility that consumer i obtains from browsing in product category j. This utility can be viewed as the sum of two components, one of which is deterministic and the other random. The deterministic component, v_{ij}, is category specific and represents the utility derived from obtaining more information about the product. This component is deterministic because we can observe that, for products of type j, the utility of search is likely to be v_{ij}. The random component, ε_{ij}, is also category specific. However, it captures those factors that affect the utility of search that are not directly related to the product's features but are due more to the consumer's characteristics, as well as the context of that consumer's search. For example, a consumer might be experienced at searching for information on the Internet and thereby derive a greater utility than someone who is not as experienced. Such differences are likely to vary randomly over a population of consumers and are therefore represented by the stochastic component.

We can define the utility of search by consumer i for product category j as

$$U_{ij} = v_{ij} + e_{ij} \qquad [1]$$

To calibrate the model, we need to make specific assumptions regarding the distribution of ε_{ij}. We assume that the stochastic component is distributed normally around a mean of zero with a variance of σ_j^2. Thus,

$$\varepsilon_{ij} \sim N(0, \sigma_j^2) \qquad [2]$$

With this specification of the utility of search, we assume that consumer i will search for information in product category j if the utility crosses a threshold. Without loss of generality, we can set this threshold equal to zero. Thus, the model that we specify for search is that consumer i would search for information on product category j if

$$U_{ij} = v_{ij} + \varepsilon > 0. \qquad [3]$$

One characteristic of ε_{ij}, which is of relevance for our objective of clustering products together, is that it is likely to be correlated across different categories. This correlation is a result of the relationships between products, so that the random components for products that are perceived as related by the consumer—whether strict or episodic substitutability or complementarity— are likely to have a stronger correlation than those that are not. If we have data on the search behavior of consumers for a group of products, by calibrating the preceding model and estimating the correlations among the random components of the utilities for different products, we should be able to identify product clusters. Products within a cluster would be suitable for forming affiliate partnerships. We therefore must rewrite our model to represent the utilities of a group of products and calibrate it on search data for the entire group rather than separately for each product. Thus, we note,

$$\overline{U} = \overline{v}_i + \overline{\epsilon}, \text{ where } \overline{\epsilon} \sim MVN(0, \Sigma), \qquad [4]$$

where $\overline{U}_i$ is the $J \times 1$ vector of utilities that consumer i gets from J different product categories, is the $J \times 1$ vector of deterministic components, and is the $J \times 1$ vector of stochastic components randomly generated from a multivariate normal (MVN) distribution with zero mean and error-covariance matrix Σ as follows,

$$\Sigma = \begin{bmatrix} \sigma_j^2 & & & & \\ & \cdot & & \cdot & \\ & & \cdot & & \\ & \cdot & & \cdot & \\ \sigma_{jk} & \cdot & \cdot & & \sigma_k^2 \end{bmatrix}. \qquad [5]$$

The diagonal terms of Σ are the variances of the stochastic terms in Equation 4, whereas the terms that are off the diagonal are the covariances between the stochastic components, $\sigma_{jk} = \text{cov}(\epsilon_j, \epsilon_k)$.

We can therefore write the likelihood for household i's online search behavior in J product categories as

$$L_i = \int\int \ldots \int_{\theta} \xi(x) dx, \qquad [6]$$

where $\xi(x) \sim MVN(0, \Sigma)$ is the MVN probability density function with a mean vector of 0 and variance Σ. The limits of integration θ in Equation 6 depend on the observed behavior of the household. Specifically, if the household searches for information on category j, $\theta = (-v_{ij}, \infty)$. Alternatively, if the consumer does not search for information on the product category, $\theta = (-\infty, -v_{ij})$.

If we have observations on the browsing behavior of a pool of N consumers searching in J product categories, the likelihood can be specified as

$$L(v, \Sigma) = \prod_N L_i .$$

[7]

By maximizing L in Equation 7, we can obtain an estimate of Σ and hence infer the relationships between different products. More formally, when an estimate of Σ is obtained, we use factor analysis to obtain the component factors of the estimated variance–covariance matrix. This approach identifies which rows (and corresponding columns) of the matrix belong to the same factor, which in turn indicates that the products in the same rows (columns) belong to the same factor, are related, and form a cluster. These products would be best suited for forming affiliate partnerships.

The Data

The data are somewhat unique in the sense that they were collected over the Internet. The Internet promises tremendous cost efficiencies, such as nearly complete elimination of paper, postage, mailout, and data entry costs. The Internet also provides a means of crossing international boundaries, which have been significant barriers to conducting surveys. The time required for mailing also can be eliminated, making it possible to get instant feedback. Moreover, the marginal cost of surveying one more respondent is almost nil, making it possible, at least theoretically, to survey the entire population. Furthermore, if the survey is properly designed, the data can be entered automatically, further reducing the cost (Dillman 2000).

The survey was advertised on Yahoo!, Netscape, and WebTV. Responses were boosted by offering three cash prizes of $250 each. Respondents self-selected to participate in the survey. The respondents were presented with a list of product categories, for which they stated whether they had searched online for information. In the context of our model, the consumers' responses can be compactly represented by a $J \times 1$ vector of zeroes and ones, where the ones indicate that consumers search. This vector becomes the dependent variable in our model and is used to estimate the category-specific unique preferences and error covariance matrix.

However, Internet surveys suffer from certain constraints. The very technological advances that enhance the capabilities of Internet surveys may prove daunting to less sophisticated respondents. Moreover, because the Internet is a new medium, not everybody has access to it. Only half of the U.S. population owns a computer with Internet access, which can probably bias the findings. Households with Internet access at present tend to be biased toward high education and high income segments of the population. Moreover, the shadows of security and confidentiality issues still hang over the Internet, and many consumers may not be as willing to part with personal information on the Internet as they would be for more traditional types of surveys (Dillman 2000).

We took care to include a variety of categories such that the set was fairly representative of the market. We surveyed the popular literature to identify the product categories that seem to be succeeding in online markets. We chose categories such as computer hardware, software, and electronics, which are the leading product categories sold on the Web (*Boston Herald* 2000). According to the Gartner Group (2000), computer products and consumer electronics retailers will continue to reap the most benefits from online retailing, with revenue in these sectors expected to grow to US$59.7 billion by 2004 from US$7.5 billion in 1999. We include both hardware and software because they differ in terms of their price and short- and long-term implications. Software seems particularly suitable for selling over the Internet because it can be delivered over the Web. According to Forrester Research (2000b), products such as software, music, videos, and books that can be digitally delivered will experience explosive growth on the Web because they offer tremendous distribution cost savings, leading to lower prices. Another reason for including books is that affiliate marketing was introduced by Amazon.com. Other figures from Nielsen NetRatings (2001), PC Data (2000), and Forrester Research (2000a) show that product categories that are normally given as gifts, such as jewelry, wine, precious metals, and flowers, have recorded impressive growth rates. By buying gift items online and having them shipped by online retailers, consumers save themselves the trouble of packaging and shipping the gifts themselves. Therefore, on the basis of these surveys, we focus on hardware, software, electronics, music, video, books, jewelry, wine, precious metals, and flowers.

All the categories are tangible, and therefore, we decided to extend the analysis to include intangible categories as well. Specifically, we selected the categories of recreation, concert, travel, investment, stock quotes, and online banking. Online banking is thriving across the world. There are 13.6 million U.S. Internet users that actively use online banking services, according to Gomez Advisors (2001). Nearly a quarter of Canadians and Europeans bank online (eMarketer 2002). According to NFO Worldgroup (2001), traffic to travel Web sites in the United States is up 27 percent among leisure travelers and 10 percent among business travelers. Entertainment and travel ticket sales on the Internet will rise from US$475 million in 1999 to more than US$10 billion by 2002, according to a report by Forrester Research (1997). According to a report by Investment Company Institute (2000), nearly

68 percent of Web users use the Web for receiving financial information, regarding stock quotes, or investment.

There were 639 complete responses for the sample. Nearly 90.6 percent of the sample had some college education, and approximately one-third (37.1%) were college graduates. The sample also included households with relatively high income, with nearly 22.1 percent of the sample earning between $50,000 and $74,999 and 13.6 percent earning more than $100,000. Turning to the distribution of the sample across men and women, men constituted more than two-thirds of the sample (68.7%). In terms of age, more than 90 percent of the sample was 55 years or younger. Some additional demographic characteristics of the sample were as follows: Nearly 45.5 percent of the sample reported living in suburbs, whereas 38.5 percent resided in urban areas, and more than 90.1 percent had in excess of one year of experience in using the Internet. Overall, this sample was quite representative of the population of Internet consumers, which is characterized by high education and income (Clemente 1998; Donthu and Garcia 1999).

Results and Discussion

We calibrated the proposed model with the data obtained. The results of this analysis are presented in Tables 11.1–11.3.

The estimates of the deterministic components of the utilities of searching in each product and service category appear in Table 11.1. A large positive estimate of the component indicates a strong preference for searching for information in that category. Conversely, a large negative estimate suggests strong reluctance to search for information. On the basis of this interpretation, the estimated deterministic components of product categories indicate that consumers are most likely to search for information on computer hardware and computer software, followed by books, music, electronics, video, flowers, wine, jewelry, and metals, in that order. Regarding service categories, consumers are most likely to search travel-related sites, followed by stock quotes, investment, bank, recreation, and concert.

The correlation matrix between the stochastic components of the utility derived from searching online in different product and service categories is presented in Table 11.2. It is difficult to arrive at a meaningful summary of the managerial implications of the results in this matrix. Instead, it is preferable to factor analyze these matrices to identify which categories have a similar pattern of variances and covariances and therefore belong together for affiliate partnerships.

We used principal component analysis to reduce the error correlation matrix

Table 11.1

Search Preferences

Categories	Unique preferences	Standard error	t-ratio
Product categories			
Hardware	0.7706	0.0578	13.32
Software	0.7130	0.0564	12.65
Wine	−1.3670	0.0766	−17.85
Books	0.4832	0.0530	9.12
Video	−0.4235	0.0532	−7.96
Music	0.3137	0.0517	6.07
Electronics	−0.0916	0.0499	−1.83
Metals	−2.0145	0.1275	−15.80
Jewelry	−1.4237	0.0796	−17.87
Flowers	−0.8300	0.0582	−14.26
Service categories			
Recreation	−0.7115	0.055	−12.91
Concert	−0.76579	0.056	−13.771
Travel	0.22957	0.050	4.584
Invest	−0.65195	0.054	−12.031
Stock quotes	−0.42925	0.051	−8.496
Bank	−0.55229	0.053	−10.449

to a smaller set. Because we chose different product categories, we cannot identify strict substitutes (strict substitutes can exist only within a product category). According to our hypothesized framework for identifying successful affiliate partners, there should be three clusters among the product categories, namely, strict complement, episode complement, and episode substitute. Therefore, we factor the error correlation matrix of products into three sets. These three factors accounted for a total of 61.18 percent of the variation. These factors were then rotated by means of varimax. The resulting rotated factor matrix is presented in Table 11.3. The factors suggest that books, video, and music form one group, whereas wine, electronics, metals, jewelry, and flowers form a second. Computer hardware, software, and electronics form a third cluster. Therefore, books, video, and music should form affiliate partnerships among themselves. Wine, electronics, metals, jewelry, and flowers can similarly form another set of affiliate partnerships.

In the case of services, because services by definition are from one provider to an end user, it is unlikely that there are any categories that are strict complements or substitutes. Therefore, only two types of clustering are possible, episode substitute and episode complement. We therefore factor the error correlation matrix of the services into two sets that account for 63.17 percent of the total variance in the data. The factors were then rotated by means of varimax, and the rotated factor matrix is presented in Table 11.3.

Table 11.2

Correlation Matrix of Stochastic Component of Product and Service Categories

Product categories	Hardware	Software	Wine	Books	Video	Music	Electronics	Metals	Jewelry	Flowers
Hardware	1	0.655 (0.046)	−0.014 (0.104)	0.282" (0.068)	0.232" (0.070)	0.249" (0.065)	0.401" (0.061)	0.288 (0.410)	0.249' (0.113)	0.04 (0.076)
Software	—	1	0.023 (0.110)	0.260" (0.065)	0.272" (0.069)	0.194" (0.064)	0.346" (0.061)	0.0536 (0.299)	0.095 (0.010)	−0.077 (0.073)
Wine	—	—	1	0.101 (0.092)	0.168' (0.082)	0.1 (0.088)	0.242' (0.079)	0.365" (0.132)	0.211 (0.141)	0.115 (0.091)
Books	—	—	—	1	0.346" (0.064)	0.416" (0.056)	0.267" (0.061)	0.33 (0.292)	0.319" (0.117)	0.241" (0.074)
Video	—	—	—	—	1	0.543" (0.052)	0.334" (0.058)	0.302 (0.232)	0.173' (0.097)	0.275" (0.071)
Music	—	—	—	—	—	1	0.327" (0.057)	0.058 (0.248)	0.072 (0.114)	0.199" (0.068)
Electronics	—	—	—	—	—	—	1	0.383' (0.159)	0.306" (0.077)	0.192" (0.068)
Metals	—	—	—	—	—	—	—	1	0.606" (0.125)	0.336" (0.107)
Jewelry	—	—	—	—	—	—	—	—	1	0.342" (0.083)
Flowers	—	—	—	—	—	—	—	—	—	1

Table 11.3

Rotated Factor Loadings for Products

| | Category grouping | | |
Categories	Episode substitute	Episode complement	Strict complement
Product categories			
Hardware	0.184	0.092	**0.845**
Software	0.154	−0.019	**0.851**
Wine	−0.117	**0.468**	0.129
Books	**0.684**	0.069	0.201
Video	**0.741**	0.049	0.201
Music	**0.781**	−0.106	0.176
Electronics	0.306	**0.504**	**0.499**
Metals	−0.022	**0.917**	−0.046
Jewelry	0.245	**0.737**	0.005
Flowers	0.421	**0.554**	−0.284
Variance explained by each factor	2.159021	2.061306	1.898137
Service categories			
Recreation	**0.49844**	0.16486	
Concert	**0.83871**	0.02228	
Travel	**0.71226**	0.22645	
Invest	0.16547	**0.91401**	
Stock Quotes	0.08086	**0.91437**	
Bank	0.29082	**0.67967**	
Variance explained by each factor	1.577686	2.212384	

Note: The bold numbers indicate that product categories load on that factor more.

These factors suggest that recreation, concert, and travel form one group, and investment, stock quotes, and bank form another.

In terms of the product classification scheme that we suggested previously, books, video, and music would belong to the episode substitute category because all are used for entertainment/leisure activities. The second group, wine, electronics, metals, jewelry, and flowers, is an episode complement category. Each can be consumed and experienced independently, but when consumed together, they magnify the joint utility, say, of wine with flowers. The first group cannot be episode complement, as consumers cannot watch a movie and listen to music simultaneously. Computer hardware and software are strict complements, as discussed previously. Electronics falls in both the second and third cluster; it is quite a wide category and can consist of a range of items. On the one hand, it might include Internet telephones, modems, or speakers that might be essential for using a computer, therefore making it a strict complement. On the other hand, electronics could be episode complements if certain electronics (such as DVD players) can enhance the experience of using the computer. Thus, electronics seems to be a combination of both strict and episode complements. In the case of services, recreation, travel, and concerts appear to be episode substitutes, in that a person can pursue any of these three activities in his or her leisure time. In contrast, investment, stock quotes, and banking appear to be episode complements, in that they can be complementary in certain consumption episodes.

To depict the relationships among the different products, we plotted the factor loadings from Table 11.3 in Figures 11.2, 11.3, and 11.4. In Figure 11.2, we plotted the factor loadings of the ten product categories along the dimensions of episode complement and episode substitute. The closer that two categories are on the plot, the closer is their relationship and the higher the chances of success of any affiliate relationship formed between them. Books, video, and music cluster along the episode substitute dimension, and metals, jewelry, flowers, electronics, and wine cluster along the episode complement dimension.

Figure 11.3 plots the product categories along the two dimensions of strict complements and episode complements. According to Figure 11.3, software and hardware cluster along strict complements, and electronics is related to both strict complement and episode complement. Wine, jewelry, metals, and flowers cluster along episode complement.

Figure 11.4 plots the product categories along the dimensions of episode substitute and strict complement. Music, videos, and books cluster along episode substitute, and hardware and software cluster on strict complement.

The relationships among the service categories can be visualized by studying Figure 11.5, which has episode complement along the abscissa and episode substitute along the ordinate. As can be clearly seen, recreation, travel, and concert cluster together on the episode substitute dimension, and investment, stock quotes, and bank cluster together on the episode complement dimension.

Conclusions

The growing acceptance of the Internet among consumers has resulted in a large number of retailers entering the online market. This large influx of retailers, in turn, has resulted in rapid growth in the use of advertising formats, such as affiliate advertising, to target consumers. Unfortunately, no guidelines exist at present on how to choose affiliate partners. We argue that affiliate partnerships should be established between businesses that retail products that are related to each other. Specifically, relationships among products could be of four types: strict substitutes, strict complements, episodic substitutes, or episodic complements.

Figure 11.2 **Product Structure Episode Complement Versus Episode Substitute**

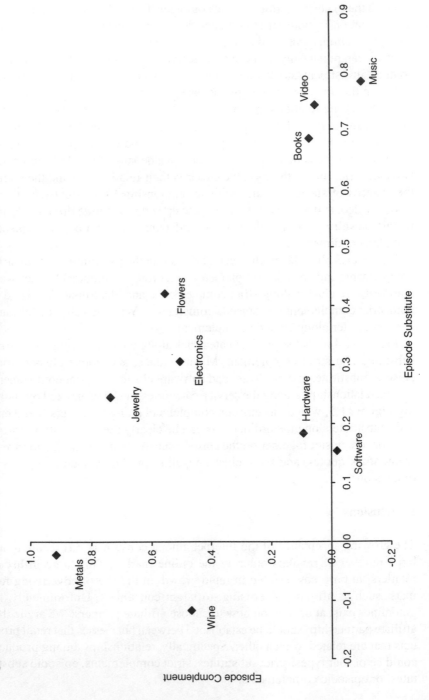

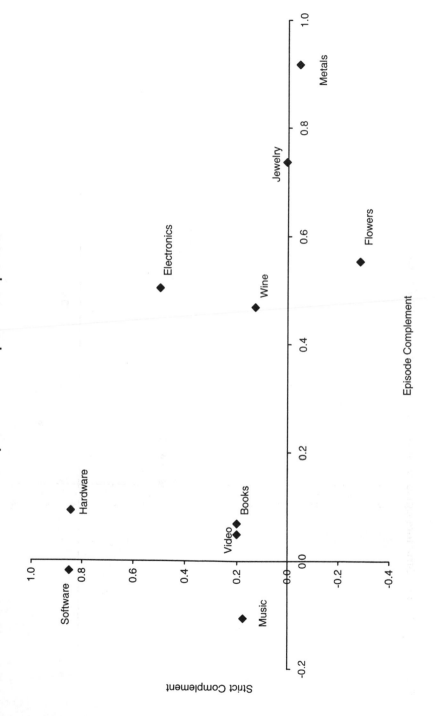

Figure 11.3 **Product Structure Strict Complement Versus Episode Complement**

Figure 11.4 **Product Structure Episode Substitute Versus Strict Complement**

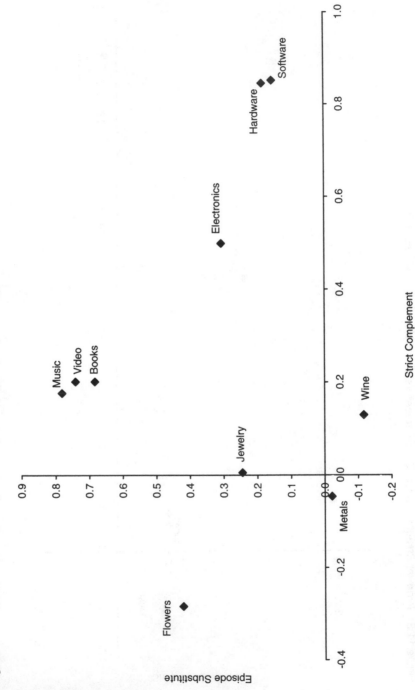

Figure 11.5   **Service Structure Episode Substitute Versus Episode Complement**

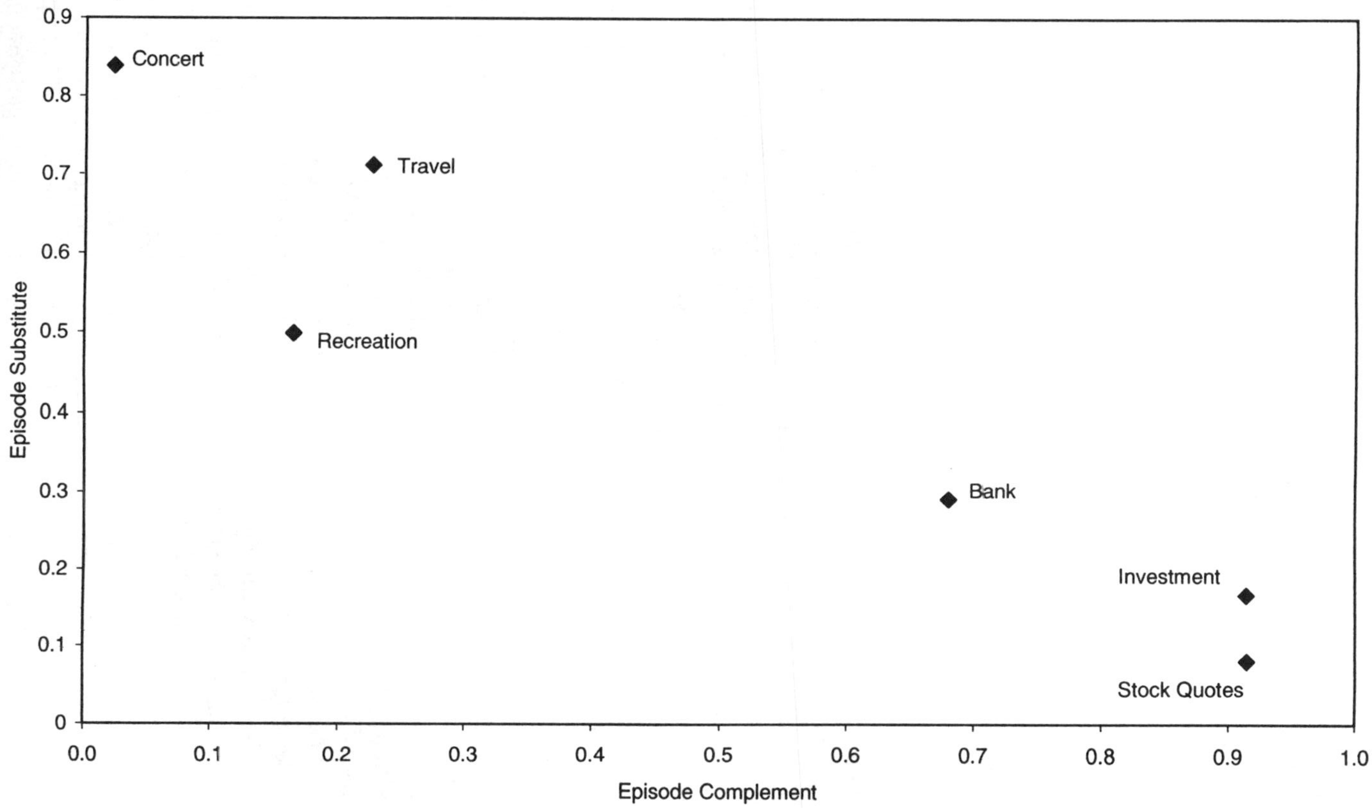

In this research, we assume that product relationships can be inferred from the way consumers collect information on the Internet. For calibrating our model, we use only data on whether consumers conduct a search. In future studies, data on the depth of information could also be collected. Although we determine the product relationships on the basis of consumers' search data, product relationships also could be inferred on the basis of product bundles, cross-elasticities, and so forth. It would be interesting to find if these different approaches yield similar relationships or different ones. Future researchers might investigate whether affiliate partnerships formed on the basis of our product relationships actually lead to purchases.

We expect managers to select affiliate partners in two steps. In the first step, they narrow down the choice to a few products, and in the second step, they choose specific firms within those categories. If the managers do everything in one step, the decision making would be unmanageable, as there are thousands and thousands of Internet-based retailers. This two-step approach would make the problem manageable. In this chapter, we have demonstrated the first step. The methodology can be easily used for the second step too. The success of affiliate advertising depends not only on whether the products are substitutes or complements, but also on the matching of brand perceptions, counterguarantees, and issues of interorganizational trust and consumer loyalty. All these issues can be incorporated into the second step.

Our framework and results raise an interesting question regarding online media planning by online retailers. Specifically, if a firm has multiple products across a variety of categories in its product mix and given that different products might have strict and episodic substitute and complementarity relationships with different products from a variety of other retailers, how should affiliate relationships be formed? Our findings suggest that, rather than choosing only one, firms might choose at least two (and if possible, three) types of affiliates for each of their products. Specifically, at least one affiliate representing each of the three types of relationships (i.e., strict complementarity, episodic complementarity, and episodic substitutability) must be used. This will expand the number of uses and thus the number of segments that each product targets. For example, a firm like Gateway might use a pure software retailer such as www.digitalriver.com in the category of strict complements, www.barnesandnoble.com as an affiliate of episodic complements, and www.3com.com as an affiliate of episodic substitutability.

It is possible, however, that not all online retailers can identify or need affiliates of all three types. For example, an online retailer of airline tickets, such as www.orbitz.com, may find an episodic complement but not a suitable affiliate as a strict complement. However, different items within a product line may also differ in whether they can have affiliate partnerships of different types. For example, whereas www.barnesandnoble.com might not be able to identify an affiliate of strict complements in general, a vendor of hardware such as www.digitalriver.com may be an affiliate for books on software, and a university might be a strict complement affiliate for textbooks.

References

Amazon (2001), "Join the Associates Program" (June 25, 2002), [http://associates. amazon.com/exec/panama/associates/ntg/browse/-/567864/002-6417984-0082434].

Betancourt, Roger and David Gautschi (1990), "Demand Complementarities, Household Production, and Retail Assortments," *Marketing Science*, 9 (2), 146–161.

Blattberg, R.C. and S.A. Neslin (1990), *Sales Promotion: Concepts, Methods and Strategies*, Englewood Cliffs, NJ: Prentice Hall.

Boston Herald (2000), "U.S. Internet Shoppers Splash Out" (November 22), [www.BostonHerald.com].

Clemente, Peter (1998), *The State of the Net: The New Frontier*, New York: McGraw-Hill.

Dillman, Don A. (2000), *Mail and Internet Surveys: The Tailored Design Approach*, 2d ed., New York: Wiley.

Donthu, Naveen and Adriana Garcia (1999), "The Internet Shopper," *Journal of Advertising Research*, 39 (3), 52–58.

eMarketer (2002), " A Quarter of Canadians Bank Online" (January 8), www. eMarketer.com.

Forrester Research (1997), "Online Ticket Sales To Reach USD10 Billion by 2001" (June 30), [www.forrester.com].

——— (2000a), "Pulling in Online Gift Buyers" (December 6), [www.forrester.com].

——— (2000b), "Spectacular Growth for Digital Delivery" (February 7) [www.forrester.com].

——— (2001), "U.S. Online Retail Sales Continue to Fall" (July 27) [www.forrester.com].

Gartner Group (2000), "U.S. B2C Sales to Top US\$ 29.3 bn This Year" (June 30), [www3.gartner.com].

Gomez Advisors (2001), "Online Banking Increasingly Popular in U.S." (September 4), [www.Gomez.com].

Henderson, James B. and Richard Quandt (1958), *Microeconomic Theory: A Mathematical Approach*, New York: McGraw-Hill.

Hoffman, Donna and Tom Novak (2000), "How to Acquire Customers on the Web," *Harvard Business Review*, 78 (3), 179–188.

Investment Company Institute (2000), "Investors Use Internet for Research" (August 11) [www.ici.org].

Kahn, Barbara and Donald R. Lehmann (1991), "Modeling Choice Among Assortments," *Journal of Retailing*, 67 (3), 274–299.

Katz, M. (1984), "Firm Specific Differentiation and Competition Among Multiproduct Firms," *Journal of Business*, 57 (1), S149–S160.

Kumar, V. and Robert Leone (1988), "Measuring the Effects of Retail Store Promotions on Brand and Store Substitution," *Journal of Marketing Research*, 21 (November), 178–185.

Moorthy, Sridhar (1984), "Market Segmentation, Self-Selection, and Product Line Design," *Marketing Science*, 3 (Fall), 288–307.

Moriarty, Mark (1985), "Retail Promotional Effects on Intra and Interbrand Sales Performance," *Journal of Retailing*, 61 (Fall), 27–47.

NFO Worldgroup (2001), "Travel Sites Continue to Thrive" (June 18) [www.plogresearch.com].

Nielsen NetRatings (2001), "Amazon, Toys 'R' Us Top Holiday eTailer List" (January 4), [www.nielsen-netratings.com].

Oren, S., S. Smith, and R. Wilson (1984), "Pricing a Product Line," *Journal of Business*, 57 (1), S73–S100.

PC Data (2000), "U.S. Consumers to Buy More Gifts Online" (December 6), [www.pcdata.com].

Russell, Gary and Wagner Kamakura (1997), "Modeling Multiple Category Brand Preference with Household Basket Data," *Journal of Retailing*, 73 (4), 439–461.

San Francisco Chronicle (2000), "Web Ads Gaining Momentum, $1.9 billion was spent in 1999, an 85.9 percent increase from 1998" (April 3), [www.sfgate.com/cgi-bin/article.cgi?file=/chronicle/archive/2000/03/31/BU100661.DTL&type=tech_article].

Walters, Rockney G. (1991), "Assessing the Impact of Retail Price Promotions on Product Substitution, Complementary Purchase, and Interstore Sales Displacement," *Journal of Marketing*, 55 (2), 17–28.

Zeff, Robin and Brad Aronson (1997), *Advertising on the Internet*, New York: Wiley.

Zenor, M.J. (1994), "The Profit Benefits of Category Management," *Journal of Marketing Research*, 31 (May), 202–213.

Part IV

Other New Media Ad Forms

12

Mobile Advertising

A Research Agenda

Virginia Rodriguez Perlado and Patrick Barwise

Despite the understandable skepticism of businesses after earlier hype, the evidence is that interactive marketing—including Internet advertising as well as permission e-mail, marketing Web sites, and mobile and other new media—is the fastest-growing area within marketing and that the reasons are long term: This is not a passing fad (Barwise and Styler 2003). There is therefore a need to extend the scope of research beyond the Internet to cover the full range of interactive marketing activities, including mobile advertising.

Because mobile advertising is such a recent development, academic research about it is only now starting to emerge. We have found just one conceptual paper (Barnes 2002a) and one empirical paper (Barwise and Strong 2002) published in academic journals. In contrast, there is already a substantial academic literature on marketing and the Internet (reviewed by Barwise, Elberse, and Hammond 2002), including research on Internet advertising as in most of the chapters in this volume.

In developing a research agenda for mobile advertising, our starting point is that most, if not all, of the issues covered by Internet advertising research are also relevant to mobile advertising. Mobile advertising—like Internet advertising—is interactive, raises questions about intrusiveness, privacy, and security, and so on. But mobile devices—cell phones, personal digital assistants (PDAs), and the like—are physically, functionally, and psychologically different from a personal computer (PC) or laptop. In this chapter, we therefore focus on distinctive aspects of mobile media and their possible implications for future advertising research.

We first review the current state of play of mobile advertising. We then briefly discuss five generic interactive advertising issues: *interactivity; intrusiveness,*

Table 12.1

Distinctive Aspects of Mobile Media: Potential Implications for Research on Five Generic Interactive Advertising Issues

Generic interactive advertising issues	Implications of distinctive aspects of mobile media for research on
Interactivity	Interactivity issues within interactive advertising
Intrusiveness, privacy, security	Intrusiveness/privacy/security issues within interactive advertising
"Rich media" content	"Rich media" content within interactive advertising
Advertising strategies	Interactive advertising strategies within interactive advertising
Measurement and effectiveness	Measurement and effectiveness issues within interactive advertising

Note: Distinctive aspects of mobile media: physical characteristics, personal identity, ubiquity, location sensitivity.

privacy, and security; "rich media" content; advertising strategies; and *measurement and effectiveness.* Almost all research on interactive advertising falls under one or more of these headings although there are, of course, many other ways of categorizing the research. Against this background, we then introduce four distinctive aspects of mobile media: *physical characteristics*—in order to be portable, mobile devices are small, have limited storage, and so on; *personal identity*—a mobile phone is part of an individual's personal identity, more like a favorite item of clothing than just a piece of technology; *ubiquity*—mobile media can be used at any time and in almost any location; and *location sensitivity*—increasingly, mobile media can signal, or respond to, their location.

In the main part of the chapter, we discuss the possible implications of these distinctive aspects of mobile media for each of the five generic interactive advertising issues (Table 12.1). We first discuss the implications of the distinctive features of mobile media for research on interactivity issues within interactive advertising; then we discuss the implications for issues concerning intrusiveness, privacy, and security, and so on. Finally, we draw these implications together into an integrated research agenda.

Mobile Advertising: The State of Play

In most countries, consumer digital mobile communications have been adopted even faster than the Internet. In the United Kingdom (UK), 85 percent of individuals owned a mobile phone in January 2003 (Merrill Lynch 2003) versus only 47 percent with access to the Internet at home (Oftel 2003). Even in the United States, where mobile penetration has been relatively slow due to a lack of standards, it is now growing fast and is likely to overtake in-home Internet penetration soon, if it has not already done so.

The original "killer application" for mobile media was voice telephony. From the early 1990s, digital (2G, i.e., "second-generation," as opposed to analog/1G "first-generation") mobile increased the quality and capacity and reduced the cost of mobile telephony, causing the market to accelerate rapidly. As a sideline, 2G also allowed users to send very short text messages to each other—up to 160 characters—using the short message service (SMS) protocol. The latter was seen as a "clunky" technology, with laborious input, limited capacity, and text-only output displayed on a tiny screen. However, just as had happened twenty years earlier with e-mail on the Internet (Hafner and Lyon 1996, 189), SMS took off far faster than expected, reflecting users' strong motivation to communicate with each other.

As with the Internet and broadband, there has also been extensive hype about mobile communications beyond 2G, focusing on higher-capacity "3G" (i.e., third-generation) technologies promising always-on service, richer content, more interactivity, convergence with the Internet, mobile e-commerce ("m-commerce"), and location-based applications that exploit the technology's ability to tailor communications to the user's specific location at the time. The past two to three years have seen a reaction against this hype as several factors have held back developments beyond 2G: the lack of compelling applications for which users are willing to pay, the lack of standards, high costs, technical problems, tough economic conditions, and a skeptical investment climate.

One of the most successful services beyond 2G is NTT DoCoMo's, iMode ("information-mode") service in Japan (Ratliff 2002). First introduced in 1999, iMode offers cell phones and PDAs with Web browsing and e-mail capabilities. In Japan, mobile phone penetration among people fifteen to sixty-five years old is 94 percent. Over 76 percent of these people use browser phones capable of accessing the Internet (Telecommunication Carriers Association 2003). When using iMode services, users do not pay for the time they are connected to a Web site or service, but are charged only according to the volume of data transmitted. iMode has become a brand and stands for key concepts like simplicity, functionality, and meeting consumers' needs (Barnes 2002b).

In summary, the current state of play is as follows. Digital (2G) mobile is a huge medium that already reaches many more global consumers than the Internet; its penetration is close to saturation in many countries and growing fast in most others. Short message service is used extensively around the world, especially by 2G users under age thirty-five who tend to be hard to reach via television and many other advertising media. U.S. usage of SMS is lower than that in most other developed countries but is growing fast, spurred by events such as AT&T Wireless's sponsorship of text voting for the reality television series *American Idol,* which generated 7.5 million texts. A third of the senders had never texted before (Budden and Moules 2003). More advanced mobile technologies are being rolled out, but the process is difficult, expensive, and fragmented. Applications include picture messaging, business and information services on PDAs, and various entertainment services for consumers.

Generic Interactive Advertising Issues

Interactivity

There has been a lot of academic discussion about interactivity, its definition and implications (e.g., Blattberg and Deighton 1991; Rust and Oliver 1994; Dutton 1996; Deighton 1996). Also the impact of information control on consumers' decision quality, memory, knowledge, and confidence has been explored some by researchers (e.g., Ariely 2000). According to Bezjian-Avery, Calder, and Iacobucci (1998), interactivity does not always enhance advertising effectiveness as it can interrupt the process of persuasion, especially when ads are targeted. However, this evidence poses a challenge because consumers are generally more responsive to targeted ads (Mehta and Sivadas, 1995). The negative effect of interactivity has also been researched by Edwards, Li, and Lee (ch. 10 in this volume), who found that intrusive Web advertisements may result in feelings of irritation or avoidance of the ads altogether.

Intrusiveness, Privacy, and Security

Issues of privacy and data protection have been important constraints on interactive marketing. Research suggests that part of consumers' low trust in online vendors arises from their perceived lack of control over Web businesses' access to their personal information and the secondary use of this information (Hoffman, Novak, and Peralta 1999). Significant research has been conducted on the Internet's influence on building trust. Some of the research reviewed by Barwise, Elberse, and Hammond (2002) highlights the Internet's contributions to relationship marketing, and especially to commitment, satisfaction, and trust (e.g., Bauer, Grether, and Leach 2002). Others go even further presenting evidence that—contrary to self-regulation efforts—

when managing consumer information, positively improving consumer trust is more effective than efforts to reduce concern (Milne and Boza 1999).

Rich Media Content

In the context of Internet advertising, advertisers are trying to find alternatives to low and declining click-through rates for conventional banner ads. "Rich media" ads (e.g., pop-ups and pop-unders) offer more sophisticated messages on the Web (Edwards, Li, and Lee, ch. 10 in this volume). However, the richer the media the greater the complexity, and therefore the higher the chances of making a mistake when making small changes (Sterne and Priore 2000). More important, there is considerable consumer reaction against these more intrusive online ad formats. Much of the growth in Internet advertising is therefore in sponsored searching, where the advertiser "buys" relevant keywords or phrases on a search engine such as Google, usually on a "cost per lead" basis (Barwise and Styler 2003).

Advertising Strategies

The Internet, as an advertising medium, can be used in many ways, for example, mass/targeted, push/pull, local/national/global (Silk, Klein, and Berndt 2001). It now includes a wide range of advertising formats, with many alternatives to traditional banner ads (Bellman and Rossiter 2001, Flores 2001). Perhaps the fastest-growing part of Internet marketing is e-mail, which has many of the benefits of direct mail, being accountable, precisely targeted, and cheap (Barwise and Styler 2003; Chaffey 2003). Researchers are starting to explore the integration of new media within marketing communications: The future challenge will be to understand not only how each medium and format works, but also how they work together (Flores 2001), including in combination with new media such as advertising on wireless devices (Barwise and Strong 2002) and interactive digital television (Brodin, Barwise, and Canhoto 2002; Mercier and Barwise 2004).

Measurement and Effectiveness

The measurement and effectiveness of online advertising have naturally been topics of great interest among advertisers and researchers. Although click-through rates are low and falling, this observation may underestimate total consumer response to banner ads (Flores 2001). In the same line of study, other researchers have also highlighted the need for a more comprehensive measure of effectiveness to obtain more insight (e.g., Briggs and

Hollis 1997; Shen, ch. 9 in this volume; Bhat, Bevans, and Sengupta, ch. 4 in this volume).

Four Distinctive Aspects of Mobile Advertising

We now turn to the four distinctive aspects of mobile advertising briefly introduced at the start of this chapter.

Physical Characteristics

Mobile phones need to be small and highly portable. In most countries—with the exception of some Asia Pacific countries—SMS is still the most common platform for mobile advertising. More complex applications and technology developments such as multimedia messaging service (MMS), incorporating improved text, color pictures, sound, and even video, will be adopted in due course. But as things stand, mobile devices have small screens and keypads and very limited memory (typically up to ten short text messages).

Personal Identity

Mobile phones belong to individuals who carry them at all times. According to the iSociety report (Crabtree, Nathan, and Roberts 2003), 38 percent of the adult population (15 and older) in Great Britain say they could not manage without their mobile phone. Cell phones are so closely identified with their owners that they are sometimes compared to a body part (Oksman and Rautiainen 2001; Hulme and Peters 2001). Mobile phones are also symbolic: They say something to other people about the individual even before they are switched on (Goffman 1959; Crabtree, Nathan, and Roberts 2003). This has enormous implications for advertisers: On the one hand, in principle it opens the door to the ultimate channel for personalized one-to-one marketing; on the other hand, it presents a potential source of perceived intrusiveness if not used with great care.

Ubiquity

The cell phone is "always on" and can be used almost anywhere. This again represents both a challenge and an opportunity for advertisers. It is a challenge because the mobile medium likely entails greater risk of intrusiveness than the fixed-line Internet. Because consumers have their cell phones with them at all times, mobile advertising may be perceived as an interruption to their normal lives (working, driving, shopping, studying, etc.). Consumers may also resent it when an advertiser sends a message, which uses up scarce text memory on the cell phone—and in some cases even generates a small financial cost to the consumer, charged by the mobile network operator. On the other hand, the ubiquity of mobile media represents the ultimate opportunity to interact with consumers at different times for different purposes, wherever they may be.

Location Sensitivity

As already noted, mobile media can be location as well as time sensitive. The location sensitivity of mobile devices represents an additional opportunity (again not without challenges) for advertisers to reach consumers by offering location-based services. According to an ARC Group report (2002), location-based services will account for 40 percent of operators' mobile data services revenue by 2007. It has been argued that third-party marketers will use location-based services to deliver extra value to customers once precise location information is available in a standardized form from all operators (Schmidt 2001). However, some issues need to be addressed beforehand: (1) operators' speed in deploying location-sensing technology varies, (2) operators' debt will slow down such deployment, and (3) standards need to be agreed upon.

We now discuss the possible implications of these distinctive characteristics of mobile media for research on the different aspects of interactive advertising, starting with interactivity itself.

Interactivity

The distinctive characteristics of mobile media make them in some ways even more interactive than the Internet. However, this potential needs to be fully understood in order for advertisers and operators to transform it into a commercial reality. The small size of mobile devices represents both advantages and disadvantages for advertisers. Consumers can carry them at all times. Furthermore, SMS, the predominant mobile advertising platform, is widely used with 58 percent of UK mobile users sending text messages (Oftel 2002a). Worldwide, 430 billion mobile messages were sent in 2002, 95 percent using basic SMS (Global Information Inc. 2003). On the minus side, the small screen, memory, and keypad of a mobile device severely limit how much information consumers are willing to read, how long they store messages, and how much they can be bothered to text back. In comparison with e-mail, SMS appears to be good for fast, simple interactivity but not for anything more complex (Barwise and Strong 2002). One growing application fits this profile: the use of SMS as a response channel for direct-response advertisements on traditional media such as television, print, and radio, and also on packaging, especially for special offers (Flytxt 2004).

The main benefit derived from the personal identity and ubiquity of mobile media is the potential to allow brands to generate and maintain a permission-based one-to-one dialogue with consumers, which in turn allows the marketer to ascertain whether the consumer is paying attention (Peppers and Rogers 1993; Godin 1999). Also, due to their personal identity, mobile media are potentially well suited to provide services that are personalized based on the user's preferences—if these can be ascertained (Barnes 2002a). However, the network charges involved to maintain that dialogue may deter consumers unless the marketer offers continuing incentives.

Related to the high usage of mobile devices for social communication, community is potentially an important aspect of viral marketing via wireless devices (Barnes 2002a). The success of mobile advertising, ringtones, and screen savers has a lot to do with the ability to show, share, and pass on. Thus, mobile advertisers are well advised to ensure that this "social content" is shared where possible.

For mobile advertising, even more than for e-mail, relevance is key (Barwise and Strong 2002). The ubiquity of mobile phones represents an opportunity to offer targeted advertising linked to consumers' interests at particular points in time. For instance, some media companies cross-sell products via SMS to target audiences or even to promote individual broadcasts or news breaking in an evening newspaper; other advertisers are using mobile advertising to target their customers at specific times of the year such as Christmas, Valentine's Day, and Mother's Day (Barwise and Strong 2002).

In the future, interactivity may be increased thanks to location-based services that allow advertisers to determine where consumers are located and accordingly send them attractive advertising messages. As Yuan and Tsao (2003) found, advertising that includes location-based services and customized recommendations is believed to affect customers' participation in advertised activities better than nonlocation-based/noncustomized advertisements.

Potential research questions here are: (1) How does mobile advertising compare with Internet advertising in terms of the typical speed of response, optimum message size, and the size of the message texted back? (2) In what contexts is a mobile device suitable as a response medium for direct-response advertising and special offers? (3) To what extent do mobile network charges deter consumers from interacting with advertisers via this medium? and (4) What is the potential of location-based advertising via mobile media? What are the pitfalls, and how can these be addressed?

Intrusiveness, Privacy, Security

The mobile medium is potentially even more intrusive than are other interactive marketing channels. The main reasons are its ubiquity and personal identity. Ubiquity becomes a potential negative if it means, say, a consumer in a business meeting receiving a text message asking her to reply immediately in order to win a holiday for two. Personal identity may become a negative if the advertiser misjudges either the consumer's product interests or the degree of personalization deemed appropriate. Some consumers dislike advertisers getting too personal: "If it said, 'Hey Steve' at the top, maybe I wouldn't like that—trying to be your friend" (Barwise and Strong 2002, 22)

Again, the mobile medium is potentially the ideal "conversational" one-to-one medium, but this also requires the marketer to follow the normal rules of conversation. For instance, as a general rule mobile advertisers should work hard (in terms of database management) to avoid sending the same message twice to the same individual—a conversational faux pas equivalent to telling the same joke twice in the pub (Barwise 2001). This is likely even more important for mobile than for e-mail marketing, and almost certainly more important than for, say, banner ads: Consumers are unlikely to resent it much if they see the same banner ad several times. The absence of clutter in the mobile medium helps maintain a "surprise factor," which may in turn reduce the perceived intrusiveness. But growth in mobile advertising may dilute the advertising message or even annoy users (Barnes 2002a).

Another potential reason for intrusiveness is the higher level of interactivity offered by the mobile medium. As Edwards, Li, and Lee (ch. 10 in this volume) found, the perceived intrusiveness of an ad should be considered a cognitive evaluation of the degree to which the advertisement interrupts a person's goals (either personal or hedonic) and different from the emotional or behavioral outcomes that may result. This insight is directly applicable to mobile advertising. The consequence of this potential intrusiveness is that relevance and permission become even more important in mobile advertising (Barwise and Strong 2002). Using permission-based marketing, the dialogue with consumers should become more like a good conversation: anticipated, personal, and relevant (Godin 1999). In terms of privacy and security, in mobile advertising it has been argued that profiling information should be collected explicitly and used judiciously (Barwise and Strong 2002).

Further research is needed to understand what causes perceived intrusiveness and how to reduce it. For example, it would be very useful for the industry to understand (both in absolute terms and relative to the Internet): (1) the antecedents of perceived intrusiveness in the context of mobile advertising, (2) the effect of explicit ("opt-in") permission on the perceived intrusiveness of mobile advertising, and (3) the appropriate degree of personalization and how this relates to different types of context.

"Rich Media" Content

Some rich media content (i.e., pictures, video, and high-quality sound) used in mobile advertising may pose the same or even more problems as in other forms of interactive advertising because of the small physical size of mobile devices. However, there is no research available on how Western consumers may react to rich media content on their cell phones, partly because the dominant platform for mobile advertising is still SMS text messaging.

The exception is Japan, where the introduction of iMode has generated very positive responses to wireless advertising. In fact, mobile advertising in Japan has more consumer appeal than advertising on the conventional Internet. Claimed click-through rates for mobile banner ads during the summer of 2000 averaged 3.6 percent, and those for wireless e-mail on iMode averaged 24 percent, while click-through rates for online banner ads on desktop PCs in Japan averaged no more than 0.5 or 0.6 percent (Barnes 2002b). Ratliff (2002) reports that wireless ads have about ten times the click-through rate of regular Web-based e-mail and banner ads, and that using iMode service in tandem with printed media makes up for the lack of information in the cell phone environment.

As already noted, the dominant mobile advertising platform in most of the world is still SMS (i.e., up to 160 characters of text message). However, this platform may change with the new mobile technologies. According to Forrester (De Lussanet 2002), messaging revenue will drop in Europe for the first time in 2004 as SMS volume stabilizes while prices continue to fall until new message types (enhanced messaging services, multimedia messaging services, instant messaging services, wireless e-mail) can compensate. According to some analysts' reports (ARC Group 2002) over 20 percent of mobile data users worldwide will use MMS by 2007.

The introduction of mobile advertising in Europe has been relatively successful due to the simplicity of SMS. However, clear, simple, and creative ad copy is essential to engage consumers (Barwise and Strong 2002). The problem is that new technologies may add complexity for consumers already overwhelmed with daily routines. On the positive side, a broader range of technologies will increase advertisers' ways of reaching different audiences or presenting different products (e.g., advertising a compact disc may benefit from using images and sounds, as opposed to advertising a book, which may require only the use of words). Another problem is the large size of mobile phones capable of displaying "rich media" content. Multimedia phones tend to be bigger and heavier than phones without MMS capabilities. This improves their picture quality and impact, but may decrease their ubiquity and portability and hence reduce advertising reach.

Location-based services, however, may be welcomed by users if they are offered in moderation in a permission-based mode and give the consumer the flexibility to choose when and when not to use them. According to iSociety (Crabtree, Nathan, and Roberts 2003), future mobile services are likely to succeed to the extent that they target users' mobility, and the specific times and places in which they are mobile. In a similar way, rich media content may be perceived as invading, even more, the personal space offered by mobile phones. Because it involves no sounds or flashy images, SMS may be potentially less annoying than richer media.

In conclusion, a new era of multimedia messaging is gradually emerging, which, in due course, will be enhanced by the next generation of mobile telephony. This will open up many more opportunities for brands to communicate with consumers in increasingly diverse and sophisticated ways (e.g., games, pictures, ringtones, music, video clips, etc.). However, there is a great deal of uncertainty about how consumers will react to new mobile technologies offering richer context. Some of the questions to be addressed are: (1) Which new mobile technologies are consumers most likely to embrace? (2) What do consumers expect from mobile technology in the next few years? (3) How do consumers react to different types of rich/multimedia mobile ads? and (4) How can advertisers best exploit the limited screen size of mobile devices in comparison with PCs and laptops? How can they exploit the potentially better sound quality?

Advertising Strategies

Mobile advertising is still at an early stage and different players are still experimenting with various formats. However, research and practice suggest that much can be achieved using simple mobile technology that is already well established (Barnes 2002a; Barwise and Strong 2002). Furthermore, mobile advertising is just one part of mobile marketing. If we take into account that relationship marketing is probably the dominant focus of interactive marketing, this trend may help grow mobile marketing expenditure given the interactivity of the medium and the portability of mobile phones. Among established interactive marketing techniques, e-mail is the closest one to mobile advertising due to the personal identity of e-mail addresses and the potential interactivity of the medium. Further, e-mail, like mobile advertising, has the advantage of low cost, fast delivery, and easy response—hence its rapid growth (Barwise and Styles 2003).

Despite the benefits presented by the mobile medium to reach audiences in new ways, advertisers have had to be creative in using this new channel as a successful marketing tool. In particular, the ubiquity and portability of mobile devices have encouraged advertisers to look for new ways to obtain consumers' permission (i.e., opt-in) to start a "mobile advertising conversation" with them. Also, the viral effects of mobile campaigns have encouraged advertisers to find creative ways to encourage users to share their mobile advertising messages. More generally, the early indicators are that the most successful users of mobile advertising have integrated the mobile channel into their marketing communications and therefore leveraged the power of combining different media to reach a wider audience and to support different stages of the purchase and postpurchase process. Commonly used mobile advertising strategies include the following:

1. *Relationship marketing/customer loyalty.* Relationship marketing is the practice of focusing resources on existing customers, especially those identified as being of high potential value, and strengthening relationships with them so that they remain loyal and end up buying more from the company (McKenna 1991). Advani and Choudhury (2001) argue that wireless technology is an ideal medium for supporting relationship marketing because of its personal, individual nature, high penetration, ubiquity, and familiar, well-established technology. For instance, wireless can be used to communicate valuable content—such as special offers, exclusive information, and games—in exchange for personal data.

2. *Media/entertainment.* This type of campaign includes any mechanism whereby, using other media as the main platform, consumers are invited to interact with the program or editorial content via a mobile phone. Examples include television voting, television quizzes, radio contests, ringtone/logo requests, editorial feedback, and so forth.

3. *Direct response-customer acquisition.* This approach includes any campaign where consumers are invited to respond via mobile phone to a promotional question. It may be supported by other media (e.g., magazine advertorials, radio competitions), an opt-in database (e.g., a sports brand sending a "Txt & Win" message to the members of a beverage brand's opt-in database), or physical presence (e.g., on-pack or in-store promotions, movie releases).

4. *Brand awareness.* This refers to a mobile advertising message where brand building is the main goal. Consumers are not necessarily invited to interact, the main purpose being to raise awareness. This category will likely become more successful as wireless technology evolves and helps to make mobile advertising more attractive to the consumer (i.e., picture messaging, m-coupons, product description, offer, etc.).

Strategies 2 and 3 are often used by brand owners to build their opt-in databases from scratch and then to evolve into a relationship marketing approach. Strategy 4 can be used as a stand-alone mechanism when a good opt-in mobile phone database is available.

In terms of market segmentation, the use of text messaging varies greatly across different demographic groups. Generally, women, younger consumers, those belonging to middle-income social groups, and homes with children most frequently send text rather than make voice calls. People over age fifty-five and, to a lesser extent, lower-spending and prepay mobile customers are among those least likely to use SMS (Oftel 2002a, 2002b). If we consider that 89 percent of fifteen to twenty-four-year-olds in the UK have a mobile phone, according to industry regulator Oftel, it is no surprise that youth brands should want to use SMS to target children and teenagers. Furthermore, research from mobile marketing agency Flytxt reveals that two-thirds of teenage mobile phone users would rather lose voice than text functionality on their phone (Flytxt 2003). Going beyond demographics, opt-in permission enables much more precise targeting in terms of lifestyle and individual interests (Barwise and Strong 2002).

Over the next few years, advertisers will also need to take account of the location sensitivity of mobile phones. Although location-based technologies are starting to emerge, there are some initial barriers, as we mentioned earlier, that service providers and advertisers will have to overcome. To accelerate this process, some advertisers may avoid the "roadblocks" by building location-sensitive services that act independently of the location-sensing technology offered by network operators. This will mean obtaining location information from other sources (e.g., affiliated sites passing location information to one another embedded in URL links, and location brokers or mobile marketing agencies supplying location information).

Research questions include the following: (1) What are the most cost-effective ways for advertisers to build an opt-in or permission-based database of mobile consumers? (2) What are the most cost-effective combinations of traditional media (e.g., for direct response advertising) and mobile media for different marketing tasks? and (3) What are mobile technology's particular strengths and weaknesses as an advertising medium, especially relative to other interactive media such as Web advertising and e-mail?

Measurement and Effectiveness

Mobile advertising is emerging as a high-potential interactive marketing tool, but it is still embryonic and experimental (Barnes 2002a). Compared to the Internet—where the ease of collecting data has resulted in a proliferation of measures, each with its own strengths and weaknesses—there is little research to date on the measurement and effectiveness of mobile advertising. The only empirical study published thus far in an academic journal is the evaluation of permission-based mobile advertising by Barwise and Strong (2002). Their main conclusions were: (1) Consumers will respond well to text advertisements that grab their attention. However, this involves getting the language, style, humor, and so forth, exactly right for the target audience. (2) The message must be relevant. Mobile is a highly personal medium suitable for one-to-one communication, but this sets high standards for targeting based on detailed profiling. It also involves combining high-speed creativity (e.g., responding to breaking news at a sport event) with excellent database management (e.g., not inadvertently sending the same message twice to the same person). (3) Response mechanisms have to be extremely simple, preferably using SMS itself and requiring little keying by the consumer. (4) For reputable, established brands, explicit permission is essential with such a personal medium.

One further factor, not present to the same extent for other interactive marketing channels, is the advertiser's dependency on mobile operators. The Internet allows seamless communication over any distance, local or global (Barwise, Elberse, and Hammond 2002). However, the mobile medium is generally constrained to the national network for reliable communication and dependent on mobile operators' technology and service quality. In some cases, delays in transmission by the network operator can cause considerable campaign disruptions.

Additional research may be helpful to understand: (1) What are the most effective mobile advertising campaigns and mechanisms for generating consumers' interest? (2) What parameters should be developed to evaluate the effectiveness of mobile advertising campaigns? and (3) To what extent can mobile advertising be evaluated using the same metrics as Internet advertising? Does it require additional metrics?

Conclusions: An Integrated Research Agenda for Mobile Advertising

Mobile advertising is an emerging topic for which almost no academic research has been done at this stage. In this chapter, we have argued that all the generic interactive advertising issues are relevant to mobile advertising but that the specific research questions differ somewhat because of the distinctive aspects of mobile media. We discussed four such distinctive aspects: the physical characteristics of mobile media, their greater degree of personal identity for the consumer, their ubiquity, and (as an emerging theme) their

Table 12.2

A Research Agenda for Mobile Advertising

Consumer response to mobile advertising
- Comparative research on mobile vs. the Internet, for example, speed of response and optimum message size.
- The impact of mobile network charges on consumer response to advertising
- Consumer response to different types of "rich media" mobile advertisements

Privacy and personalization
- The antecedents of perceived intrusiveness
- The effect of explicit permission on perceived intrusiveness
- The appropriate degree of personalization

Advertising strategy and execution
- Mobile medium channel as a response for direct-response advertising
- The strengths and weaknesses of mobile as an advertising medium, especially relative to the Internet
- Cost-effective strategies for building an opt-in database of mobile consumers
- Evaluation and metrics for mobile advertising

New mobile technologies
- Consumers' likely uptake of more advanced mobile technologies ("3G," etc)
- The potential of location-based mobile advertising

potential location sensitivity. Perhaps the first advice we might give to scholars potentially interested in researching this new medium is to explore one or more of these characteristics further than we have had space to do is this chapter.

Based on these characteristics, we suggest a range of issues as an initial research agenda for mobile advertising. These are drawn together in Table 12.2.

Doubtless reflecting our own interests, this agenda focuses on practical issues of interest to advertisers. A complementary agenda might be developed that focuses on the development and testing of theory.

Again, this should probably aim to build on existing research on Internet advertising, rather than trying to build theory from scratch.

References

Advani, R. and K. Choudhury (2001), "Making the Most of B2C Wireless," *Business Strategy Review*, 12 (2), 39–49.

ARC Group (2002), Press release, January 30, 2003 [www.arcgroup.com.homepage.nsf/prs/pro302030v].

Ariely, D. (2000), "Controlling the Information Flow: Effects on Consumers' Decisionmaking and Preferences," *Journal of Consumer Research*, 27 (2) (September), 233–248.

Barnes, S.J. (2002a), "Wireless Digital Advertising Nature and Implications," *International Journal of Advertising*, 21, 339–420.

——— (2002b), "The Mobile Commerce Value Chain: Analysis and Future Developments," *International Journal of Information Management*, 22, 91–108.

Barwise, P. (2001), "Stop Me If I've Told You This B4," *Financial Times Creative Business* (August 7), 3.

Barwise, P., A. Elberse, and K. Hammond (2002), "Marketing and the Internet," in *Handbook of Marketing*, Barton A. Weitz and Robin Wensley, eds., 527–557. Thousand Oaks, CA: Sage, [www.marketingandtheinternet.com].

Barwise, P. and C. Strong (2002), "Permission-Based Mobile Advertising," *Journal of Interactive Marketing*, 16 (1) (Winter), 14–24.

Barwise, P. and A. Styler (2003), *The MET Report: Marketing Expenditure Trends*, London Business School [www.london.edu/marketing/met].

Bauer, H.H., M. Grether, and M. Leach (2002), "Building Customer Relations Over the Internet," *Industrial Marketing Management*, 13 (2), 155–163.

Bellman, S. and J.R. Rossiter (2001), "The Web Ad Schema," working paper, Graduate School of Management, University of Western Australia.

Bezjian-Avery, A., B. Calder, and D. Iacobucci (1998), "New Media Interactive Advertising vs. Traditional Advertising," *Journal of Advertising Research* 38 (4), 23–32.

Blattberg, C.R. and J. Deighton (1991), "Interactive Marketing: Exploring the Age of Addressability," *Sloan Management Review*, 33 (Fall), 5–14.

Briggs, R. and N. Hollis (1997), "Advertising on the Web: Is There Response Before Click-Through?" *Journal of Advertising Research* (March–April), 33–45.

Brodin, K., P. Barwise, and A.I. Canhoto (2002), "UK Consumer Responses to iDTV," Future Media Report, London Business School, [www.idtvconsumers.com].

Budden, R. and J. Moules (2003), "Thumbs Up, at Last," *Financial Times* (July), 11.

Chaffey, David (2003), *Total E-mail Marketing*, Elsevier Butterworth-Heinemann [www.elsevier.com].

Crabtree, J., M. Nathan, and S. Roberts (2003), "MobileUK, Mobile Phones and Everyday Life," *iSociety*.

Deighton, J. (1996), "The Future of Interactive Marketing," *Harvard Business Review* (November–December), 151–162.

De Lussanet, M. (2002), "Mobile Messaging's Next Generation," *Forrester Research Report*, (March).

Dutton, W.H. (1996), *Information and Communication Technologies: Visions and Realities*, New York: Oxford University Press

Flores, L. (2001), "Internet Advertising Effectiveness: What Did We Learn and Where Are We Going?" [www.poolonline.com/archive/issue16/iss16fea3.html].

Flytxt (2004), [www.flytxt.com/productscontent.htm].

——— (2003), "Responsible SMS Campaigns to Kids," *Marketing* (April), [www.flytxt.com].

Global Information Inc. (2003) (March) [www.gii.co.jp/press/te112779_en.shtml].

Godin, S. (1999), *Permission Marketing—Turning Strangers into Friends and Friends into Customers*, New York: Simon and Schuster.

Goffman, E. (1959), *The Presentation of Self in Everyday Life*, New York, Doubleday.

Hafner, K. and M. Lyon (1996), *Where Wizards Stay Up Late: The Origins of the Internet*, New York: Touchstone.

Hoffman, Donna, Thomas P. Novak, and M.A. Peralta (1999), "Building Consumer Trust Online," *Communications of the ACM*, 42, 80–85.

Hulme, Michael and Sue Peters (2001), "Me, My Phone and I: The Role of the Mobile Phone," paper presented at the CHI 2002 Workshop on Mobile Communications, March 30–April 5, Seattle [www.cs.colorado.edu/~palen/chi_workshop].

McKenna, R. (1991), *Relationship Marketing*, Reading, MA: Addison-Wesley.

Mehta, R. and E. Sivadas (1995), "Direct Marketing on the Internet: An Empirical Assessment of Consumer Attitudes," *Journal of Direct Marketing*, 9 (3) (Summer), 21–32.

Mercier, P. and P. Barwise (2004), "The Evolution of Digital TV" Future Media Report, London Business School, [www.idtvconsumers2.com].

Merrill Lynch (2003), "Carphone Warehouse Report" (January).

Milne, G.R. and M.-E. Boza (1999), "Trust and Concern in Consumers' Perceptions of Marketing Information Management Practices," *Journal of Interactive Marketing*, 13 (Winter), 5–24.

Oftel (2002a), "Consumers' Use of Mobile Telephony," *Oftel Report* (May), [www. ofcom.org].

——— (2002b), "Consumers' Use of Mobile Telephony" *Oftel Report* (November), [www.ofcom.org].

——— (2003), "Consumers' Use of the Internet," *Oftel Report* (July), [www.ofcom. org].

Oksman, Virpi and Pirjo Rautiainen (2001), "Perhaps It Is a Body Part: How Mobile Phone Became an Organic Part of Everyday Lives of Children and Adolescents," paper presented at the Nordic Conference for Media, August 11–13, Reykjavik, Iceland.

Peppers, D. and M. Rogers (1993), *The One-To-One Future*, New York: Doubleday.

Ratliff, J. (2002), "NTT DoCoMo and Its i-mode Success: Origins and Implications," *California Management Review*, (Spring), 55–71.

Rust R.T. and R.W. Oliver (1994), "The Death of Advertising," *Journal of Advertising* (23), 71–77.

Schmidt, C. (2001), "Shortcuts to Mobile Location Services," *Forrester Research Report* (May), 1–21.

Silk, A. J., L.R. Klein, and E.R. Berndt (2001), "The Emerging Position of the Internet as an Advertising Medium," *Netnomics*, (3) 129–148.

Sterne, J. and A. Priore (2000), "E-mail Marketing: Using E-mail to Reach Your Target Audience and Build Customer Relationships," Wiley Computer Publishing [www.wiley.co.uk/compbooks/index-nojs.html].

Telecommunications Carriers Association (2003) (March), [www.tca.or.jp/index-e.html].

Yuan, S.-T. and Y.W. Tsao (2003), "A Recommendation Mechanism for Contextualized Mobile Advertising," *Expert Systems with Applications*, (24) 399–414.

13

Mobile Promotional Communication and Machine Persuasion

A New Paradigm for Source Effects?

Thomas F. Stafford

Introduction

Only a few years have passed since the pronouncement that m-commerce had arrived and was *the* compelling new business model for the "on-the-go" society of today (e.g., Feldman 2000; Senn 2000). Looking back, with the advantage of hindsight, we see a mobile sector that has not built out as quickly, nor in quite the way that was predicted or expected. For example, it was predicted that at about this point in time, the majority of cell phone users would be accessing data online (Feldman 2000); wireless application protocol (WAP) has certainly not lived up to its promise as a protocol for enabling mobile e-commerce via the cell phone (Batista 2002; Feldman 2000). As it is, the best working example of an in-place fully functional m-commerce system would be NTT DoCoMo's "iMode" service, and even this has remained rather a Japanese phenomenon, despite attempts to bring the service to the United States with AT&T (Stafford and Gillenson 2003).

What mobile devices will really bring to marketing remains to be seen, as new innovations in cellular technology and software support for e-commerce purposes are developed. What is generally considered by pundits, scholars, and the practice, alike, as "m-commerce" includes a full range of for-pay information services delivered by cellular phone or phone-enabled mobile computing device, in addition to the obvious "buy on the fly" product purchase scenarios. However, as is readily becoming apparent, the key use of mobile devices in consumer marketing will be for information services that support, supplement and facilitate economic transactions—not so much the product purchase transactions themselves. In other words it is hard to sell shoes and socks on a cell phone screen (Feldman 2000). Even with modern expanded-size color screens, mobile devices still are not entirely a rich medium, and the user input interface leaves much to be desired as compared to standard keyboard/mouse combinations on desktop computers.

Because wireless services *are* generally salable events, in and of themselves, anything one does with a cellular-enabled device can be conceived of as a commercial transaction—as a sale—even if only for the airtime and handset use necessary for the wireless event. Hence, the m-commerce moniker is a good (and comfortingly familiar) general catchall for the range of mobile activities connected to and involved with market transactions, even if actual products are not always bought in each airtime event, or even if the phone device is simply being used for information transmission.

We will use m-commerce as the broad general term to describe the commercial use of mobile devices to facilitate, support, and even sell goods and services, but the primary m-commerce activity— aside from the sale of specific information products—is expected to be promotional in nature and mobile devices are best thought of as on-the-go *facilitators* for all sorts of business events, serving as a very useful source of information to consumers in *support* of their purchase and consumption activities (Feldman 2000). The reality is that mobile devices are superb promotional tools, and their finest use is likely to be in support of purchases realized elsewhere and elsewise.

To that end, the wireless mobile device is likely to be the greatest sales promotion tool of the decade, and in its role as persuader, reminder, and notifier related to potential purchase activity, the credibility of its message flow will be a critical aspect of advertising and promotional strategies developed for this emerging promotional medium. This chapter examines some of the issues related to m-commerce promotional activity, or m-promotion, and the likelihood of it being accepted, acted upon, and having the desired commercial effect upon consumer purchase activity.

M-Commerce, M-Promotion, M-Confused?

The potential exchange of products and/or services for value is implicit in the concept of e-commerce; goods and services are targeted to audiences and offered for sale via the network. In comparison, m-commerce is probably better thought of as a facilitating technology or as an aspect of enhanced network access; m-commerce sessions can certainly culminate in sales, but m-commerce can also serve as a potent facilitator, or promotional device for other aspects of business, and this seems to be the distinctive feature of the business form (Stafford and Gillenson 2003).

Given the facilitational role of m-commerce in the pantheon of all that is "e," the potential for innovations in customer service, information, convenience, and tracking via mobile devices is very good indeed. With regard to discussing mobile promotion as a highly relevant subset of m-commerce, however, it is probably unwise to coin the term "m-advertising." The ultimate acronym that is likely to arise from such a name would not be fortuitous. Also, the display and interface limitations of mobile devices militate against traditional format advertising, as we know it from richer mass media; the likeliest analogue for mobile ads is a billboard, given the display and format limits of the medium, and what art director realistically prides him- or herself for their prize-winning narrow-market billboards, to the exclusion of a splendid mass market television spot for, say, the Super Bowl?

A most basic division between what is commerce and what is promotion in the mobile arena is in the distinction between transactions and access. E-commerce, despite its mode of access and delivery, is, in a least-common-denominator sense, transactional. It is really all about the consummation of an exchange between a buyer and a seller, or at least the effort to come to that conclusion. Mobile commerce may be a misnomer, insofar as most electronic commerce will take place online with standard computers, and given the likely promotional utility of the mobile device in supporting and facilitating transactions in other venues. Mobile *promotion* and information services appear to be the leading applications for mobile devices.

E-commerce is about buying things, while the emerging mobile market m-commerce concerns learning what to buy, where to buy, how to buy, and so on. The power of the mobile device lies in the ability to use location-based information services pushed out to device users for promulgating targeted last-minute sales promotion messages to on-the-go wired consumers. It is less likely, however, to be the new analogue to televisions or desktop computers for advertising presentation purposes. The medium is not rich enough to support the sorts of ads we have become familiar with. Nor is the mobile world likely to be cluttered with the sort of venal commercial froth that e-mail has fallen victim to, for reasons to be discussed herein. It is as much a function of convenience as it is a matter of legitimacy and economic necessity to channel the connection between businesses and mobile device users through a trusted intermediary, be it the phone company itself, as is frequent practice in Europe and Japan, or through emerging "mobile portals" that will serve as personally tailored information filtering and retrieval services for mobile device users. In fact, for mobile information services to have any meaning or utility, they must have some ability to interact with users in order to serve their needs on the go. Something very like the personalized Web site services provided across the

Internet now can serve a similar purpose in the world of mobile promotion and information services.

M-Promotion: The Frontiers of Information Efficiency

Just as e-commerce gave people the convenience and efficiency of shopping from home (or alternatively, shopping from wherever they wished, outside of the store), mobile promotion gives marketers the potential to reach their prospective customers on the go, presumably as the customers are in the process of seeking commercial satisfaction on the open market. Mind you, the potential is nascent and will be realized only by skillful and customer-oriented marketers; the ability to reach people at the point of purchase is not the same as the *effective* contact of customers at that point in time. Busy consumers may not take kindly to unsolicited and un-opted "push" promotional efforts. Issues of privacy and theft suggest themselves with regard to the totally uninvited promotional communication directed to a personal device that is regulated as a public utility (at its heart, it is a telephone); the recent "do not call" regulatory initiative is but one example of the sort of limitations that can be placed on unsolicited promotion in this emerging venue.

Even so, marketers will have the *opportunity* to use targeted mobile device messages (meaning messages sent to customers with demonstrated interest) to steer customers to the business location where desired products are on sale. The metaphor of global positioning system (GPS)-enabled cell phones ringing with news of special promotions as users pass technologically enabled storefronts in the shopping districts of modern cities is a scenario that has been discussed for several years now (Stafford and Gillenson 2003), with visions of GPS-enabled devices (which are already available) that can tell you the nearest location of different kinds of stores (and let the nearest stores know you are in the neighborhood).

These are scary scenarios; some network operators are planning to beam advertisements directly to consumer mobile devices, promising ready discounts at nearby stores in exchange for an immediate shopping visit (Herman 2000). On the one hand, mobile devices that can provide such functionality are the ultimate mobile promotional tool: Location-based sales promotions are generated on the fly, potentially reaching and inducing visits and purchases from busy consumers even as they enter the shopping district. On the other hand, they could be the ultimate intrusion on consumer privacy. Clearly, trusted intermediaries will be an important part of the emerging business model for mobile promotions; such intermediaries, best thought of as "mobile information portals," can both certify the "goodness" of incoming mobile promotions to receivers, and authenticate customers to marketers as legitimate and desirous targets for such promotions.

The "portal play" in mobile commerce and promotion (e.g., Volkov 1999) will be important insofar as recent developments that integrate artificial intelligence technology make it possible for advertisers to create contextualized mobile advertising based on locations of potential customers, customer needs of the moment, and the types of devices being used by customers (Yuan and Tsao 2003). Marketers will be able to anticipate virtually every need of customers with mobile devices, it would appear, but there are sharp distinctions in the phone-based mobile arena between knowing what a customer might like and forcing your message upon them in the absence of some signal that the message is welcomed.

Consider Athens, Georgia, and the "Wired Downtown" (Shamp 2002), where an entire entertainment district of a high-tech college town has been enabled with Wi-Fi (Wireless High Fidelity: high bandwidth wireless Internet access using the IEEE 802.11b networking protocol) to allow mobile device users to receive and view informative and promotional messages from the various venues downtown; rather than checking the paper, customers for bars, restaurants, and music venues can log in and view ads for dinner specials, special events, and entertainment listings, all on their mobile devices. This can be a very convenient information service for an Athens consumer who wishes to know where the interesting entertainment events are located. Even so, the customer must log on to the network in order to receive the information; it does not automatically deliver itself to the mobile device uninvited.

M-Promotion and the Information-Support Effect

High-volume mobile services users around the world seem to use their devices more to support commerce than to transact it. Hence, we have the emerging view of mobile promotion as a pathway through which to provide on-the-go consumers with the information they need to effectively navigate the daily events of their busy lives. The "always-on" opt-in model of information/entertainment mobile Internet service, as contrasted to the transaction-based perspective of trying to sell goods over mobile devices, is synergistic, in that providing customers with high-quality information has been considered as a key determinant for the success of the mobile Internet (Chae et al. 2002).

NTT DoCoMo's iMode service remains a powerful working example of both the business and the technology of mobile Internet service provision (Anwar 2002). The iMode packet-based radio service has taken the consumer information and entertainment route while circuit-switched service providers (with lower bandwidth and less functional flexibility) have generally concentrated on the business market (Baldi and Thaung 2002). With iMode, customers specifically select desired information and entertainment services for purchase and can authorize automatic updating and downloads of the selected information and entertainment services, as required, because the packet-based services are essentially "always on"—able to receive incoming data at any time the phone is powered up (Herman 2000).

Most cellular phone switching is circuit based, requiring a dedicated connection for each complete data or voice transmission, from start to finish; the only transmissions received when a call is not specifically switched are tower location routines that ensure the phone is always getting a phone system signal from a nearby cell, in the event that a call *is* switched to it. This switched-circuit connection method can be an inefficient use of bandwidth, but packet-based switching, which is also the protocol used by the Internet, connects only momentarily in order to transmit small portions of each message by the quickest available route. Of course, packet-based devices connect and disconnect many times per second, as message fragments (packets) making up a compete transaction are dispatched over momentary connections via the fastest available route.

Packet switching is a more efficient use of bandwidth, insofar as connections are made only for the instant in which data packets are transmitted, and this approach also matches the underlying switching protocol of the Internet itself, ensuring better compatibility. This approach also provides for the capability to economically monitor the network in an "always on" configuration for *incoming* data, so that information updates such as e-mail and location-based promotions can be received even if the phone device is not currently engaged in a voice call. Even if the phone is engaged in a voice call, data packets may still be received and sent at the same time, which means you can receive e-mail and other downloads while calling home at the same instant in time.

The Mobile Internet Abroad

In areas where mobile Internet service is prospering, specifically Japan and Finland, frequently mentioned offerings include banking, booking or buying tickets, shopping, and real-time news (Barnes 2002). In Japan, it is expected that within ten years, all cell phones will handle 3-D visual data, so people can window-shop on the go without actually going to stores (Dvorak 2003); by that time, it is anticipated that over 80 percent of all phone users in Japan will be using wireless Internet phones.

Currently, reading news and checking bank balances and financial statements are popular Japanese mobile services provided on cell phone handsets (Wessel 2000), although mobile users also trade stock shares, get weather forecasts, and receive travel updates such as train and air schedules on the go with their iMode phones (Barnes 2001). These information-based commercial services are highly indicative of what works well for the busy consumer in a market where packet-switched cell phones are heavily diffused. While the Japanese are the premier mobile device entertainment and information consumers, consumers in Finland are on the forefront of *location-based* mobile services. In restaurants, to which you can easily get immediate directions based on a phone company location service that matches your active cell tower to local business offerings, waiters can place your order into production directly from the table back to the kitchen via wireless device, and can also prepare and present your credit card payment at the table after the meal (no trip to the cash register to ring up the bill!), using a wireless device (Salonen 2003; Wessell 2000). In Finland, one might well have paid the parking meter in front of the restaurant with a cell phone-enabled eWallet, which is an excellent real world example of how mobile devices facilitate commerce as a payment source and information conduit, if not the actual online transaction itself (LaTour 2002).

In Finland, customers leaving a restaurant at the peak of rush hour can avail themselves of traffic guidance services over their mobile device, because the mobile services provider tracks customer signals in automobiles and is able to provide highly accurate traffic updates and routing information based on mobile signal information from the entire traffic flow at key traffic peak periods (*Wall Street Journal* 2003). These are not unusual uses for mobile devices in a nation that boasts more wireless than wired phone users, and that shortly expects the majority of Internet use to be via wireless device (Rytkönon 2000). Even so, the mobile promotion and services example continues to be that of mobile information services *supporting* and *facilitating* commerce, much like sales promotion, since the ability to actually make purchases with a mobile phone is considered by the highly wired Finns to be the least important feature of the mobile Internet (Koivumäki 2002).

Machine-Mediated Channels

Mobile Internet service is not just a new distribution channel for selling products or providing highly useful promotional information in support of sales. It is a new aspect of consumerism and powerful way to speak with consumers, and the mobile Internet revolution will put pressure on present e-commerce business models, resulting in entirely new value propositions in many industries (Evans and Wurster 1997). Consumers are defined by lifestyle variables when they are reached on the move, and it is likely that a portal model of customer contact and support (where trusted sites seek to attain and retain a constant real-time connection to consumers via mobile devices) will arise in mobile channels, as the business practice spreads (Nohria and Leestma 2001). Portals are central points of contact and information distribution, where users can define their information needs for providers, establish an addressable online identity, and be assured that they have a known and trusted source for Internet connectivity and services.

Yahoo!, Netscape, MSN, and AOL have all made use of the "portal play" in the provision of standard Internet services. The necessity of such portals for mobile services is clear: Consumers need a trusted mediator for the information directed to their mobile devices if they are not to be overwhelmed with offerings (DiPietro and Mancini 2003; Volkov 1999). Hence, we tend to believe that one of the more powerful business models that will arise in the growth and emerging maturity of the mobile Internet market will be a promotional model: with the mobile device either as an immediate and on-the-go contact point for microsegmented customers, or as a constantly present always-on information portal that keeps buyers and sellers fully informed of market circumstances regardless of (and often, in special context of) their physical locations in travel.

That being the case, we anticipate that the greatest challenges in m-promotion and related m-commerce will not be access issues, or media-related issues such as bandwidth and media richness. These things come with time, and many are already prototyped for commercial exploitation. The interesting concern is what consumers will think about the persuasive attempts that are directed to them ubiquitously by their mobile devices across a wireless Internet. The question is, will this increasing flow of promotion and commercial communication to consumers' wireless devices be accepted in accordance with communications models that we are familiar with, or will some new dynamic be in effect? We suspect that mobile device persuasion will convey characteristics of machine-mediated persuasion, as opposed to the more visible and conceptually familiar mediated interpersonal persuasion process.

The question of interest is will m-promotion operate from the basis of the source effects models we are familiar with, or will the juxtaposition of an intimate, yet avowedly mechanical device in the mediated chain of promotional communication result in some new process of source perceptions in the persuasive process? Successful promotion, as any form of communication, is subject to the processes of perception and persuasion, among which are the important source-based effects that lend to or detract from the credibility of a promotional message.

Machine Promotion and Source Credibility

Source credibility has typically been defined as aspects of a communications source that positively influence receiver message acceptance (Ohanian 1990). Credibility, defined this way, is a critical aspect of the persuasive process that promotional communication depends upon for its success. From the early days of source effects research in mass communications, source effectiveness as been considered a multidimensional construct. We consider credibility to be generally dependent on the trust audience members have for communicators (Hovland, Janis, and Kelley 1953), although the problem in mobile advertising is to determine *who* the communicator is. The most visible manifestation of the communicator and/or the message in mobile promotion would be represented through a small mobile device liquid crystal display; it is not as though you can fully represent the qualities of human sources in the display formats typical of such devices.

Iterations of the classic "Yale School" view (e.g., McGuire 1969) describe source credibility as being a synthesis of two critical constructs: a trustworthiness/expertise component, which will depend on perceptions of source knowledge and honesty, and a similarity/attractiveness/likeability component, which depends greatly on perceptions of the source's general appearances and potential interpersonal appeal to audience members. Early research focuses on the importance of communicator similarity to the intended audience (Berscheid 1966; Brock 1965); indeed, it has been noted that machine sources that are anthropomorphic (such as animated characters) generally produce higher perceptions of credibility (cf. Cowell 2001; Weaver 1999; see also trade character research in Kirkpatrick 1953; Phillips 1996).

Of course, devices like phones and other mobile devices are not as capable of rich media presentations such as the animated characters used in some machine credibility studies (e.g., Cowell 2001; Weaver 1999), so other issues are more important in determining how users might judge the credibility of information provided through "lean media" such as those provided on mobile devices. McGuire (1985) noted that there are differences in credibility ascribed to different media, with the generalization that more vivid (analogously, rich) media are generally better liked and believed more. He also notes that cues to credibility become particularly important when perceivers are low involved and accept or reject information based simply upon source cues—a scenario that seems a good fit with the likely attention and involvement levels of busy on-the-go consumers. For these reasons it is very important to understand the influences of credibility in machine-mediated environments such as those provided by the mobile promotions channel discussed here.

Traditionally, trust is the critical component in credibility (e.g., Hovland

and Weiss 1951–52; McGinnies and Ward, 1980; Friedman and Friedman 1979). Trust, we come to find, tends to evolve from audience perceptions of the source's expertise on the topic at hand (Chawla, Dave, and Barr 1994), and is a critical aspect of the advertising persuasion process. Yet, the power of attractive sources cannot be overlooked as an important part of persuasion (Chaiken 1979; Kamins and Gupta 1994; Patzer 1983), in light of McGuire's (1985) observations about media appearance and subsequent credibility. Another consideration is the power of a source to withhold or provide rewards in exchange for compliance (McGuire 1985), which has been part of some credibility conceptualizations.

If trust is an important aspect of credibility, it is important to understand how media are trusted, or not. Media credibility has been waning in recent years (Anonymous 1996; Dickson and Topping 2001), and the Internet itself is not necessarily a reliable source of professionally developed information when anyone with software and bandwidth can be a publisher (Eastin 2001). In Internet communications, not only the sender but also, to a great degree, the *medium* are considered as communication sources (Sundar and Nass 2001), and perceivers even employ the social rules they would use with humans in dealing with machine sources of information. This tends to reinforce the importance of source attractiveness-related issues, in view of the findings considered above on anthropomorphic animations on computers.

However, these human-like qualities are difficult to portray, discern, and even *transmit* in the lean media venue of the small handheld device. This new advertising venue is inherently *poor* in production values, simply because of the small display size, limited memory and processing power, and highly finite power reserves that mobile devices have as an inherent aspect of their very mobility. Granted, emerging third-generation phone devices are equipped with cameras and color displays, and the graphic display capabilities of mobile devices are increasing, but because graphics are inherently a function of processor power and memory storage capability, portable devices will always have limitations that larger, more powerful permanently sited devices will not have (Chae et al. 2002). If the presentation values are an aspect of the credibility of a presentation across a medium, as McGuire (1985) has suggested, then in the mobile arena, one must look to aspects of credibility other than those impacted by the presentation and actual user interface alone.

Source Effects in the Computer Age

The recent work of Fogg on machine-mediated persuasion (cf. Fogg and Tseng 1999; Tseng and Fogg 1999; Fogg 2003) provides some guidance on how to consider credibility in machine-mediated channels. Fogg's work has focused on computer-mediated persuasive technologies—something he has coined the term "captology" to describe. The main idea of his work on source credibility effects and persuasive efficacy in computer-mediated communications is that communication via computers is qualitatively different from other forms of human interaction.

With computers the rules of persuasion seem to be different because perceivers do not attribute credibility characteristics to sources that are mediated through computers in the same way that they do through more traditional media; moreover, Fogg has not yet been able to replicate the traditional source credibility variables in a computer context. They do not seem to quite fit; credibility is *different* with computer-mediated communication.

Mobile Promotion: The Challenges of Machine Credibility

Where computers were once considered infallible arbiters of information, that magic quality of computer accuracy seems to be fading in the modern day, much to the detriment of communications that are judged by the credibility of computer-mediated channels (e.g., Fogg and Tseng 1999). As people gain more experience with computers, they become more knowledgeable about their potential shortcomings and likely failures; they are no longer the magic calculation and storage boxes that they seemed to be to the uninitiated in the past. Of course, given the generally declining trend of credibility for media at large (Anonymous 1996; Dickson and Topping 2001; Meyer and Zhang 2002), this decline in the "magic box" sense of computer infallibility may not result in such a steep decline in credibility or effectiveness for machine-mediated channels after all, because computers as sources are held to be at least as credibile as news editors in many cases (Sethuraman 1995).

It does seem, based on Fogg's research, that trustworthiness and expertise are the credibility dimensions most applicable to machine-mediated communications (cf. Fogg and Tseng 1999; Tseng and Fogg 1999), to the exclusion of similarity/likeability/attractiveness components (cf. McGuire 1969) that depend on specific identification of a human source for a message.

Machine Credibility: Critical Components

Fogg (2003) makes an interesting point about machine-mediated persuasion, and the credibility issues surrounding it: Perceivers must both *notice* something about the communication (a quality he calls prominence), and they must *make a judgment* about what they have noticed (the quality of interpretation). If both of these things do not happen, there may be no credibility assessment.

Noticing that a communication is coming from a source that requires a credibility assessment (Fogg's quality of prominence) is a function of involvement, the message topic, what the perceiver might do with the information (task specificity), user experience with the computing medium, and individual differences that typically accrue (such as need for cognition, literacy, etc.). In this view, if a perceiver does not realize that a message is coming from a computer, there may be no credibility assessment. As strange as it seems, even though computers are more suspect as message sources these days thanks to the proliferation of Internet advertising, embedded computing devices can send messages in "under the radar" if consumers do not realize that they are attending to a computing device. Take a cell phone, for example. It could well be that ads coming to consumers through their phones will not be subjected to the same scrutiny that ads arriving on desktop computers would receive. This effect relies, of course, on the embedded nature of the computing device. If the device is recognizably a computer, as desktop machines are (and converged palmtop/phone combos), then the prominence of the communication is naturally much higher.

Much of Fogg's prominence effect depends on user involvement. If they are involved with the device or the utility that the device provides, perceivers are much more likely to notice factors of the communication. Take the example of a busy Web search for information; users rarely welcome pop-up ads when they are in a hurry to make a travel reservation online and simply want to execute the transaction. Also consider the salience of information sought through computer devices: much has been made of the potential for mobile devices to provide important information transactions supporting mobility. If users rely heavily on their mobile device for critical information, such as voice mail, travel guidance, or business updates, they may not welcome interruptions, either.

Aside from noticing a computer-mediated communication, the *ability and will* to interpret the communication must also be present for credibility assessments to transpire (Fogg 2003). The usage context influences this (expectations, usage situations, etc.) as do the user's skill and ability level with the technology and the assumptions that guide all human perception in the form of culture, heuristics, and past experience.

Musings on Mobile Promotion Effectiveness

The picture of computer device credibility, as it might influence the effectiveness of mobile promotion, is interesting. Mobile devices are lauded for their ability to keep users informed, connected, and up to date, all while on the go in a busy and highly mobile society. Hence, much of what mobile commerce and subsequent mobile promotional efforts might consist of will be informational in character: advice, guidance, decision support, and so forth. However, the literature tends to support a view of computer credibility that leverages rich media and familiarity effects in favor of familiar desktop machines; mobile devices are limited to much leaner media in presentations and interfaces and are not yet as ubiquitous as our personal computers (PCs). Leanness, or lack of "signaling capacity" limits the credibility of a communication across Internet channels (Haas and Wearden 2003).

In the guise of mobile phones, there will certainly be some familiarity with the basic device, if not the new potential use, but the presentation format is highly limited. In the form of personal digital assistants (PDAs)—small wireless-enabled handheld computers), the media presentation possibilities are only just slightly richer, and the interface is not noticeably different from the standard phone keypad—except for devices equipped with the Palm operating system and WINDOWS Compact Edition devices, which use stylus input in lieu of keystrokes on thumb-operated mini-QWERTY pads or standard numeric phone keypads. In either case, as compared to PCs, the display size is minuscule and the interface is rudimentary. This paucity of media richness is the price users pay for high portability.

Because the device itself can be considered as both a source and the channel that feeds the device (cf. Greer 2003; Ogianova 1997; Sundar and Nass 2001), the best approach to boosting credibility in mobile promotion messages would seem to be a concentration on the delivery channel as opposed to the terminating access device. Look at the content provider/provision channel rather than the mobile device as the platform for impacting credibility assessments. This is the sense of the "portal play," in which mobile users might be expected to affiliate with trusted sites or Internet portal locations, such as Yahoo!, AOL, Netscape, Google, and others, as specifically authorized delivery sources for directing trusted mobile information to their devices.

Insofar as the process of affiliating with a portal typically involves user opt-in processes that set profiles for desired information feeds and services, this portal-play approach would provide two advantages, one to each side of the mobile promotions exchange. First, customers would potentially be shielded from unchecked barrages of location-based wireless spam (imagine how many messages you would get walking down a "wired" shopping district storefront area if this sort of portal filtering were not in place!); second, providers would have a ready segmented and prequalified group of consumers identified by the portal for messaging purposes. Naturally, one expects the portal will charge its own fees for access to consumers who match desired profiles, but that is already the practice in Web-based portal advertising anyhow.

Fogg (2003) cautions that when information from a computing device becomes noticeably unreliable, perceivers judge them less credible. He gives the specific case of airport kiosks that give information only about client hotels and restaurants and do not provide general information access to the range of choices possible. Just as in many areas of advertising, shading the truth, pushing too hard, or being too boastful, can all be signals in mobile promotion that will give rise to the prominence/interpretation process that leads to specific credibility evaluations of messages and sources. The airport kiosk example is just one demonstration of how a portal-play approach can be misused; presume too much on the user's goodwill and intelligence, and you lose the capability to access them in the future. Though Fogg's kiosk example is not the sort of portal envisioned here, it serves the same kind of gatekeeper role that lends such huge impact to its potential credibility, or lack thereof, in the delivery of information resources.

The reality of effective mobile promotion seems to be that information that supports user goals will be welcomed, and might not even be questioned for credibility. It is the source of this information that we must look to, and the channel/content provider role of opt-in Internet portals are eminently suited to serving the creditable and credible source/gatekeeper role for mobile consumers. As shown in Figure 13.1, if mobile promotion arrives from a user-opted Internet portal (route 3) on an embedded device like a cell phone, and if it supports the user requirements for information and support in a busy mobile environment, it looks as if the promotional message will be received in an atmosphere highly conducive to assimilation and subsequent persuasion. If, on the other hand, the mobile promotion interferes with the orderly and efficient transmission of important information to and from a mobile device, and does so obtrusively or brazenly (route 2, the direct obtrusive contact), it is likely that credibility assessments will be made to the detriment of the effectiveness of the promotional message as well as the mobile channel (e.g., Sundar and Nass 2001). There is also the case of the user-initiated service contact, where ads would be considered a normal aspect of contacting a provider for a "free" service (route 1, direct contact by user).

We do not want our mobile devices taking "station breaks" and requiring us to listen to a pod of commercials before we get an information service we desire, even though a likely commercial model for mobile information services will be promotions supported. We do not want unchecked barrages of mobile information directed at our devices based on where we happen to be or what we happen to be doing; users of mobile devices are likely to be far too busy and impatient to stand for commercial interruptions, so a model of commercial sponsorship of information service products is required that sufficiently promotes the sponsor of the information while sufficiently meeting

Figure 13.1 **Three Routes to Computer-Mediated Persuasion**

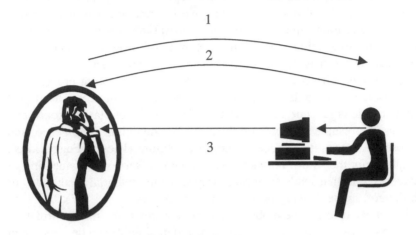

1 = direct route, source is directly contacted, ads accepted as a
    condition of contact
2 = direct route, receiver is directly and intrusively contacted,
    credibility evaluated
3 = indirect route—portal play—credibility preestablished, user
    opts in, promotion embedded and limited

the needs for quick and accurate information delivery on the part of the user.
The portal is one such approach that has already shown promise and profit in
conventional Internet service. Sponsorship of information, even *access* to
the information consumer, would be mediated by wireless-enabled Internet
portals in this business model. Consumers, as members of portals, would
have the ability to tailor their information needs and information feeds based
on what they want and find compelling. This approach would be much more
likely to satisfy and compel users of mobile devices than the alternative laissez-
faire model that presently dominates e-mail service on standard Internet channels. We dare not let mobile promotion devolve into another device-choking
flurry of widecast and unsolicited spam.

A sponsorship model that could also work would be the user-initiated
access approach. This contrasts to the portal approach to the extent that the
portal would be authorized to provide automated feeds of information ap-
proved by prior opt-in processes, where the user initiation approach would
be something like the process encountered on the present-day telephone when
a user calls the local time/temperature automated phone number to get the

correct time. The "correct time" service is not a free public service. In most areas the function is operated at a profit by a local business that uses the opportunity of the time update to play users a brief commercial for a sponsor while waiting for the time information. As a consequence of receiving an accurate update of the present time, callers are also informed that "Captain D's Time is now 12:25." This is an equitable trade of ad exposure for information service: Users probably do not care if it is Captain D's time, or McDonald's time, or the Canadian Pacific Railroad's time . . . they just want to know the time quickly, and are willing to let the service provider characterize it as a service belonging to the promotional sponsor. This sort of sponsorship of an information service is a model that consumers are already aware of, and accepting of, and it appears to be a useful analogue for the provision of basic sponsored information services over mobile devices. The critical aspect is that the contact is *customer*-initiated, so the ad is not necessarily viewed as intrusive or objectionable.

Concluding Thoughts: One Last Word from Your Sponsor

We will have to rethink advertising and promotion for mobile devices, just as we have rethought promotions for online environments. The interface qualities and the typical information processing styles of users in these environments call for a different approach. Given the purpose that the mobile device fills in the busy consumer's life, it hardly seems wise to waste their time with extended advertisements. In fact, given the usual operating environment (how many people use mobile phones in cars these days?) it might well limit potential liabilities to keep promotional messages short, sweet, and easy to attend to. This might not only enhance credibility but also represent an actual user effectiveness issue in certain mobile environments.

Aside from the time-and-temperature metaphor for user-initiated contact, think of billboard-style art direction for mobile promotions directed to users through mobile portals. Format-wise, whatever works for billboards ought to work for electronic mobile devices. One picture and no more than seven words in text for visual messages, as the billboard "truism" goes, is a format that seems workable in the lean media mobile environment. There are real-world parallels and synergies: you can already use your mobile device on the road to contact the police in the event of an emergency— "Dial * HP for roadside assistance" is a frequently seen sign on national highways directing travelers to the highway patrol. Roadside billboards are already including exhortations to key in special characters for follow-up information, should the message catch your eye. Cell phones already provide a ready channel of customer direct response with the currently utilized advertising and promotional media; mobile devices go a step further by permitting the message to reach out to the customer, as well as permitting (even inviting) immediate response.

As we begin our experimentation with mobile promotion, we can be sure that there will be as many missteps, false starts, and charlatans on the loose as there were when Internet advertising started up. The temptation for sellers of goods and services to signal every passing mobile device, using system location capabilities that already exist, will be enormous. However, we have already seen the impact of unchecked mass promotion across the Internet. Moreover, the leading location-based mobile promotion users in the world, citizens of Finland, have already demonstrated the best possible approach: The provider (in this case the phone company) tracks them, and the information related to their location is available at the tap of a key—it is a user choice to access, not an incoming message to potentially avoid. Best to keep this model in mind as we think about ways to effectively serve our mobile customers; marketing cannot afford another spam debacle.

It is quite likely that if there are inherent credibility challenges with mobile promotion, simply as a function of the computer-mediated medium through which messages will arrive, the credibility issues will be exacerbated through the inevitable confusion that will reign during the learning process, as business attempts to understand and deliver promotional offerings that suit the requirements and needs of the mobile-enabled consumer. Understanding the issues related to the several sources that can be evaluated in mobile promotion is a good start to building mobile promotions and information services that meet the evolving customer need for timely information in support of busy mobile lifestyles.

References

Anonymous (1996), "Media Credibility Sinking: Survey," *Editor and Publisher* 129 (43) 19.

Anwar, S.T. (2002), "NTT DoCoMo and M-commerce: A Study in Market Expansion and Global Strategy," *Thunderbird International Business Review*, 44 (1) 139–164.

Baldi, S., and H. Thaung (2002), "The Entertaining Way to M-Commerce: Japan's Approach to the Mobile Internet—A Model for Europe?" *Electronic Markets* 12(1), 6–13.

Barnes, S.J. (2001), "iMode and the Mobile Internet," *Journal of Information Technology Theory & Application*, 3 (4) 27–32.

——— (2002), "The Mobile Commerce Value Chain: Analysis and Future Developments," *International Journal of Information Management*, 22 (2), 91–108.

Batista, E. (2002), "Crappy WAP Bridging Gap," [www.wired.com/news/wireless/0,1382,51516,00.html].

Berscheid, E. (1966), "Opinion Change and Communicator-Communicatee Similarity and Dissimilarity," *Journal of Personality and Social Psychology*, 4 (6), 670–680.

Brock, T.C. (1965), "Communicator-Recipient Similarity and Decision Change," *Journal of Personality and Social Psychology*, 1 (6), 650–654.

Chae, M., J. Kim, H. Kim, and H. Ryu (2002), "Information Quality for Mobile Internet Services: A Theoretical Model with Empirical Validation," *Electronic Markets* 12 (1), 38–46.

Chaiken, S. (1979), "Communicator Physical Attractiveness and Persuasion," *Journal of Personality and Social Psychology*, 37 (8) 1387–1397.

Chawla, S.K., D.S. Dave, and P.B. Barr (1994), "Role of Physical Attractiveness in Endorsement: An Empirical Study," *Journal of Services Marketing*, 10 (2) 203–215.

Cowell, A.J. (2001). "Increasing the Credibility of Anthropomorphic Computer Characters: The Effects of Manipulating Nonverbal Interaction Style and Demographic Content." Ph.D. dissertation, University of Central Florida, Orlando.

Dickson, T. and E. Topping (2001), "Public Trust, Media Responsibility and Public Journalism: U.S. Newspaper Editors and Educators' Attitudes about Media Credibility," *Asia Pacific Media Educator* 11, 72–86.

DiPietro, R., and L. Mancini (2003), "Security and Privacy Issues of Handheld and Wearable Wireless Devices," *Communications of the ACM*, 46 (9), 75–79.

Dvorak, Phred (2003), "Calling all Gadgets Geeks," *Far Eastern Economic Review* 166 (32), 58.

Eastin, M.S. (2001), "Credibility Assessment of Online Health Information: The Effects of Source Expertise and Knowledge of the Content," *Journal of Computer-mediated Communication*, 6 (4), [www.ascusc.org, jcmc/vol6/issue4/eastin.html].

Evans, P.B. and T.S. Wurster (1997), "Strategy and the New Economics of Information," *Harvard Business Review*, 75 (5), 70–82.

Feldman, S. (2000), "Mobile Commerce for the Masses," *IEEE Internet Computing*, 4 (6), 74–75.

Fogg, B.J. (2003), "Prominence-Interpretation Theory: Explaining How People Assess Credibility Online," *Proceedings of the CHI 2003 ACM Conference on Human Factors and Computing Systems*, 722–723.

——— and H. Tseng (1999), "The Elements of Computer Credibility," *Proceedings of the CH 99 ACM Conference on Human Factors and Computing Systems*, 80–87.

Friedman, H.H., and L. Friedman (1979), "Endorser Effectiveness by Product Type," *Journal of Advertising Research* 19 (5), 63–71.

Greer, J.D. (2003), "Evaluating the Credibility of Online Information: A Test of Source and Advertising Influences," *Mass Communications and Society*, 6 (1) 11–28.

Haas, C., and S.T. Wearden (2003), "E-Credibility: Building Common Ground in Web Environments," *L1—Educational Studies in Language and Literature*, 3 169–184.

Herman, J. (2000), "The Coming Revolution in M-commerce," *Business Communications Review*, 30 (10) 24–25.

———, I.L. Janis, and H.H Kelley (1953), *Communication and Persuasion.* New Haven: Yale University Press.

Hovland, C.I. and W. Weiss (1951–52), "The Influence of Source Credibility on Communication Effectiveness," *Public Opinion Quarterly* 15, 635–650.

Kamins, M.A. and K. Gupta (1994), "Congruence Between Spokesperson and Product Type: A Matchup Hypothesis Perspective," *Psychology & Marketing* 11 (6), 569–586.

Kirkpatrick, C.A. (1953), "Trade Characters in Promotion Programs," *Journal of Marketing*, 17 (1), 366–371.

Koivumäki, T. (2002), "Consumer Attitudes and Mobile Travel Portal," *Electronic Markets*, 12 (1), 47–57.

LaTour, A. (2002), "Mobile Phones Become Wallets in New System," *Wall Street Journal* (March 14), B4.

McGinnies, E. and C.D. Ward (1980), "Better Liked than Right: Trustworthiness and Expertise as Factors in Credibility," *Personality and Social Psychology Bulletin*, 6 (3), 467–472.

McGuire, W. (1969), "The Nature of Attitudes and Attitude Change," in *Handbook of Social Psychology*, G. Lindsey and E. Aronson eds., Reading, MA: Addison-Wesley.

————— (1985), "Attitude and Attitude Change," in *Handbook of Social Psychology*, G. Lindsey and E. Aronson eds., New York: Random House.

Meyer, P. and Y. Zhang (2002), "Anatomy of a Death Spiral: Newspapers and their Credibility," paper presented at the 2002 AEJMC Conference.

Nohria, N. and M. Leestma (2001), "A Moving Target: The Mobile-Commerce Customer," *Sloan Management Review*, 42 (3) 104.

Ogianova, E.K. (1997). "Audience Processing of News and Advertising in Computer-Mediated Environments: Effects of the Content Provider's Perceived Credibility and Identity." Ph.D. dissertation, University of Missouri, Columbia.

Ohanian, R. (1990), "Construction and Validation of a Scale to Measure Celebrity Endorsers' Perceived Expertise, Trustworthiness, and Attractiveness," *Journal of Advertising* 19 (3), 39–52.

Patzer, G.L. (1983), "Source Credibility as a Function of Communicator Physical Attractiveness," *Journal of Business Research* 11 229–241.

Phillips, B. (1996), "Advertising and the Cultural Meaning of Animals," *Advances in Consumer Research* 23, 354–360.

Rytkönon, K. (2000). *Mobile Commerce and WML.* [www.infoloom.com/gaconfs/WEB/paris2000/S13–01/htm], (September 9, 2003).

Salonen, R. (2003), "Finnish Telecommunications," *World Trade* 16 (5), 40.

Senn, J.A. (2000), "The Emergence of m-Commerce," *Computer*, 33 (12) 148–151.

Sethuraman, S. (1995). "Effects of Source on the Perception and Evaluation of Online News." Ph.D. dissertation, Stanford University, Palo Alto, CA.

Shamp, S. (2002), "The WAGz Story: How the Wireless Athens Georgia Zone Came to Be, [www.nmi.uga.edu/research/wagzstory.asp].

Stafford, T.F. and M. Gillenson (2003), "M-Commerce: What It Is and What It Could Be," *Communications of the ACM*, 46 (12), 33–34.

Sundar, S.S., and C. Nass (2001), "Conceptualizing Sources in Online News," *Journal of Communication*, 51 (1), 52–72.

Tseng, S. and B.J. Fogg (1999), "Credibility and Computing Technology," *Communications of the ACM* 2 (5), 39–44.

Volkov, V. (1999). "Personalized Content Aggregation at Web Portals: Tailoring the Content Bundle Based on Content Providers' Credibility." Ph.D. dissertation, Georgia State University, Atlanta.

Wall Street Journal (2003), "Traffic Study Tracks Mobile Phones in Cars" (March 25), D6.

Weaver, E.R. (1999). "Reactance or Impression Management: The Role of Expert

System versus Human Expert Advice in the Interpretation of Resistance to Policy Persuasion." Ph.D. dissertation, Duke University, Durham, NC.

Wessel, D. (2000), "Gadget Envy: Masters of the New Economy, Americans Must Go Abroad to Find the Coolest Toys," *Wall Street Journal Eastern Edition* (August 3), B1.

Yuan, S.T. and Y.W. Tsao (2003), "A Recommendatiion Mechanism for Contextualized Mobile Advertising," *Expert Systems with Applications*, 24 (4), 399–414.

14

Brand Recall in the Advergaming Environment

A Cross-Country Comparison

Monica D. Hernandez, Michael S. Minor,
Jaebeom Suh, Sindy Chapa, and Jose A. Salas

Introduction

Advertisers continually seek new, captivating, and persuasive environments
to attain impact on their target audience and maximization of their investment. Electronic games are gaining increasing attention among companies
around the world as a new and captivating advertising medium. Electronic
games provide an environment with the capability of maintaining players'
full attention during the time the game is being played, and represent an
excellent niche for advertising. The increasing popularity of electronic games
is another reason to consider the use of this medium. In the United States
alone, the number of online-game players exceeded 50 million in 2002, and
it is expected this number will increase to more than 80 million by 2005
(Fattah and Paul 2002). Players use the medium extensively: According to
YaYa (2003), online players spend on average thirteen hours a week playing
games. In sum, electronic games are increasingly popular, and the engagement of players is both intensive and extensive.

Electronic games involve consumers in ways not possible with other media. Traditional methods of Internet advertising, such as banners and pop-up
windows, have not been effective (Olsen 2001; Rodgers 2002). In contrast,
advertising in electronic games—also called advergaming—emerges as an
alternative advertising technique that offers companies an opportunity to build
brand awareness through the promotion of their brands within the graphics
of a computer game, gaining prolonged exposure to a target market.

Advergaming should not be perceived as simply an evolution of online advertising or a substitute for an e-mail campaign. Its interactive nature provides many advantages. Among advergaming's advantages are an immersive brand experience and unlimited exposure frequency at a reasonable price, the possibility of logging valuable customer information through registration, viral interactive promotion through e-mail, and the possibility of displaying detailed information on the product or service, providing the consumer with the opportunity to make informed choices (Hernandez and Minor 2003). As suggested by Hernandez and Minor (2003), an additional advantage for global companies in considering advergaming is the overcoming of language limitations. Because of their graphic nature, most games require very little wording, thus overcoming the language limitations encountered by other media. Our first contribution is an attempt to empirically test this assumption by comparing samples of countries with different languages and writing systems.

Advergaming is gaining recognition among advertisers and companies pursuing effective promotion of their brands. However, very little is known about the effectiveness of those ads. Advertising effectiveness has traditionally been measured by memory-based awareness measures, through brand recognition and brand recall (Nedungadi and Hutchinson 1985). To assess the effectiveness of product placements in electronic games, a recent study by Nelson (2002) addressed short- and long-term brand recall and attitudes toward brand placements in a racing game, but only for a small group of American players. No previous study has compared recall of brand placements and attitudes toward brand placements in electronic games across countries. In particular, the study of the impact of this new medium on the rapidly growing emerging economies in Asia and Latin America is timely in order to appropriately target these segments. Our second contribution addresses these issues by the inclusion of Asian and Latin American countries in the study.

Games are attracting a diverse group of consumers who demand a variety of game genres to satisfy different tastes. This increasing demand captures electronic game players with distinct levels of expertise. As such, hard-core and casual players are equally included in this group of consumers. Novice gamers are considered casuals, who play games occasionally. In contrast, expert gamers play for several hours a day. No research has been conducted to determine the impact of level of expertise and perceived goal difficulty on brand recall. Our third contribution focuses on these issues.

We accomplish these objectives by assessing, through brand recall, the effectiveness of the display of brands in two different online games across groups of players from four different countries: the United States, South Korea, Chile, and Mexico. The chapter is organized as follows: First, an electronic game and advergaming conceptual framework is presented. Next, a brief description of the current situation of electronic game usage in the countries selected for the study follows. The sampling procedure, instrument, experimental stimuli, and procedure of the data collection methods are described in the subsequent section. We follow with descriptive statistics and hypothesis testing. Finally, managerial implications and future research directions are discussed.

Conceptual Framework

Electronic Games and Advergaming Framework

Electronic games require special hardware and software to be played. Typically, the hardware is classified based on two main platforms: stored and online. Stored games are played on consoles, such as Sony's PlayStation and PlayStation 2, Microsoft's Xbox, and Nintendo's GameCube and GameBoy. In its basic mode, a video-game console is a hardware system dedicated to video game play, usually connected to the television. Recent models also can play DVDs, which are designed to be part of an entertainment system. Most of the games played on consoles can also be linked over the Internet. The online—also called Internet-based—games require a personal computer (PC) or a Web-based device, such as a cell phone. Games can be designed for specific or multiple platforms. Although most of the growth in gaming is occurring on the Internet, consoles are also an important medium for advertising. To take advantage of the online market growth, the leading console companies are launching online console gaming services (Elkin 2002).

Electronic game software can be broadly classified into several genres, including: action, adventure, driving, puzzle, role-playing game, simulation, sports, and strategy (Gamespot 2002). Adventure games emphasize exploration or strategy elements through use of player-oriented or fixed-camera viewpoints. Action games are fast and intense, such as Nabisco's Extreme Power Bike (www.nabiscoworld.com/games/nt_shock_ntpb.htm). Role-playing games involve complex storylines and interaction with other characters (i.e., Siemens' Spinopolis [spinopolis.yaya.com/]). Sports games simulate real life sports (e.g, Altoids Billiards, [www.altoids.com/index.aspx?area=arcade&]). Puzzle and strategy games give a player control over multiple units, which are engaged in conflict with one or more opponents (e.g., Burger King's Drive Thru, [www.bk.com/bigkids/fungames.html]). Simulation and driving games represent the user-vehicle interaction (e.g., BMW's X3 Adventure, 146.145.203.221).

There is a great deal of variation in the way advergaming is conceptualized and defined. For the purpose of this chapter, the definition to be utilized is that proposed by Hernandez and Minor (2003, 6), which encompasses the objective and benefits of this technique: "Advergaming is the use of electronic games to deliver advertising messages in order to build brand awareness, to offer product information, and to provide a means to compare similar products, for the purpose of developing lasting exchange relationships with the customers."

Appropriateness of Recall Measures in Assessing Product Placement Effectiveness

Product placement refers to the practice of including a brand-name product, package, signage, or other trademark merchandise within a communication medium. Product placement effectiveness through memory recall measures has recently been studied with respect to American television (Russell 2002) as well as in American movies (Brennan, Dubas, and Babin 1999). The assessment of the effectiveness of this practice is also of interest in other geographic areas. For instance, Gould, Gupta, and Grabner-Krauter (2000) analyzed product placement in movies in a cross-cultural study.

The traditional approach to advertising effectiveness focuses on specific effects of the ad. Aided and unaided recall of the brand name is a commonly used measure to assess those effects (Reynolds, Olson, and Rochon 1997; Wright-Isak, Faber, and Horner 1997). Because recall is a cognitive and not a behavioral measure (Jones 2002), the measure is suitable for assessing brand awareness. Brand awareness is a measure of cognitive effect, and it could be measured either spontaneously or by being prompted (Jones 2002). Specifically, brand awareness is understood as the ability to identify a brand or package within a category in sufficient detail to stimulate a response to the brand (Percy and Rossiter 1992).

Similarly, short-term effectiveness is best assessed by demonstrating a chain of effects that might include awareness or attitudes (Wright-Isak et al. 1997). Therefore, the measurement of the short-term effectiveness of product placements utilized for this study is appropriate for assessment in the advergaming environment.

Country Sampling Rationale

Each of the countries selected for this study makes a contribution to our understanding of advergaming. South Korea and Chile were selected for the study because of their large high-speed connection penetration. The United States and Mexico were selected because of their large number of users.

By 2002, South Korea possessed the largest high-speed Internet market penetration in the world (French 2002). According to the Organization for Economic Cooperation and Development, an estimated 7.5 million South Korean households have broadband, which represents 44.8 percent of the total households (onlinegamegurus.com 2002). In comparison, while broadband penetration in the United States is less than 11 percent, broadband subscribers reached nearly 13 million by July 2002 (Federal Communications Commission 2002).

Electronic games have become the second largest entertainment industry in South Korea, after broadcasting (Global Information 2002). Figures for sales of PC games and mobile subscribers using high-speed wireless Internet services are unparalleled around the world. This South Korean gaming phenomenon is valued at $3 billion a year (Chon 2002). As President Sung Jae Hwan of the state-funded Korea Game Promotion Center pointed out, the online game wave is an important factor raising the Korean economy (Moon 2001).

Electronic game playing has extended to South Koreans of all ages and it is no longer considered to be just for the youthful population. About 55 percent of game players are twenty-one to thirty years old (Vikas 2003). The gender disparity is also declining, with 36.5 percent of gamers being female (Kushairi 2003). The study of advergaming in South Korea is particularly timely for companies promoting their products and services in this fast-growing online gaming market.

The exploration of the electronic game phenomenon in other emerging economies—such as Latin America—is also beneficial. Latin America has the fastest growing Internet user population in the world (eMarketer 2003). Chile's Internet users have reached 3.1 million. Specifically, Chile has a penetration rate of over 20 percent, the highest in the region. It is expected that due to its small population, Chile will reach saturation faster than other countries. The number of Mexican Internet users has exceeded 3.6 million, ranking second in the number of users in Latin America (Instituto Nacional de Estadística, Geografía e Informática 2002). These statistics set the stage for the fast growth of the online gaming audience. At the same time, there is very little information about the Latin American online gaming audience. By the inclusion of Latin American samples, the present study provides valuable information about these emerging markets.

Specifically, our study addresses differences in language systems. Previous studies addressing these differences have compared either two Western languages or one Eastern language versus one Western language. Luna and Peracchio (2003) compared English and Spanish, concluding that Westerners perceived images as more concrete and less conceptual than words. Tavassoli and Han (2001) compared the basic process of alphabetic and logographic scripts utilized by the Korean language. Schmitt, Pan, and Tavassoli (1994) compared Chinese and English, and found that Chinese consumers recalled better when the visual memory instead of the phonological memory evidence was retrieved. In the same vein, Tavassoli (1999) compared Chinese and English, concluding that differences in information processing result from relative differences in dependence on short-term memory components. Our research extends previous analysis of language systems by providing comparison of recall by natives of one Eastern language (Korean) versus three groups of natives of two Western languages (Spanish and English) simultaneously.

Hypotheses

Previous research concluded that language differences do affect consumer information processing (Tavassoli 1999). Tavassoli (1999) found that temporal memory for pictorial information was superior to that for words, regardless of language. Additionally, Luna and Peracchio (2003) reported evidence supporting the claim that pictures might reduce the processing load involved in second-language acquisition. They suggest that the presence of congruent pictures increases bilinguals' comprehension of second language wording. Indeed, better recall was obtained among Asian subjects by incorporation of pictorial stimuli (Leong, Ang, and Tham 1996).

Alphabetic scripts heavily rely on phonological short-term memory, while logographic scripts rely more on visual short-term memory. The English and Spanish languages are based on the Latin alphabet, which consists of symbols representing sounds. The Korean language uses both alphabetic and logographic scripts, labeled *hangul* and *hancha*, respectively. Tavassoli and Han (2001) found that spatial memory was better for logographic *hancha* words than for the same words written in the alphabetic *hangul*. Tavassoli (2003) found that differences in processing alphabetic and logographic scripts could extend to processes involved in memory. Specifically, differences in visual attention among stimuli in advertising displays are expected insofar as spatial memory is better for logographic words than for alphabetic words. Thus, we expect that, because of South Koreans' greater experience in processing logographic information:

> H1: South Korean subjects will have better brand recall than the American, Chilean, and Mexican subjects.

A distinction among the players based on frequency of playing could have an effect on brand recall. Previous studies had found a significant correlation between domain expertise and memory recall after a brief exposure time (Hutchinson 1983; Vicente and Wang 1998). Specifically, a study by Hong and Liu (2003) found differences in the analytical thinking of electronic game experts and novices. Greenfield et al. (1994) found that expert electronic games players possess skills that allow monitoring of several locations on the screen. Thus, the following hypothesis is stated:

> H2: Across all countries, subjects who perceive themselves as expert players will have better brand recall than novice players.

Locke and Latham (1990) claimed that specific, difficult goals lead to higher performance than do easy and vague goals. Additionally, these findings hold consistently when participants have feedback concerning progress in relation to their goals. This situation could be paralleled to electronic games, in that game goals are always specific and usually provide a certain degree of difficulty in order to offer a challenge to the player. Furthermore, electronic games usually display scores in order to let players know their progress in relation to the game goal.

Gellatly and Meyer (1992) found that arousal and cognitive mechanisms might mediate the goal-difficulty-performance relation. According to Locke and Latham (1990), cognitive mechanisms also mediate the allocation of attentional and information-processing resources during task performance. In facing new tasks, the early stages of skill acquisition demand more of the individual's attentional resources necessary for on-task activity, and therefore, resources for the self-regulatory activity are distracted. Perceived difficulty is viewed as a function of the degree of skill already achieved and the task's objective demands (Rellinger et al. 1995). Hence, it is expected that players allocate attentional resources when coping with the early stage of skill acquisition of a new game, and consequently, they might not recall details in the game environment, such as brand placements. Therefore, based on goal theory, the following hypothesis is investigated:

> H3: Across all countries, subjects who perceive a low level of game difficulty will have better brand recall than the subjects perceiving it as too difficult.

Method

Experimental Stimuli

Sports sponsorship has been demonstrated to possess a substantial nonverbal component in promoting a company's brand in an international context (Quester and Farrelly 1998). Because the sports games genre simulates real-life sports, this nonverbal component extends to the electronic game setting, and it is particularly useful for our hypothesis testing. Hence, sports games with different characteristics and pace were selected for the study. Racing players compete against each other to reach a goal, usually under a time constraint. In comparison, golf is a solitary and slow-paced game where players battle par, rather than a human opponent directly. These different characteristics appeal to different segments of players.

Free online games were selected for the study in order to obtain the four samples playing the same games. Because the objective of the study is to assess online advergaming effectiveness, no commercial games were used to conduct the study. The games selected were Arctic 3D Racer (www. nabiscoworld.com/games/nw_shock_nwar.htm) and Mini Mini Golf (www.nabiscoworld.com/games/nw_shock_nwmm.htm) from nabisco world.com. The Nabisco site was selected because it is one of the ten highest traffic gaming sites, ranking fourth in time usage (Fattah and Paul 2002). Another criterion considered in the selection was that Nabisco is a multinational company and offers the same brands in these four countries. In addition, it was particularly appropriate for our hypothesis testing that Nabisco games do not provide different levels of difficulty because they are aimed at all types of players.

The game Arctic 3D Racer (game A) is a snowmobile racing game exhibiting three brand products and one corporate brand. The brand products are Chips Ahoy! Cremewiches, X-treme Jello, and LifeSavers Kickers. The corporate brand is Nabisco. The brands are visible on the skymobile, helmet, driver jacket, dashboard, obstacles, signs, signal flags, and on the walls along the road. Additionally, the products are displayed along the snow road as part of the game play. Background music and sound effects (driving, crashing, shooting) are heard during the gameplay. Arctic 3D Racer is a rapid game requiring quick fingers and reflexes.

The game Mini Mini Golf (game B) promotes six brand products and one corporate brand. The brand products are Ritz Bits Sandwiches, Mini Chips Ahoy! Nutter Butter Bites, Mini Oreos, Cheese Nips, and Fun Fruits. The packages of the product exhibiting the brand names are shown as part of the obstacles of the game. Each brand is shown one by one in the different holes. The brands are always visible in the frame of the play window. Sound effects are heard when the ball hits the obstacles. Mini Mini Golf is a slow-paced game, and it requires avoiding obstacles by carefully timing shots.

Instrument

Based on the exploratory nature of the study, in addition to closed-ended questions, a series of open-ended questions was included in the questionnaire. Some of the questions included in the instrument were those addressing free and aided brand recall and subjects' attitudes toward product placement as they were used by Nelson (2002), modifying where needed. Two open-ended questions assessed brand recall. Attitudes were measured by three questions utilizing a seven-point Likert-type scale and one open-ended question. Three questions were added to address game genre preference and two questions used a seven-point Likert scale to address perceived game difficulty. Appendix Table 14.1 shows the English version of the questionnaire used.

The instruments were presented in English in the United States and South Korea, and in Spanish in Mexico and Chile. The questionnaires were translated and backtranslated to achieve construct equivalence across nations. Completing the full survey took participants about ten minutes.

Measures

The variables reported for each country were free and aided recall of brands after game play, attitudes toward product placement, perceived goal difficulty, and genre preference. In addressing hypothesis testing, the recall means for each game were compared across groups of players by ability in processing logographic information, level of expertise, and perceived goal difficulty.

The free recall scores were determined by summing all the brands recalled without the cue provided in aided recall. The number of brands differs considerably for both games. The maximum score for game Arctic 3D Racer was four and the maximum score for game Mini Mini Golf was seven. We did not expect that the players of the Mini Mini Golf game would recall all brands, because the assigned exposure time of the game was not intended to encompass all holes.

Aided recall was addressed with six open-ended questions. Three questions addressed each game. For game A, we asked about recall for brands of cookies, candy, and gelatin. For game B, we asked about recall for brands of crackers, cookies, and candy. The format of the question asked was: "What brands of product do you recall seeing in game A?"

The level of expertise was determined based on the frequency of playing. Frequency of playing was addressed by a seven-point Likert scale question. We classified subjects who selected one (never) to four in the scale as novice players, while those subjects who selected five to seven (very often) were classified as expert players. Similarly, the groups based on perceived goal difficulty were divided according to their perception of each game. Therefore, the subjects perceiving the game as having high to moderate difficulty selected one (too difficult) to three in the scale, and they constituted one group. Those subjects perceiving the game as having somewhat to low difficulty selected four to seven (too easy) in the scale, and they were classified in the second group.

Samples

Convenience samples were used for the study representing both groups of players, both sexes, and various age categories. Two hundred sixty subjects from four countries voluntarily participated in the study. The entire sample included subjects from the United States, South Korea, Mexico, and Chile. The same procedure was used in the recruitment of subjects. All subjects were recruited from selected universities in each country. Only undergraduate students participated. Specifically, the subjects were senior-level students in South Korea, Chile, and Mexico. American freshmen participated in the study. Business majors were recruited in the United States, South Korea, and Chile. Manufacturing majors participated in Mexico.

United States. The American participants were seventy-one subjects attending a large southwestern university in Edinburg, Texas, ranging from seventeen to forty years old. Forty-two percent were male, and 90 percent were students. Eighty percent of the subjects classified themselves as novice players.

Mexico. Seventy-two subjects from Matamoros, Mexico, ranging from eighteen to thirty-nine years old took part in the study. Eighty-two percent were male, and 91 percent were students. Seventy-seven percent classified themselves as novice players.

Chile. Forty-five subjects from Talca, Chile, ranging from nineteen to thirty-two years old participated in the study. Twenty-seven percent were male, and 96 percent were students. Eighty percent classified themselves as novice players.

South Korea. Seventy-two subjects from Seoul, South Korea, ranging from twenty to thirty-two years old participated in the study. Fifty-eight percent were male, and all participants were students. Sixty-three percent classified themselves as novice players.

Data Collection Procedure

Data were collected during spring 2003. Lab experiments were conducted in university computer labs in the United States, Mexico, Chile, and South Korea. Subjects participated on computers assigned individually. To avoid demand artifacts, the participants were told this was a consumer behavior study. They were provided with instructions to the games in English in the United States and South Korea, and in Spanish in Mexico and Chile. The participants were instructed to play each game for ten minutes. During a total of twenty minutes of playing, the subjects were exposed to the brands several times. Following the game play, participants completed the questionnaires independently.

Results

South Koreans' Ability to Process Logographic Information

Multivariate analysis of variance (MANOVA) was performed to test hypothesis H1 addressing differences in visual attention among stimuli in advertising displays. The sum of brands recalled in game A and sum of brands recalled in game B were used as dependent variables. The independent variable was language script type. The sample was classified based on the language script type. American, Mexican, and Chilean subjects formed the alphabetic script group, which was compared with the logographic script group constituted by South Korean subjects. The Wilks' lambda test result for the effect by language script type shows a significant difference in brand recall means (Wilks' lambda = 0.95133, exact $F = 6.57464$, significance = .002). Analysis of variance (ANOVA) tests for each game assessed whether mean differences were significantly different for each dependent variable (brand recall of game A and brand recall of game B) considered alone. Results indicate significant differences in recall for game B, $F(1,258) = 8.684$, $p < .01$. Results of recall for game A indicate no significant difference, $F(1,258) = 0.292$, $p = .623$. Therefore, our sample provided partial support for H1.

Expert and Novice Players

To address H2, a t-test was performed for the entire sample. The group of expert players consisted of 65 subjects, and 192 subjects constituted the novice players group. To assess the difference between two independent samples identified by level of expertise, brand recall means were compared across the expert group and novice players group for both the Arctic 3D Racer and Mini Mini Golf games. The means, standard deviation, and statistical significance for the t-test are shown in Table 14.1. t-test results show that for the two games, group means are not significantly different. Therefore, our sample failed to support H2.

Perceived Goal Difficulty

To test H3, t-tests for each game assessed the difference between two inde-

Table 14.1

Players Classified by Level of Expertise

	Game A: Arctic Racer	Game B: Mini Golf
Mean recall		
Expert players' group (n = 65)	1.25	1.43
Novice players' group (n = 192)	1.44	1.56
df	255	255
t-test results	1.39	0.70
Statistical significance (2-tailed)	0.166	0.484

Table 14.2

Players Classified by Perceived Goal Difficulty

	Game A: Arctic Racer	Game B: Mini Golf
Mean recall		
Low difficulty group	1.41[a]	1.55[b]
High difficulty group	1.37[c]	1.44[d]
df	257	254
t-test results	−.364	0.685
Significance (2-tailed)	0.716	0.494

Notes: [a]n = 94; [b]n = 135; [c]n = 165; [d]n = 121

pendent sample means classified by perceived goal difficulty. One hundred sixty-five subjects (64%) perceived the goal of game A as difficult, and ninety-four (36%) perceived the game as having none to low difficulty. Results showed no significant difference between the two groups for game A. One hundred twenty-one subjects (47%) perceived game B as difficult and 135 (52%) did not. The *t*-test result showed no significant difference between the two groups for game B. The means, standard deviation, and statistical significance for the *t*-test are shown in Table 14.2. Therefore, H3 was not supported.

Additional Exploratory Analysis

Additional exploratory analysis addressed free and aided brand recall, attitudes, and perceived difficulty as dependent variables. In addition, genre preferences were also listed by country. Table 14.3 contains a summary of

Table 14.3

Overall Exploratory Results and Differences by Country

Mean	United States ($n = 71$)	Mexico ($n = 72$)	Chile ($n = 45$)	South Korea ($n = 72$)	Total ($n = 260$)
Free recall					
Racing	2.00	0.88	1.29	1.33	1.38
Mini golf	1.39	0.88	2.16	1.90	1.52
Attitudes[a]					
Deceptive	3.97	5.15	4.62	4.17	4.47
Realism	3.57	4.80	4.22	4.08	4.16
Interrupt	4.82	5.27	4.79	4.55	4.86
Perceived difficulty[b]					
Racing	3.72	4.40	4.16	4.01	4.07
Mini golf	3.41	4.13	3.73	3.12	3.59
Genre preference	Driving	Driving	Driving	Sports	
	Sports	Action	Strategy	Role-playing	
	Action	Sports	Adventure	Strategy	

[a]Seven-point Likert scale (1–deceptive, 7–not deceptive; 1–it does not add to the realism, 7–it adds to the realism; 1–it impairs/interrupts, 7–it does not impair/interrupt).
[b]Seven-point Likert scale (1–too difficult, 7–too easy).

means classified by dependent variable and country, including a listing of genre preference as well.

Free and Aided Brand Recall

Overall, recall of brands ranged from zero to four in the racing game (mean = 1.38), and zero to six in the Mini Mini Golf game (mean = 1.52). In exploring differences in recall by country, ANOVA was performed for each game. Results showed that there were differences in recall among countries. Statistical significance was found for the Arctic 3D racing, $F(3,256) = 20.407$, $p < .01$. Post hoc tests revealed that a difference in recall was found in the United States, which showed recall superiority in this game. A significant ANOVA result was also found for the Mini Mini Golf game, $F(3,256) = 13.391$, $p < .01$. A post hoc test indicated that a difference in recall for this game was found for Mexican respondents who exhibited the poorest recall among the four countries in the study.

United States. The range of responses varied from zero to four in the racing game. The range varied from zero to five in the golf game. The average recall was 2.00 and 1.39, respectively. Aided recall did not help the players' recall.

South Korea. The responses varied from zero to three for the racing game (mean = 1.33) and zero to five for the Mini Mini Golf (mean = 1.90). Aided recall did not help the players' recall.

Mexico. The range of responses varied from zero to two in the racing game. The range varied from zero to one in the golf game. The average recall was 0.88 and 0.88, respectively. Aided recall did not help the players' recall.

Chile. The range of responses varied from zero to three in the racing game (mean = 1.29). For the golf game, the range of responses was zero to six (mean = 2.16). Overall, aided recall did not help the players' recall.

Brand recall across countries. The percentages of recall frequencies across countries (35% for game A and 22% for game B) were comparable with Nelson's (2002) findings (25–30%) in the short-term assessment of a sample of American subjects. The percentages of recall frequencies across countries were obtained considering the ratio of the total score of brands recalled divided by the maximum score any player could get for recall. In particular, the brands with superior recall were Chips Ahoy! (63%) and Ritz Bits Sandwiches (47%). These brands appeared first in game A and game B, respectively, providing a cross-national instance of the primacy effect. Chips Ahoy! and Ritz Bits Sandwiches brands are placed in the default background of each game. For instance, if the player followed the usual sequence of the golf game, starting in hole 1, the brand Ritz Bits would be the first to appear and it would have longer exposure during the experiment.

Attitudes Toward Product Placements

In exploring differences in attitudes by country, ANOVA was performed for each item addressed in attitudes. A statistically significant difference was found in perception of deceptiveness, $F(3,255) = 7.309$, $p < .01$. Post hoc tests revealed that the difference was in Mexico, indicating that Mexicans perceived the product placement as deceptive. A significant difference was also found in perception of whether product placements add to the realism of the game, $F(3,253) = 5.362$, $p < .01$. Again, the difference was found in Mexicans, who thought the ads in games add to the realism. ANOVA results for the perception of interruption indicated no statistically significant difference among the four countries, $F(3,252) = 1.852$, $p = .138$. In general, players from the four countries perceived the product placement as somewhat interrupting the experience.

United States. Overall, Americans showed a neutral attitude toward product placements. They were neutral toward the practice of deceptiveness (mean = 3.97). They were inclined toward the opinion that product placement does not add to the realism of the game (mean = 3.57). However, Americans did not think that the practice impaired or interrupted the game play (mean = 4.82). The great majority of the answers to the open-ended question tended toward a positive attitude toward product placements as long as the advertising made sense in the context of the game.

South Korea. Overall, South Koreans showed a neutral attitude toward product placements. They showed a neutral attitude toward the deceptiveness of the practice (mean = 4.17). They were neutral as to whether advergaming adds to the realism of the game (mean = 4.08). They thought that product placements in electronic games do not impair the game-playing experience (mean = 4.55).

Mexico. Mexicans did not consider the practice deceptive (mean = 5.15). They did not think that product placement impaired or interrupted the game play (mean = 4.80). They thought that advertising in games adds to the realism of the experience (mean = 5.27). The open-ended question revealed that 69 percent of the respondents considered product placement in games as a good practice. Thirty-one percent of the respondents found product placement irrelevant, emphasizing the importance of the game play. Overall, the results showed that the players were positive in their attitude toward product placement.

Chile. Overall, Chileans had a positive attitude toward product placement. They did not consider the practice deceptive (mean = 4.62). They were somewhat neutral on the question of whether product placement adds to the realism of the game (mean = 4.22). They did not think that product placement impaired or interrupted the game play (mean = 4.79). Sixty-three percent of the respondents considered product placement in games as a positive and novel practice.

Attitudes across countries. Overall, Mexicans and Chileans showed a positive attitude toward product placement, while South Koreans and Americans were neutral concerning this practice. The open-ended questions revealed several points that were consistent across samples. Some players indicated they were not able to recall because they were focused on playing the game and they did not pay attention to the environment. The great majority of participants recommended slow-paced games for advergaming, such as puzzles or strategy games, in order to direct attention to the brand placement and not to control of the vehicle. Another point the players highlighted was the relevance of the placement with the game environment. They would like to see advertising that makes sense in the context of the game.

Perceived Difficulty

In exploring differences in perceived difficulty by country, ANOVA was performed for each game. No statistical significance was found for the Arctic 3D Racer game, $F(3,255) = 2.223, p = .086$. However, statistical significance was found for the Mini Mini Golf game, $F(3,252) = 5.230, p < .01$. Post hoc tests revealed that the difference was found in South Korea, where the players rated the game as more difficult than the players from other countries did.

United States. Americans found the golf game (mean = 3.41) more difficult than the racing game (mean = 3.72). Overall, the games were perceived as having average difficulty. The pace of the game did let the players watch the advertising in both games.

South Korea. South Koreans found the golf game (mean = 3.12) more difficult than the racing game (mean = 4.01). Overall, they rated the games as having some degree of difficulty to moderate difficulty. They found the golf game to be more difficult than the other national groups did.

Mexico. In assessing perceived difficulty, Mexicans found the games to be of average difficulty. They found the racing game a little more difficult (mean = 4.40) than the golf game (mean = 4.13). Mexicans rated both games as easier than the other national groups did.

Chile. Chileans found the games to have average difficulty. They rated the golf game as more difficult (mean = 3.73) than the racing game (mean = 4.16).

Genre Preference

United States. Americans prefer driving, sports, and action genres. Almost all the participants indicated a preference for games that let them compete against friends.

South Korea. Sports games are the South Koreans' preferred games, followed by role-playing and strategy games. Fifty-nine percent of them favored competition among friends.

Mexico. Among the favorite games they play, the Mexicans favored driving, action, and sports genres. The great majority indicated a preference for games that let them compete against friends.

Chile. Driving, strategy, and adventure are the preferred games genres among the Chileans. Sixty-eight percent of the participants favor competition among friends.

Conclusions and Directions for Future Research

Our findings imply practical implications for companies using the Internet as an advertising medium. The Internet is a central factor in approaching globalization. As Luna, Peracchio, and De Juan (2003) point out, a large number of Internet users are bilingual, and their attitude-formation processes are influenced by both the graphic and cultural congruity. Images and language are merely two codes for representing thought. As Scott and Batra (2003) pointed out, the thought itself is in neither form and the current accepted relationship of language to thought would be questionable. Thus, the study of language becomes crucial when attitudes toward the ad and advertising effectiveness are under scrutiny.

This study assessed the effectiveness of product placement in online games through brand recall across groups of players from the United States, South Korea, Chile, and Mexico. Effectiveness was assessed by free brand recall after brief exposure during game play. Although no difference was found between level-of-expertise groups and between perceived-difficulty groups, partial support was found for the hypothesized difference between subjects speaking an alphabetic language only (Spanish and English) versus subjects speaking a combined alphabetic and logographic language (Korean).

Although our sample failed to provide support for the hypothesis that expert players would recall better than novice players, the outcome is encouraging. The fact that expertise has no effect on recall indicates that advergames represent an effective medium to reach both expert and novice segments of users. The lack of support for the hypothesis that subjects perceiving low goal difficulty would recall better than subjects perceiving the goal as too difficult might indicate that the early stages of skill acquisition demand more individual attentional resources, leading to poor recall. Future research could address this issue by exposing the subjects to a game previously played, in order to ensure that cognitive resources were redirected to attention following the skill acquisition stages.

We hypothesized that the recall superiority demonstrated in one game by the group of South Koreans over the American, Chilean, and Mexican subjects was due to language factors. However, alternative explanations are available. For instance, in our sample, all South Korean subjects had a computer at home. This situation could have some influence in familiarity with games. As discussed earlier, the popularity of electronic games in South Korea has made the practice so familiar that we might expect to see better brand recall than elsewhere. In addition, other cognitive factors might influence their memory. Future research could explore closely the South Korean outcome by controlling specific factors that might affect the cognitive aspects involved in recall measures.

Some brands were better recalled than others. We suggest that exposure time could have some influence in brand recall. Future research could address this issue by exposing the subjects to a larger period of time or to subsequent short exposures, in order to evaluate the exposure time as a possible factor influencing recall. Another possible factor influencing this outcome is that the games selected for the study promote brands of an international corporation with considerable time in the market. Therefore, respondents might have retrieved brand information based on past experience rather than based on the exposure in the advergame. Future work could develop hypothetical brands and test them in the same context to ensure that the findings hold.

Mexican subjects were readily able to recall an average of about 0.88 (standard deviation = 0.71) brands in the racing game, and an average of 0.88 (standard deviation = 0.82) in the golf game. However, it is important to note a special situation when they were asked to list the brands. Though they were not able to recall a high percentage of the brands placed in the games, they were able to recall similar products produced and distributed by the Mexican competition of these products. For instance, instead of recalling the Chips Ahoy! brand, they mentioned Chokis, which are chocolate chip cookies produced and distributed by Gamesa in Mexico. Similarly, a large percentage of subjects recalled the objects. Thirty-six percent of the subjects described the cookies they recalled. For example, Mexicans described the "chocolate chip cookies" in association with the Chips Ahoy! brand. Previous work addressing brand confusion in printed media by Brengman, Geuens, and De Pelsmacker (2001) concluded that brands heavily supported by advertising, especially by more than one media type, are less likely to suffer from brand confusion. In the case of Mexico, our study was conducted in a northern city, close to Gamesa headquarters. Thus, we believe the strong advertising in the surrounding area might influence brand confusion. In addition, the attitudes of Mexicans toward the advergames were more favorable than those of any other country group. This might also influence brand confusion. The advergame might overwhelm the brand, similar to the way in which celebrities' endorsement has led to exaggeration of the properties of the advertised product (Ross et al. 1984). Future work could address assessment of the package characteristics recall in order to differentiate between the product advertised and the product actually associated with recall.

Sponsored Web sites, promotional contests, push-strategy e-mail updates, and brand placement represent a combination of advertising and media content (Nelson 2002). Although advergaming provides many advantages, this study did not directly compare advergaming with these types of advertising. For instance, advergaming is considered as an agent of viral interactive promotion through e-mail (Hernandez and Minor 2003). However, this capability is practically unexploited. None of the subjects of our sample indicate they play games received by e-mail. The participants indicate they play either online games or they buy games at the store. Future work could address comparison of the effectiveness of these areas.

Though academic attention to product placement effectiveness in the electronic game medium has been limited, the increasing tendency to place brands in electronic games is very well known (Richtel 2002; Rowan 2002), deserving careful attention by practitioners and academicians. This study provides a starting point in addressing some cognitive mechanisms behind the effectiveness measures of product placement in electronic games. In addition, the study provides insight into the effectiveness of advergaming across Latin American and Asian countries.

Appendix Table 14.1

Questionnaire

Dependent variables	Questions included
Free recall	What products or brands do you remember seeing in game A? List any or all below.
	What products or brands do you remember seeing in game B? List any or all below.
Aided recall	What brands of *product* do you recall seeing in game A?
	What brands of *product* do you recall seeing in game B?
Attitudes toward product placement	How do you feel about product placements/advertising in games?
	Do you think it is deceptive/not deceptive?
	Do you think it adds to the realism of the game/does not add to the realism of the game?
	Do you think it impairs or interrupts the game-playing experience/does not impair or interrupt the game-playing experience?
Perceived difficulty of game play	How difficult was it to reach the goal of game A? (Too difficult, about right, too easy.)
	How difficult was it to reach the goal of game B? (Too difficult, about right, too easy.)
	Did the game play let you watch the advertising in game A?
	Did the game play let you watch the advertising in game B?
Genre preference	What is your favorite game (if any)?
	Do you like games that let you compete against friends?
	Please select your preferred game genre among the following: action, adventure, driving, puzzle, role-playing game, simulation, sports, strategy.
Open-ended questions	Which game genres do you think are better suited to product placement?
	Why?
	Comments

Demographics	Age
	Sex
	Occupation
	Do you have a computer at home?
	Do you own a console?
	How often do you play games?
	What kind of games do you play? (Free online games, received by e-mail, buy at the store.)
	When do you play games?
	For how long (hours per day)?
	E-mail

References

Brengman, Malaika, Maggie Geuens, and Patrick De Pelsmacker (2001), "The Impact of Consumer Characteristics and Campaign Related Factors on Brand Confusion in Print Advertising," *Journal of Marketing Communications*, 7 (4), 231–243.

Brennan, Ian, Khalid M. Dubas, and Laurie A. Babin (1999), "The Influence of Product-Placement Type and Exposure Time on Product-Placement Recognition," *International Journal of Advertising*, 18 (3), 323–337.

Chon, Gina (2002), "Korea Battles Its Online Warriors," *Fortune (Asia)* (July 22), 146 (2), 21–22.

Elkin, Tobi (2002), "Digital Gamescapes Lure Major Marketers," AdAge.com, [www.adage.com/news.cms?newsId=34888].

eMarketer (2003), "Latin America Online: Demographics, Usage and E-Commerce," [www.emarketer.com/products/report.php?latin_am].

Fattah, Hassan and Pamela Paul (2002), "Gaming Gets Serious," *American Demographics*, 24 (5), 38–43.

Federal Communications Commission (2002), "Federal Communications Commission Releases Data on High-speed Services for Internet Access," *News Federal Communications Commission* (December 17).

French, Howard W. (2002), "South Korea's Real Rage for Virtual Games," *New York Times* (October 9) [www.nytimes.com/2002/10/09/technology/09KORE.html].

Gamespot (2002), "Gamespot Splash Page," [www.gamespot.com].

Gellatly, Ian R. and John P. Meyer (1992), "The Effects of Goal Difficulty on Physiological Arousal, Cognition, and Task Performance," *Journal of Applied Psychology*, 77 (5), 694–704.

Global Information, Inc. (2002), "Report on The Korean Electronic Games Market Selling Game Content and Applications to the World's Most Avid Electronic Games Players," [www.gii.co.jp/english/vc11944_korean_games.html].

Gould, Stephen J., Pola B. Gupta, and Sonja Grabner-Krauter (2000), "Product Placements in Movies: A Cross-Cultural Analysis of Austrian, French and American Consumers' Attitudes Toward This Emerging, International Promotional Medium," *Journal of Advertising*, 29 (4), 41–58.

Greenfield, Patricia M., Patricia deWinstanley, Heidi Kilpatrick, and Daniel Kaye (1994), "Action Video Games and Informal Education: Effects on Strategies for Dividing Visual Attention," *Journal of Applied Developmental Psychology*, 15, 105–123.

Hernandez, Monica D. and Michael S. Minor (2003), "A Decision Tool for the Assessment of Advergaming Suitability," Paper presented at the 2003 American Marketing Association Summer Educators Conference, Chicago (August 17).

Hong, Jon-Chao and Ming-Chou Liu (2003), "A Study on Thinking Strategy Between Experts and Novices of Computer Games," *Computers in Human Behavior*, 19, 245–258.

Hutchinson, J. Wesley (1983), "Expertise and the Structure of Free Recall," *Advances in Consumer Research*, 10 (1), 585–589.

Instituto Nacional de Estadística, Geografía e Informática (2002), "Usuarios de Internet por Paises Seleccionados 2000–2002," [www.inegi.gob.mx/est/contenidos/espanol/tematicos/mediano/med.asp?+=tinf142&c=4870].

Jones, John P. (2002), *The Ultimate Secrets of Advertising*, Thousands Oaks, CA: Sage.

Kushairi, Admad (2003), "More Girls Take to Net Gaming," *New Straits Times-Management Times* (January 23).

Leong, Siew Meng, Swee Hoon Ang, and Lai Leng Tham (1996), "Increasing Brand Name Recall in Print Advertising among Asian Consumers," *Journal of Advertising*, 25 (2), 65–81.

Locke, Edwin A., and Gary P. Latham (1990), *A Theory of Goal Setting and Task Performance*, Englewood Cliffs, NJ: Prentice Hall.

Luna, David and Laura A. Peracchio (2003), "Visual and Linguistic Processing of Ads by Bilingual Consumers," In *Persuasive Imagery: A Consumer Response Perspective*, Linda M. Scott and Rajeev Batra, eds., Mahwah, NJ: Lawrence Erlbaum Associates, 153–173.

———, ———, and Maria Dolores De Juan (2003), "The Impact of Language and Congruity on Persuasion in Multicultural E-Marketing," *Journal of Consumer Psychology*, 13 (1&2), 41–50.

Moon, Ihlwan (2001), "The Champs in Online Games," *Business Week* (July 23), Issue 3742, 51.

Nedungadi, Prakash and J. Wesley Hutchinson (1985), "The Prototypicality of Brands: Relationships with Brand Awareness, Preference and Usage," *Advances in Consumer Research*, 12 (1), 498–503.

Nelson, Michelle R. (2002), "Recall of Brand Placements in Computer/Video Games," *Journal of Advertising Research*, 42 (2), 80–92.

Olsen, Stefanie (2001), "Major Brands Play for Attention," News.com [http://news.com.com/2102–1023–256982.html].

Percy, Larry and John R. Rossiter (1992), "A Model of Brand Awareness and Brand Attitude Advertising Strategies," *Psychology and Marketing*, 4 (4), 263–274.

Quester, Pascale and Francis Farrelly (1998), "Brand Association and Memory Decay Effects of Sponsorship: The Case of the Australian Formula One Grand Prix," *Journal of Product and Brand Management*, 7 (6), 539–556.

Rellinger, Elizabeth, John G. Borkowski, Lisa A. Turner, and Catherine A. Hale (1995), "Perceived Task Difficulty and Intelligence: Determinants of Strategy Use and Recall," *Intelligence*, 20, 125–143.

Reynolds, Thomas J., Jerry C. Olson, and John P. Rochon (1997), "A Strategic Approach to Measuring Advertising Effectiveness," in *Measuring Advertising Effectiveness*, William D. Wells, ed., Mahwah, NJ: Lawrence Erlbaum Associates, 337–355.

Richtel, Matt (2002), "Product Placements Go Interactive in Video Games," *New York Times* (September 17), C1.

Rodgers, Anni Layne (2002), "More Than a Game," *Fast Company* (May), 46–48.

Rowan, David (2002), "Will That Be Fries with Your Sims? David Rowan Looks at How Product Placement Has Invaded Video Games," *The Times* (United Kingdom) (September 25), 9.

Russell, Cristel A. (2002), "Investigating the Effectiveness of Product Placements in Television Shows: The Role of Modality and Plot Connection Congruence on Brand Memory and Attitude," *Journal of Consumer Research*, 29 (3), 306–318.

Schmitt, Bernd H., Yigang Pan, and Nader T. Tavassoli (1994), "Language and Consumer Memory: The Impact of Linguistic Differences between Chinese and English," *Journal of Consumer Research*, 21, 419–431.

Scott, Linda M. and Rajeev Batra (2003), "Introduction," in *Persuasive Imagery: A Consumer Response Perspective*, Linda M. Scott and Rajeev Batra, eds., Mahwah, NJ: Lawrence Erlbaum Associates, ix–xxi.

Tavassoli, Nader T. (1999), "Temporal and Associative Memory in Chinese and English," *Journal of Consumer Research*, 26, 170–181.

——— (2003), "Scripted Thought," in *Persuasive Imagery: A Consumer Response Perspective*, Linda M. Scott and Rajeev Batra, eds., Mahwah, NJ: Lawrence Erlbaum Associates, 141–152.

——— and Jin K. Han (2001), "Scripted Thought: Processing Korean Hancha and Hangul in a Multimedia Context," *Journal of Consumer Research*, 28 (3), 482–493.

Vicente, Kim J. and JoAnne H. Wang (1998), "An Ecological Theory of Expertise Effects in Memory Recall," *Psychology Review*, 105 (1), 33–57.

Vikas, Bajaj (2003), "Online Gaming Captivates S. Korean Youths; Emphasis on Teamwork Counter to Playing Habits in US," *Dallas Morning News* (January 18), 1H.

Wright-Isak, Christine, Ronald J. Faber, and Lewis R. Horner (1997), "Comprehensive Measurement of Advertising Effectiveness: Notes from the Marketplace," in *Measuring Advertising Effectiveness*, William D. Wells, ed., Mahwah, NJ: Lawrence Erlbaum Associates, 3–12.

YaYa (2003), "Why Games?" [www.yaya.com/why/index_why.html].

15

Advergame Playing Motivations and Effectiveness

A "Uses and Gratifications" Perspective

Seounmi Youn and Mira Lee

As electronic games have become an ingrained part of consumers' recreational life, advertisers have focused their attention on using online game-related advertising tactics (Emling 2001; Freeman 2001; Ghose and Dou 1998; Neff 2001). According to Jupiter Media Metrix, some 35.1 million people play online games, and this number is estimated to grow to 104.9 million by 2005 (Hopper 2002). With this potential increase in online gamers, advertisers have been experimenting with the strategic idea of advertising-as-entertainment or advergames by incorporating advertising messages into interactive games on commercial Web sites (Nelson 2002). Advergames, designed to blend a company's brand with entertainment, are expected to have a lot of benefits for online advertisers (Emling 2001). Advertisers hope that these advergames will capture online users' attention to get their message across. They also hope that the play value of advergames will improve the attitude toward the game, the site, and the game sponsor.

Advertisers have offered advergames on their Web sites as a new vehicle to reach consumers while decreasing budgets as a percentage of sales and increasing fragmentation of mass media (Neff 2001). At the virtual theme park site created by Nabisco, online users can play all sorts of games including a Ritz ball toss (Emling 2001). One good example of advergames is Nabisco's snowmobile racing game. Using a computer keyboard's directional buttons, consumers drive a snowmobile through a track. The snowmobile is plastered with Nabisco brands and every advertisement seen along the track's billboards is for Nabisco products.

These cases demonstrate the growing tendency to use interactive entertainment on the Internet as a new form of advertising campaign. However, despite advertisers' recent and frequent use of advergames, little empirical research to date has been conducted on why online users participate in playing advergames and what the possible consequences of advergame playing are. While online advertisers recognize advergames as a powerful tool, they also raise questions about the communicative effectiveness of advergames (Neff 2001). Thus, it seems likely that understanding advergame players' motivations and advergame effectiveness will benefit academic and applied researchers who are eager to unravel this kind of advertisement's potential.

This study applies a uses-and-gratifications approach to improve the understanding of advergame-playing consumption. This chapter presents two studies. Study 1 was conducted to find out advergame-specific motivations by using open-ended questions. The primary interest was to examine what types of motivations people actually have for advergame play. Study 2 was undertaken to validate items developed from Study 1 and to investigate how the motives for playing advergames are related to the effectiveness of advergames. In Study 2, a path model is proposed to determine the relationships between motivations and advergame effectiveness. This study proposes a new construct of attitude toward the advergame (A_{AG}) as a way to assess advergame effectiveness. Just as attitude toward the ad (A_{AD}) is a key indicator of advertising effectiveness in traditional mass media advertising (Aaker and Stayman 1990; Brown and Stayman 1992; MacKenzie, Lutz, and Belch 1986), we assume that attitude toward the advergame (A_{AG}) will be an important indicator of advergame effectiveness. This study conceptually defines attitude toward the advergame as a player's predisposition to respond in a favorable or unfavorable manner to a particular advergame on a commercial Web site. In this study, motivations for advergame playing were explored as antecedents, while attitude toward the site, relationship building, and purchase intention were examined as consequences. This conceptual model of the antecedents and consequences of attitude toward the advergame is then tested with a path analysis using LISREL 8 (Jöreskog and Sörbom 1993).

Uses-and-Gratifications Application to Advergame Play

Uses-and-gratifications (U&G) research has proved fruitful in explaining the motives for, and consequences of, consuming media (Eighmey 1997; Eighmey and McCord 1998; Korgaonkar and Wolin 1999; Rubin 1984; Sherry et al. 2001). Uses and gratifications is a psychological communication perspective that shifts our focus from understanding what the mass media do to people to examining what people do with the media (Rubin 1994). The primary interest is to identify what functions the media serve for active audiences, with an emphasis on individual use and choice of media. One of the basic tenets of uses and gratifications is the assumption of the active audience (Katz, Blumler, and Gurevitch 1974). Audience activity represents the intentionality, selectivity, and involvement of the audience with the media or content (Rubin 1994; Blumler 1979). Audiences intentionally participate in and select media or content from alternatives to satisfy their needs or desires. This audience activity concept is particularly important when investigating advergame players' motivations for playing games on commercial Web sites.

Advergame players take the initiative in playing advergames, choosing which games to play, when to play, who to play with, and whether or not to return to the site. These interactive features allow players to personalize and customize their gaming experiences by selecting from various options. The gaming experience can go on as long as the player stays interested (Emling 2001). The interactive role of game players enhances the active, voluntary, and self-selective consumption context. This is congruent with the audience activity assumed in the U&G perspective.

Focusing on the concept of audience activity, Katz, Blumler, and Gurevitch (1974) stated three objectives of the U&G perspective: They are to explain the ways that audiences use media to fulfill their needs, to explore motives for media consumption, and to discover consequences that result from needs, motives, and behavior. The current study is particularly interested in exploring the last two objectives, that is, to examine *motives* for advergame play and *consequences* that follow from advergame play. Drawing from a U&G framework, Study 1 attempts to examine what motivates online users to play advergames that are built around commercial Web sites.

Study 1

Advergames in commercial Web sites are advertisements disguised as games, thus blurring the line between commercial persuasion and entertainment. Participating in advergames on the company's Web site is a playful activity as well as a branding experience. Because playing advergames is considered a new form of entertainment media consumption on the Web, a review of consumers' motives for both new media technologies and gaming consumption may help understand what motivates online users to play advergames.

New Media Consumption

Because a basic assumption of the uses and gratifications perspective is that users are actively involved in media usage and interact highly with the media to gratify needs or wants, the U&G model has been regarded as one of the most effective conceptual bases to identify the motivations and perceived benefits of Internet use (Eighmey 1997; Ferguson and Perse 2000; Korgaonkar and Wolin 1999; Luo 2002; Papacharissi and Rubin 2000; Stafford and Stafford 1998). Among various motivations of Internet use, the most common are information and entertainment seeking, which have also frequently been found in various traditional media usage contexts (Eighmey 1997; Ferguson and Perse 2000; Hammond, McWilliam, and Diaz 1998; Korgaonkar and Wolin 1999; Luo 2002; Papacharissi and Rubin 2000; Rodgers and Sheldon 2002; Stafford and Stafford 1998). Other traditional media-like motivations include pass time (Ferguson and Perse 2000; Papacharissi and Rubin 2000), relaxation (Ferguson and Perse 2000), social escapism, and socialization (Korgaonkar and Wolin 1999). In addition, a number of studies also found Internet usage-specific motivations such as convenience (Papacharissi and Rubin 2000), interactive control, and economic motivation (Korgaonkar and Wolin 1999). Rodgers and Sheldon (2002) argue that these various motivations for Internet use can be grouped into four primary categories: research, entertainment (e.g., surfing), shopping, and communication (e.g., socialization).

In contrast to the fairly abundant studies on audience use of the Internet, uses-and-gratification research on gaming consumption has been relatively scant, despite the great popularity of gaming behavior.

Gaming Consumption

Selnow (1984), in a survey of 244 children aged ten to fourteen, uncovered five reasons for playing arcade video games: Video games are preferred over human companions, video games teach about other people, video games provide companionship, playing games makes me part of the action, and video games provide solitude/escape. This study identified the video-specific gratification, such as a direct and personal involvement in the action of the game. Sherry and his colleagues (2001) found six main reasons people play video games using a twenty-eight-item scale. Specific motivations for playing video games are as follows: competition (to be the best player), challenge (to push oneself to beat the game), social interaction (to play as a social experience with friends), diversion (to pass time), fantasy (to experience what cannot be experienced in real life), and arousal (to play for the excitement).

Previous studies on video-game playing motivations provide guidelines in identifying why online users play games. However, they are of limited use for describing motivations for advergame playing insofar as they do not take into consideration Internet usage context. For example, unlike the video-game playing situation, online users may play advergames spontaneously on the commercial Web sites while browsing the Internet. In addition, some gamers may look for monetary incentives in return for good scores. Because online game playing is a different type of entertainment than video-game playing, it is worthwhile to find game motivations specific to advergame playing. Thus, this study attempts to examine what motivates online users to play advergames on commercial Web sites, presuming that a distinction must be made between the motivations of online and offline gaming consumption. An overall research question that explores motivations for advergame playing is posed as follows.

RQ1: What motivates online users to play advergames on commercial Web sites?

Avoidance of Media Use

Uses-and-gratifications research, by extension, suggests that individuals have specific motives for media disuse. People are actively engaging in avoiding certain media behavior to fulfill specific needs and desires. For example, Stafford and Stafford (1996) examined the reasons why individuals actually engage in mechanical commercial avoidance such as zipping or zapping. For both types of commercial avoidance, four motivations were identified: enjoyment, boredom, relaxation, and commercial overload. For zapping behavior, a fifth factor, curiosity, was found. By utilizing the U&G framework, they found that specific motivations for avoiding commercials are significantly related to both zipping and zapping behaviors. In a related vein, people tend to avoid advertising when they perceive that advertising does not provide value (e.g., information and/or entertainment) (Pasadeos 1990). People also engage in advertising avoidance when ads are perceived as intrusive or disturbing (Abernethy 1991; Edwards, Li, and Lee, ch. 10 in this volume).

Together, these studies argue that it is important to understand the reasons why people do not engage in particular media behavior because such understanding helps practitioners develop strategies for reducing avoidance activity. The current study takes a similar approach. Because playing advergames is a relatively new form of entertainment media consumption, an examination of what motivations prevent this media activity seems critical to advertisers who currently employ advergames as a promotional tool. Just as advertisers explore the motives that drive gaming consumption online to better gratify players' needs or wants, they should attempt to discover the reasons these players have for not playing advergames built around commercial sites in order to increase nonplayers' participation in advergame play. For this reason, the following research question is offered.

RQ2: What motives prevent people from playing advergames on commercial Web sites?

Method

Insofar as motivations for advergame playing have not yet been studied, Study 1 was conducted to obtain a list of motivations germane to advergame playing online. Open-ended questions were used to capture motivations for playing advergames on a company's Web site. Because Study 1 was exploratory, it seemed appropriate to utilize open-ended questions in an attempt to develop a complete list of motivations (Stafford and Stafford 1998). Such a list is useful not only in advancing an initial understanding of motivations for advergame play, but also in providing specific measures to be used in Study 2. In Study 1, the reasons for *not* playing advergames were also examined in nonplayers using open-ended questions.

Answers were collected from 125 college students at two large midwestern universities (players = 37, nonplayers = 88). It should be noted that college students were considered appropriate for this study. Today's college students are the first generation to grow up with computer technology and video/computer games (Sherry et al. 2001). Recent research conducted by the Pew Internet and American Life Project (2003) showed that 70 percent of 1,162 college students who participated in the project reported playing video, computer, or online games at least once in a while. Some 65 percent of college students reported being regular or occasional game players. Accordingly, online marketers are anxious to use advergames to microtarget younger consumers, including college students (Emling 2001; Ghose and Dou 1998).

Multiple responses to the open-ended questions were listed and tallied. To capture a comprehensive list of motivations, up to four multiple responses were counted. Responses are ranked by frequency of responses.

Results

Motivations for Playing Advergames

The first research question (RQ1) was to find out what motivates online users to play advergames on company Web sites. Thirty-seven students gave a total of sixty-three responses and about twenty-five different reasons for playing advergames emerged. Fifteen responses indicated fun, entertainment, and enjoyment of playing games. The next most important motivations appeared to be "to relieve boredom" (seven responses) and "to waste time" (six responses). These findings indicated that primary motives for playing advergames, such as excitement, boredom relief, escape, and passing the time, are similar to motives for using new media or playing offline videogames (Papacharissi and Rubin 2000; Selnow 1984; Sherry et al. 2001).

Interestingly, advergame players also pointed out that they enjoy participating in advergames because the games were free (five responses). Free play is perceived to be one of the primary benefits for advergame players. Players also mentioned the chance to win prizes or cash, which indicates promotion-related motivation (four responses). Although the chance of winning does not rank high on the list, it is noteworthy that some players consider the monetary incentive as a motive for playing advergames. In addition, it appeared that catchy graphics (three responses), curiosity (two responses), and browsing the Internet (two responses) served as motives for playing advergames. Most of these motivations are advergame-specific. For more detail, see Table 15.1.

Playful consumption in the marketplace has been explained by two types of motivations elsewhere (Ward and Hill 1991). Deci (1975) stated that behaviors stimulated by pleasure, enjoyment, or excitement are intrinsically motivated. Such behaviors are experienced for their own sake. Intrinsically motivated consumption is rewarded by internal states that are related to positive affect. Scholars have argued that playful consumption would appear to be an emotional response; to state it simply, playing is fun (Holbrook et al. 1984). In contrast, behaviors deriven by a desire for external rewards such as monetary incentives or social approval are extrinsically motivated. The findings in Study 1 may be characterized in terms of intrinsic and extrinsic motivations. Entertainment, fun, boredom relief, escape, or diversion to pass time can be classified as intrinsic motivations, while free play or the chance of winning prizes or cash can be identified as extrinsic motivations.

Reasons for Not Playing Advergames

Study 1 also explored why online users do *not* participate in advergames (RQ2). Eighty-eight nonplayers gave a total of 105 responses for not playing advergames, with nineteen different answers. The primary reason for *not* participating in advergames was the negative attitude toward gaming itself. Online users do not play advergames because they do not have any interest (twenty-seven responses) or time to play games (twenty-three responses). Another notable reason that may be useful to advertisers was "a lack of experience" or "a lack of knowledge of advergames" (ten responses). Because advertisers have just started to adopt advergames as an advertising tool, it seems reasonable that consumers do not know of their existence or have not yet seen them on commercial sites. This implies that advertisers need to communicate with online users to make them click the game options available on their Web

Table 15.1

Motivations for Playing Advergames on Commercial Web Sites

	No. of responses	% of cases[a]
It is fun and entertaining.	15	40.5
Play when I am bored.	7	18.9
It passes the time away/It wastes my time.	6	16.2
It is free.	5	13.5
It gives me the chance to win prizes.	4	10.8
Games are visually stimulating/Graphics.	3	8.1
I am curious.	2	5.4
I like to browse around on the Internet.	2	5.4
It is easy.	2	5.4
So I get away from what I'm doing/Relieve stress.	2	5.4
I like variety.	1	2.7
It is sometimes informative.	1	2.7
Games are quick/I don't wait a long time to play.	1	2.7
Games are easy to download.	1	2.7
When I have nothing better to do.	1	2.7
It is something to do while the page loaded.	1	2.7
I like the product.	1	2.7
Just try it when I am on the Internet for other reasons.	1	2.7
Make myself feel smart.	1	2.7
I can play with other people.	1	2.7
To see who can tally the highest score.	1	2.7
I can try a product virtually on the Internet without buying it.	1	2.7
People tell me about the game/send the addresses where I can find them.	1	2.7
Others	2	5.4
Total responses	63	170.3

[a]Percent of cases: No. of responses (4)/No. of players (37).

sites. The next frequently mentioned reasons were "I don't use the Internet that much" (nine responses), "I'm online for a specific reason" (six responses), "I don't like games" (three responses), and so on (see Table 15.2).

Study 2

The two main objectives of Study 2 are to test motivation-related items generated from Study 1 and to investigate how the motives for playing advergames are related to the effects of advergames. In Study 2, players' motivations for advergame playing are considered the antecedents of attitude toward the advergame, while advergame effectiveness is regarded as the consequences of attitude toward the advergame.

Table 15.2

Reasons for *Not* Playing Advergames on Commercial Web Sites

	No. of responses	% of cases[a]
I don't have interests for games/I don't play games.	27	31.4
I don't have time for games/I am busy for games.	23	26.7
I haven't been to a site that had games/haven't come across any game.	10	11.6
I don't spend much time on the Internet/I don't use the Internet.	9	10.5
When I am online, I'm on for a specific reason.	6	7.0
Games waste my time.	4	4.7
I haven't visited sites with online games.	4	4.7
I don't like games.	3	3.5
It is usually not very interesting.	3	3.5
Because games are slow due to slow connection.	3	3.5
I have better things to do with my time.	2	2.3
I haven't thought of it.	2	2.3
Companies try to sell me something.	2	2.3
I don't want to register for all of those things.	2	2.3
I stick to sites I've been to before.	1	1.2
I don't like games for the use of ads.	1	1.2
I don't have much access to the Internet.	1	1.2
Others	2	2.3
Total responses	105	122.1

[a]Percent of cases: No. of responses (4)/No. of nonplayers (88).

Antecedents of Attitude Toward the Advergame (A_{AG})

The summative findings gathered from the literature suggest that motivations for media use influence attitudinal and behavioral outcomes of media use (Palmgreen, Wenner, and Rosengren 1985). In particular, prior studies showed that motivations for using the Internet are associated with the attitude toward the Internet. Papacharissi and Rubin (2000) identified the following five motives for using the Internet: interpersonal utility, passage of time, information seeking, convenience, and entertainment. In examining how these motives influence attitudinal and behavioral outcomes of Internet use, they discovered that the interpersonal-utility motivation significantly predicted Internet affinity. Further, Ducoffe (1996) found that perceived gratifications of using Internet advertising such as informativeness, entertainment, and irritation are significant predictors of how consumers assess the value of Internet advertising. People rating Internet advertising as high in value held favorable general attitudes toward it. In a similar vein, Luo (2002) also found that Internet users who perceived the Web as entertaining and informative showed a positive attitude toward the Web, while those who perceived the Web as irritating indicated a negative attitude toward the Web.

In a promotional game context such as sweepstakes or contests, Ward and Hill (1991) also proposed that intrinsic and extrinsic motives affecting the decision to participate in a promotional game may positively influence attitude toward the game. Based on this discussion, motivations for advergame playing are hypothesized to have an impact on attitude toward the advergame in this study. That is, it seems likely that an *initial* response to advergame playing involves forming an attitude toward the advergame, which in turn has an impact on the effects of advergames. In other words, an understanding of online users' motives for advergame playing enhances the explanation of advergame effects.

In conjunction with advergaming behavior, Study 1 found motivations for playing advergames through open-ended questions directed to actual game players: entertainment, fun, boredom relief, escape, diversion to pass time, free play, and the chance of winning prizes or cash. Study 2 expects that online users would be motivated to participate in advergames and such motivations would influence the players' attitudes toward the advergame. These considerations help develop the following hypothesis:

H1: Motivations for advergame playing will be significantly associated with the attitude toward the advergame.

Consequences of Attitude Toward the Advergame (A_{AG})

Traditional mass media advertising research has shown that attitude toward the ad (A_{AD}) is the most noteworthy indicator of advertising effectiveness and outcomes (Aaker and Stayman 1990; Harley and Baldinger 1991). Numerous studies have examined relationships between the attitude toward the ad and other constructs of interest in order to understand the hierarchy of effects of advertising (e.g., MacKenzie, Lutz, and Belch 1986). One of the most common relationships is that attitude toward the ad tends to directly impact the attitude toward the brand, which in turn tends to positively affect purchase intention. In a similar manner, this study proposes that a new construct, attitude toward the advergame (A_{AG}), plays an important role in predicting the hierarchy of effects of the advergame as an advertising tool.

Players' responses to the advergame seem likely to influence their attitudes toward the site where brands are promoted. Players may generate affective reactions to the advergame and the game-generated affective responses may influence subsequent attitudes. Thus, it is expected that players' positive attitudes toward the advergame induced by game playing may carry over to their attitude toward the site in which the game is incorporated.

In addition, a positive attitude toward the advergame may lead to building a relationship with the site or the company (Coupey 2001). Players who hold a favorable attitude toward the advergame will revisit the site sponsoring the game in the future and feel satisfied with the service provided by the site. Thus, they may be inclined to establish a relationship with the site or the game sponsor (Hopper 2002; Schmitt 1999). Altogether, these speculations suggest the following hypotheses:

> H2a: Attitude toward the advergame will be positively associated with attitude toward the site.
> H2b: Attitude toward the advergame will be positively associated with relationship building on the site or with company.

As mentioned above, attitude toward the ad is considered an important predictor of an advertisement's effectiveness in traditional advertising literature (Aaker and Stayman 1990; Harley and Baldinger 1991; Walker and Dubitsky 1994). Harley and Baldinger (1991), in the study of the Advertising Research Foundation's (ARF) Copy Research Validity Project, found a strong relationship between the positive attitude toward the ad and effect on sales in the marketplace. Walker and Dubitsky (1994) reported that attitude toward the ad was significantly correlated with intent to purchase the brand and persuasion scores. Similarly, researchers found attitude toward the Web site as a key determinant in explaining Web marketing effectiveness (Bruner and Kumar 2000; Chen and Wells 1999). It is argued that consumers who have a positive attitude toward the site will be more likely to purchase the promoted product on the site (Bruner and Kumar 2000).

The interactive nature of the Web provides the company with opportunities to build a relationship with its consumers by producing a brand experience and maintaining contact with its consumers (Jo, Kim, and Jung 2001; Kent and Taylor 1998). Because interactivity in the form of a game can increase the players' involvement with a Web site, online gaming tactics can be used to influence the early stages of a relationship with players (Coupey 2001; Hopper 2002). Building a relationship with site visitors is considered to be a strategy employed by marketers to increase consumer loyalty to the site and, eventually, boost sales. A relationship that is built on psychological engagement such as playing value may help enhance players' site loyalty, and thereby link them to the potential to purchase the product or service promoted by the site (Bruner and Kumar 2000; Ducoffe 1996;

Korgaonkar and Wolin 1999). Therefore, the hypotheses are developed as follows:

H3a: Attitude toward the site will be positively associated with purchase intention.

H3b: The relationship building with the site or company will be positively associated with purchase intention.

All constructs and relationships described in the hypotheses are shown in Figure 15.1.

Method

Sample

As in Study 1, college students at two large midwestern universities participated in Study 2. Respondents were recruited from the Mass Communication, Economics, Education, Electronic Engineering, and Finance departments in order to reflect diversity in terms of majors. Overall, 605 students participated in this survey. Most respondents (96%) were between the ages of eighteen and twenty-five, with a mean age of twenty-one. Fifty-five percent of respondents were female. On average, respondents stay online for about 110 minutes a day (mode: sixty minutes a day). One hundred fourteen respondents (19%) reported that they have played advergames on a company's Web site before, while 491 (81%) were nonplayers.

Measures

The survey instrument included several statements designed to measure the motivations for playing advergames. The list of motivations examined was derived from those found in Study 1. This ensured that motives were directly related to advergame play rather than just general gaming behavior. Of the twenty-five different motivations for game playing found in Study 1, twenty items were used in Study 2. Several of these were modified or polished for Study 2, but the original meaning of each item was kept. Motivations viewed as unique or idiosyncratic were not used in Study 2. We also reviewed and adapted the items used in prior studies on new media as well as video-game uses and gratifications (Eighmey 1997; Selnow 1984; Sherry et al. 2001). As a result, four other items were added to the twenty items generated from the first study. A total of twenty-four items were measured using a five-point Likert scale ranging from 1 = "strongly disagree" to 5 = "strongly agree."

Figure 15.1 **A Path Model of Attitude Toward the Advergame**

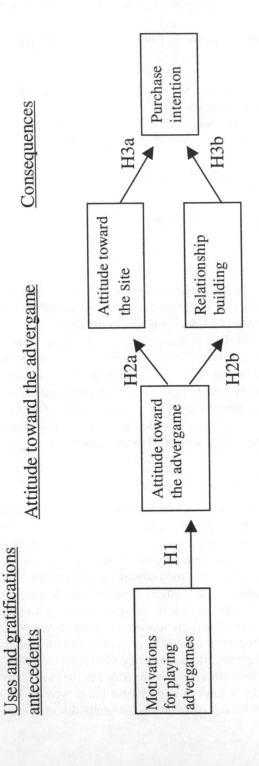

To determine how motivations for playing advergames influence advergame effectiveness, players were asked to indicate the name of the company Web site on which they played games most recently. Subsequently, they were asked to answer the questions assessing attitude toward the advergame, attitude toward the site, relationship building, and purchase intention. Specifically, players' attitudes toward the advergame were measured by seven items, which were developed for this study (e.g., "I felt the time I spent playing the games on this site was worth it"). When constructing the survey items specific to attitude toward the advergame, we selected and modified the items in prior Internet-related studies (e.g., Chen and Wells 1999; Korgaonkar and Wolin 1999), and further developed new items to address the evaluative dimension associated with the distinctive features of the advergame. To assess attitude toward the site, this study included three of the six items developed by Chen and Wells (1999) (e.g., "I would like to visit this Web site again in the future"). With regard to building a relationship with the site or the company, two items were developed (e.g., "Playing games on this site gets me involved with this Web site"). Purchase intention was measured with a single item (e.g., "It is very likely that I will buy the product that this site promotes"). All measures were assessed using a five-point scale with 1 = "strongly disagree" and 5 = "strongly agree" (see Appendix Table 15.1). All constructs were considered sufficiently reliable with the following coefficient alpha estimates: attitude toward the advergame = .92, attitude toward the site = .72, and relationship building = .74. Multiple items representing each construct were aggregated for further analysis.

Analysis and Results

Motivations for Advergame Playing

To test the hypothesized path model, it is necessary to identify the motivations for advergame playing. To identify the motivations underlying advergame play, an exploratory factor analysis with Varimax rotation was executed over the twenty-four items. Only players were included in this analysis ($n = 114$). The number of factors was limited to those with an eigenvalue above 1.0. Three criteria were used for an item to be included in a factor: (1) a cut point of factor loading of .40 or higher, (2) no significant cross loading, and (3) corrected item-total correlation of .30 or higher. After refining the items, an exploratory factor analysis was conducted again over the remaining eighteen items. This analysis produced five interpretable factors, accounting for 68.3 percent of the total variance: escapism, competition, boredom relief, fun, and curiosity. The first three factors yielded alphas ranging from .73 to .81 and were considered to have achieved an acceptable level of reliability for an exploratory study (Nunnally 1978). The last two factors consisted of only two items each and are best assessed by looking at the correlations of the items. The correlation coefficients for the items in the two factors were .42 for fun and .35 for curiosity. Each factor's raw scores were summed and then divided by the number of items for subsequent analysis. Along with mean scores for individual items, factor analysis results are presented in Table 15.3.

The first factor, labeled "escapism," stands for play's diversion value from what people are doing. This factor also represents virtual experiences such as trying a product (e.g., "I can try a product virtually on the Internet while playing games"). The second factor, named "competition," had items representing players' motivation to beat other players. This factor is linked to extrinsic motivations of advergame playing that reflect competition, social approval, or monetary incentives such as prizes. The third factor, "boredom relief," had strong loadings on items indicating that advergames offer gratifications such as relieving boredom or passing time. The fourth factor was labeled "fun" because highly loaded items reflect the hedonic value of advergames such as entertainment or pleasure. The first four motivations are similar to arousal, social interaction, competition, and diversion motivations found in the study by Sherry and colleagues (2001). "Escapism," "boredom relief," and "fun" are considered intrinsic motivations involving hedonic and playful consumption, while "competition" is linked to extrinsic motivations of advergame playing that reflect competition, social approval, or monetary incentives such as prizes.

The final fifth factor is related to "curiosity" with items such as "to see what kinds of games are on the site" or "games are just something to look at." This factor is unique in that it was not found in previous studies that explored the motivations for playing video games (Selnow 1984; Sherry et al. 2001). It seems likely that this factor was generated from the very act of browsing the Internet. Overall, these five factors represent the major motivations identified in Study 1 with the exception of "free play." Motivation for free play did not emerge as a separate factor in Study 2.

Hypotheses Tests

Table 15.4 presents the correlations among motivations, attitude toward the advergame, attitude toward the site, relationship building, and purchase intention. As expected, the correlations among the variables are sizable, significant, and in the expected directions. One exception occurs with the

Table 15.3

Factor Structure of Motivations for Advergame Play and Mean Scores of Items

Factors and items (players: 114)	Mean	% of variance	Alpha	Factor loading
Factor 1: Escapism	**2.77**[a]	29.7	0.81	
I play games on the site, so I can forget about other things.	2.54			0.83
I play games so I can get away from what I'm doing.	3.19			0.79
Playing games on the site relaxes me.	3.04			0.72
I can try a product virtually on the Internet while playing games.	2.47			0.70
The games on the site are visually stimulating.	2.86			0.61
The games on the site are thrilling.	2.60			0.60
Factor 2: Competition	**2.51**	13.7	0.80	
I play games on the site to do better than an opponent.	2.57			0.87
I play games on the site to beat others.	2.56			0.83
I play online games on the site because I can play with people around the world.	2.50			0.57
I play games on the site because of the chance to win prizes.	2.40	0.82		
Factor 3: Boredom relief	**3.77**	10.6	0.73	
I play games when I have nothing better to do.	3.71			0.87
I play games when I am bored.	4.09			0.73
I play games when I have a little extra time.	3.63			0.67
Playing games on the site passes the time away.	3.64			0.62
Factor 4: Fun	**3.55**	7.7	0.56 (r = 0.42)	
Playing games on the site is fun.	3.44			0.81
Playing games on the site entertains me.	3.67			0.67
Factor 5: Curiosity	**3.25**	6.6	0.52 (r = 0.35)	
The games on the site are something to look at.	3.20			0.85
I play to see what kinds of games are on the site.	3.29			0.72
Cumulative % of variance		68.3		

[a]The boldface numbers represent mean scores for each factor and were divided by the number of items. Each item was measured with a five-point Likert scale ranging from 1 = "strongly disagree" to 5 = "strongly agree."

"curiosity" factor, which shows a weak relationship with attitude toward the advergame.

To test the structural model investigating the relationships among the variables, the hypothesized paths were estimated via LISREL 8 (Jöreskog and Sörbom 1993). The model was tested with the correlation matrix as input. The results are presented graphically in Figure 15.2 and parameter estimates for causal paths are reported in Table 15.5. The overall fit indices for the model were acceptable, revealing a good fit of the model to the data ($\chi^2 = 26.57$, 17 df, $p = $ ns; $NFI = .90$, $CFI = .95$; $GFI = .95$; $AGFI = .87$; $IFI = .96$; $RMSEA = .072$).

Hypothesis H1 stated that motivations for advergame playing would be significantly related to attitude toward the advergame. The expected relationships were supported with the significant t-values for each path: escapism (2.291); competition (2.981); boredom relief (2.078); fun (3.001); and curiosity (–2.588). A t-value of greater than 2.0 for each coefficient showed that these estimates were statistically significant (Anderson and Gerbing 1988). It is noteworthy that curiosity motivation led to a negative attitude toward the advergame. Curiosity may induce initial play of advergames resulting from some browsing experience, and such accidental exposure did not contribute to shaping a favorable attitude toward the advergame. This finding illustrates the importance of online users' voluntary and selective motivations for playing advergames. Overall, these results support hypothesis H1, which predicts that the motivations for playing advergames significantly explain attitude toward the advergame.

Next, it was stated in hypotheses H2a and H2b that attitude toward the advergame would be positively associated with attitude toward the site and relationship building with the site. The path coefficient for the relationship between attitude toward the advergame and attitude toward the site was positive and highly significant ($t = 8.533$, $p < .001$). The path between attitude toward the advergame and relationship building was also highly positive ($t = 6.277$, $p < .001$). These results confirmed expectations that players' attitudes toward the advergame have a significant impact on their attitudes toward the site and relationship building with the site.

The final hypotheses H3a and H3b stated that attitude toward the site and relationship building would be positively related with purchase intention, respectively. The attitude toward the site–purchase intention path coefficient was .077 with a t-value of 0.798, which indicates a nonsignificant relationship between these variables. Our expectation that attitude toward the site may lead to purchase intention was not supported in this study. On the other hand, the relationship building–purchase intention path estimate was .269 ($t = 2.780$, $p < .01$), indicating a positive and significant relationship between

Table 15.4

Correlation Matrix (players = 114)

	ES	CO	BO	FU	CU	A_{AG}	A_{ST}	RB	PI
Escapism	1.00								
Competition	0.44[c]	1.00							
Boredom relief	0.29[b]	0.24[a]	1.00						
Fun	0.38[b]	0.37[c]	0.51[c]	1.00					
Curiosity	0.15	0.04	0.11	0.03	1.00				
A_{AG}	0.43[c]	0.47[c]	0.41[c]	0.52[c]	-0.13	1.00			
A_{ST}	0.25[b]	0.27[b]	0.21[a]	0.42[c]	-0.15	0.63[c]	1.00		
Relationship building	0.36[c]	0.39[c]	0.19[a]	0.27[b]	0.09	0.52[c]	0.40[c]	1.00	
Purchase intention	0.25[b]	0.24[a]	0.21[a]	0.19[a]	0.21[a]	0.14	0.19[a]	0.30[c]	1.00
Mean	2.77	2.51	3.77	3.55	3.25	2.67	3.44	2.51	2.29
SD	0.69	0.97	0.70	0.68	0.80	1.00	0.80	0.98	1.09

Mean: For each construct, raw scores were aggregated and then divided by the number of items.
[a] $p < 0.05$; [b] $p < 0.01$; [c] $p < 0.001$.

Figure 15.2 **Antecedents and Consequences of Attitude Toward the Advergame: Model Test Results**

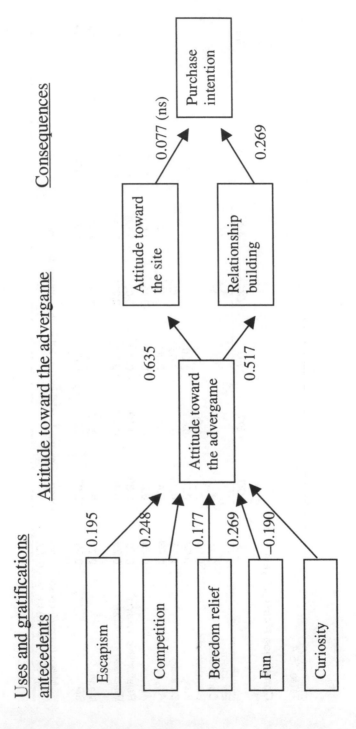

Note: The numbers represent standardized parameter estimates.

Table 15.5

Parameter Estimates for Paths

Hypotheses	Paths		Measurement item	Standardized parameter estimates	Standard error	t-value
H1	Motivations	→	Attitude toward the advergame			
	Escapism	→	A_{AG}	0.195	0.085	2.291
	Competition	→	A_{AG}	0.248	0.083	2.981
	Boredom relief	→	A_{AG}	0.177	0.085	2.078
	Fun	→	A_{AG}	0.269	0.090	3.001
	Curiosity	→	A_{AG}	−0.190	0.074	−2.588
H2a	A_{AG}	→	Attitude toward the site	0.635	0.074	8.533
H2b	A_{AG}	→	Relationship building	0.517	0.082	6.277
H3a	A_{ST}	→	Purchase intention	0.077	0.097	0.798
H3b	Relationship building	→	Purchase intention	0.269	0.097	2.780

Goodness-of-fit statistics: $\chi^2 (17) = 26.57$, $p = $ ns; $NFI = .90$; $CFI = .95$; $GFI = .95$; $AGFI = .87$; $IFI = .96$; $RMSEA = .072$.

two variables. Thus, hypothesis H3 concerning purchase intention was partially supported.

Discussion

Studies 1 and 2, by applying the uses and gratifications framework, identified online users' motivations for playing advergames on company Web sites and explored the influences of respective motivations on advergame effectiveness. The list of motivations reported in Study 1 served as the basis for building a motivation scale of advergames in Study 2. An exploratory factor analysis in Study 2 yielded five factors underlying advergame playing motivations. In Study 2, these motivations were considered the antecedents of attitude toward the advergame, while attitude toward the site, relationship building, and purchase intention were explored as the consequences of attitude toward the advergame. This structural model was tested with a path analysis via LISREL 8 and the results supported most of the relationships hypothesized in this study except for the relationship between attitude toward the site and purchase intention.

The findings of the two studies offer several important implications to academicians and practitioners. The understanding of advergame playing motivations helps explain effectiveness of the advergame as an advertising or promotional tool. In the path model of Study 2, escapism, competition, boredom relief, and fun showed positive relationships with attitude toward the advergame. On the contrary, the curiosity factor was negatively related to attitude toward the advergame. Intrinsic motives such as escapism, boredom relief, and fun significantly affect attitude toward the advergame in a favorable way, and thus shape a positive attitude toward the site and help build a relationship with the site (and possibly increase purchase intention). The findings support the speculation that a pleasurable feeling generated from gaming experiences may transfer to attitude toward the site and relationship building, confirming that entertainment value is an important indicator of users' attitude toward the Web (Eighmey and McCord 1998; Lee 2001; Luo 2002). This indicates that it is important for advertisers to enhance the greater hedonic value of playing by incorporating advergames on their site.

Intrinsic motivations identified in this study can also be characterized in terms of process gratifications posited by Cutler and Danowski (1980). They classified gratifications from media use into content versus process. Content gratification results from the use of the message itself because it provides the audience with the direct value of the message, while process gratification stems from the experiential aspect of communication behavior (Cutler and Danowski 1980). Online users are more likely to play advergames for entertainment or passage of time resulting from being involved in the communication process itself. Process gratification is important for online advertisers because prior work showed that hedonic motivations such as entertainment or fun play a significant role in explaining advertising effectiveness online (Ducoffe 1995, 1996; Luo 2002).

Among motivations for advergame playing, curiosity seems to stem from the navigational feature of the Web. While browsing the Web without any specific purposes, online surfers may encounter and try options for advergames. This accidental exposure leads to the initial playing of advergames, triggering spontaneous participation of advergames. Such spontaneous play due to curiosity is not likely to form a favorable attitude toward the game. This finding implies that, as McGuire (1974) argued, this initial play should be developed into continued play, which in turn may shape a favorable attitude toward the game and the site. Increasing the holding power of advergame playing, which allows online surfers to stay longer and to return to the site, would be of primary interest for advertisers.

It is worthwhile to note that extrinsic motivation, such as beating others or winning prizes, appeared to be a distinctive factor in accounting for the attitude toward the advergame. Along with hedonic pleasure, this implies that players perceive external rewards to be important incentives for engaging in advergames. Accordingly, advertisers need to actively communicate or cultivate the potential attractions such as prizes, free games, or social approval that advergames can offer.

Furthermore, the current study found that the attitude toward the advergame was positively linked to the attitude toward the site. Recent studies argued that a site with higher levels of interactivity and vividness may lead to more positive attitudes toward the site (Coyle and Thorson 2001; Ghose and Dou 1998). One way to enhance interactivity and vividness may be to employ online games on Web sites because online games can create a rich product experience by placing a product in games or by stimulating a virtually direct experience with a product. This provides many potential marketing opportunities to improve consumers' positive attitudes toward the site. Online games on company sites can also be used to promote visitor involvement with the Web site or the company. The results that are drawn from this study support this proposition by showing a positive relationship between attitude toward the advergame and relationship building. Advertisers can use online gaming tactics to establish consumers' relationships over the long run by encouraging them to visit the site more frequently and for longer periods of time.

Advergame effectiveness depends on the extent to which a game accomplishes its objectives. Greater sales might be one of its objectives. To achieve this, online users must be motivated to participate in the advergame, and playing the advergame should result in positive feelings toward the advergame. This in turn helps to enhance attitude toward the site and to build a relationship with the game sponsor. Subsequently, these lead to an increase in purchase intention. In Study 2, relationship building with the site or game sponsor appeared to be an important predictor of purchase intention. These findings imply that the effects of advergames on purchase intention work well through players' involvement or relationship with the site. However, this study did not find any significant relationship between attitude toward the site and purchase intention. This may be explained by the indirect effect model (or dual mediation model) found in the traditional advertising studies (Brown and Stayman 1992; MacKenzie, Lutz, and Belch, 1986). MacKenzie, Lutz, and Belch (1986) found that attitude toward the ad has an indirect effect on purchase intention through attitude toward the brand, arguing for no direct attitude toward the ad–purchase intention link. In a similar fashion, favorable attitude toward the site created by playing an advergame may carry over indirectly to an increase in purchase intention. Unfortunately, this study cannot test this alternative explanation because it did not include a measure of attitude toward the brand. Future work should measure attitude toward the brand and test an indirect relationship between attitude toward the site and purchase intention.

This study also investigated motivations for not playing advergames among nonplayers. These included such reasons as negative attitudes toward games, a lack of familiarity, and specific use of the Internet. Psychological avoidance such as disinterest, disparage, and lack of time appeared to be major obstacles. These findings echo Greenberg's (1974) and Rubin's (1984) studies on affinity with the medium, which refer to individuals' perceptions of the importance of the medium in their lives. The reason that online users do not participate in advergames is due to their low affinity toward games. This argument was supported by additional data regarding general attitude toward video/computer games in Study 2. Study 2 determined the respondents' general attitudes toward electronic games by using five statements with a five-point scale and found significant differences between advergame players and nonplayers ($M_{players}$ vs. $M_{nonplayers}$ 16.50 vs. 14.52; $t = 4.43$, $p < .001$). It is a big challenge for advertisers to overcome the low affinity toward games among nonplayers.

A lack of familiarity or experience is another important aspect that advertisers need to pay attention to (Ducoffe 1996). This may lead to skeptical or negative attitudes toward the advergame that could result in a reduction of its perceived value. Because advergames are relatively recent occurrences, familiarity or experience with advergames cannot be assumed for the majority of online users at this time. Among college students in Study 2, 19 percent have played advergames on company sites before. This suggests that familiarity or experience may play a pivotal role in stimulating advergame participation and enhancing the expected effectiveness. To attract online users who are less knowledgeable, but possibly interested, advertisers need to utilize attention-getting message tactics and promote availability and incentives of advergames to this segment by placing the option for games on the home page.

Advergames are a promotional tactic that blurs the line between commercial persuasion and entertainment. Such a seamless mix is attractive to advertisers because it can offer a branding experience that is also fun. Additionally, advergames can be a valuable asset for advertisers when collecting consumer data, in that players are often asked to register to play (Chen and Ringel 2001). However, these features may raise a possible backlash against the companies and their advergame practices. Some may criticize the subliminal effect of persuasive messages on unsuspecting players as well as the invasion of online privacy (Emling 2001; Freeman 2001). In response to these concerns, advertisers need to pay careful attention to appropriate use of online disclaimers that separate advertising from editorial content and statements of privacy policy.

Limitations, Future Research, and Conclusions

Several limitations of the current study are noteworthy. First, the data collected from college students may limit the ability to generalize the findings because college students are not representative of all online game players. Although younger online users, including college students, are assumed to be a prime target audience for advergames, the path model tested in this study should be additionally validated using a larger, random sample of online users. Future research will also need to examine attitude toward the brand as the consequence of attitude toward the advergame. As discussed earlier, the current survey did not include a direct measure of attitude toward the brand. Attitude toward the site, building a relationship with the site, and purchase intention can be indicative of attitude toward the brand, but the effects of advergames on attitude toward the brand are worthwhile to look at separately in future research.

This study developed items to assess motivations for playing advergames from Studies 1 and 2. The initial items came from self-reports of actual advergame players in Study 1 and the literature review of prior studies in this field. The final items were selected and refined through a series of exploratory factor analyses with the data collected in Study 2, which were also used for model testing. However, more work should be done in the future to refine and validate the items with different data sets.

Appendix 15.1

Measurement Items

Items	Mean	Alpha
Attitude toward the advergame		0.92
I will spend more time playing games on the company's Web site.	2.60	
I would e-mail this game to my friends.	2.42	
I felt the time I spent playing the games on this site was worth it.	2.65	
I'd like to play the games on this site again in the future.	3.10	
I would tell my friends about the games I played on this site.	2.87	
I would not mind registering my name to play games like this.	2.54	
I would bookmark this Web site on my browser to play this game again.	2.54	
Attitude toward the site		0.72
I would like to visit this Web site again in the future.	3.36	
I'm satisfied with the service provided by this Web site.	3.49	
Compared with other Web sites, I would rate this one as (one of the worst—one of the best).	3.45	
Relationship building		0.74
The games built around this Web site make me build a relationship with this company.	2.25	
Playing games on this site gets me involved with this Web site.	2.78	
Purchase intention		
It is very likely that I will buy the product that this site promotes.	2.29	—

Profiling online gamers would be a promising endeavor for future researchers. As advertising tools, advertisers are eager to figure out the right target audience to reach with advergames. Knowledge of demographic and psychographic characteristics differentiating players from nonplayers will be useful for planning effective marketing communications in terms of targeting and advergame designing. Future research is also needed to examine the effectiveness of advergames using a different research method such as an experiment. By simply manipulating the presence or absence of advergames on the site, we can compare the effects of advergames on players' attitudes and behavioral intentions. In addition, we could also assess players' mood states that are derived from playing games and then investigate how their mood states moderate the relationship between gaming activity and its effects.

As online users become more and more annoyed with banner ads, pop-up ads, or unsolicited e-mail, advertisers have been looking for new ways to promote their products on the Web. As an alternative, advergames have the potential to grow in their popularity because of online users' voluntary and selective participation. Although preliminary, this study is the first intended to explore antecedents and consequences of attitude toward the advergame. The findings take a step toward advancing our knowledge on the effectiveness of advergame playing and provide valuable information for building a more pleasurable and effective site, which may contribute to consumer satisfaction and site loyalty.

References

Aaker, David A. and Douglas M. Stayman (1990), "Measuring Audience Perceptions of Commercials and Relating Them to Ad Impact," *Journal of Advertising Research*, 30 (4), 7–17.

Abernethy, Avery M. (1991), "Physical and Mechanical Avoidance of Television Commercials: An Exploratory Study of Zipping, Zapping and Leaving," in *Proceedings of the American Academy of Advertising*, Rebecca Holman, ed., 223–231. New York: D'Arcy Mas-Benton and Bowles, Inc.

Anderson, James C. and David W. Gerbing (1988), "Structural Equation Modeling in Practice: A Review and Recommended Two-Step Approach," *Psychological Bulletin*, 103 (3), 411–423.

Blumler, Jay G. (1979), "The Role of Theory in Uses and Gratifications Studies," *Communication Research*, 6, 9–36.

Brown, Steven P. and Douglas M. Stayman (1992), "Antecedents and Consequences of Attitude toward the Ad: A Meta-analysis," *Journal of Consumer Research*, 19 (1), 34–51.

Bruner II, Gordon C. and Anand Kumar (2000), "Web Commercials and Advertising Hierarchy-of-Effects," *Journal of Advertising Research*, 40 (January/April), 35–42.

Chen, Jane and Matthew Ringel (2001), "Can Advergaming Be the Future of Interactive Advertising?" [www.kpe.com].

Chen, Qimei and William D. Wells (1999), "Attitude toward the Site," *Journal of Advertising Research*, 39 (September/October), 27–37.

Coupey, Eloise (2001), *Marketing and the Internet*, Englewood Cliffs, NJ: Prentice Hall.

Coyle, James R. and Esther Thorson (2001), "The Effects of Progressive Levels of Interactivity and Vividness in Web Marketing Sites," *Journal of Advertising*, 30 (3), 66–77.

Cutler, Neal E. and James A. Danowski (1980), "Process Gratification in Aging Cohorts," *Journalism Quarterly*, 57 (Summer), 269–277.

Deci, Edward L. (1975), *Intrinsic Motivation*, New York: Plenum.

Ducoffe, Robert H. (1995), "How Consumers Assess the Value of Advertising," *Journal of Current Issues and Research in Advertising*, 17 (1), 1–18.

——— (1996), "Advertising Value and Advertising on the Web," *Journal of Advertising Research*, 36 (September/October), 21–35.

Eighmey, John (1997), "Profiling User Responses to Commercial Web Sites," *Journal of Advertising Research*, 37 (May/June), 59–66.

——— and Lola McCord (1998), "Adding Value in the Information Age: Uses and Gratifications of Sites on the World Wide Web," *Journal of Business Research*, 41, 187–194.

Emling, Shelley (2001), "Marketers Advertise with Online Games," *Star Tribune* (September 6), E8(4).

Ferguson, Douglas A. and Elizabeth M. Perse (2000), "The World Wide Web as a Functional Alternative to Television," *Journal of Broadcasting and Electronic*

Media, 44 (2), 155–174.

Freeman, Laurie (2001), "BubbleCase Floats Online Ad Potential: Nickelodeon's Interactive Game Sets Stage for New Marketing Concepts," *Advertising Age* (February 12), 72, S12.

Ghose, Sanjoy and Wenyu Dou (1998), "Interactive Functions and Their Impacts on the Appeal of Internet Presence Sites," *Journal of Advertising Research*, 38 (March/April), 29–43.

Greenberg, Bradley S. (1974), "Gratifications of Television Viewing and Their Correlates for British Children," in *The Uses of Mass Communications: Current Perspectives on Gratifications*, Jay G. Blumler and Elihu Katz, eds., Beverly Hills, CA: Sage, 71–92 .

Hammond, Kathy, Gil McWilliam, and Andrea N. Diaz (1998), "Fun and Work on the Web: Differences in Attitudes between Novices and Experienced Users," *Advances in Consumer Research*, 25, 372–378.

Harley, Russell I. and Allan L. Baldinger (1991), "The ARF Copy Research Validity Project," *Journal of Advertising Research*, 31 (April/May), 11–32.

Holbrook, Morris B., Robert W. Chestnut, Terence A. Oliva, and Eric A. Greenleaf (1984), "Play as a Consumption Experience: The Roles of Emotions, Performance, and Personality in the Enjoyment of Games," *Journal of Consumer Research*, 11 (September), 728–739.

Hopper, John (2002), "The (Online) Game People Play," *Brandweek* (January 7), 43 (i1), 16.

Jo, Samsup, Yungwook Kim, and Jaemin Jung (2001), "The Effect of the WWW on Relationship Building," paper presented at the Association for Education in Journalism and Mass Communication, August, Washington DC.

Jöreskog, Karl G. and Dan Sörbom (1993), *LISREL 8: Structural Equation Modeling with the SIMPLIS Command Language*, Chicago: Scientific Software International.

Katz, Elihu, Jay G. Blumler, and Michael Gurevitch (1974), "Utilization of Mass Communication by the Individual," in *The Uses of Mass Communication: Current Perspectives on Gratifications Research*, Jay G. Blumler and Elihu Katz, eds. Beverly Hills, CA: Sage, 19–32.

Kent, Michael L. and Maureen Taylor (1998), "Building Dialogic Relationships through the World Wide Web," *Public Relations Review*, 24 (3), 321–334.

Korgaonkar, Pradeep K. and Lori D. Wolin (1999), "A Multivariate Analysis of Web Usage," *Journal of Advertising Research*, 39 (March/April), 53–68.

Lee, Mira (2001), "Commercial Web Sites Search: Its Driving Forces and Outcomes," paper presented at the poster session in the twentieth annual Advertising and Consumer Psychology Conference.

Luo, Xueming (2002), "Uses and Gratifications Theory and E-Consumer Behaviors: A Structural Equation Modeling Study," *Journal of Interactive Advertising*, 2 (2), [http://jiad.org/v0l2/n02/luo].

MacKenzie, Scott B., Richard J. Lutz, and George E. Belch (1986), "The Role of Attitude toward the Ad as a Mediator of Advertising Effectiveness: A Test of Competing Explanations," *Journal of Marketing Research*, 23 (2), 130–143.

McGuire, William J. (1974), "Psychological Motives and Communication Gratification," in *The Uses of Mass Communications: Current Perspectives on Gratifications Research*, Jay G. Blumler and Elihu Katz, eds. Beverly Hills, CA: Sage, 167–196.

Neff, Jack (2001), "Seeking Click with Consumers Online," *Advertising Age* (April 23), 30.

Nelson, Michelle R. (2002), "Recall of Brand Placements in Computer/Video Games," *Journal of Advertising Research* (March/April), 80–92.

Nunnally, Jim C. (1978), *Psychometric Theory*, 2d ed., New York: McGraw-Hill.

Palmgreen, Philip C., Lawrence A. Wenner, and Karl E. Rosengren (1985), "Uses and Gratifications Research: The Past Ten Years," in *Uses and Gratifications Research: Current Perspectives*, Karl E. Rosengren, Lawrence A. Wenner, and Philip C. Palmgreen, eds., Beverly Hills, CA: Sage, 11–37.

Papacharissi, ZiZi and Alan M. Rubin (2000), "Predictors of Internet Use," *Journal of Broadcasting and Electronic Media*, 44 (2), 175–196.

Pasadeos, Yorgo (1990), "Perceived Informativeness of and Irritation with Local Advertising," *Journalism Quarterly*, 67 (1), 35–39.

Pew Internet and American Life Project (2003), "Let the Games Begin: Gaming Technology and Entertainment Among College Students," [www.pewinternet.org].

Rodgers, Shelly and Kennon M. Sheldon (2002), "An Improved Way to Characterize Internet Users," *Journal of Advertising Research* (September/October), 85–94.

Rubin, Alan M. (1984), "Ritualized and Instrumental Television Viewing," *Journal of Communication*, 34 (3), 67–78.

———— (1994), "Media Uses and Effects: A Uses-and-Gratifications Perspective," in *Media Effects: Advances in Theory and Research*, Jennings Bryant and Dolf Zillmann, eds., Hillsdale, NJ: Lawrence Erlbaum Associates, 417–436.

Schmitt, Bernd (1999), "Experiential Marketing," *Journal of Marketing Management*, 15, 53–67.

Selnow, Gary W. (1984), "Playing Videogames: The Electronic Friend," *Journal of Communication*, 34 (2), 148–156.

Sherry, John, Kristen Lucas, Stephany Rechtsteiner, Christi Brooks, and Brooke Wilson (2001), "Video Game Uses and Gratifications as Predictors of Use and Game Preference," paper Presented at the International Communications Association Convention, Washington, DC, May.

Stafford, Marla R. and Thomas F. Stafford (1996), "Mechanical Commercial Avoidance: A Uses and Gratifications Perspective," *Journal of Current Issues and Research in Advertising*, 18 (2), 27–38.

Stafford, Thomas F. and Marla R. Stafford (1998), "Uses and Gratifications of the World Wide Web: A Preliminary Study," in *Proceedings of the American Academy of Advertising*, Darrel D. Muehling, ed., Lexington, KY: Washington State University, 174–182.

Walker, David and Tony M. Dubitsky (1994), "Why Liking Matters," *Journal of Advertising Research*, 34 (May/June), 9–18.

Ward, James C. and Ronald Paul Hill (1991), "Designing Effective Promotional Games: Opportunities and Problems," *Journal of Advertising*, 20 (3), 69–81.

Part V

Conclusion

16

The Future of Consumer Decision Making in the Age of New Media Promotions and Advertising

Ronald J. Faber and Marla Royne Stafford

As advertising enters a new age, it is accompanied by the rapid development of new media. This is an exciting and unpredictable time, and it may signal a considerable change in the way marketers interact with consumers and how consumers use information to make product and brand decisions. However, it is important to remember that just as history has shown that advertising changes with the development of each new medium, so too will advertising continue to grow and morph to fit the continually changing information environment.

The technological changes inherent in the new media have allowed media advertising to move full circle from a growing "massification" of the audience back to greater individuality. Newspapers provided an initial way of reaching large numbers simultaneously. The advent first of magazines, followed by network radio and television, made this even easier. With a single media buy, an advertiser could reach a huge audience throughout the United States. This ease in reaching large audiences, however, did not come without a cost. To communicate with a mass audience meant that homogenous, undifferentiated messages appealing to the largest common denominator needed to be used. Such messages came to dominate advertising. As a result, advertising became more distant from the unique characteristics of audience members.

A change to more targeted appeals began with the arrival of cable television and the fragmentation of its audience. Carefully targeted messages to specific segments became more critical in advertising strategy. The fragmentary nature of Internet sites provides an even greater ability to place unique appeals in specifically selected locations. More important, new media can provide a quantum leap in our ability to selectively craft messages to match specific characteristics of the receiver and to make the audience member feel more connected to the brand.

In 2000, Rodgers and Thorson identified five types of advertising formats found on the Internet: banner ads, interstitials and pop-ups, sponsorships, hyperlinks, and Web sites. While banner ads, pop-up ads, and Internet sponsorships can potentially reach a broad audience, they can also be more targeted to the specific concerns or interests of the receiver. For example, banner ads on search engine pages can be generated based on the keywords consumers enter. Specific ads can also be altered on the basis of prior Internet traffic patterns. It has been argued that this ability to deliver the type of information consumers desire, at the time it is desired, has the potential to dramatically enhance the value of such advertising (Dou, Linn, and Yang 2001).

Because hyperlinks and Web sites are under the control of the user, they allow for more useful and personalized information to the consumer. Here, users can choose the information they want to see on a Web site and be given more detailed information based on the specific concerns and interests that matter to them. This allows for a more targeted and personalized form of information and an advertising message that is relevant to the specific consumer.

In the past few years, the five initial formats identified by Rodgers and Thorson (2000) have been improved and joined by additional formats made possible by changing technology. Added bandwidth has made it possible to add more animation to banner ads, provide more visual enhancements to Web sites, and foster additional advertising formats such as 3-D advertising and advergames. Future bandwidth improvements are likely to make audio and video commercials more prominent on the Internet as well as further the development of short films featuring specific brands. Wireless communication is also likely to lead to additional changes in advertising formats, allowing for the delivery of appropriate messages based on the location of the audience member (see chs. 12 and 13 in this volume). These potential technological developments suggest important changes in channel characteristics that can influence advertising effects.

Changes in Channel Characteristics

Schudson (1984) argued that the most important brand choice information for consumers comes from their prior experience. If consumers do not have relevant prior experience, they are likely to rely on interpersonal communication. Mass media advertising is used only when sufficient information is unavailable from both of these other sources (Arndt and May 1981). Advertising effects might, therefore, be stronger if ads can more closely resemble direct experience or interpersonal communication. Emerging research on new media advertising has shown that various formats can approximate direct experience and contain characteristics of interpersonal communication.

New Media as Direct Experience

Telepresence has been defined as the simulated perception of direct experience (Coyle and Thorson 2001). As reported in chapter 7, consumers can feel an increased sense of virtual experience from 3-D advertising. When consumers have a heightened feeling of presence from advertising, they have increased confidence in their attitudes toward the brand and are more persuaded to buy it (Choi, Miracle, and Biocca 2001; Kim and Biocca 1997; Li, Daugherty, and Biocca, ch. 7 in this volume). With increasing technological changes, it is possible that more and more new media advertising will begin to take on characteristics that allow consumers to feel as if they are actually seeing and/or trying a brand.

New Media as Interpersonal Communication

In comparison to mass communication, interpersonal communication is seen as better able to tailor the message to the needs, concerns, and prior experiences of the receiver. Additionally, the two-way communications inherent in both interpersonal communication and new media allow the sender to utilize feedback from the receiver in developing the message. These characteristics have been identified as reasons why interpersonal communication is more effective in changing attitudes than is mass communication (McGuire 1969; Rodgers 1995). These characteristics give both interpersonal and new media communication greater information flexibility to better fit the needs of the receiver (Faber, Lee, and Nan, in press). Information flexibility in the new media can be achieved through actions of both the sender and the receiver.

Online advertisers and marketers can customize messages by utilizing information gathered from the consumer. For example, the advertiser can use cookies to determine where the receiver has been online and tailor information sent to this receiver based on this knowledge. Additionally, consumers are often asked to provide personal information when they register to use a Web site and a profile of each customer can be used to determine what appeals are sent to that individual. Finally, prior purchases and behaviors can help direct relevant advertising messages. Retail sites, such as Amazon.com, can use past purchases of consumers to identify their interests and tastes.

This allows them to provide highly focused promotional messages for related items. Travel sites can utilize a person's travel destination to direct promotional communications about hotels, restaurants, and attractions in the city being visited. In each case, knowledge of the consumer's personal tastes helps to guide the production of advertising messages. The use of this information about the receiver to select and target a particularly meaningful message is similar to the way we develop appeals to match what we know about the receiver in interpersonal communication.

With new media, consumers are also able to create flexibility in the messages they receive to match their interests and concerns. This is due in large part to the interactive nature of the new media, which is one of the fundamental features that distinguish it from more traditional media. The vast capacity of the Internet allows an advertiser to store and transmit a wide range of promotional content. Messages regarding a host of different attributes can be created. The receiver is then able to select just those that match his or her interests. This allows each receiver, with just a few clicks, to select the information that is most relevant and to ignore anything that is considered unimportant or not useful.

The ability for new media advertising to more closely resemble the attributes of interpersonal communication suggests the possibility of altering the way communication typically flows. Early work in diffusion of information suggested a two-step flow model of communication for political and consumer choices (Katz and Lazarsfeld 1955; Lazarsfeld, Berelson, and Gaudet 1948). These authors claimed that individuals, who were termed "opinion leaders," gathered new information from the mass media and then transmitted it to others. Thus, brand knowledge would move from the media to opinion leaders and then to the general public. Later research, however, began to question the idea of the two-step flow, and instead suggested that rather than passively waiting for information to come from opinion leaders, the opinion followers actually sought out information from opinion leaders. (Gatignon and Robertson 1991; Robinson 1976). Additionally, followers were able to gain some knowledge directly from the media. This came to be known as the multistep flow of communication (O'Guinn and Faber 1991; Schiffman and Kanuk 2000).

New media allow consumers to more easily and directly search the media to find relevant content. They no longer need to wait for others to do this for them, nor do they have to go through other people to learn this information. The advent of Web searching allows people to quickly and easily find relevant information both directly from the manufacturer and from third-party sources. Approximately half of all Web users say they currently use search engines (Overture 2003) and this is sure to grow in the future. The use of these engines will allow consumers to bypass some of the traditional inter-personal mediators of knowledge.

Characteristics Important in New Media Persuasion

The ability of new media to replicate and replace some of the characteristics of interpersonal communication and direct experience make it a particularly powerful potential source of consumer information. However, this increased reliance on new media sources will lead to the enhanced importance of some variables in explaining new media effects. Two factors, credibility and intrusiveness, may serve as barriers to a new media vehicle's impact on consumer choice. Two others, personalization and added value, may be seen as potentially enhancing impact. Finally, the biggest change to result from the development of new media advertising and promotion techniques may be a shift in the way most consumer decision making is done.

Credibility

Consumers have long found the credibility of advertising to be suspect. Since the 1930s, about 70 percent of the American public has indicated doubts about the veracity of advertising claims (Calfee 1997). The unregulated nature of the Internet has added to concerns about the believability of promotional information from this medium. The ability of anyone to post a Web site, to make up a name that might be confused for some brand, and to sound trustworthy has made many consumers suspicious. Additional concern may stem from the blatant efforts of advertisers using banner ads to fool consumers into clicking on them. Further credibility issues regarding electronic promotions stem from problems of fraud and identity theft that have plagued the Internet. Thus, establishing trust with the consumer may be a critical initial goal for any advertiser.

Promotional techniques used on the Internet should be careful to avoid creating doubt and distrust among consumers. For example, paying search engines to place listings near the top or paying for links on Web sites that are not clearly identified as being paid promotions may further erode consumers' trust. Greater research on the criteria consumers use to determine the trustworthiness of an advertiser and the impact such evaluations have on brand attitudes and behavior are likely to be important topics in the future.

Intrusiveness

One of the major complaints about Internet ads is their intrusiveness (see ch. 10). This is especially true for pop-up ads (GartnerG2 2002) because they occur without warning and interrupt the user's focus by taking them away from the material they wanted to examine. Anything that interrupts a user's flow is likely to be seen as irritating and undesirable (Rodgers and Thorson 2000). Additionally, these ads are frequently for products that do not interest the user. It is, therefore, not surprising that users have strong negative attitudes toward this type of advertising.

Although intrusive ads may be considered irritating, that does not necessarily mean they are ineffective. For example, the law of extremes states that whether consumers like or dislike an ad is less important than the intensity of their feelings (Robertson, Zelinski, and Ward 1984). Thus, a strong negative response to an ad may be preferable to a weak pleasant response. A famous example of this was the Wisk laundry detergent "ring around the collar" ad campaign that was rated as one of the most irritating and annoying ad campaigns, but lasted fifteen years and contributed to the success of what was a sinking brand. Empirical evidence has also shown that extremely unpleasant ads can outperform weakly positive ones (Silk and Vavra 1974). Certainly, there are large risks to be taken with using irritating ads. The widespread demand for "do not call" lists and for protection against spam as well as the technological innovations by online providers to suppress pop-up ads show that intrusive advertising engenders strong feelings among consumers and leads to efforts to prevent these forms of promotions. Research on when ads are perceived as intrusive in new media and when this hurts or helps a brand may be a valuable area for future investigation.

Two important ways to reduce intrusiveness are to make the ad more relevant to consumers and to make consumers feel they are more in control. New media alternatives that are more effectively targeted in terms of content, channel, and time may go a long way to reducing perceptions of intrusiveness. Advertising based on tracking information and wireless communication that can allow for information to be requested and/or delivered closer to the point of purchase are ways of accomplishing this. Another potentially valuable strategy may be to give consumers control over selecting the information they receive. Web sites that allow consumers to sign up for targeted e-mail promotions avoid the feelings of intrusiveness that come with unwanted messages. This notion of permission marketing (Godin 1999) may provide a sense of control that alters the effectiveness of such electronic advertising; future research may address this question.

Personalization

One factor that may help the success of new media advertising is increased personalization. Research on banner ads found that personalizing these messages increased the likelihood that people would click on them and result in enhanced attitudes toward the Web site and sponsor (Nowak et al. 1999). The ability for consumers to personalize a company's Web site to make it more relevant and useful is also likely to increase return visits and improve the value of the site as a marketing communication tool. The same is likely to be true for search engines that can customize the information they bring to the consumer to match his or her specific interests. Interactivity, along with database management and consumer tracking can enhance personalization and make this a variable of growing importance in advertising and promotion.

Value-Added Content

One of the major issues in the future will be how to best target and reach the desired audience. The Internet has the ability to fragment audiences into millions of different segments of people who can choose from an unimaginably large variety of sites. One of the biggest challenges for advertisers will be to reach the selected target market. To help accomplish this, advertisers and Web site designers will need to offer a compelling reason for the Internet surfer to select, and periodically return to, their particular site; clearly, to achieve this, sites must offer the consumer something extra. Thus, an important element of new media advertising may be the notion of added value.

Examples of adding value to a Web site are already evident; retail store sites like Amazon.com offer the consumer personalized help in finding additional relevant items. Service sites like Northwest Airlines (nwa.com) offer help and links in finding related services such as hotels or rental cars. Additional helpful information may also be offered. For example, these consumers may receive an e-mail with the weather forecast for their destination the day prior to traveling. Some company Web sites offer consumers games, special offers, extras such as manuals, tips, instructions, or recipes utilizing their brand in order to help entice customers. Each of these adds to the consumers' use and enjoyment. They provide potential reasons for the consumer to return to the Website and/or enhance positive affect for the brand.

Ads themselves can also provide consumers added value. For instance, visual metaphors may add to the enjoyment consumers experience in looking at ads. Visual metaphors occur when pictures are used to suggest that one object is figuratively like another, although they are literally very different (Phillips 2003; Stern 1990). For example, a brand of toothpaste may show a picture of a string of pearls in its ad. When readers encounter this ad, they initially recognize that the image in it deviates from expectations and does not make literal sense. To interpret the ad, they must process it figuratively and discern what it may mean. In this case, a reasonable interpretation would be that this toothpaste would get your teeth "pearly white." Research on visual elements in ads has shown that consumers are more likely to notice ads that contain visual rhetoric (McQuarrie and Mick 2003) and experience enjoyment and a sense of accomplishment from figuring out the meaning of rhetorical figures (Peracchio and Meyers-Levy 1994; Phillips 2000). This can lead to more positive attitudes toward the ad (McQuarrie and Mick 1999; Phillips 2000). Games and puzzles within ads such as those frequently appearing in print ads for brands like J&B Scotch whiskies, and Absolut vodka, are other examples of an added value that visuals in ads can provide. The interactive nature of new media communications may increase the possibilities for visual games and decoding tasks that audiences may find enjoyable or satisfying.

Consumer Information Environment

Perhaps the greatest change to come from the development of new media will not be in the form or content that advertising takes, but in the overall characteristics of the consumer information environment. These changes may dramatically impact the way we typically make brand decisions.

Economists have long considered humans to be rational beings. Under ideal circumstances, they would make the best possible choices to maximize utility. However, such ideal circumstances have rarely existed. Therefore, the notion of bounded rationality was developed to indicate that human beings have limitations on their ability to process information and make ideal decisions (Simon 1955). For consumers, these limitations have typically been caused by the nature of the information environment at the point of both learning and retrieval.

To make optimal decisions, one would like to have comparative information about all possible choices and each of their attributes. However, the typical marketplace environment makes acquiring such information difficult, if not impossible. From prior experience, we may have tried more than one brand, but these trials were usually done at different points in time, making a direct comparison of the brands on all important attributes very difficult. Additionally, given that many products change models, ingredients, price, or other factors over time, the appropriateness of such comparisons can be questioned. An even greater problem occurs if one is relying on advertising for such information. Any given ad generally presents only positive information about a few attributes of one brand. This requires consumers to acquire, remember, sort, reorganize, and retain information from many different ads in order to make comparisons of specific attributes across brands.

Bettman and Kakkar (1977) argue that consumers process information in the fashion that is easiest given the way the information is displayed. They found that when information was organized by brand, brand processing was generally used. On the other hand, attribute formats led to more attribute processing. As previously discussed, traditional mass media advertising focuses on a single brand and thus offers information organized by brand. Much online information may also be provided this way. However, the online environment is beginning to offer more information organized by attribute or presented across brands. Many online retail stores (e.g., www.bestbuy.com; www.dealtime.com; www.saveonphone.com) offer information matrices comparing the brands they sell across a number of attributes. Individuals with particular interests have also developed independent Web sites about specific products and provide comparisons across brands. For example, aficionados have posted Web sites that compare brands and retail outlets for products such as flat-screen plasma televisions, audio equipment, wines, coffee, and even lap and pedal steel guitars (e.g., Brad's Page of Steel; Bob's Steel Guitar Pages). Finally, search engines allow consumers to select a product category and get information from many brands at one time, facilitating the comparison of information across attributes. All of this may lead to a greater use of attribute-based processing. Attribute-based information presentation may enhance the ability of consumers to engage in more compensatory and more complex decision-making strategies.

Consumer decisions can also be categorized as stimulus based or memory based (Lynch and Srull 1982). When all information to make a brand choice must be retrieved from one's prior knowledge, it is a memory-based decision. When all the relevant information is available externally such as in a catalogue, store display, or summary table, it is considered to be stimulus based. Not surprisingly, few decisions are considered to be purely one or the other, but instead are labeled as mixed types (Bettman, Johnson, and Payne 1991). The degree to which decisions are memory based adds difficulty to making rational decisions. In relying on memory, consumers usually consider only a few brand alternatives. In this way, consumers save cognitive effort. However, this comes at the potential risk of overlooking the "best" alternative.

In contrast, new media can provide a vast amount of both brand and attribute information. Peterson and Merino (2003) argue that because of the relatively low cost and high entertainment value of information search on the Internet, consumers will engage in more general information searching (i.e., nonpurposeful, hedonic searching) online than they will offline. This suggests consumers will be more knowledgeable when the time comes for them to make brand decisions. Additionally, new media sources can aid in searching for relevant information when consumers are seeking it to make decisions. Browsers, search engines, and intelligence agents (e.g., bots) can all help in this effort. It was estimated that 36 percent of Americans over the age of three used the Internet to search for products or services in 2001 (U.S. Department of Commerce 2002) and this percentage has been growing rapidly (Peterson and Merino 2003). Having information available at the time of purchase allows decision making to become more stimulus based rather than memory based. This can benefit consumers by providing a larger consideration set and more comparative information on specific attributes. The ease and availability of such information may encourage the use of complex decision-making strategies. Gathering such information from multiple sources or from independent third-party sites rather than from manufacturers may enhance the perceived credibility of the information and further support the use of information-based decisions. Future research should attempt to determine whether new media advertising and promotion actually do alter the criteria and strategies consumers use to make decisions.

Low-Involvement Decisions

Most of the literature describing the impact of new media information on consumer decisions has stressed high-involvement brand choices. These are predicated on the belief that consumers will seek out or attend to brand information. However, reliance on external search is thought to be influenced by at least four factors: (1) ability to search; (2) motivation to search; (3) the cost of searching; and (4) its perceived benefits (Schmidt and Spreng 1996). As noted above, new media can reduce the cost of searching and increase the consumer's ability to do so. However, if the perceived benefits of searching are low, or if one is not motivated to engage in searching behavior, decisions will be made on the basis of simple heuristics or stimulus-based information. In these situations new media content can still be important, but in different ways.

The two most important marketing factors influencing nonsearch-based consumer choices are brand awareness (typically achieved through repetition) and the use of sales promotion techniques. Familiarity with a brand will make it more accessible in memory and help it be perceived as a safe decision. Thus, advertisers will still need to get their brand's name in places where consumers will see it frequently. This suggests that formats such as banner ads, links, paid search listings, and sponsorship may still be important for some product categories. However, it will be important for consumers to notice these messages. This may present a challenge to advertisers because consumers have learned to focus their attention away from such ads.

Research on factors that lead to an orienting response on the Internet to gain attention to these messages is likely to become increasingly important. Eye-tracking studies may be a valuable way to determine this.

To gain an audience, the sites for promotional messages for low-involvement purchases will need to provide some value to consumers. One potential avenue to achieving this is for a low-involvement product to be placed within an entertainment activity. Brand placements in advergames or online videos may become more common. These possibilities are especially likely as bandwidth improves. Interactivity may also promote efforts among advertisers to have consumers develop Internet material that incorporates the brand. Efforts to sponsor short videos starring a brand have already begun.

Increased consumer accessibility may also be an important element influencing low-involvement purchases. Accessibility refers to the users' ability to control when and where information is available (Faber, Lee, and Nan, in press). With the Internet and wireless technology, brand and product information can be accessed from almost any location on earth and at any time. Other forms of new media can use satellite tracking and cell phone or wi-fi technology to provide consumers with information about the closest location to purchase a brand or provide a list of possible alternative consumption choices. For example, a hungry traveler can use a cell phone or other handheld device to request a listing of Chinese restaurants within a one-mile radius of where he or she is standing. A couple looking for something to do one night can request a listing of the five top-grossing movies from the past week and the nearest location where each is playing. Such technological possibilities change the role advertising needs to play in fostering top-of-mind awareness and may well change the way people make decisions.

If consumers are not engaged in information searching, stimulus-based information can be particularly important. One of the most important and effective forms of stimulus-based information is sales promotion. These techniques are designed to reach the consumer at the time and place of purchase (Schultz, Robinson, and Petrison 1994) and are aimed at directly influencing behavior by providing a reason to buy one brand over another (Blattberg and Neslin 1990). New media have the ability to replicate, and even improve on, many consumer sales promotion activities.

Several sales promotion techniques such as coupons, cents-off offers, bonus packs, and refunds or rebates provide a direct monetary incentive to the consumer. The assumption is that the consumer will make decisions based on either the lowest-cost brand or on the basis of a price-to-value relationship. Many Internet retail sites help consumers who want to rely on these price-based decision-making rules. These sites (e.g., CNET.com) allow consumers to organize competing choices by price or by price within specific categories. This facilitates choosing the cheapest brand or the lowest cost brand possessing a desired attribute. The existence of such displays makes brands compete on actual price and reduces the need to utilize price-based promotional activities. However, one of the reasons for using price-based promotions is to increase demand in times of high inventory. To compensate for this online, manufacturers are likely to alter their prices far more frequently. It may not be uncommon to see companies reevaluating their prices several times a day and changing them to reflect changes in inventory.

To encourage trial, especially for new brands, package goods frequently use sampling. These samples can be delivered via direct mail, door-to-door, or in heavily trafficked areas. The Internet is also capable of providing samples of some goods. The most typical examples are music, films, software, and games. Limited-term play and abbreviated forms of these products can be downloaded and experienced by the consumer. Advances in 3-D and other new technologies hold promise for allowing consumers to experience a range of new products and determine whether each is something the consumer would like to purchase.

Some manufacturers have used premiums to promote brand loyalty. Continuity premiums require consumers to make multiple purchases to acquire gifts or rebates. Loyalty programs by retail stores (e.g., buy ten and get the next one free) and services (e.g., airline frequent-flyer miles) also promote repeat purchases. Similar loyalty programs are likely to become common on the Internet.

Contests and sweepstakes are another form of sales promotion used by marketers to grab attention, build excitement, and stimulate action (Schultz, Robinson, and Petrison 1994). Similar techniques can readily be incorporated in online promotions. Games, puzzles, and contests provide the consumer with added value for visiting a site as well as for engaging in a specific action such as purchasing or filling out registration information. Additionally, games and sweepstakes may tie products purchased from brick and mortar stores to online promotions. For example, the once-classic scratch-off sweepstakes tickets now often require consumers to enter information from the sweepstakes ticket online to determine whether the ticket is a winning one.

Conclusions

Advances in new media are likely to alter the form that advertising and promotion can take in the future. Many of these changes are likely to allow for a more direct and personal form of communication with consumers. They are also likely to promote more immediate communication and more stimulus-based decision-making. As a result, the temporal distance between promotional message content and choice is likely to decrease.

While many changes are likely in the form of consumer information and the buying environment, some elements of human decision making are likely to remain constant. Even with greater access to information, many consumer decisions will still take place using simple heuristics. Changes may be more a matter of degree or frequency than of complete changes in behavior. Regardless, changes are certain and the savvy advertiser will identify, respond to, and monitor those changes to most effectively and efficiently reach their target market. Clearly, we are living in interesting and exciting times for advertisers, consumers, and researchers alike.

References

Arndt, Johan and Frederick D. May (1981), "The Hypothesis of a Dominance Hierarchy of Information Sources," *Journal of the Academy of Marketing Science*, 9, 337–351.

Bettman, James R., Eric J. Johnson, and John W. Payne (1991), "Consumer Decision Making," in *Handbook of Consumer Behavior*, Thomas S. Robertson and Harold H. Kassarjian, eds., Englewood Cliffs, NJ: Prentice Hall, 50–84.

Bettman, James R. and P. Kakkar (1977), "Effects of Information Presentation Format on Consumer Information Acquisition Strategies," *Journal of Consumer Research*, 3, 233–240.

Blattberg, Robert C. and Scott A. Neslin (1990), *Sales Promotion: Concepts, Methods, and Strategies*, Englewood Cliffs, NJ: Prentice Hall.

Calfee, John E. (1997), *Fear of Persuasion*, Mannaz, Switzerland: Agora.

Choi, Y.K., Gordon E. Miracle, and Frank Biocca (2001), "The Effects of Anthropomorphic Agents on Advertising Effectiveness and the Mediating Role of Presence," *Journal of Interactive Advertising*, 2 (1) [www.jiad.org].

Coyle, James R. and Esther Thorson (2001), "The Effects of Progressive Levels of Interactivity and Vividness in Web Marketing Sites," *Journal of Advertising*, 30 (3), 65–78.

Dou, W., R. Linn, and S. Yang (2001), "How Smart Are Smart Banners?" *Journal of Advertising Research* (July/August), 23–30.

Faber, Ronald J., Mira Lee and Xiaoli Nan (in press), "Advertising and the Consumer Environment Online," in *American Behavioral Scientist*.

GartnerG2 (2000), "Unpopular Pop-Ups Won't Stop" (December), [www.gartnerg2.com].

Gatignon, Hubert and Thomas S. Robertson (1991), "Innovative Decision Processes," in *Handbook of Consumer Behavior*, Thomas S. Robertson and Harold H. Kassarjian, eds., Englewood Cliffs, NJ: Prentice Hall, 316–348.

Godin, Seth (1999), *Permission Marketing*, New York: Simon and Schuster.

Katz, Elihu and Paul F. Lazarsfeld (1955), *Personal Influence*, New York: Free Press.

Kim, Taeyoung and Frank Biocca (1997), "Telepresence Via Television: Two-Dimensions of Telepresence May Have Different Connections to Memory and Persuasion," *Journal of Computer-Mediated Communication*, 3 (2), [www.ascusc.org/jcmc/vol3/issue2/kim.html].

Lazarsfeld, Paul F., Bernard Berelson, and Hazel Gaudet (1948), *The People's Choice*, New York: Columbia University Press.

Lynch, John G. and Thomas K. Srull (1982), "Memory and Attentional Factors in Consumer Choice: Concepts and Research Methods," *Journal of Consumer Research*, 9 (June), 18–37.

McGuire, William J. (1969), "The Nature of Attitudes and Attitude Change," in *The Handbook of Social Psychology*, 2d ed., Gardner Lindsey and Elliot Aronson, eds., Reading, MA: Addison-Wesley, 136–314.

McQuarrie, Edward F. and David G. Mick (1999), "Visual Rhetoric in Advertising: Text-Interpretive, Experimental, and Reader-Response Analyses," *Journal of Consumer Research*, 26 (June), 37–54.

——— and ——— (2003), "Visual and Verbal Rhetorical Figures under Directed Processing versus Incidental Exposure to Advertising, "*Journal of Consumer Research*, 29 (March), 579–587.

Nowak, Glen J., Scott Shamp, Barry Hollander, and Glen T. Cameron (1999), "Interactive Media: A Means for More Meaningful Advertising?" in *Advertising and the World Wide Web*, David W. Schumann and Esther Thorson, eds., Mahwah, NJ: Lawrence Erlbaum Associates, 99–118.

O'Guinn, Thomas C. and Ronald J. Faber (1991), "Mass Communication and Consumer Behavior," in *Handbook of Consumer Behavior*, Thomas S. Robertson and Harold H. Kassarjian, eds., Englewood Cliffs, NJ: Prentice Hall, 349–400.

Overture (2003), "History and Evolution of Search Marketing," available from http://adage.com.

Peracchio, Laura A. and Joan Meyers-Levy (1994), "How Ambiguous Cropped Objects in Ad Photos Affect Product Evaluations," *Journal of Consumer Research*, 21 (June), 190–204.

Peterson, Robert A. and Maria C. Merino (2003), "Consumer Information Search Behavior and the Internet," *Psychology and Marketing*, 20 (2), 99–121.

Phillips, Barbara J. (2000), "The Impact of Verbal Anchoring on Consumer Response to Image Ads," *Journal of Advertising*, 29 (1), 15–24.

——— (2003), "Understanding Visual Metaphor," in *Persuasive Imagery: A Consumer Response Perspective*, Linda M. Scott and Rajeev Batra, eds., Mahwah, NJ: Lawrence Earlbaum Associates, 297–310.

Robertson, Thomas S., Joan Zelinski, and Scott Ward (1984), *Consumer Behavior*, Glenview, IL: Scott, Foresman and Co.

Robinson, John P. (1976), "Interpersonal Influence in Election Campaigns: Two Step-Flow Hypotheses," *Public Opinion Quarterly*, 40 (3), 304–319.

Rodgers, Everett M. (1995), *Diffusion of Innovations*, 4th ed., New York: Free Press.

Rodgers, Shelly and Esther Thorson (2000), "The Interactive Advertising Model: How Users Perceive and Process Online Ads," *Journal of Interactive Advertising*, 1 (1) [www.jiad.org/vol1/no1/rodgers].

Schiffman, Leon G. and Kanuk, Leslie L. (2000), *Consumer Behavior*, 7th ed., Upper Saddle River, NJ: Prentice Hall.

Schmidt, J.B. and R.A. Spreng (1996), "A Proposed Model of External Consumer Information Search," *Journal of the Academy of Marketing Science*, 24, 246–256.

Schudson, Michael (1984), *Advertising, Uneasy Persuasion*, New York: Basic Books.

Schultz, Don E., William A. Robinson, and Lisa A. Petrison (1994), *Sales Promotion Essentials*, 2d ed., Lincolnwood, IL: NTC Business Books.

Silk , Alvin J. and Terry G. Vavra (1974), "The Influence of Advertising's Affective Qualities on Consumer Response," in *Buyer/Consumer Information Processing*, G. David Hughes and Michael L. Ray, eds., Chapel Hill: University of North Carolina Press, 157–187.

Simon, H.A. (1955), "A Behavioral Model of Rational Choice," *Quarterly Journal of Economics*, 69, 99–118.

Stern, Barbara B. (1990), "Beauty and Joy in Metaphorical Advertising: The Poetic Dimension," in *Advances in Consumer Research*, Marvin E. Goldberg, Gerald Gorn, and Richard W. Pollay, eds., Provo, UT: Association for Consumer Research, 71–77.

U.S. Department of Commerce (2002), *A Nation Online: How Americans Are Expanding Their Use of the Internet*, Washington, DC: Government Printing Office.

About the Editors and the Contributors

Editors

Ronald J. Faber (Ph.D., University of Wisconsin) is professor of Mass Communications and co-director of the Communication Research Division at the School of Journalism and Mass Communication, University of Minnesota. He is a member of the Editorial Review Board of several leading journals, including *Journal of Consumer Research* and *Journal of Advertising*. His current research interests focus on new media advertising, advertising effectiveness, and impulsive and compulsive buying.

Marla Royne Stafford (Ph.D., University of Georgia) is professor of Marketing at the Fogelman College of Business and Economics, University of Memphis. She is the associate editor of the *Journal of Consumer Affairs* and is a member of the Editorial Review Board for the *Journal of Advertising, Journal of the Academy of Marketing Science, Journal of Interactive Advertising, Marketing Theory,* and *Journal of Current Issues and Research in Advertising*. Her current research interests include new media advertising, online consumer behavior, and services advertising.

Contributors

Patrick Barwise is professor of Management and Marketing at London Business School.

Michael Bevans is senior product marketing manager at WebEx Communications.

Subodh Bhat is professor of Marketing at San Francisco State University.

Amit Bhatnagar is assistant professor of Marketing at the University of Wisconsin–Milwaukee.

Frank Biocca is SBC Professor of Telecommunication and director, M.I.N.D. Labs, Michigan State University

Sindy Chapa is a Ph.D. candidate at The University of Texas–Pan American.

Terry Daugherty is assistant professor in the Department of Advertising at The University of Texas–Austin.

Steven M. Edwards is associate professor at Michigan State University.

Monica D. Hernandez is a Ph.D. candidate in International Business at The University of Texas–Pan American.

Morris B. Holbrook is W. T. Dillard Professor of Marketing at the Graduate School of Business, Columbia University.

Jang-Sun Hwang is a full-time instructor at Chung-Ang University, Seoul, Korea.

John D. Leckenby holds the Everett D. Collier Centennial Chair in Communication at The University of Texas–Austin.

Joo-Hyun Lee, is director, Brand Marketing Institute, Cheil Communication, Seoul, Korea.

Mira Lee is assistant professor in the Department of Advertising at Michigan State University.

Hairong Li is associate professor of Advertising at Michigan State University,

Yuping Liu is assistant professor of Marketing at Old Dominion University.

Sally J. McMillan is associate professor at the University of Tennessee.

Satya Menon is assistant professor of Marketing at the University of Illinois at Chicago.

Michael S. Minor is professor of Marketing and International Business and Ph.D. program director at The University of Texas–Pan American.

Purushottam Papatla is associate professor of Marketing at the University of Wisconsin–Milwaukee.

Virginia Rodriguez Perlado is a researcher at the Centre for Marketing, London Business School.

Shelly Rodgers is assistant professor in the School of Journalism at the University of Missouri.

Jose A. Salas is professor of Accounting at Universidad de Talca, Talca, Chile.

Sanjit Sengupta is professor and chair of the Marketing Department at San Francisco State University.

Fuyuan Shen is assistant professor in the College of Communications at Pennsylvania State University.

L.J. Shrum is associate professor of Marketing at The University of Texas–San Antonio.

Dilip Soman is associate professor of Marketing at Hong Kong University of Science and Technology.

Thomas F. Stafford is assistant professor of Management Information Systems at Fogelman College of Business, University of Memphis.

Barbara B. Stern is professor and chair of the Marketing Department at Rutgers Business School.

Jaebeom Suh is assistant professor of Marketing at Kansas State University.

Seounmi Youn is assistant professor of Marketing Communication at Emerson College.

George M. Zinkhan is Coca-Cola Company Chair of Marketing at the University of Georgia.

Index